STRANGE
LIKENESS

THINKING LITERATURE
A series edited by Nan Z. Da and Anahid Nersessian

Strange Likeness

DESCRIPTION AND
THE MODERNIST NOVEL

Dora Zhang

The University of Chicago Press
Chicago and London

PUBLICATION OF THIS BOOK HAS BEEN AIDED BY
A GRANT FROM THE BEVINGTON FUND.

The University of Chicago Press, Chicago 60637
The University of Chicago Press, Ltd., London
© 2020 by The University of Chicago
All rights reserved. No part of this book may be used or reproduced
in any manner whatsoever without written permission, except
in the case of brief quotations in critical articles and reviews.
For more information, contact the University of Chicago Press,
1427 East 60th Street, Chicago, IL 60637.
Published 2020

29 28 27 26 25 24 23 22 21 20   1 2 3 4 5

ISBN-13: 978-0-226-72249-8 (cloth)
ISBN-13: 978-0-226-72252-8 (paper)
ISBN-13: 978-0-226-72266-5 (e-book)
DOI: https://doi.org/10.7208/chicago/9780226722665.001.0001

Library of Congress Cataloging-in-Publication Data

Names: Zhang, Dora, author.
Title: Strange likeness : description and the modernist novel /
   Dora Zhang.
Other titles: Thinking literature.
Description: Chicago : University of Chicago Press, 2020. | Series:
   Thinking literature | Includes bibliographical references and
   index.
Identifiers: LCCN 2020004310 | ISBN 9780226722498 (cloth) |
   ISBN 9780226722528 (paperback) | ISBN 9780226722665 (ebook)
Subjects: LCSH: Woolf, Virginia, 1882–1941—Criticism and
   interpretation. | James, Henry, 1843–1916—Criticism and
   interpretation. | Proust, Marcel, 1871–1922—Criticism and
   interpretation. | Fiction—History and criticism. | Description
   (Rhetoric)
Classification: LCC PN3365 .Z47 2020 | DDC 808.3—dc23
LC record available at https://lccn.loc.gov/2020004310

FOR RYAN AND KAI

Contents

LIST OF ABBREVIATIONS ix

INTRODUCTION · "That Ugly, That Clumsy, That Incongruous Tool" 1

ONE · Toward a Theory of Description 35

TWO · James's Airs 61

THREE · Proust and the Effects of Analogy 87

FOUR · Feeling with Woolf 117

FIVE · The Ends of Description 144

ACKNOWLEDGMENTS 173

NOTES 177

BIBLIOGRAPHY 219

INDEX 237

Abbreviations

Specific edition information is given in the bibliography.

D	Virginia Woolf, *The Diary of Virginia Woolf*
E	Virginia Woolf, *The Essays of Virginia Woolf*
GB	Henry James, *The Golden Bowl*
JR	Virginia Woolf, *Jacob's Room*
LC	Henry James, *Literary Criticism*
MD	Virginia Woolf, *Mrs. Dalloway*
PP	William James, *Principles of Psychology*
PPH	Bertrand Russell, *Problems of Philosophy*
RTP	Marcel Proust, *À la recherche du temps perdu*
SLT	Marcel Proust, *In Search of Lost Time*
TL	Virginia Woolf, *To the Lighthouse*
W	Virginia Woolf, *The Waves*
WD	Henry James, *The Wings of the Dove*

"That Ugly, That Clumsy, That Incongruous Tool"

[INTRODUCTION]

Suppose you are a writer. How do you go about describing a character? If you're Honoré de Balzac, introducing a devoted father before he is mercilessly fleeced for money by his unfeeling daughters in Restoration-era Paris, you might say, "Usually dressed in a cornflower-blue coat, he changed his white piqué waistcoat every day, and as his massive pearshaped paunch swayed beneath it, a heavy gold chain hung with trinkets bobbed up and down.... He wore his hair in pigeon-wing style, coming down in points over his low forehead and setting off his features to advantage; the barber from the École Polytechnique came in every morning to powder it."[1] This is how we first meet the unlucky père Goriot in Balzac's eponymous 1835 novel. If you're Henry James, introducing a different devoted father, an American industrialist turned collector of Old World valuables at the dawn of the twentieth century, you might say of this man, whose singular wealth is oddly belied by a lack of all distinction, "His neat colourless face, provided with the merely indispensable features, suggested immediately, for a description, that it was *clear*, and in this manner somewhat resembled a small decent room, clean-swept and unencumbered with furniture, but drawing a particular advantage, as might presently be noted, from the outlook of a pair of ample and uncurtained windows" (*GB* 161). This is how we meet Adam Verver in *The Golden Bowl* (1904). The first of these passages follows expected protocols for describing a person, detailing physical features and items of dress and grooming that function recognizably as indexes of socioeconomic position and moral character. But what of the second passage? What does it mean to say that Adam Verver's face *resembles* a small decent room, clean-swept and unencumbered with furniture? In what way does this work as a description? And what kind of work does such a description do?

These two passages go some way toward indicating the variety and historicity of literary descriptive modes, something that does not always go remarked in discussions of the novel. As one of the most basic elements of "bringing the unthought of into awareness" and setting it before us, how we describe something—as "a table" or as "a brown oblong mass," to take a simple example—determines in crucial ways how that thing is subsequently understood.[2] Description is thus always a form of translation rather than transcription, a way of *giving*, not recording, the given even as its ideological power derives precisely from masking this fact.[3] Michel Foucault makes this point clear in *The Order of Things*, where he argues that a shift in the way beings were described in the early modern period reveals a shift in the conception of history itself. Before the emergence of the field of natural history in the mid-seventeenth century, "To write the history of a plant or an animal was as much a matter of describing its elements or organs as of describing the resemblances that could be found in it, the virtues that it was thought to possess, the legends and stories with which it had been involved, its place in heraldry, the medicaments that were concocted from its substance," and so on.[4] By the time Johnston's *Natural History of Quadrupeds* was published in 1657, however, the animal semantic field had drastically diminished, a process of reduction that by the early eighteenth century culminated in the simplicity of the Linnaean taxonomy.[5] Once certain features no longer determined how an organism was understood, there was no thought of including them in a description of that organism. Foucault's remarks make clear that the seemingly simple, neutral task of describing is determined by a whole host of assumptions about what is worthy of attention, what is relevant and irrelevant, what the salient features are by which objects should be identified and categorized; in short, what is able to emerge into visibility at all.

This is no less true in novels. At least since the rise of realism in the nineteenth century, description has been an indispensable means of world making: sketching in settings, painting figures, materializing objects, and generally establishing the parameters of a novelistic universe. This also means that, as Susan Stewart writes, "It is not lived experience which literature describes, but the conventions for organizing and interpreting that experience, conventions which are modified and informed by each instance of the genre."[6] In the case of the Balzacian description, the specificities of Goriot's dress and manner all serve to locate him in a sociocultural-moral matrix evincing a familiar realist descriptive mode that Balzac himself did so much to establish and for which he served as the exemplar to many. In the case of James, whose description of Adam Verver is far less obviously situated in a sociocultural world, it is not that this world no longer matters but that how a person is located there has shifted. As I elaborate in chapter 2, James inherits the Balzacian social hermeneutic descriptive project, but it is keyed to a different aspect of the real and a more elusive dimension of social experience. Moreover, the likening of Adam Verver's face to a small decent room also alerts us to the fact that the very standard of likeness has changed. Although description has long been understood as a form of textual visualizing, the vivid images conjured up in modernist descriptions direct us to "see" something other than how the world looks.

Before going on, I want to pause over the status of description in studies of the novel. It is a thoroughly familiar term, one that is usually taken for granted as a central feature of the novel, yet it has received surprisingly little critical attention. Because of its very ubiquity and its unobtrusiveness, description tends to recede into the background, if readers do not skip over it entirely in order to get to the action. From another angle, even as we use the term without hesitation, it can be hard to circumscribe description and to say exactly what it is. After all, what piece of text doesn't in some way contain a descriptive element? Even as scholars have subjected a variety of narrative elements to critical scrutiny, description has largely been treated as incidental or ancillary, often invoked but usually taken for granted and rarely discussed as a subject in its own right. So it is that Michel Beaujour calls its history "that of a continuous and seemingly undeserved misfortune."[7]

This misfortune can take different guises. In seventeenth- and eighteenth-century rhetorical treatises, it was considered a picturesque ornament when used sparingly but always an interruption of narrative momentum that had to be held in check lest it bring everything to a halt. In the twentieth century, our major theories of the novel—whether formalist, structuralist, Marxist, or psychoanalytic—have all identified the genre closely with narration, defined broadly as the telling of actions. Because description remains messily mired in particulars and resistant to structural analysis, it has been ill suited to the methods of narratologists—from Vladimir Propp to Gérard Genette—who seek to abstract common properties across a range of narratives and to order them in schemas and taxonomies.[8] Moreover, in the wake of Roman Jakobson's influential work on poetics, structuralist semioticians installed an antireferential view of literature as a self-reflexive and self-organized system, assigning meaning or signification to the textual codes of narration while relegating description to the outmoded task of reference.[9] Meanwhile, for more psychoanalytic narrative theorists like Peter Brooks, narrative is defined by the inextricable connection between desire and plot, to which descriptive pauses seem only to be an obstacle or an afterthought.[10] And for a Marxist critic like Georg Lukács (whom I discuss in greater detail in chapter 1), description is a technique that mortifies its objects, turning them into still lifes that symptomize the reification wrought by capitalist modernity.[11] The consequence of these varied positions, ranging from indifference to hostility, is that the continent of nonnarrative novelistic features remains unmapped.[12]

In this book I argue that the near-universal devaluation of description has prevented us from recognizing the heterogeneity of descriptive practices and their centrality to the novel and that it is high time we attend to their modes and effects. *Strange Likeness* aims to reinvigorate our understanding of literary description and to do so specifically by tracing its development in Anglo-French modernist fiction, in particular in the works of Henry James, Marcel Proust, and Virginia Woolf. At first blush modernism may seem like an odd place to explore this problem. In the history of the novel, description is overwhelmingly associated with nineteenth-century realism, while critics have remained virtually silent on its fate in the period of intense experimentation in the early twentieth century.[13] Compounding the matter, modernist writers were themselves among the most vocal critics of description. But despite these disavowals, description is an important site of attention—and experimentation—for a number of early twentieth-century writers. And it is just their experimentation that makes modernist novels an ideal corpus for refreshing our ideas about this most basic of novelistic features.

To begin with, these works help us move beyond the terms that have overwhelmingly dominated understandings of description: its opposition—and subordination—to narration. In this basic schema of narrative theory, narration deals with the primary order of events and actions, while description concerns itself with secondary matters, objects and beings. Whereas narration stresses the temporal, dramatic aspect, description, "because it lingers on objects and beings considered in their simultaneity, and because it considers the processes themselves as spectacles, seems to suspend the course of time and to contribute to spreading the narrative in space."[14] Although he makes the divide between the two an "internal" border, Gérard Genette nevertheless calls the division one of "the major features of our literary consciousness," one in which *description* is always the subordinate term.[15]

When the dichotomy of narrate or describe falls by the wayside, critical defenses of description no longer need to limit themselves to arguing that it does serve a narrative function, as most previous accounts have done.[16] We are thus freed to think about the potential uses of description beyond those defined by narrativity. As Ludwig Wittgenstein reminds us in *Phil-*

osophical Investigations, "What we call 'descriptions' are instruments for particular uses. Think of a machine-drawing, a cross-section, an elevation with measurements, which an engineer has before him. Thinking of a description as a word-picture of the facts [*Wortbild der Tatsachen*] has something misleading about it: one tends to think only such pictures as hang on our walls."[17]

From tourist guides to military field reports, descriptive writing has always served a variety of pragmatic functions, and this is no less true within the genre of the novel.[18] For Balzac, the need to carefully visualize settings and objects is a way to convey the information embedded in the material world for those able to read it—so the imbrication of character and surroundings is such that, as he writes of Madame Vauquer and her pension in *Père Goriot*, "her whole person is an explicit comment on the boarding house, just as the boarding house is implicitly suggestive of her."[19] For Gustave Flaubert, the famously strange description of Charles Bovary's hat at the beginning of *Madame Bovary* is a metafictional moment, already undoing the reliability and referentiality of this method. Description's sociological indexes intensified in naturalism with its commitment to thorough depictions of milieus, but, as Fredric Jameson has recently argued, sensory impressions and bodily affects also become increasingly free floating and autonomous in Émile Zola's works, no longer subsumable entirely to an allegorical function.[20]

In spite of its wide-ranging forms, our standard conception of description remains quite narrow. Derived from a realist paradigm, it is identified largely with inventories of the material world and often simply synonymous with a "prose of things." Modernist fiction does not abandon the realist descriptive project, but it shifts its focus toward objects that are less solid: the atmosphere of a room, analogies of relations between disparate phenomena, affective states and sensations. James, Proust, and Woolf inherit from realism the world-establishing tasks of novelistic description, but they reimagined this practice as an open process of association, one whose social analogue is a nondetermined mode of relationality. Through their intensifications and modifications of realist practices, these modernist writers make clear the heterogeneous repertoire of functions that novelistic description has always performed, allowing us to see more clearly its ramifying history.

Even as Wittgenstein suggests that it is misleading to think of description as simply providing "a word-picture of the facts," that task is not always so easy. In the early twentieth century, it was by no means clear how to know and represent a common world or just what "the facts" were much less how to provide a word picture of them. The results of the rapid social and technological changes that characterize modernity are well known—

epistemological skepticism, alienation, the breakdown of traditional canons of authority, urbanization, new forms of social mobility, changing class and gender relations, imperial expansion, and increased migration, to name a few. If the world would not sit still for its portrait to be painted, if a stable, shared, perceptual reality could no longer be taken for granted, what effects did this have on descriptive form? In this book I suggest that in responding to this problem, James, Proust, and Woolf seek to describe states of affairs without reifying them, saying how the world *was* by saying what it was *like*. Taken together, their descriptive practices direct us to perceive not so much objects but *relations*—social, formal, and experiential—between disparate phenomena. It is for this reason that I call these writers *relational modernists*, constituting a strain of modernist literary production that shares a set of conceptual and thematic concerns as well as formal strategies.

Faced with questions about how sensory perceptions could be shared and a desire to bring elusive facets of experience into the realm of novelistic representation, relational modernists call our attention to the fact that description always makes its objects available in particular ways, reminding us that far from merely recording the world, description makes it up.[21] Describing something involves picking it out as perceivable *in a particular way*; to describe anything is always to describe it *as* something.[22] Since so much of what modernist fiction seeks to describe is something intangible or ineffable, it crystallizes the work of making-it-up that is inherent to all forms of description. By determining how the given is *given*, as it were, description plays an active role in shaping the possible ways of being and acting available to us.[23]

This point has been made more influentially in disciplines outside of literary studies. In the philosopher Elizabeth Anscombe's well-known work on intention, an act can be considered intentional only under certain descriptions (e.g., raising an arm) but not others (e.g., "a certain contraction of muscles"). Thus, in order to speak of intentional actions, we must speak of them as "actions under a description."[24] "This is not mere lingualism," Ian Hacking comments, "for descriptions are embedded in our practice and lives. But if a description is not there, then intentional actions under that description cannot be there either." Because of the intimate connection between the things we do and how we describe those things (unlike, say, bacterial action, which is indifferent to how it is described), it follows that "if new modes of description come into being, new possibilities for action come into being in consequence."[25] Mieke Bal puts this point in literary terms when she reminds us that although description seems to presuppose a stable object that preexists it, the object is in fact "written into existence by the description that purportedly 'renders' it."[26] Thus, all kinds of "naturalizing" devices have to be employed in order to maintain the illusionistic effect for the reader (so a character looks at their reflection in a mirror in order for their portrait to be sketched, as in Zola's *La bête humaine*, or a carriage ride through a landscape licenses its description, as in Flaubert's *Madame Bovary*). This point becomes especially visible in modernism, which not only estranges many of these naturalizing devices but is also preoccupied with phenomena—social and psychic dynamics like the atmosphere of a room or an affective state—whose limning might more readily be called expression, materialization, display, or even incarnation rather than description.[27] But redescribing these moments *as* description allows us to see that modernism is the place where certain potentialities of description in making up its object come to occupy center stage, potentialities that are, moreover, present in a whole range of other texts.[28]

The rest of the book elaborates the particular ways in which James, Proust, and Woolf turn description toward immaterial, intangible phenomena, remaking it in the process. But first, I want to look at why modernist fiction, unlike realism, has not been associated with description. That entails looking at the objections to description among modernist writers as well as some of the aesthetic, technological, and institutional contexts in which novelistic description came under attack—and became altered—in the early twentieth century. We will then be in a position in the next chapter to see how modernism can reinvigorate thinking about descriptive form more generally.

"Stop! Stop!"

Although we now expect novels to thoroughly visualize rooms, landscapes, and people, literary historians have noted that this is a relatively new expectation—and, I will argue, a relatively short-lived one. In eighteenth-century fiction, descriptions are (to the modern readers' eye, at least) sparse, tending to simply mention or allude to objects rather than detailing their properties and appearance with any degree of fullness.[29] By the mid-nineteenth century, however, things were quite different. Balzacian pensions and Victorian parlors were rendered down to their last pouf, and these rooms were inhabited by characters whose buttons were "sewn on as the Bond Street tailors would have it" (*E* 4:160). Description, typically in the form of elaborate depictions of houses and thorough catalogs of furniture, became a constitutive hallmark of the realist novel. But in spite of its new prominence, a dictionary from 1881 gives this definition: "Description: there are always too many of them in novels."³⁰ The dictionary is that of *idées reçues*, published as an appendix to an unfinished satire of the great Enlightenment project of cataloging all knowledge, *Bouvard et Pécuchet*. Its author, Flaubert, was himself both hailed and harangued for the detail and volume of his own descriptions. Flaubert's sly definition makes clear that by the later nineteenth century, description had become essential to the novel, but in its increasingly exhaustive inventories of the material world, it had outstayed its welcome not long after its arrival.

Received though the idea may be, it finds no lack of proponents in Flaubert's wake. Henry James chastises Balzac for his "choking dose[s] of brick and mortar" and admonishes Flaubert himself for his pictorial renderings of chimney pots and duchesses' shoulders, making human life "before all things a spectacle, a thing to be looked at, seen, apprehended, enjoyed with the eyes" (*LC* 2:170).³¹ Proust, taking as his immediate target Jules and Edmond Goncourt's heavily descriptive *Journal*, inveighs against "the realists and naturalists worshipping the offal of experience, prostrate before the epidermis."³² And Woolf, decrying Arnold Bennett's fascination with describing villas, puts it most forcefully in "Mr. Bennett and Mrs. Brown" when she writes: "'Stop! Stop!' and I regret to say that I threw that ugly, that clumsy, that incongruous tool out of the window" (*E* 3:432).

This feeling was shared in avant-garde quarters. In the first "Manifesto of Surrealism" (1924) André Breton sneered at the "purely informative style" that had made the realist novel a degraded record of a false reality and the vehicle for a bourgeois morality and ideology. "And the descriptions! There is nothing to which their vacuity can be compared; they are nothing but so many superimposed images taken from some stock catalogue."³³ Citing Dostoevsky's "school-boy description" of a room in *Crime and Punishment*, Breton flatly refuses to go in.³⁴ Given this denunciation, it may be surprising that fellow surrealist Louis Aragon's take on the novel, *Le paysan de Paris* (1926), devotes its better part to a lengthy, detailed description of a Parisian arcade about to be torn down to make way for a new boulevard. Reflecting on the work years later, Aragon notes that he perversely constrained himself to write in "precisely the way that would, without fail, seem intolerable to my intimate judges: that is, to adopt a descriptive tone."³⁵ Description was, it would seem, the most effective way to *épate les surréalistes*. By the time we get to *Molloy* (1951), Samuel Beckett makes clear the exhaustion of this practice. Molloy asks of the woman he calls "Lousse" and the house she lives in, "Must I describe her?" "Must I describe it?" He concludes "I don't think so. I won't, that's all I know, for the moment. Perhaps later on, if I get to know it."³⁶ And by the end of *The Unnamable* (1953), the disembodied narrative voice cries, "Help help, if I could only describe this place, I who am so good at describing places, walls, ceilings, floors, they are my speciality, doors, windows.... If I could describe this place, portray it, I've tried, I feel no place, no place round me, there's no end to me, I don't know what it is."[37]

As these examples make clear, in a range of early twentieth-century Anglo-American and French aesthetic tracts, description's status suffers a precipitate fall. For many realist writers, descriptive passages functioned as sites for the display of perceptual acuity; hence, comprehensiveness of detail was a measure of a novelist's powers of observation. Such details also functioned as alibis for a fiction's claims to truth—so Balzac claims to write a natural history of French society, and Flaubert refutes critics who questioned the accuracy of *Salammbô*'s fictional Carthage by daring them to go to the Orient, where they would see that the pavements glittered in the moonlight exactly as he described.[38] For many early twentieth-century writers, however, the descriptive impulse became an expression of epistemological naivete and misplaced ontological emphasis. The proliferation of visual reports and inventories of objects formed the arch expression of what they saw as a naive positivism and vulgar materialism, and for them the descriptive instinct had transformed the writer into an auctioneer, a real estate agent, an archivist, and a fact-checker. The drive to carefully observe and faithfully record the surfaces of things was derided as the expression of an obsolete belief that looking at the world was a reliable way of knowing it.

We might well be surprised at this disavowal on the part of modernist writers. First, as anyone who has read the work of James, Proust, and Woolf knows, they are intensely, minutely, sometimes exhaustingly descriptive. Second, one of the best-known commonplaces about modernist experiments with novelistic form is that they dispensed with the traditional structures and supports of plotting. In turning away from inherited conventions for telling stories, we might expect this antinarrative impulse to result in a turn toward the possibilities of description, at least if we accept the narrate/describe paradigm.[39] This book grows out of a desire to understand what was at stake in the decline of description's reputation and what happens to its fate in modernism. Because for all the talk of throwing the clumsy, obsolete tool out of the house of fiction, the fact is that descriptions *don't* disappear in early twentieth-century novels. Rather than being abandoned, the very idea of what it means to describe becomes reconceptualized such that a new standard of likeness emerges, one that breaks from visual depiction and directs us to "see" the relations between things. The chapters that follow elaborate the ideas of likeness at work in a set of authors who remain committed to an intensified kind of realism, who inherit the realist tools of description even as they turn these tools to their own ends.

If the fact that description matters to modernism has largely gone unremarked, this can be attributed not only to these writers' own disavowals but also to the close association of description with objects and the material world, making it appear opposed to modernism's ostensible "inward turn." This is certainly true for the midcentury critics who canonized that version of modernism. So in Leon Edel's 1957 introduction to the English version of Édouard Dujardin's *Les lauriers sont coupés* (1888, translated as *We'll to the Woods No More*), the novel praised by Joyce as inventing interior monologue, Edel notes that Dujardin's experiment in stream of consciousness posed a challenge for rendering the external world. "What is he to do with descriptive detail, that sense of immediate material things of which Balzac made fiction singularly aware? How describe the room, the street, the house and still remain 'inside' Daniel Prince?"[40] Notable here is Edel's conflation of description with "that sense of immediate material things" as well as the idea that it was antithetical to novelists interested in exploring the terrain of subjective life.

In the last few decades the new modernist studies has dispelled the myth of a modernism turned solely inward toward solipsistic interiorities, and one strand of that work has involved attending to the material objects that populate the novel and the global networks of production and exchange in which they are embedded.[41] While a study of description would seem ideally suited to that project, which has enlarged our understanding of literary production and material culture, that is not my concern here. Instead, I am interested in the ways in which modernist fiction invites us to question our habitual conflation of description with the prose of things as well as our assumption that it works first of all to visualize the material world.

Accordingly, *Strange Likeness* is concerned with tracking what happens when description turns toward the immaterial and the intangible. We should not forget the simple point that the object being described affects the form that description takes, sometimes in ways that obscure its status as a description. In a discussion of how we talk about sensations, Wittgenstein asks, "Isn't the beginning the sensation—which I describe?—Perhaps this word 'describe' tricks us here. I say 'I describe my state of mind' and 'I describe my room.' You need to call to mind the differences between the language-games."[42] Wittgenstein calls attention here to the fact that the contexts in which a description takes place affects both its forms and functions. In the case of the novel, we have made certain realist protocols for describing a room (themselves relatively recently developed, as we have seen) synonymous with description tout court, and we have tended not to see descriptions of mind or sensation *as* descriptions at all. The ontologizing of this difference means we have largely overlooked an important continuity between modernism and realism while also failing to recognize modernist innovations in the practice of novelistic description.

The descriptive experiments studied in this book are spurred in no small part by the banal fact that James, Proust, and Woolf turn their attention to what does not look like anything at all: things in the air, formal or structural resemblances between disparate phenomena, intensities of affect, and the qualitative feels of experience. It is not that there had been no descriptions of the immaterial and intangible in older novels, but by focusing prominently and insistently on things that are barely there, modernist works activate the making-it-up potential that is always present in description, shifting what we mean by the term as well as revealing potentialities in it that are less obvious when we focus on its referential function. Importantly, however, this turn to what hovers on the edge of materiality and visibility did not mean a turn away from the real world toward solipsistic interiorities. Instead, James, Proust, and Woolf showed that what is real is not exhausted by what is physical, expanding the field of descriptive attention while evincing a more thoroughgoing kind of empiricism. Moreover, calling the limning of psychic states and vibes in an interaction instances of description not only allows us to see modernism's continuity with nineteenth-century realism, it also has the capacity to reilluminate realist texts by showing that the range of description has always been broader than the prose of things.

In the following chapters, I explore the ways in which modernists used description to register an atmosphere, produce likenesses, attune readers affectively, and create new communities of understanding. But first let us look at a few more reasons for the backlash against this practice in order to understand what was at stake in its rejection: first the increasing skepticism in the early twentieth century facing the visual epistemology that undergirds the prose of things, and then the changing landscape of writing pedagogy and the struggle to establish the novel as a serious art.

Making Us See

A basic assumption derived from classical ekphrasis and carried through Renaissance rhetoric to nineteenth-century realism is that description aims to bring an image before the audience's eye. Even as scholars have shown the contested nature and meaning of ekphrasis—typically understood as a verbal representation of a visual image—the assumption nevertheless remains that description's "primary function is to make us *see*."[43] The meaning of descriptive likeness is thus closely tied up with questions of visuality and the image, a relationship that is especially fruitful and complex in the modernist period with its close imbrications of literature and the visual arts.⁴⁴ It is difficult to talk about description without addressing questions of visuality, but the well-documented relationship of literary and visual modernism is only obliquely my subject here. I discuss specific visual technologies in individual chapters, but my focus is on how these technologies spurred writers to rethink visuality *in language*. This book is primarily interested in what happens when description does *not* concern the realm of the visible. If a governing assumption about novelistic description is that it functions to visualize the material world, what happens to the descriptive "image" when its referent is an atmosphere, a sensation, or a relation? Conversely, what is it that modernist descriptions are trying to make us see?

Before addressing these questions directly, it is worth looking briefly at description's entanglement with visuality and the epistemic authority of visual information leading up to the modernist period in order to understand the historical dimensions of this shift. The prominence of descriptive passages in the realist novel goes hand in hand with the dominance of visual inspection in the nineteenth century. It was the narrative mode for an age that witnessed the establishment or flourishing of the great museums of America and Europe, the popularity of world's fairs and exhibitions on both sides of the Atlantic, and, importantly, the invention of photography. As Nancy Armstrong has argued, the proliferation of photographic images beginning in the 1850s collaborated with realist fiction to instate an epistemology in which what was real came to be understood as what could be seen, or, what *could*—and probably would—be photographed.⁴⁵ At the same time, the rise of the new "sciences of man" such as physiognomy, phrenology, and criminal anthropology all arose within—and reinforced—an epistemic paradigm that assumed internal moral traits were legible on the surfaces of the body. The visualizing imperative was, moreover, reinforced by an explosion in the number of things to inspect. The nineteenth century was also "the Age of Property," as E. M. Forster put it, and the descriptive gaze was applied with special intensity to the growing piles of material commodities accumulating in bourgeois drawing rooms.⁴⁶ In order for fiction to qualify as a reliable guide to the real world, it had to detail certain kinds of information in the form of visual descriptions.

The nineteenth century's compulsive visualizing instinct began to encounter challenges in that century's later half, as the evidence of the senses, especially of vision, became less reliable. The invention of photography in 1839 spawned a veritable cult of images in the following decades, but although photographs (such as Eadweard Muybridge's famous images depicting locomotive processes) were hailed for revealing what the eye could not see, these also had the effect of increasing skepticism about the reliability of "natural" vision. At the same time, even as visual technologies like photography and later the stereoscope were praised for their realism, they were also linked from the beginning with the capacity to create illusions—thanks to retouching and manipulation—that cast doubt on their claim to unmediated truth.[47] As Martin Jay argues, "In the long run, the invention of the camera may well have helped undermine confidence in the authority of the eyes."[48]

At the same time that the authority of visual information was being undermined, scientific developments such as James Clerk Maxwell's work on electromagnetic radiation and widespread ideas about the invisible medium of the ether led to an increasing sense that the ultimate constituents of reality were nothing like the world perceived by the eye.[49] By the early twentieth century, the physical world had never seemed less solid or substantial. Physicists, especially Einstein and other proponents of relativity, "have been making 'matter' less and less material," Bertrand Russell wrote in 1921. "Their world consists of 'events,' from which 'matter' is derived by a logical construction."[50] The interest of modernist writers in the new sense of the immateriality of reality is exemplified in an 1898 letter from Joseph Conrad to Edward Garnett at the time that he was working on *Heart of Darkness*. In the letter, Conrad recounts a visit in Glasgow with Dr. John McIntyre, one of the first radiologists, in which, in front of "a Röntgen machine" that was X-raying a fellow guest's ribs, talk turned to "*the secret of the universe and the nonexistence of, so called, matter. The secret of the universe is in the existence of horizontal waves whose varied vibrations are at the bottom of all states of consciousness.*" Conrad asks the doctor whether it is true that all matter is "only that thing of inconceivable tenuity through which the various vibrations of waves (electricity, heat, sound, light, etc.) are propagated, thus giving birth to our sensations—then emotions—then thought."[51] He is both excited and perturbed by the doctor's confirmation that "there is no space, time, matter, mind as vulgarly understood," and, punning on the "matter" of a house he is trying to sublet from Ford Madox Ford ("there's no matter," he writes parenthetically), he concludes wryly, "I hope I may get it. If I don't I shall vanish into space (there's no space) and the vibrations that make up me, shall go into making up some other poor fool."[52] For Conrad there is something at once exciting and terrifying about the idea that what appears to be solid matter—including ourselves—is actually vibrations of waves. As we will see in the exploration of James's interest in atmospheres in chapter 2, the sense that a description of the real world need not only involve a prose of things leads to an expansion rather than an abandonment of realism's empiricist commitments.

The dematerialization of reality and the demotion of the epistemic authority of visual knowledge went hand in hand in the early twentieth century. But my argument is not that modernist descriptions are therefore simply not visual—it is rather that their aim is not to prompt the reader to visualize a scene, thus undermining description's ekphrastic conventions. To be sure, there are notable ekphrastic moments in literary modernism, such as the scene with the Hubert Robert fountain near the beginning of *Sodom and Gomorrah*, and the baroque, explicitly framed description of Robin Vote the first time she appears in Djuna Barnes's *Nightwood*. But these scenes tend to place into question the assumptions of ekphrasis even as they situate themselves in the genre.[53] Most often when modernist descriptions concern visual appearance, it is to make the point that these appearances are continually shifting, whether because of the effects of time or shifts in perspective. This is perhaps nowhere clearer than in Proust's descriptions of the "petite bande" of girls at Combray, which continually thematize the failure to fix their faces—moles wander, freckles appear and disappear, eyes change color, and facial features disaggregate and recompose themselves with surprising frequency.[54]

As is already clear, the altered meaning of descriptive visuality in modernist fiction developed in no small part in response to the popularization or invention of new visual technologies in the nineteenth and early twentieth centuries—photography and film, but also, as we saw with Conrad, the X-ray—which reconfigured the matrices of perception and contributed to the discontinuity between seeing and knowing.[55] Writers responded to these technologies and the sense of intermedial competition they sometimes prompted in a variety of ways, ranging from wariness to fascination, hesitant caution to unbridled enthusiasm. Their responses, which often hinged on questions of medium specificity, prompted a revival of the old *ut pictura poesis* debate as laid out by G. E. Lessing in the eighteenth century, where painting and poetry were enjoined to respect the constraints of their own mediums.[56] Scholars of modernism across the arts have often noted borrowings of formal techniques from one medium to another, arguing, for instance, that writers adapted cinematic forms such as the montage and the close-up for their own purposes.[57] But for some writers, description, precisely because it was the verbal feature most closely aligned with the visual, seemed to be entirely superseded in literature by technologies that gave better visual likenesses of the world. Although this was not the response of James, Proust, and Woolf, I want to look briefly now at this more antagonistic attitude, exemplified by Valéry and Breton, that was also influential in the modernist period. Representing an extreme version of the reservations expressed by James, Proust, and Woolf around description's status as a positivistic form, Valéry and Breton claimed that the need for literary description had been obviated, even as, as we will see, this claim was undermined in their own literary experiments.

Valéry's hostility toward literary description derived from its association with photography, which he both devalued as positivistic on the one hand and celebrated on the other for freeing literature from the constraints of referentiality. In an essay on the centenary of photography, Valéry notes that initially it seemed as if this "marvelous invention" might displace writing altogether, since "it is practically illusory to claim that language can convey the idea of how an object looks with any degree of precision."[58] However skilled at her craft, the writer who depicts a landscape or a face will suggest as many different visions as she has readers. "Thus the existence of photography discourages us, rather, from wanting to describe what can inscribe itself of its own accord."[59] But by this same token it also encourages writers to exploit the means of expression and production proper to them and them alone—for him, the pure qualities of language, exemplified in poetry. Echoing Lessing's injunction that poetry and painting should respect the constraints of their mediums, Valéry reasons that if the photograph furnishes the visual description of the world par excellence, then the novel should describe something other than the world seen. He associates photography with history, both of which know only what took place: history comprises things seen, moments witnessed, things that could have been captured on camera. In contrast, "*All the rest is literature*. All that is left consists of those components of the story or of the thesis that are products of the mind and are consequently imaginations, interpretations, or constructions, bodiless things by nature imperceptible to the photographic eye or the phonographic ear, which thus could not have been observed and transmitted in their purity."[60] Here, Valéry recapitulates a Romantic-Baudelairean critique where observation of fact is distinguished from—and made inferior to—the work of aesthetic imagination, and he recasts this distinction as one between media.[61] Many critics have subsequently put to rest any naive equation of photography with referentiality or fact, but it was an influential view in the early twentieth century.[62] What I want to highlight here are the ways in which this understanding of photography—and film—prompted modernist writers to rethink visuality *in language*, with consequences for the kinds of visual frameworks underwriting novelistic descriptions.

What Valéry dreams of in theory, André Breton, his onetime disciple, put into practice in his novel *Nadja* (1928), which includes photographs of empty Parisian street scenes and portraits as well as drawings ostensibly by Nadja herself.⁶³ Although this surrealist experiment differs in many ways from the novels of James, Proust, and Woolf, it provides an interesting point of contrast with respect to description. In the preface to a revised edition in 1963, Breton writes that the "photographic illustrations" were aimed at "eliminating all description," counting this as one of the principal "anti-literary" imperatives guiding the text.⁶⁴ (From this we can see how much description had become identified with literature, specifically the novel.) The claim of displacement or supersession is interesting because unlike images manipulated through surrealist techniques such as collage, solarization, and double exposure, the photos in *Nadja* are straightforward, unremarkable, and by most assessments, banal, especially when contrasted with the novel's much more dreamlike prose.⁶⁵ In the first surrealist manifesto, Breton identified the realism afflicting the novel as the product of too much description, but his own reinvention of the genre entailed not abstaining from describing but paradoxically eliminating it by doing it *even better*—in a medium that was hailed for its realism and with images that themselves could have come from a stock catalog.⁶⁶

This dream of intermedial replacement does not, it will come as no surprise, meet with success. Breton himself acknowledges the "insufficiency" of the images in *Nadja*'s final section, which takes place after an interval of time and finds him reflecting on the preceding events. Going back to places mentioned earlier in the narrative, Breton writes late in the novel, "I wanted in fact—with some of the people and some of the objects—to provide a photographic image of them taken at the special angle from which I myself had looked at them. On this occasion, I realized that most of the places more or less resisted my venture, so that, as I see it, the illustrated part of *Nadja* is quite inadequate."⁶⁷ Failing not only to successfully "illustrate" the text, the photographs also fail Breton's stated aim in the preface, since verbal description is in fact *not* eliminated from *Nadja*. Having refused to go into Dostoevsky's room in the manifesto, in his own novel Breton recounts his frequent visits to the Théâtre Moderne in the Passage de l'Opéra in some detail. Even though this theater is a site that seems primed to yield the ultimate surrealist desideratum—the marvelous—the space is described in classic realist fashion: "this hall with its great, worn mirrors, decorated toward the base with gray swans gliding among yellow reeds, with its grillwork loges entirely without air or light, as suspicious-looking as the hall itself where during the performance rats crept about, running over your feet."⁶⁸ This passage would seem to be a prime candidate for a visual illustration, but the Théâtre Moderne was torn down the year before *Nadja*'s publication, thus underscoring the transience of the modern city undergoing rapid transformation and undermining photography's association with preservation and monumentalization.

Although he faults description for being a servile copy of the real world, Breton's novel in fact ends up demonstrating how little this is true. I am not here asserting the authenticity or privilege of language over and against the image; instead, I am arguing that *Nadja* highlights the incommensurability—and necessary translation work—of any kind of description, regardless of medium. At the same time, the desire to eliminate description from literature exemplified by Valéry and Breton conforms to an agonistic model of intermedial competition in the early twentieth century where the advent of one kind of technology displaces another. It is a position summed up by Friedrich Kittler when he writes, "Ever since December 28, 1895, when the Lumières presented their cinema projector, non-filmability has been an unmistakable criterion for literature."[69] Even if this account is too neat to be entirely accurate, it remains true that as the element of the novel most closely tied to visualizing, practices of description were rethought in response to modernist writers' encounters with new visual technologies—sometimes as foil, sometimes as spur. As I will detail at length in the following pages, James, Proust, and Woolf turned their descriptive attention toward what hovers on the edge of visibility but without Valéry's dream of moving towards a pure language or Breton's ambition of intermedial supersession. The likenesses fashioned by their descriptive images are aimed above all at enabling us to "see" the relations between disparate phenomena.

The Art of the Novel

The association of describing with the recording instrument of the camera reveals not only an aesthetic problem but also a coded problem of social distinction, thus raising questions about the politics of description in the modernist period. This was the time when the Anglo-American novel cemented its status as a "fine art" and as a conduit for aesthetic elevation, and it did so at times by performing a certain opposition to mass culture even as scholars have pointed out that its relationship to popular forms was dialectical.[70] Given that photography and especially cinema was in the early twentieth century associated with popular entertainment enjoyed by the lower classes, aligning description with these media also placed it low on the novel's internal aesthetic hierarchy. As we have seen, the modernists who decried their predecessors' proclivities to overdescribe made their critiques on the grounds that this was bad writing: the Balzacs and the Bennetts had been unable to stop themselves from weighing down their novels with unnecessary detritus. But these critiques were also launched on another front: describing was too easy, and so, too accessible, too democratic.

A certain snobbery at workmanlike descriptive prose is evinced at moments by James, Proust, and Woolf, but perhaps the most explicit articulation of this position appears in Willa Cather's 1922 manifesto, "The Novel Démeublé." Adopting a by now familiar line, Cather begins, "The property-man has been so busy on its pages, the importance of material objects and their vivid presentation have been so stressed, that we take it for granted whoever can observe, and can write the English language, can write a novel."[71] But, she adds, "every writer who is an artist knows that his 'power of observation,' and his 'power of description,' form but a low part of his equipment."[72] The "lowness" that Cather attributes to description is nothing new. Even in the nineteenth century, the period of its greatest ascendancy in the novel, description was still often associated unfavorably with the genres of landscape and still life and especially with the detailed scenes of ordinary life typical of seventeenth-century Dutch painting.[73] So when Valéry observes a "remarkable parallel" between the rise of description and the rise of landscape painting in the nineteenth century, he adds that both led to the diminution of the "intellectual" element in painting and literature.[74] Not only its association with surface appearance but also the perceived ease and accessibility of descriptive practices made it a prime target for disavowal by modernists erecting their art on the altar of intellectual seriousness.

If we look more closely at the contexts in which these antidescriptive pronouncements were issued, a further dimension emerges that had to do with changes in the professionalization of authorship and the pedagogy of writing. James's first major programmatic theory of the novel, "The Art of Fiction" (1884), was written in response to a widely discussed essay of the same name by Walter Besant, an English antiquarian and popular novelist. Meanwhile, Woolf's polemic, "Mr. Bennett and Mrs. Brown," was spurred partly by a review of *Jacob's Room* written by Arnold Bennett.[75] It is no accident that Besant and Bennett, both popular writers, approached the art of writing in a matter-of-fact way that assumed it could be taught to anyone. Both men produced popular instruction manuals and, in the case of Besant, also established professional author societies aimed at protecting intellectual property.[76] James's rejoinder to Besant, much like Woolf's later rebuttal to Bennett, championed instead the necessity of the novel's freedom from prescriptive rules and conventions, arguing that the genre's greatest asset was its elasticity. But the defense of the novel's need for formal freedom was at the same time a denial that anyone could become a novelist by learning a set of rules. The attempt to preserve, or indeed to establish, the distinction of novel writing as a serious, "high" art entailed refuting the idea that whoever "can write the English language, can write a novel."[77]

In the decades just before Cather pronounced those lines, a similar set of ideas had in fact been put into practice with the widespread rise of writing instruction in the modern American university. The 1870s to 1910s were decades of transition as older, more ad hoc programs of traditional rhetoric gave way to a standardized curriculum of modern composition. The most influential handbooks of this period, including those by Barrett Wendell at Harvard and John Genung at Amherst, separated writing into four or sometimes five rhetorical styles: description, narration, exposition, argument, and persuasion.[78] Each style had its own aim, and that of description was to enable one's reader to imagine or picture a scene, although, as in classical rhetoric, it was always subordinate to other aims, centrally those of narrative. Importantly, description was also often the baseline starting point in such courses of instruction because it seemed the simplest to do.[79] When Cather calls the power of observation and the power of description a low part of the writer's equipment, she is adhering to a Romantic-Baudelairean aesthetic hierarchy that pits poetic imagination above and against empirical observation. But her critique should also be understood in a contemporaneous pedagogical context, when description was considered the most basic element in teaching students how to write.[80]

In France, meanwhile, the case for the novel's aesthetic autonomy had been made earlier by Flaubert, and there was already a tradition of novelistic theorizing in the later nineteenth century, notably in Zola's "The Experimental Novel" and by critics such as Ferdinand Brunetière. But the late nineteenth and early twentieth century also saw educational reforms that affected the way writing was taught. Philippe Hamon argues that the gradual acceptance of description in nineteenth-century belles lettres was due in part to the fact that, relatively autonomous and extractable, descriptive passages became favored selections for the "explication de texte," a pedagogical practice that arose with public education expansion and reform in 1880.[81] This reform entailed moving away from an older rhetorical model, where texts served as means for understanding rhetorical figures and producing them in imitative writing, to a more hermeneutic model, where texts came to be studied for their own sake. The emphasis shifted, accordingly, from learning how to write as an end in itself, achieved largely through imitation, to writing considered "as a way in which to convey ideas and to discuss other texts."[82] Nevertheless, the older model persisted even after the 1880 reform, and Proust, for one, who began attending the Lycée Condorcet in 1882, received a largely nineteenth-century education, one where "the great texts of Greek, Latin, and French literature were not only . . . objects of study, but also and in the most direct manner, *models to imitate*."[83] Under the older rhetorical model of pedagogy, the main exercise was one of *amplificatio*, the production of writing on a subject or theme through "enrichment," which counts description among its first techniques.[84] So when Antoine Albalat, the author of a popular 1901 rhetorically based writing manual, turns from preliminary considerations to "the matter that constitutes style itself," the first consideration is "le style descriptif."[85] Although the major postreform exercises, the *explication de texte* and the *dissertation*, were more analytical in nature, they arguably also contained a descriptive component insofar as they required the student to give an account of what was happening in a text.[86] Even more strongly influenced by classical rhetoric than the American model of composition, description remained a basic building block of learning to write in the French case as well.

Outside of institutional contexts, we find similar instructions to begin learning to write by practicing the art of description. In his own influential "Art of Fiction," Walter Besant posits as the novel's first principle that "everything in Fiction which is invented and is not the result of personal experience and observation is worthless."[87] Although selection of details is important later on in the composition process, the writer had to begin by honing his art of observation, the stylistic correlate of which is the art of description. "It seems easy to describe; any one, it seems, can set down what he sees. But consider. How much does he see? There is everywhere, even in a room, such a quantity of things to be seen. . . . The unpractised eye sees nothing, or next to nothing. . . . But to the observant and trained eye, the intelligent eye, there lies before him everywhere an inexhaustible and bewildering mass of things to see."[88] In Besant's terms, keenness of observation means being able to see *more*. This was a common wisdom echoed in contemporaneous and subsequent handbooks of rhetoric as well as in general writing manuals, all of which advised would-be writers to begin by honing their senses. For Besant, such training in visual attention had two models, painting and natural history, and he commends aspiring novelists to undertake "daily practice in the description of things, even common things, that they have observed, by reporting conversations, and by word portraits of their friends," analogous to drawing exercises, in order to cultivate through practice the faculties of seeing, hearing, and noticing.[89]

James echoes the need for observation in his response to Besant's essay, but where attention is directed, what it *means* to be an observant, what it means to see—these have all shifted in meaning from one art of fiction to another.[90] Whereas for Besant observation meant a careful and thorough inventory of details, for James the mark of a writer's perceptual skill was precisely the ability to "see" what was *not* visible, including, as I will suggest, the myriad of things in the air. In subsequent chapters, we will see

Proust's formidable powers of observation directed toward the perception of similarities and Woolf's toward the evocation of affects and sensations. Thus, it was not that these writers repudiated the empiricist epistemic virtue of close observation of phenomena, or indeed even aesthetic virtues of descriptive skill, but rather that the very meaning of these terms shifted. It is also for this reason that I group them together in this book as representing a particular strain of modernist literary aesthetics. Rather than making a break with a kind of empiricist realism—as did, for instance, Joyce, Stein, or the avant-garde—the writers of my study inherit the realist project of prioritizing observation of experience while rendering their descriptive likenesses of the world recognizable but a little strange.

The following chapters will detail the ways in which these changes worked, but for now suffice it to note that recommended as it was by literary authorities in how-to manuals as well as institutionalized in freshman composition courses, practicing the art of describing was one of the first ways in which the public learned to become writers and, perhaps, novelists. It was an accessible practice of writing available to anyone, and like prose itself, it was sometimes juxtaposed against not only the difficulty but also the aristocracy of older forms of art, including poetry.[91] In the next chapter we will see a quite different argument for the "literary democracy" of modern fiction put forth by Jacques Rancière. For him, the rise of descriptive elements in the nineteenth-century novel led to a kind of leveling that overturned the classical hierarchy of narrative, which was also a social hierarchy. In varied ways, then, description was a democratizing form of writing in the later nineteenth and early twentieth centuries. And even as modernist writers decried its very accessibility, which they sometimes perceived as intellectual and aesthetic inferiority, I will argue that their own descriptive practices sought to reimagine a more open, less determined relationship of word to world, a way of saying how things are without thereby reifying existing states of affairs.

Perceptual and Affective Mimesis

We have thus far considered some of the contexts for the backlash against description in modernism: the emergence of new visual technologies that demanded a rethinking of visuality in language alongside a new discontinuity between seeing and knowing, and changes in institutional pedagogy and the professionalization of writing as an art that could be taught. I want now to turn to some broad contours of how modernist descriptions operate. The issue of perception will in turn open onto a central issue of description in the modernist period: worries about the communicability of individual experience and the ability to establish a common perceptual world.

Insofar as descriptions seem designed to enable readers to visualize a scene or a setting, they might be read as instances of what Elaine Scarry calls "perceptual mimesis." In *Dreaming by the Book*, Scarry observes that "we habitually say of images in novels that they 'represent' or 'are mimetic of' the real world," but in fact "the mimesis is perhaps less in them than in our seeing of them."[92] In other words, the mimesis concerns not the object, the thing we are directed to imagine, but rather the mental *act* of imagining itself. Thus, when we read (as when we daydream) we are continually imagining acts of perception; that is, we are performing acts of perceptual mimesis.[93] These imagined perceptual acts can feel vivid in spite of the actual paucity of sensory data in literature (which are just black and white marks on a page, after all), and Scarry attributes this vivacity to the work of instruction. "When we say 'Emily Brontë describes Catherine's face,' we might also say, 'Brontë gives us a set of instructions for how to imagine or construct Catherine's face,'" and in so doing, "we perform a mimesis of actually seeing a face."[94] For Scarry, literature is filled with implicit (and erased) imperatives for the performance of perceptual mimesis, such as "picture this" or "look closely here" or "let your eyes drift over there." Although she does not explicitly locate the issuing of instructions in any particular feature of the novel, it is clear that such imperatives are found prominently in passages we usually call *descriptive*.[95]

In Scarry's account, these directives decompose a visual tableau into parts that are described in order that the reader can then recompose it in the imagination. Such a characterization may work for tableau-like passages that indicate spatial positions within a bounded frame, such as this example from Thomas Hardy's *Far from the Madding Crowd*:

> [Norcombe Hill] was a featureless convexity of chalk and soil—an ordinary specimen of those smoothly-outlined protuberances of the globe which may remain undisturbed on some great day of confusion.
> The hill was covered on its northern side by an ancient and decaying plantation of beeches, whose upper verge formed a line over the crest, fringing its arched curve against the sky, like a mane.[96]

But to return to the example with which we began, in what way can the description of Adam Verver's face as resembling "a small decent room, clean-swept and unencumbered with furniture" be said to function as an instruction for imagining his face? However vivid the image is in its own right, it actually *obstructs* us from picturing a face, directing us forcefully instead toward imagining an empty room. Indeed, the room, the sentence goes on, "draw[s] a particular advantage . . . from the outlook of a pair of ample and uncurtained windows." The comparison of eyes to windows is a cliché, but the addition of the qualifiers "ample and uncurtained" at once defamiliarizes the expression by rendering these figurative windows oddly concrete.[97] If we try to imagine a face, it can only be a surreal one. In fact, something similar is already at work at the end of the Hardy passage cited above, where the line of beeches is likened to a mane. In such moments we are confronting a different descriptive mode—and a different notion of mimesis—than in the familiar portrait that enumerates properties one by one or that moves across a frame from top to bottom or left to right.[98]

James was singled out by critics both in his time and ours for "underdescribing," failing to provide sufficient visual details of his houses and his characters. But his description also insists that it is in some way a more exact characterization of what Adam Verver's face is *like* even as it fails to conjure up an image of that face. To expand the idea of perceptual mimesis, we can ask what it is that such descriptions instruct us to perceive if we remove the reflexive identification of perception with visualization. Insofar as the Jamesian passage functions as an instruction for an imagined perceptual act, it is for an indirect one. In analogy to the imperatives Scarry finds, such as "look closely here" or "let your eyes drift over there," the imperatives in the Jamesian description would be something more like "when you look at this thing, see that other thing." What we are really instructed to "see" is not the object itself, Adam Verver's face, but the likeness of one thing to another; that is, we are directed to see *relations* rather than things.

At work in the modernist descriptions that I track here is a nonmimetic or nonrepresentational notion of likeness resulting in "images" that appeal to experiential homology, structural or formal correspondence, or what I will call *affective matching*, rather than visual resemblance. In fact, Woolf identifies James's resistance to visualization as a turning point in her idiosyncratic literary history "Phases of Fiction" (1929). When we take up *What Maisie Knew*, she writes, we have the sense of having left every familiar world behind. "The visual sense which has hitherto been so active, perpetually sketching fields and farmhouses and faces, seems now to fail or to use its powers to illumine the mind within rather than the world without." James's method, as Woolf puts it, is "to find an equivalent for the processes of the mind, to make concrete a mental state. He says [of Maisie] she was 'a ready vessel for bitterness, a deep little porcelain cup in which biting acids could be mixed.' He is forever using this intellectual imagery" (*E* 5:64). "Intellectual" here means both taking mental acts as objects of representation and something like nonpictorial, where the descriptive image is based not on visual resemblance but instead on some more abstract, conceptual correspondence. At the same time, the descriptions I take up in this book retain a commitment to what could be called verisimilitude, albeit one whose standards have shifted from its realist incarnation. Unlike the self-consciously dreamlike juxtapositions of the surrealists or Gertrude Stein's cubist portraits of objects, food, and rooms in *Tender Buttons*, the descriptive modes employed by James, Proust, and Woolf do not break with mimesis so much as shift the kind of correspondence between description and its object. Noticing this has the effect of both establishing the continuity of these archmodernist authors with their predecessors and illuminating the strangeness of their quasi-realist descriptions, a strangeness that may be less obvious than the experiments of more avant-garde writers.

Importantly, the perceptual mimesis at stake in modernist descriptions is also an *affective* mimesis. When writers turn their descriptive attention to things not quite material, what we are often instructed to perceive is not so much an image but a feeling. So when, walking through a thoroughly modernized London on his way to Clarissa's party, Peter Walsh feels that "The cold stream of visual impressions failed him now as if the eye were a cup that overflowed and let the rest run down its china walls unrecorded," this striking, Buñuelian image conveys a hard-to-summarize affective state by means of a cross-modal perceptual homology between the feeling of sensory saturation and the fullness of liquid in a cup (*MD* 164). In linking affect with description and emphasizing its prominence in modernism, I am concurring with a claim made by Fredric Jameson in *Antinomies of Realism*. There, Jameson posits two dueling impulses whose tension sustains the realist novel. One impulse is that of the *récit*, or narrative, to which belongs a temporal order of past-present-future, while the other impulse includes everything that halts the *récit*'s movement, including description, the "scene," and "affect."[99] According to Jameson, the gradual takeover of the narrative pole by the affective one is what leads to the dissolution of the realist novel.[100] If it is true that the affective pole becomes increasingly dominant in the early twentieth century, my interest here is with how affect is registered at the level of form. Usually theorized as resisting nomination, language, or representation, affect seems to present a particular challenge to mimesis.[101] But as I will argue with Woolf in chapter 4, describing feeling requires evocation via a particular mode of "matching" that relies on correspondence rather than imitation across perceptual modes. So intensity, for instance, can be felt across the vividness and saturation of a color, the brightness of a light, or the forcefulness of a gesture. Accordingly, affective "mimesis" should be understood in this altered sense. The comparative energies of simile making, I argue, can be turned toward finding ways to *match* rather than to represent an affective experience.

Likeness and Relational Modernism

If description determines how and under what conditions something emerges into the field of visibility, what are the descriptive modes of modernist fiction, and what are their logics? Perhaps the most common or familiar mode is what we could call *enumerative* description, which works by listing the predicates of an object. This is description understood as "a textual fragment in which features are attributed to objects," where, as Mieke Bal writes, the "aspect of attribution is the descriptive function."[102] A key stylistic strategy common to James, Proust, and Woolf's rethinking of the notion of likeness is a shift to what I call *relational* descriptions, which liken by analogy or comparison. Whereas an enumerative phrase like "the room was small, bare, and cold" considers an object in its integrity, detailing its qualities or inventorying its contents, a relational phrase like "as sometimes happens when a cloud falls on a green . . . so Cam now felt herself overcast" (*TL* 168) works by drawing a connection between one thing and another. Rather than attributing properties to an object considered as an integral, bounded whole, relational descriptions forge connections between one thing and another. Rather than defining, they liken, prioritizing approximation while reinventing standards of precision. If these descriptions attribute features to objects, they do so only in a tentative mode, preferring the *as* to the *is*. We see such comparative strategies prominently in all the writers studied here, but the work of analogy and simile become explicit subjects in chapters 3 and 4.

To be sure, comparative strategies are by no means exclusive to modernism, being as old as poetry itself, and modernists often explicitly hearken back to older forms, such as the epic simile. But the dominance of comparative descriptions in certain authors during this period is distinctive. Taken together, it reveals a changed expectation: in the works of James, Proust, and Woolf, describing how something *is* involves describing what it is *like*. If for modernists the world could not be pinned down and captured in a static portrait, relational descriptions are a way of registering how things are without hypostasizing them. We are thus directed to perceive a world traversed by an unfolding web of relations, often with surprising connections drawn between disparate phenomena.

It is for this reason that I call the writers of my study *relational modernists*. The novel of consciousness that intensifies in the early twentieth century has been accused of tending toward monadic interiorities, but the descriptive forms of relational modernists evince an understanding of the world in which nothing can be understood as an autonomous whole or an integral unified object but only in connection to other things. Of course, the nineteenth-century realist novel is also characterized by its interest in sprawling forms of relationality as well as its attempt to comprehend a social totality—one need only think of George Eliot, Charles Dickens, Balzac, and Zola, to take just a few examples. The writers of my study demonstrate an important continuity with that realist project even as they approach the thinking of relations through different forms.

The concept of relation operates in a number of ways in this book: as the formal principle of operation in modernist description; sometimes as the thematic focus of the novels themselves; and as the central argument about the possibilities of modernist description. For Lukács, who remains the most powerful critic of description, the authentic realist novel (for him exemplified by Tolstoy and Balzac) showed the truth of social relations in their totality through the mode of narration. I contend that the protagonists of my study find ways to make relations susceptible not only to narration but also to description. In one familiar critical view, James, Proust, and Woolf are interested only in the rarefied precincts of individual consciousness (in contrast to socially oriented novelists such as Dickens or Zola), and it is undoubtedly true that their characters and milieus tend to be of limited scope. I argue here, however, that they are no less interested in the web of relations making up the social world, but that they work through these—abstractly rather than representationally, and at the level of form rather than at the level of theme—in the mode of description. By delimiting things by way of other things and directing us to perceive likenesses rather than objects, James, Proust, and Woolf make description into a mode that reaches outward toward open associations. In a variety of ways, relational modernists attuned descriptions to the mediations that compose experience, fashioning forms capable of rendering the world without reifying it, preserving openness to ongoing judgments of value. My account thus seeks to vindicate description against Lukács's critique of its reifying effects while showing that modernist writers were in fact engaged with social relations broadly construed, albeit via a route that would have been for Lukács unimaginable.

Relationality has recently been theorized under a variety of rubrics. It is, of course, a central concern of Lukács and the Marxist tradition to which he belongs. It also animates Bruno Latour's actor-network theory and associated notions of "assemblages" in posthumanism and new materialism.[103] Among ecocritics, Timothy Morton calls "the ecological thought" the thinking of the vast, interconnected mesh that infects a range of discourses from quotidian relationships between humans and nonhumans to energy policies.[104] It has also been an abiding concern of queer theory. Noting that the root meaning of the word *queer* is "across,"

Eve Kosofsky Sedgwick writes of "the immemorial current that *queer* represents," "keenly, it is relational, and strange."[105] Relationality is key as well to certain traditions of psychoanalytic thought, especially the British object-relations school, for whom "the world of social relations outside of us is reflected and mediated by a world of object relations within us."[106] Among recent studies of the novel, my thinking about the capacities of certain descriptive forms resonates with Alicia Mireles Christoff's *Novel Relations*, which reads Victorian novels alongside object-relations psychoanalytic theory. I do not adopt any single theoretical framework in sustained fashion in this book, drawing from a number of the ones cited above (as well as affect theory, analytic philosophy of language, early sociology, and developmental psychology) in strategic fashion, but I share Christoff's faith in "the vibratory energy that ... really does emanate from the striking together of two texts, like the prongs of a tuning fork set ringing."[107] At the same time, I argue that faith in open, nondetermined relationality is also precisely what is displayed by the often-surprising points of contact in the descriptive forms of James, Proust, and Woolf.

It hardly needs to be said that modernism is a heterogeneous field, and the authors discussed here make up only one strand within it. There is, of course, no such thing as "the" modernist novel, although I have kept that term in this book's subtitle for the sake of convenience. As I began to suggest above, James, Proust, and Woolf retain the commitment to beginning from experience and hewing closely to it, to *recording* reality rather than *inventing* it, and this accounts for their continued interest in description. In contrast, the urge to invent or to create reality (for instance, by plumbing the depths of the unconscious or looking to machines) is evident in the surrealists and futurists on the one hand and on the other in what Charles Altieri has called a Nietzschean strain of modernism represented by W. B. Yeats, James Joyce, Ezra Pound, and Mina Loy, who saw the artist's version of the will to power as imposing values strong enough to become later accepted as facts.[108]

Altieri's list is mostly made up of poets, and indeed many of the problems I am concerned with in this book are more familiar as problems in poetics than in studies of the novel, the latter of which tends to place less emphasis on issues of figuration. Description in poetry has its own history, and descriptive poetry, of which James Thomson's poem cycle *The Seasons* (1726-1730) is an exemplar, was for a while a distinct and popular genre.[109] Analogy and simile are, of course, important features of modernist poetic movements such as imagism, and a wider account of the role of description in literary modernism would no doubt benefit from a consideration of these poets (as well as H.D., William Carlos Williams, Jean Toomer, and

Francis Ponge). In this book, however, I am concerned specifically with the problems and possibilities of novelistic description, which means both considering it in a history of the novel and in relation to novelistic features such as narration, character, and point of view even as I hope not to be determined by these categories.

Establishing the Common

If a certain strain of modernist description directs us to perceive relations rather than things, what is such perceptual mimesis for? By way of answering I want to turn to Fredric Jameson's discussion of a description that includes, quite explicitly, exactly the kind of instructions for perceptual mimesis that Scarry argues literature is filled with, albeit usually erased. The novel in question is Balzac's *La vieille fille* (*The Old Maid*, 1836), and Jameson reads this paradigmatic example of realist description as a site where the libidinal investment of the narrative apparatus is made clear, particularly in relation to point of view.

> On the balustrade of the terrace, imagine great blue and white pots filled with wallflowers; envision right and left, along with the neighboring walls, two rows of square-trimmed lime-trees; you will form an idea of this landscape filled with demure good humor, with tranquil chastity, and with modest homely [*bourgeois*] vistas offered by the other bank, and its quaint houses, the trickling waters of the Brillante, the garden, two rows of trees lining its walls, and the venerable edifice of the Cormon family. What peace! What calm! Nothing pretentious, but nothing transitory: here everything seems eternal. The ground-floor, then, was given over to reception rooms for visitors. Here everything breathed the Provincial, ancient but unalterable.[110]

Although Balzacian description is well known for its social metonymic functions, Jameson finds it charged here with a different task: "to validate or accredit the object as desirable."[111] For him it is crucial that we cannot attribute the particular desire for Mademoiselle Cormon's house expressed in this description to any individual subject. "Biographical Balzac, Implied Author, this or that desiring protagonist: none of these unities are (yet) present, and desire here comes before us in a peculiarly anonymous state which makes a strangely absolute claim on us."[112] Rather than focalized through a particular character, as becomes increasingly common from the later nineteenth century on, this Balzacian description is reported by an anonymous narrator. Generalized and free floating, it becomes allegorical of desire as such, before "the pretext or theme of such desire" is "relativized and privatized by the ego-barriers that jealously confirm the personal and purely subjective experience of monadized subjects they thus separate."[113] Focused here on the fantasy of landed property away from the business and social struggles of Paris ("a Utopia of the household"), the description "solicits the reader not merely to reconstruct this building and grounds in some inner eye, but to reinvent it as Idea and as heart's desire."[114]

According to Jameson, the need for description to solicit desire differentiates Balzac's work from classical quest narratives; by his time, the desirability of an object ("gold, princess, crown or palace") is no longer simply determined by its narrative position—it has become necessary "to secure the reader's consent."[115] By the time we get to modernism, not only desire but the very possibility of a shared perceptual reality could not be taken for granted, and my own focus in this book is on description's role in establishing a common world. As Auerbach puts it, in the early twentieth century it could no longer be assumed that "so much clearly formulable and recognized community of thought and feeling remained in [European] countries that a writer engaged in representing reality had reliable criteria at hand by which to organize it."[116] The tempo of change in experience, knowledge, ideas, and forms of possible existence—begun in the sixteenth century—had by the beginning of the twentieth accelerated so tremendously that these changes could not be surveyed as a whole.[117] Or in Wittgenstein's terms cited above, it was no longer clear how to give a "word-picture of the facts."

The uncertainty over how a common world could be known and represented, a familiar condition of modernity, was also tied to an increasing sense in the early twentieth century not only that sensory experience was not always reliable but also that it might not be shared. New experiments in the physiology of sensation in the later nineteenth century pioneered by scientists such as Hermann von Helmholtz included measuring different people's reactions to the same stimuli in a laboratory environment. These early revelations of experimental psychology showed the variation in perceptual experience, and they put to rest any idea of sensing as passive receptivity, demonstrating instead how actively we contribute to our sensory impressions.[118] These are the kind of discoveries that made "a theory of natural seeing" impossible, and so, as Raymond Williams argues, necessitated a new kind of realism.[119] "When we thought we had only to open our eyes to see a common world, we could suppose that realism was a simple recording process.... We know now that we literally create the world we see, and that this human creation... is necessarily dynamic and active."[120] If sensory experience could not be shared, or more precisely, if shared sensory experience could not be assumed with any certainty, it was no longer possible to assume a common world that could be known and represented through standard means of description.

There was, moreover, a further barrier to establishing a common perceptual reality, one already noted by Helmholtz in 1868.

> When we say that we "know" a man, a road, a fruit, a perfume, we mean that we have seen, or tasted, or smelt, these objects. We keep the sensible impression fast in our memory, and we shall recognize it again when it is repeated, but we cannot describe the impression in words, even to ourselves. And yet it is certain that this kind of knowledge [*Kennen*] may attain the highest possible degree of precision and certainty, and is so far not inferior to any knowledge [*Wissen*] which can be expressed in words; but it is not directly communicable, unless the object in question can be brought actually forward, or the impression it produces can be otherwise represented—as by drawing the portrait of a man instead of producing the man himself.[121]

Helmholtz lays out here a conundrum: that which we know best, the sensible impressions belonging to *das Kennen*, whether of men, roads, fruits, perfumes, or anything else, is at once the most precise and certain kind of knowledge and also that which cannot be put into words.[122] This gap between what we know and what we can express was observed in a number of quarters in the early twentieth century. A worry about the potential epistemic privacy of sense perception and the inability to fully communicate one's own experience of the world to others led Gottlob Frege and Bertrand Russell to posit ideal languages and symbolic notations capable of expressing greater exactitude and precision than ordinary words.[123] And the conundrum laid out by Helmholtz is also one facing the novel, which aims to make available sense experiences that are not our own in the medium of language. The frequent thematization of misunderstanding and incommunicability between characters in modernist novels arises from not knowing directly—or being able to share—what others are thinking or experiencing. This epistemological and linguistic problem thus also puts into question the possibility (and limits) of intersubjectivity as well as the grounds for establishing community. If, as Williams puts it, "reality . . . is that which human beings make common, by work or language," what are the modes by which a common reality can be posited or described?[124]

In order to understand the ways in which modernist writers, foremost among them Woolf, dealt with the limits of description, I read them alongside the philosophers, who explored these problems more systematically. Like Helmholtz in the passage above, Russell also posits two different ways of knowing, by acquaintance and by description, terms that had in fact been used by William James a few decades earlier. Acquaintance refers to our immediate knowledge of our own experience, while description is the means by which we come to know everything else outside of ourselves. For both Russell and James, although it cannot match the certainty offered by acquaintance, description is a crucial step toward transcending the boundaries of our own immediate sense experience and epistemologically securing the social. But there remain "sharp points" marking the boundary, words that register the "essential privacy of each individual's experience" and thus the limits of describability in language.[125] These sharp points are indexicals—words like *this*, *here*, and *now*—that shift referents according to contexts of use, and I will argue that they constitute the culmination—both apogee and end—of modernist description. The strategic deployment of such words comes to a head in Woolf, careful reader of both James and Proust, who thought most explicitly about these issues and who in many ways stands at the center of this book.

Of course, the fracturing of the "community of thought and feeling," the fragmentation of perspectives, and the thematizations of alienation described above are precisely the features of modernism decried by Marxist critics from Lukács to Jameson.[126] In *The Political Unconscious*, Jameson contrasts the descriptive passage from Balzac's *La vieille fille* discussed earlier with a similar passage from *Sister Carrie*, Theodore Dreiser being the American author whose lust for commodities most resembles that of Balzac. Whereas the Balzacian passage created an anonymous, generalized state of desire, in Jameson's account Carrie becomes merely a "point of view." Written in a later period of capitalism, the thoroughly commodified object meets its counterpart in a thoroughly monadized subject, now regulated by the laws of "psychology." Unlike in Balzac, with Dreiser we are situated outside Carrie's desire for luxuries and fine goods, "which is represented as a private wish or longing to which we relate ourselves as readers by mechanisms of identification and projection," or to which we may relate ironically, thanks to the intervention of Flaubert and *bovarysme* in the intervening period.[127] Although both Lukács and Jameson critique the dominance of point of view in modernism, which they associate with the bourgeois ideology of a monadic subject, in chapter 5 I will argue that Woolf takes such an ideology to its limit, which will also be its dissolution. As we will see, the bare gesture of ostension offered by *this* or *there* at once affirms the absolute privacy of experience (the monad locked in its room) and simultaneously undoes it by emptying it of content while conscripting the reader into its sphere of reference.

As the preeminent means of establishing the novelistic world, description draws boundaries between who is included and who is not, that is, who recognizes this common world and who does not. This extends to characters, some of whom are in the know, like James's "sensitive feelers" who can "read" the atmosphere, and some of whom, like Proust's clumsy social climbers, are not. And it also extends to readers, directing us to perceive the novel's world or occluding it from us. As we will see, indexicals that mark the limits of intersubjective understanding can be deployed to exclude characters and readers (ultimately I cannot have access to your *this* nor you to mine), but they can also, as I argue in the case of Woolf, invite the reader to participate in the process of meaning making precisely because they are semantically empty and thus cannot be tested. Their emptiness enables them to create communities of linguistic understanding not formed according to predetermined concepts or established lines of resemblance. The use of the demonstrative is thus the ultimate response to the question of how to describe the world without reifying it into mortified still lifes on the one hand and without collapsing into private, monadic, incommunicable viewpoints on the other. Estranging exactitude, relational modernists sidestepped the problem of verifiability and correspondence through fashioning new kinds of matching and attunement. In so doing, they sought new ways to imagine nondetermined modes of relation.

Chapter Overviews

Chapter 1 begins by reexamining the place of description in novel theory, returning to Lukács's still influential critique in "Narrate or Describe?" and reading it against Jacques Rancière's recent account of modern fiction, in which the rise of description indicates a new kind of literary democracy. The second part of the chapter then moves beyond the narrate/describe binary, rethinking description in relation to form and scale, examining its temporality, and looking to affective intensity and proportion to find nonnarrative types of dynamism and flux. I conclude by looking at the recent debates about critical reading practices in literary studies and asking what it might mean to read for description.

Departing from the turn away from visualizing and from the prose of things discussed above, chapter 2 takes seriously Henry James's pervasive attention to things "in the air" in his late works, challenging the prevailing critical opinion that James "underdescribes" by asking not only what kind of perception is blocked by his vague descriptions but also what kind of perception is enabled by them. I track his interest in describing atmosphere, which in his novels is capable of exerting influence and producing effects on the world while remaining ontologically elusive. James both brings this dimension of social experience within the descriptive scope of the novel and uses the metaphorics of atmospheric and spatial inhabiting to describe the affective qualities of social relations.

Chapter 3 widens the consideration of how description can render relations by turning to Proust's ubiquitous use of analogical techniques in *In Search of Lost Time*. I look at Proust's dismissal of description and its association with the superficial vision of camera in contrast to his valorization of metaphor, which he aligns with the penetrating vision of the X-ray but whose surface/depth dichotomy is less straightforward than it appears. Rather than the landmark moments associated with metaphor, such as the madeleine episode, which bring together the same sensation felt at different times under the sign of identity, my chapter highlights the passing, ordinary descriptive analogies that are omnipresent in the text. These, I contend, reveal Proust's greater penchant for things that are alike rather than the same, which amounts to a critique of the logic of identity. If James's atmospheres turned description toward relations that hovered uncertainly in the air, Proust amplifies this by using analogies that point out parallels not between two substantives or objects (A is like B) but between two sets of relations (A is to B as C is to D). Through ubiquitous strategies of likening, Proust makes description a technique capable not only of representation but also of discovery and critique.

Chapter 4 turns to Woolf and the question of how to describe a feeling. Like James, Woolf, too, is concerned with the representational challenges of describing the immaterial, which she worked through paradoxically via an engagement with the visual media of painting and the cinema. Like Proust, of whom she was a careful reader, Woolf also favors similes, but she turns them squarely toward the task of conveying affects, which in her novels often float free of particular characters and plots. I elucidate her descriptions of feeling through the work of psychoanalyst and developmental psychologist Daniel Stern, who argues that "affect attunement," that is, sharing another's feeling, entails not directly imitating a behavior but matching some formal feature of it (e.g., intensity, rhythm, shape) in a different perceptual mode. This nonmimetic, nonrepresentational model of creating likeness both explains with new precision how affects can be conveyed in language and also alerts us to an important role of description in the novel: that of enabling moments of shared feeling.

Whereas chapter 4 explores the paths toward affective communion offered by novelistic descriptions of feeling, chapter 5 is its negative counterpart, looking at the limits of what can be communicated in words. In modernism, I propose, descriptive failure is caused not by confrontation with a Romantic sublime beyond comprehension but rather with the particularities of sensations that we ourselves know all too well. Such idiosyncratic experiential qualities escape full expression in language even as they call forth ever more descriptions. Reading Woolf alongside Russell and William James' philosophy of language, I contend that in demonstratives such as "this," "here," and "now," modernism finds the "name" of the indescribable.

Toward a Theory of Description

[CHAPTER ONE]

Most novel readers today are likely to agree with Henry James's assessment in "The Art of Fiction" that it is impossible to really separate description and narration. "People often talk of these things as if they had a kind of internecine distinctness," James writes, "instead of melting into each other at every breath, and being intimately associated parts of one general effort of expression" (*LC* 1:54). Who can imagine in a novel worth discussing "a passage of description that is not in its intention narrative, a passage of dialogue that is not in its intention descriptive?" And yet our major theories of the novel in the twentieth century, echoing an older rhetorical tradition, have insisted on this partition as virtually axiomatic.[1] Indeed, even if this separation seems artificial and difficult to maintain with any strictness, it is also not hard to see why "The house is white, with a slate roof and green shutters" is called descriptive whereas "The man went over to the table and picked up a knife" is called narrative.[2] The former (both examples come from Gérard Genette and I will return to them later in this chapter) deals with a state of affairs, whereas the latter deals with an action. Correspondingly, the first sentence contains very few verbs of action, favoring instead predications of qualities, enumeration of parts, and a sense of duration or simultaneity. These are all features that we associate with description in contrast to the telling of sequential actions unfolding in time that characterizes narration. We thus face something of a conundrum: although the strict separation of description from narration is a kind of fiction, this distinction also seems impossible to entirely dispense with, not least because the dichotomy has so structured our thinking on this topic. Even if we want to leave it behind, it seems to be a necessary point of departure.

In part 1 of this chapter, I reexamine this classic divide in novel theory. I first return to Georg Lukács's influential critique of the politics of description and read it against Jacques Rancière's more recent, differing account of modern fiction and its growing disproportions of descriptive elements from the mid-nineteenth century onward. After reappraising the narrate versus describe framework, in part 2 I then move beyond that dichotomy in order to consider some alternate ways of thinking about description outside the confines of narrativity, which also bear on our ideas of literary form more generally. Finally, in light of recent debates about critical reading practices in literary studies in which it has enjoyed a new prominence, in part 3 I consider what it might mean to take description not as a critical method but instead as a critical object, that is, not description as a form of reading but rather reading *for* description.

Part I: Narrate or Describe, Still?

In the twentieth century no critic did more to entrench the separation of narration from description and to devalue the latter term than the Marxist philosopher and aesthetician Georg Lukács. For Lukács, the issue is not merely one of aesthetic preference but of the different logics underlying the two narrative modes, which he pegs to the specific sociohistorical development of two periods of capitalism in the nineteenth century. As he writes in "Narrate or Describe?" (1934), authentic realism, governed by the mode of narration and exemplified by Balzac and Tolstoy, preserves the "significant and vital aspects of social practice" found in epic art, making "the wheel of events," characters, and their actions the decisive elements.[3] After 1848, however, authentic realism gives way to a fallen naturalism, dominated by the mode of description and embodied by Zola and Flaubert. According to Lukács, although Balzac was in fact the novelist who elevated description to prominence, his descriptive practices subordinated details to the greater whole and were driven by the need to accurately represent new social phenomena. Since the relationship of the individual to his class became more complicated than it had been in the seventeenth and eighteenth centuries, the precise delineation of the filth, smells, and meals in the Vauquer pension was necessary "to render Rastignac's particular kind of adventurism comprehensible and real."[4] With Flaubert and Zola, in contrast, description was severed from the sphere of human action and practiced for its own sake, painting only still lifes.[5] The results could hardly be more disastrous. The growth of descriptive elements turns the novel into a simple succession of sketches rather than a work organized by a narrative logic that can establish causal relationships and make of it an organic unity. Details proliferate, the whole disintegrates, all significance is leveled, and any view of a social totality is lost.

For Lukács, the dominance of the descriptive mode in literature after 1848 evinced a new relationship to society evident in both naturalist authors and protagonists, who were no longer active participants but instead passive observers. Correspondingly, social conditions were no longer portrayed as the result of struggle and flux, shown in their development and thus presented as capable of change. Instead, the status quo appeared as immutable, already-achieved "social facts, as results, as *caput mortuum* of a social process."[6] Because narration alone is concerned with the unfolding of human actions, for Lukács it is the sole means of conveying the dynamism and flux of historical becoming. Description, by contrast, can only mortify the dialectical movement of history; human beings thus become objectified while objects are lavishly depicted for their own sake. Importantly, in spite of superficial differences of style, in Lukács's view modernism was continuous with naturalism: both took a static and sensory approach to reality rather than the "dynamic and developmental" one of an authentic realism.[7] On this account, modernist protagonists alienated and withdrawn from society express a view of the human as incapable of realizing her existence as a social being and deprived of the agency to create narrative—or historical—change. Thus, although Lukács's limits his critique of description to naturalism, its continuity with modernism raises the question of what happens to this mode in the early twentieth century.

The charges laid at description's door in "Narrate or Describe?" do not begin or end with Lukács. With respect to the danger of descriptive autonomy, he echoes a long line of thinking derived from Aristotelian poetics, carried through eighteenth-century rhetoricians, and extended into the twentieth century. For earlier rhetoricians, the trouble with unchecked description was that it posed a threat to the internal unity and necessity of the text because such passages could potentially be skipped over without consequence, violating the principle that every part of the work should derive its sense from its place within the whole.[8] For Lukács, meanwhile, the autonomy of description was symptomatic of reification and commodity fetishism; for this reason he scorns the possibility of a "poetry of things."[9] But despite the differences between a belletristic view of the work and a Marxist one, in both cases description constitutes a troublesome kind of part, a fragment that always needs to be subordinated to other ends in order to neutralize its threat of disintegrating the whole. In effect, the place of description within the novel—its perpetual desire to become autonomous—has entailed a kind of "l'art pour l'art" debate captured in miniature. The specter of its autonomy challenges the unity and integrity of the work as a whole. Thus, description has been conceived as a kind of "textual cyst," dismissed as minor but paradoxically always remaining a concern, a perpetual foreign body allowed to exist as long as it assimilates into the larger entity, but which always aspires to take over the host.[10]

In addition to echoes of older belletrists and rhetoricians, there is also a striking formal similarity between Lukács's critique of naturalism and the modernists' own critique of earlier realist description. This similarity turns on an opposition of surface to depth that was everywhere in modernist thinking.[11] So, for instance, James urges the writer to look "beneath and behind" that which presents itself to the eye, and Woolf praised Joyce for revealing the flickerings of the "innermost flame" (E 3:34). Of course, this version of depth—as moral ambiguity and psychological interiority— was decried by Lukács as a false one. Whereas the modernists charged their predecessors with failing to penetrate beyond surface appearances in their descriptive inventories of the material world, for Lukács it was the modernists themselves who were unable to see how surface phenomena were produced by underlying social relations and class conflict. According to him, they mistook the subjective view as the true and only one, negating an objective or external standpoint and thus rendering themselves unable to adopt a perspective that grasped society in its totality and in the flux of history.[12] But although Lukács and the modernists operate with different understandings of what the deeper, truer reality is, they both critique description by aligning it with mere appearance, and this shared opposition is significant. For Lukács, the novel was the genre for an age in which totality was no longer possible but was still the goal, and he saw the growth of description in the later nineteenth century onward as thwarting the novel's rightful search to represent that totality or that deeper reality.[13] For the modernists, the disavowal of surfaces was symptomatic of their own desire for a reality, truth, or essence behind appearances at the very moment when it becomes most apparent that any such stable reality is no longer tenable.[14] In both cases, the disavowal of description indexes a continued investment in certain classical ideas of truth, wholeness, and unity. The difference is that modernists' descriptive practices constitute an attempt to articulate an idea of wholeness that is not totalizing or modeled on an organic unity. From the diffuse, unlocalizable figure of atmosphere in James to the culminating point or gasp in Woolf, my contention is that modernist writers seek out a new model of a whole through the very mode—description—that seems to undo it.

"THE EQUALITY EFFECT"

What appears on the surface of experience is a succession of particulars— fleeting, momentary sense experiences unconnected by strong relations of cause and effect. Although Lukács finds in the descriptive impulses of modern fiction an inability to grasp the truth of historical becoming and a failure to convey the causality of human actions, the advocates of modern fiction themselves saw in the constraints of traditional narrative and its logic of cause and effect a false tyranny. So Woolf complains of the "powerful and unscrupulous tyrant" who compels the writer "to provide a plot, to provide comedy, tragedy, love interest, and an air of probability embalming the whole" (*E* 4:160). Instead, she famously enjoins the modern novelist to record the "incessant shower of innumerable atoms" as they fall on the mind, for "there is no proper stuff of fiction" (*E* 4:164). Taking up Woolf's injunction, Jacques Rancière argues that traditional poetic structures and definitions of action are predicated on a rigid social hierarchy of who is capable of acting. This idea leads Rancière to a different anatomy of modern literature, one that I want to juxtapose against Lukács's account to yield an alternative reading of the politics of description.[15] Like Lukács, Rancière locates a shift in the proportions of modern fiction beginning with Flaubert, but for him this new "disequilibrium between the immobilities of description and the dynamics of action" constitutes not a fall from historicity but instead a new egalitarian logic entailing a "redistribution of the sensible [*partage du sensible*]," a shift in the very parameters of what is perceptible, and by whom.[16] Whereas Lukács sees the proliferation of description as evidence of realism's fall out of history and action, Rancière sees this flattening or leveling as evidence of a profound shift toward the democratization of experience where what is lost is not all sense of human action and significance but instead only one particular understanding of action and one particular way of "linking action and significance."[17]

The traditional way of linking action to significance is traced to Aristotle, who established fiction as first and foremost a "structure of rationality: a mode of presentation that renders things, situations or events perceptible and intelligible; a mode of liaison that constructs forms of coexistence, succession and causal linkage between events, and gives to these forms the characters of the possible, the real or the necessary."[18] For Aristotle, the poetic structure of rationality is a matter of narration: "a succession of actions, linked by necessity or verisimilitude," the coherent telling of events with a beginning, a middle, and an end.[19] In this way, poetry differs from history, which deals with *kath'hekaston*, "the succession of facts as they arrive, one after another, whereas poetry has to do with the generality of things grasped in their ensemble (*ta katholou*)."[20] A divide is thus set up: either the empirical succession of individual facts one after the other or an arrangement of events linked by causal relations cohering in an organic whole. The revolutions of modern fiction were upsetting, Rancière argues, precisely because they broke with this model of fiction as a totality where the parts are subordinated to the whole and events unfold as a chain of causes and effects governed by necessity or verisimilitude.

Accordingly, critiques of the new disproportions of modern fiction—attributable in no small part to the swelling of description over action—were driven by a continued adherence to a traditional Aristotelian poetic rationality and a continued investment in classical ideas of action and totality.[21] This was true regardless of where the critique was politically situated. Conservative nineteenth-century critics found Flaubert's descriptive meanderings to be an assault on rationality in both art and life, connecting it to the overturning of social order. So Barbey d'Aurevilly faulted *Sentimental Education* for being a series of tableaux strung one next to another lacking any higher plan and proceeding without any suspicion "that life . . . under the diversity and apparent disorder of its coincidences, has its own logical and inflexible laws and its necessary engenderments."[22] And in 1857 Armand de Pontmartin called the reign of detail in Flaubert's work "democracy in literature" because it rendered all episodes equally significant (or insignificant).[23] Leftist twentieth-century critics such as Roland Barthes and Jean-Paul Sartre did not accuse Flaubert of being too democratic, but they were no less critical of the growth of description in the realist novel, which they, much like Lukács, saw as expressive of capitalist reification, a bourgeois fascination with commodities, and a flight from social praxis through petrifying gestures and actions.[24] In "The Reality Effect," Barthes famously argues that realism gives rise to the narratively superfluous descriptive detail (such as a barometer hanging on a wall), which, however, signifies a fiction's reality by virtue of its very uselessness. But, as Rancière points out, Barthes thus reintegrates the useless detail into the narrative economy, betraying a continued commitment to the old organic model of a whole.[25] Barthes, no less than Barbey, takes issue with a "fictional fabric made up of 'details' without narrative function in the narrative totality."[26] In each case, what is at stake is a certain understanding of the work as an ordered, bounded, determined whole made up of subordinated parts, and in each case the prominence of description was seen to upset this order and upend the larger plan.[27]

Crucially, Rancière argues that Aristotle's distinction between two kinds of connections between events—poetic rationality versus historical empiricity—corresponds to a social distinction between two different types of humanity. When critics denounce the loss of action that is entailed by a rise in description, the very understanding of what constitutes action turns on a particular division of the sensible that excludes certain people from the order of ends. "There are active men who live at the level of the totality, able to conceive grand ends and to seek to accomplish them in contention with other wills and the blows of fortune. And there are men who simply have things happen to them one after the other, able only to live day to day in the mere sphere of life's reproduction."[28] What was really upsetting, according to Rancière, about the lack of structure and proportion in the form of *Madame Bovary* or *Sentimental Education* was that it overturned an entrenched social order by redistributing capacities for sensible experience and dismantling established divisions of who could feel what. In this way, whereas "an entire progressist tradition has seen in the modern revolutions of fiction a process of fragmentation of the human totality or of dethroning of action in favour of the passivity of things," Rancière urges us to "see in it something else altogether: a destruction of the hierarchical model subjecting parts to the whole and dividing humanity between an elite of active beings and a multitude of passive ones."[29] Viewed this way, the later century's proliferation of descriptive details evinces a shift towards "literary democracy."[30]

For Rancière, the importance of literature derives from the fact that it operates on the same plane as politics by intervening "in the carving up of space and time, the visible and the invisible, speech and noise. It intervenes in the relationship between practices and forms of visibility and modes of saying that carves up one or more common worlds."[31] But literary democracy should not thereby be understood as equivalent to political democracy. "The equality specific to the new fiction belongs to this redistribution of forms of sensible experience, in which the forms of worker emancipation also participated, as did the multiplicity of rebellions that assailed the traditional hierarchy of forms of life. But it did not for all that express political aspirations for democracy or social emancipation."[32] The equality of literary democracy is limited to capacities for feeling, breaking down the division between "life doomed to utility" and "existences destined for the grandeurs of action and passion."[33] Emma Bovary, along with Felicité in "A Simple Heart" and other later nineteenth-century figures like Germinie Lacerteux, all belong to "the formidable species of those daughters of peasants capable of doing anything to sate their most sensual passions or their most ideal aspirations."[34] No longer reserved for aristocratic souls, after Flaubert, workers' sons and peasants' daughters could read about forms of life in books not meant for them and aspire to experience lives that did not match their identity. "From now on, anyone whomsoever can experience any emotion or passion whatsoever."[35] And this redistribution of the sensible is reflected in the new proportions—or disproportions—of novelistic form. The egalitarianism or indifference to beings, things, and situations, all open to being seen, "leaves no place for the selection of meaningful characters and the harmonious development of a plot."³⁶ Anything could be important, including a barometer mentioned offhand. For Rancière, the "reality effect" becomes "an equality effect."³⁷

We could certainly wonder just how far this "equality effect" extends. The time of those living in "the mere sphere of life's reproduction" is after all not just the time of workers and ordinary people but also specifically that of women (as Rancière's own examples of Emma, Félicité, and Germinie attest) and of subjugated people. The hierarchy of poetic rationality over unordered empiricity also expresses a hierarchy of subjects considered more or less capable of reason, and it should not be surprising that the absence of a plan or plot for which Flaubert drew criticism is a charge that has also been leveled at "minor" genres, which are often associated with marginalized subjects. The nineteenth-century genre of literary sketches, for instance, which was primarily practiced by women, was considered a nonnarrative, descriptive genre in ways that marked it as intellectually inferior.³⁸ And as W. J. T. Mitchell notes, slave narratives, in which description is a dominant rhetorical feature, were often characterized as "assemblages of 'scenes' and 'sketches' linked in an episodic structure that confines temporality to particular 'incidents'" rather than complex plots.³⁹ The validity of Rancière's account of the redistribution of the sensible outside the high-European realist context in which he is working is open to question, but his account is nevertheless valuable for giving us a different way to understand the meaning of the disproportions introduced by description and its threat to the unity of a whole, a criticism that underlies virtually all discussions of the subject.⁴⁰

Of course, it is also not the case that all order or design disappears after Flaubert. In the absence of the old hierarchies, the novel is still faced with the task of linking one sentence and one narrative event to another, and in the following pages I trace the ways various writers responded to the modern novelist's task of spinning "a wandering thread, lightly joining one thing to another" while attempting to fashion a kind of whole not modeled on organic unity.⁴¹ My point is not that the descriptive mode simply dissolves the form of modernist fiction altogether; instead, I mean to emphasize that attending to description makes us rethink the signal categories of novelistic form.

Although he does not frame his account in terms of "narrate or describe," Rancière's recasting of Lukács's agon allows the rise of description in the novel to lead to something quite different from the mortifying effects of reification. Indeed, for him the dominance of the concept of reification in accounts of modern fiction's break with the old logic of action has obscured the meaning of this break. "This concept [of reification] places at modernity's core the loss of a totality of lived experience. But this 'totality' was one of a world strictly divided into two worlds of experience without communication. And the democracy of modern fiction works to revoke this division."[42] Rather than nostalgia for a lost totality that results in too much description, Rancière urges us to subject that idea of totality itself to critique.

Moreover, the idea that the novelist (or critic) could access that totality by taking a position of omniscient and comprehensive vision and narrating history involves taking a stance outside history itself. This is why it is so important for Lukács that realism recount events in the past and why it is problematic for him that description renders everything contemporaneous.[43] But such retrospective recounting presumes the achievement of an authoritative self looking back at something completed. As Jennifer Fleissner argues in a brilliant and revisionary account of American naturalism, "If anything . . . it is the appealing 'realist' dream of history as forming a story, as opposed to naturalism's stuckness in ongoing description, that has the problematic effect of making history appear a foregone conclusion."[44] Although for Lukács only realist narrative can express the movement of history, Fleissner points out that it is precisely "narrative that covers over the truth of history's incompletion and thus the possibility for change."[45] Whereas Fleissner turns her attention to the peculiar creativity she finds in the "stuck" descriptions of naturalism, my focus here is on the relational and comparative energies of modernist forms, but it remains true that description is capable of being a historical, agential mode (sometimes by questioning these very terms), albeit one that differs from the causal logic of the plot.

One final point deserves mentioning here. Fleissner defends the apparent immobility of naturalist description by positioning women at the center of American naturalism—in her reading, the naturalist heroine embodies a trajectory not of decline or triumph but of "on-going, nonlinear, repetitive motion" that is mirrored in naturalism's "compulsive" descriptions.[46] Although it is not always flagged as a keyword, gender (and, to a degree, sexuality) is an important issue in this book as well, beginning with Lukács's implicitly masculinist valorization of history, progress, action, and health against a feminized stasis, commodification, observation, and degeneration.[47] Nor is he alone in the gendering of his antidescriptive stance, as evidenced by the long-standing association of description with the everyday, the miniature, the domestic, and the ornamental, all feminized terms (this history has been discussed influentially by Naomi Schor in the context of the detail).[48] Issues of gender inflect my readings of the descriptive practices of all the writers studied here as well, from James's differential distribution of perceptual sensitivity and consequent feminization of his own authorial position to the importance Proust accords to women's work in his social panorama to Woolf's valuing of presence as a kind of feminist resistance to modernity's cult of speed and progress. I would not want to simply associate description with the feminine (or to celebrate such an association uncomplicatedly) in modernism, but a certain alignment of the two is a thread that runs quietly but persistently throughout this book.

Part II: Description beyond Narration

For novel theorists of diverse stripes, the battle of narrate or describe is staged on the field of nineteenth-century realism. But if we accept that by the early twentieth century, the classical model of action and significance identified with the logic of the plot is no longer tenable, it follows that the logic of description can no longer be understood simply as narration's foil. In the foregoing I have been concerned with recovering the possibilities and politics of description *within* that influential binary. I want now to consider ways of thinking about it as not determined solely by the purposes of narrativity. Whereas most defenses of description thus far have made their case on the grounds that it *is* in fact narrative (at least in whatever author is being discussed at the time), I proceed by assuming not that a distinction between the two does not exist but that such a distinction is not always determining or even especially important. In what follows, I want to lay out a set of categories according to which we can consider description anew: its challenges to our prevailing assumptions about novelistic form, the heterogeneous temporalities it can introduce into the work, the dynamism it can create through modulations in affective intensity, and the strange effects of its elongated proportions. Some of these strands will be taken up more extensively in subsequent chapters, but my main aim in this section is to suggest some ways of thinking about description that don't take its opposition to narration as its principal determining feature. All of this will lead in part 3 to the question of what we might gain by reading for description.

FORM AND SCALE

If, as we have seen, description has always threatened the organic unity of a work, this raises a host of questions about how we conceive of novelistic form. As Nicholas Dames notes in *Physiology of the Novel*, we habitually conceive of form in synchronic, structural terms rather than temporal, processual ones. Indeed, literary formalism has had to seek a variety of ways "to still time in order to detect structure."[49] This view of the novel as a complete, static object, Dames argues, is bequeathed to Anglo-American criticism in no small part by Percy Lubbock, a disciple of James.[50] Dames seeks instead to recover an earlier tradition of thinking about the novel (formulated by G. H. Lewes, Alexander Bain, E. S. Dallas, and Vernon Lee, among others) that conceived of it as "a process rather than a structure."[51] Taking a cue from this alternate tradition, which Dames calls "physiological novel theory," can open up our thinking about the place of description. Physiological novel theorists imagined novelistic form as "produced by reading in time, particularly in the rhythms of attention and inattention, slow comprehension and rapid skipping ahead, buildups and discharges of affect."[52] Accordingly, for them, "formal investigation ... was usually grounded on the identification of recurrent units (sounds, themes, effects) over time, rather than the attempt to form a spatial map of such units or to shape them into a totality."[53] The data of reading, Dames argues, was precisely what Lubbock excised, in so doing inaugurating a tradition of regarding the novel as an object whose form and design could only be seen from a certain level of abstraction and distance, since that was the only way to see it as a whole.[54]

We have now become so accustomed to thinking of narrative as a spatially extended object—because only in this way can we see the full sequence of events and understand their significance—that we tend to forget that this sense of the plot is only visible from a particular vantage point, namely, retroactively and at a distance. This is especially true in the case of dense, elliptical modernist works. Think of how hard it is to know what is happening at any given moment in a late James novel when you're actually reading one; it is usually only with some degree of retrospect that we can grasp a given sequence of events and say what has actually happened in a given section. Modernist novels in particular have been associated with "spatial form" ever since Joseph Frank's influential argument, which posited that these works were spatially rather than temporally organized and replaced narrative sequentiality with a sense of simultaneity.[55] But modernist writers themselves were attuned to the tension between comprehending a novel's form as a whole and the temporal process through which that form is actually encountered. In an essay titled "The Love of Reading" (1931), Woolf observes

> During the actual reading new impressions are always cancelling or completing the old. Delight, anger, boredom, laughter succeed each other incessantly as we read. Judgment is suspended, for we cannot know what may come next. But now the book is completed. It has taken a definite shape. And the book as a whole is different from the book received currently in several different parts. It has a shape, it has a being. And this

shape, this being, can be held in the mind and compared with the shapes of other books and given its own size and smallness by comparison with theirs. (*E* 5:272–73)

Writing in a post-James, post-Lubbock landscape, Woolf intimates that something is lost as well as gained when a work is conceived as a complete whole. It gains a shape and a being, but it is by that token something different from the book experienced in the process of reading, that is, in its parts.

Thinking about novels as a temporal process of unfolding effects allows us to see that our received view of description, specifically the narrate/describe binary, depends on a spatialized idea of a novel's form as a bounded container viewed from above.[56] On a sentence-by-sentence level in the actual process of reading, however, there is nothing in a novel that is *not* descriptive. Here the issue of analytical scale becomes crucial. Take Genette's example of a descriptive versus narrative sentence given at the beginning of this chapter: "The house is white, with a slate roof and green shutters" and "The man went over to the table and picked up a knife." These sentences actually lead Genette to conclude that it is in fact easier to conceive of a purely descriptive text than a purely narrative one. After all, in "The man went over to the table and picked up a knife," the three substantives in that sentence, however little qualified, are nevertheless descriptive of the beings they designate. "Even a verb can be more or less descriptive, in the precision that it gives to the spectacle of the action (one has only to compare 'grabbed a knife,' for example, with 'picked up a knife'), and consequently no verb is quite exempt from descriptive resonance."[57] The question of whether any words at all are free from descriptive resonance is a problem I will take up in chapter 5 via the philosophies of Bertrand Russell and William James. But for now what I want to highlight is the significance of the fact that Genette's example is a single phrase, for it is at this microlevel that the descriptive is ubiquitous, indeed, impossible to eliminate. Even when we are reading passages that recount actions, the individual words and sentences that are doing the narrating also inevitably contain important descriptive information that cannot be extricated from the narration. Thus, description cannot be singled out as an isolable feature except when it reaches a certain threshold of dominance, which requires a larger scale of analysis, for instance, a paragraph, a page, or a scene. Only in larger units does it make sense to call a passage "narrative" rather than "descriptive"; on a smaller scale the distinction is impossible to maintain. That the binary has been so influential is due to the fact that novel theory tends to work at macroscales, and description's marginality can also be explained by the fact that larger textual units are (typically) the scale at which description is *not* pervasive. Rather than an ontological division made on the basis of the objects it covers (things versus events), which can then be extrapolated to worldviews (e.g., passive versus active), description and narration should instead be considered a matter of degree or emphasis that depends on the scale of critical analysis, which will be determined in turn by the questions being asked.

Even considered at the scale of a work as a whole, the preponderance and distribution of narrative and descriptive elements will of course vary such that it may be easier or harder to draw a line between the two.[58] It is no accident that the critics who have most entrenched the narrate/describe binary have been primarily working with a nineteenth-century corpus that features relatively autonomous descriptive set pieces, such as those that occur at the beginning of the work or a chapter, or every time a new setting or character is introduced. Established by Balzac, these passages are what Genette calls "extratemporal descriptions," where "the narrator, forsaking the course of the story . . . makes it his business, in his own name and solely for the information of his reader, to describe a scene that at this point in the story no one, strictly speaking, is looking at."[59] A celebrated, paradigmatic example would be the opening description of the Vauquer boardinghouse in *Père Goriot*, which sets the stage before the action proper begins.

In modernism, such set pieces of mise-en-scène tend either to disappear or to become defamiliarized. The latter strategies can take the form of a self-consciously baroque or cubist style, as in the ekphrastic scene when we first meet Robin Vote in Djuna Barnes's *Nightwood*, or in Wyndham Lewis's descriptions of Bertha Lunken in *Tarr*. Alternately, the semi-autonomy of descriptive passages can be intensified by being explicitly separated from the main body of the text and its characters, as in the italicized seascapes in *The Waves* or the "Time Passes" section of *To the Lighthouse*. And when descriptions do occur in the body of texts, they are usually interwoven with narration. So Genette observes that Proust's descriptions in *In Search of Lost Time* "never bring about a pause in the narrative, a suspension of the story or of (according to the traditional term) the 'action.'"[60] Instead, the action at hand is just the labor of perception, which is the "story" these descriptions narrate. Although Genette, like other critics who have written on the subject, see this as evidence that what we call description is in fact narrative, it takes very little to push the argument in the other direction, to say that narration is just the description of action. My point is not to advocate for a simple inversion of the hierarchy, or even to generate "a description-bound narratology of the novel" but rather to point out that our axiomatic sense of the divide itself depends on a particular view of the work.[61] Since modernist texts make this division difficult to sustain, they are well positioned to help us think about description in other terms.

TEMPORALITY AND RHYTHM

One of the first charges against description is that it is static, and it is easy to see why when it is juxtaposed against the propulsive forward pull of plot. But even if it is true that a descriptive passage may have a different pace than that of a passage recounting a series of actions, something more like a durative dwelling than a moving flow, this is a distinction between different temporalities, not a difference between something temporal and something not. Notably, in Genette's influential work of narratology, *Narrative Discourse*, the only discussion of description appears under the rubric of temporality. Specifically, the discussion concerns variations in speed, which is determined by the duration of narrative events relative to the space (in paragraphs or pages, for instance) devoted to telling them—a relation known as rhythm. Theoretically, Genette argues, "there exists a continuous gradation from the infinite speed of ellipsis, where a nonexistent section of narrative corresponds to some duration of story, on up to the absolute slowness of descriptive pause, where some section of narrative discourse corresponds to a nonexistent diegetic duration."[62] The "nonexistent diegetic duration" is why description is thought to arrest the flow of narrative: no time elapses in the story, but lots of time elapses in the discourse, as in the multipage description of the Vauquer pension at the beginning of *Père Goriot*. As a response, conceits such as following a character moving around a space developed in an attempt to motivate descriptions and to integrate them into narrative time.[63] The apparent stasis of description also goes hand in hand, I would argue, with the reason that it is so liable to be skipped entirely. It repels the absorption commanded by the *récit*, which pulls us along in its past-present-future movement. This resistance to absorption is what is signaled when we say we can't "get into" a book—leisurely reading can easily become boredom.

But the "absolute slowness" of the descriptive pause, even if we accept this characterization and even if it risks tedium, does not always have the same character or the same effects. Rather than viewing description simply as pulling a work away from temporality, which belongs solely to narrative, we might reconsider—and revalue—the temporality of description itself, including varied forms of stillness. For instance, Amy M. King argues that the swelling of novelistic description in Victorian works borrowed a structure and ethical justification from the close observational practices of natural history and its debt to natural theology, which valued close attention to the minute and the quotidian.[64] Thus, for Mary Mitford and others, the temporality of descriptive stillness had a moral justification. Meanwhile, Claire Jarvis argues in another study of Victorian fiction that the stasis of description is central to the representation of a particular kind of charged sexual desire. "When an author translates sexual tension into a scene, there is little emphasis on future action or the possibility of change. Instead, the narrative halts, producing a descriptive *tableau vivant* in which characters' physical and sartorial attributes take on significance."[65] The frozen, suspended qualities of the kind of sexuality Jarvis calls "exquisite masochism" can only be achieved through descriptive form, one in which stasis itself becomes pleasurable. Thinking of pleasure another way, the often-dilatory rhythms of descriptive passages can also be an invitation to linger, resulting in moments of what we could call readerly leisure. This need not take the form of a morally virtuous close attention such as the one sanctioned by natural theology but rather a kind of acceptable mental drift in the face of a surfeit of details that prevents systematic recall or ordering. As Nicholas Dames argues, when the novel form is understood first as a temporal process of unfolding effects over time, room is made for distraction and periodic attention as an inevitable feature of any extended temporal process.[66] Moreover, long, lyrical descriptions that are rife with figurative invention and play can also function as moments of respite from a novel's feeling of doom or its shocking plot, as Alicia Mireles Christoff shows in a reading of Hardy's *Tess of the D'Urbevilles*.[67]

However conceived, as rest, distraction, sexually charged tension, or sustained attention, descriptive temporality, unlike a narrative one, asks to be read not in order to get from one thing to the next. In this respect it amounts to the kind of temporality that Alexander Kluge calls "the insurrection of the present against the other temporalities," one that chafes at serving as a mere stage of transit on the itinerary from past to future.[68] As we will see in chapter 4, the refusal of perpetual momentum and the attention to presence solicited by description can constitute a critique of masculinist notions of action and historical progress everywhere in modernity.

AFFECT AND INTENSITY

In defending description against the charges of stasis and immobility, critics have often argued that it is in fact narrative, and therefore, dynamic. But this denies description its own forms of fluctuation and change, making narrativity the sole ground of dynamism. Affect, I propose, offers a way to think about modulation and flux within description that isn't solely dependent on narrative. Affective modulation and intensity forms another axis along which especially longer descriptive episodes can generate their own variability and interest.

Consider the nine italicized interludes in *The Waves*, made up of descriptive scenes of a house and seascape at different hours of the day, that are juxtaposed with the chronological development of human life told in the main body of the text by the six characters. These interludes have a strong quality of stillness not simply by virtue of being descriptive but thanks to features such as repeated allusions to small motions in place, as when we read "The red curtains and the white blinds blew in and out, flapping against the edge of the window" (*W* 183), or "In the bucket near the house the tap stopped dripping, as if the bucket were full, and then the tap dripped one, two, three separate drops in succession" (*W* 165). Additionally, references to blankness and the impersonal, scenic use of the preterit—"The birds sang their blank melody outside" (*W* 8); "The pool on the top of the moor lay blank" (*W* 207)—give the effect of an eternal present very much along Jamesonian lines.

But however powerful their impression of stillness, these descriptions also display movement both internally within a single section and also across their dispersal throughout the work as a whole. The most obvious way this happens is thematically, since the interludes are organized chronologically across different times of day (although we can also note its multiple temporal scales: human, meteorological, and ecological). Dynamism is also achieved through linguistic means, for instance, through the use of adverbs of time, such as the Woolfian favorite "now . . . now . . . ," which create sequence and variation while remaining in an oddly persisting present.

Another important motor of movement and variation in these descriptive sections is the modulation of affects and affective intensity. So in the third interlude, the initial playfulness of some birds' flight, "singing as they chased each other, escaping, pursuing, pecking each other" (*W* 73-74) gives way to a sense of decadence and disgust as their pecking at "the soft, monstrous body of the defenceless worm" leads to a description of sticky, oozing textures. "Down there among the roots where the flowers decayed, gusts of dead smells were wafted; drops formed on the bloated sides of swollen things. The skin of rotten fruit broke, and matter oozed too thick to run. Yellow excretions were exuded by slugs and now and again an amorphous body with a head at either end swayed slowly from side to side" (*W* 74-75). The swaying of the amorphous two-headed body is another instance of the aforementioned references to motion in place that create a sense of stillness, but the shifts in affective tone, from playful (if tinged with violence) to grotesque, as well as the dialing up of affective intensity in the later passages, make this descriptive interlude varied and dynamic. Throughout the nine interludes the still, impersonal descriptions of sun, waves, birds, and light create an uncanny eeriness, not to say ominousness, that is not without suspense but that is not, however, resolved narratively by any turn of events. At times this uncanny, eerie feeling intensifies, as in the evocations of rotten fruit and oozing excretions, while at other times it diminishes, as happens when things are said to be resting, motionless, or blank. Although it is less pertinent in the case of the interludes in *The Waves*, this descriptive-affective mode of fluctuation may also cut against or supplement narrative fluctuations.

Finally, thinking about affect leads us to an issue touched on already but rarely considered in novel theory even as it belongs to discussions of craft and indeed of ordinary reading experience: the pleasure of descriptions. We need only contrast the poet Mark Doty's meditation on the necessity and the pleasure of bringing words "tuned to their highest ability" to "the project of saying what's before us" with Lukács's remark that in spite of the thoroughness and virtuosity of his descriptions, Zola produced nothing in the horse race scene in *Nana* but a monograph on modern turf.[69] Mieke Bal observes that "the gap between a criticism that applauds description" as concrete, visionary, lyrical, moving, and so forth and "a narrative theory that marginalizes it, appears to come from the 'experience' of reading versus the logic of structure."[70] This gap is similar to the one drawn earlier between the physiological novel theory view of the novel considered as a temporal process of unfolding and the James-Lubbock view of the novel as a completed spatial plan. Needless to say, the pleasure of description can take many forms: it can appeal to our appetites and our senses, it can produce the thrill of recognition, and it can lead to the shock of discovery, to name just a few. In this book I will approach the issue in two ways. In chapter 3 we will see that Proust's compulsive habit of describing by analogizing, which I read as an exercise of what Walter Benjamin calls the "mimetic faculty," is not only a cognitive habit but also an affective orientation toward finding likenesses that constitutes at once a critique of identity (what is alike is precisely what is not the same) and evidence of a sensibility geared toward understanding the world in terms of relations. Then in my discussion of affect attunement in chapter 4, I will consider how descriptions of feeling in particular can lead to a sense of feeling-with, which is an integral part of the pleasure of reading.

PROPORTION AND ORDER

Perhaps the single greatest fault singled out by virtually all critics of description is its liability to take on a life of its own. When it is charged with an allegorical function or when it works to supplement the narration—in other words, when it is subordinated to other ends—description is praised. But even when details of clothing, physiognomy, and furniture all function as social indexes, there is always the possibility of excess. Even in the case of Balzac we could ask if we need all *eight* pages describing "une de ces maisons provinciales" to get the point that Monsieur Grandet is a miser—

would six or seven have done? As often as he has been hailed as an exemplary allegorical describer (by Lukács, Auerbach, and Jameson, for instance), Balzac has been charged by critics during his time and later with an inability to select from among details and a tendency to overstuff his novels by throwing them all in. This drive toward descriptive comprehensiveness may be attributed partly to his intention to be the natural historian of French society, but it also stems from something inescapable about description itself: the inability to determine with any intrinsic necessity where to start and when to stop.

As we saw last chapter in the remarks of Valéry, this kernel of arbitrariness has rendered description suspect, but we could also see in the always-hovering threat of descriptive excess the anarchic element that contains the possibility for disruption even when it is marshaled for other purposes. Philippe Hamon suggests as much when he writes that the essence of the descriptive, insofar as there is one, is to resist "the constraining linearity of the text."[71] In this sense the growing autonomy of description from the service of the plot beginning in the later nineteenth century—especially descriptions of "microsensory events," to use Rancière's phrase—could be read as resistance to the encroaching logic of rationalization and efficiency that was becoming increasingly dominant. The ineliminable threat of arbitrariness and excess in any description, its inability to be fully integrated into a narrative economy, its aforementioned stillness or attention to presence—these could be read not as symptoms of total reification but rather as challenges to teleology and instrumentality. The very features that have led to description's devaluation may also be the places where we can locate its aesthetic importance and its political promise.

In assessing what qualifies as "excess" in a description, questions of proportion and length come to the fore. We have seen Rancière's account of how the growth of description in the nineteenth century upended the classical proportions of narrative. This descriptive growth also contributed importantly to an expansion of the novel's girth as it swelled with "filler," elements that make text but do not constitute a turning point in the story.[72] With respect to length, modernist novels tend toward two extremes: on the one hand, doorstoppers such as *In Search of Lost Time*, *Ulysses*, *Parade's End*, the *Pilgrimage* cycle, the *U.S.A.* trilogy, and *The Man without Qualities*; and on the other hand, the slim economy of works such as *Heart of Darkness*, *The Good Soldier*, *Mrs. Dalloway*, *Passing*, *The Great Gatsby*, and *Nightwood*. This is not to say that descriptions can only be excessive in long novels—more salient is the question of proportion within a given work, and my subsequent chapters look at novels that fall into both camps.

Length *is* key to excess, however, within a description, and while such excess is often faulted for its tedium, in modernist works length usually has an estranging effect. We see this especially clearly in James's late works, where descriptions often begin with a conventional image that by being extended longer than we might expect ends up becoming much more unpredictable. A good example comes from *The Golden Bowl* when, on the eve of his marriage to Maggie Verver, the Prince first sees again his old flame, Charlotte Stant. "He knew above all the extraordinary fineness of her flexible waist, the stem of an expanded flower, which gave her a likeness also to some long loose silk purse, well-filled with gold pieces, but having been passed empty through a finger ring that held it together. It was as if, before she turned to him, he had weighed the whole thing in his open palm and even heard a little the chink of the metal" (*GB* 73). Beginning with a familiar comparison of the feminine figure to a flower, the moment when this description becomes strange is not when the second comparison appears, the well-filled silk purse, but when the purse passes empty through a finger ring. The woman herself is miniaturized into a possession held in the beholder's palm by mobilizing both a tactile sense and an acoustic one—feeling the weight of the purse in his hand and hearing the sound of the coins clinking against one another. Charlotte's objectification by the Prince's appraisal of her physical parts is just one of the many instances of people being turned into commodities in James, especially in *The Golden Bowl*. But what does she become here? A bag, a container that exists only to hold other objects, something whose function depends on its emptiness. And what is this bag filled with? Gold, at once the embodiment of materiality and abstraction insofar as its utility depends on the purity of its physical makeup but also on an exchange value that is not correlated with its use value. Even in cases when their narrative utility is clear, modernist descriptions can end up diverting their own expository work by going on a little too long, like a joke whose initially predictable punchline is extended so far that it ends up somewhere else entirely. Rather than simply evidence of prolixity or inability to select pertinent details, they invite us to ask not only about the effects of descriptive proportion within a work as a whole but also the effects of length and proportion within a description itself.[73]

Part III: Reading for Description

If modernist fiction invites us to rethink conventional wisdom about description in relation to categories such as form and scale, temporality and rhythm, affective intensity, and proportion, we might also ask what effect it has on our methods. What might it mean, in other words, to read for description? In this final part of the chapter I want to lay out my own method of reading in this book, consider some further potential yields of attending to descriptive form, and situate my project in relation to recent debates about description as a critical method.

In the preceding section I discussed how moving away from thinking of the work as a spatialized whole opens up our ideas about novelistic form. An aerial perspective that can, as Woolf put it, hold a shape and a being in mind and compare it with those of other books is important and necessary. But taking the work at the level of the whole also inevitably misses what is in many ways most salient about descriptions: their particular textures, determined by varied aspects of language, syntax, phonetics, rhythm, imagery, and so forth—all the elements that tend to be grouped under that elusive and old-fashioned term *style*. To see these elements and their effects requires dwelling at a more local scale. Reading for description seems to commit us to attending to particulars or parts, making it difficult to ascend to the level of the totality or to achieve a unified account of a whole. It is for this reason that my method in the ensuing chapters is not to present comprehensive interpretations of single novels, which also means I am not focused primarily on questions of plot, theme, or character, although of course it is impossible to ignore these in any discussion of a work. But I am primarily interested in tracing recurrent patterns and structures across descriptive passages, often across multiple works by an author, in an effort to isolate the assumptions these forms embed and to trace the effects they create. So I track James's persistent invocation of things "in the air," Proust and Woolf's deployments of analogy and comparison, and Woolf's pervasive use of indexicals—what I am after are philosophies of descriptive composition.

Strange Likeness concentrates on a select group of authors intensely engaged with this problem in the modernist period, and the scope of the book is thus necessarily limited. But the ambit of description as an analytic problem is virtually limitless, which is what makes it both a difficult and generative topic. What might we gain by attending to descriptive practices? It could give us new ways to carve up the literary field, rewriting our received periodizations as well as opening up new lines of comparative study across national traditions and genres. It could, for instance, provide a new view onto familiar divides, such as the one between realism and modernism that I try to recast here. We could also track particular descriptive forms, for instance, what I call enumerative and relational descriptions, across periods much in the same way that we talk about the marriage plot equally in Victorian fiction and the contemporary novel. In chapter 4 I suggest that Woolf's comparative strategies hearken back to an older tradition of epic similes; we could also conduct a study of how certain basic descriptive forms, such as the list or catalog, have persisted across time or moved from one tradition to another, much as we do with something like free indirect discourse.

It would also be well worth investigating the valuations of description in different national literatures as well as their different histories of development, for instance, by looking at the prose and verse descriptions in *The Tale of Genji*, usually considered the first Japanese novel, alongside its counterparts in the European tradition.[74] Comparative work might also proceed along genre lines. For example, how does description function differently in a realist text than in speculative fiction or utopian literature? In a study of the latter, Phillip Wegner argues that "utopias are too often read as static descriptions of a place, real or ideal, with 'description' being implicitly understood to be the 'other' to the temporal, or process, orientation of narrative. However . . . in forms like the narrative utopia, description itself serves as what in other contexts we think of as action or plot, so that social and cultural space and communal identity slowly emerge before our eyes by way of a process Roland Barthes calls 'semiosis.'"[75] By "semiosis" Wegner is referring to a class of texts concerned not with mimesis but with "'the performance of discourse,' the very activity of making the world through language."[76] In this book I take as a premise that all description makes—and makes up—the world through language, but its world-making imperatives and effects surely change when it is freed from mimetic expectations of corresponding recognizably to actual places.

The centrality of descriptive practices to world making can also lead us to ask about its place in world literature. If, as Toral Gajarawala has suggested, description "has been the singular narrative device by which we know the other," how have writers responded to the discursive violence of the colonial descriptive gaze?[77] The postcolonial novel often works with the trope and topos of "the rural, the peasant, and the pastoral," which is understood to be ahistorical and timeless.[78] At the same time, the evocation of locale and surroundings take on particular importance in works that feature narratives of immigration and exile. If, as Gajarawala writes, "for so long what 'the third world' had was 'description' rather than 'narration,'" and "the settler makes narrative because he makes history," how do the forms of postcolonial fiction rewrite our understanding of the Lukácsian binary and the relationship of description to historicity?[79] Relatedly, we could also ask about the imperatives and expectations around ideas of documentary and authenticity, not to mention voyeurism and consumption, that attend descriptions by writers of color who have to be aware of "representing" a minoritized group to a dominant audience. I regret that I have not taken up these questions here due to my limited scope, but they are essential to further understanding.

Finally, not only genre fiction but also fiction as a genre may gain new purchase when scrutinized with respect to description.⁸⁰ In the foundational (in an Anglo-American context) novel theories formulated by James and Lubbock, drama appears insistently as a counterfactual genre against which to identify the distinctive features of the novel. Commenting on the Vaubyessard ball scene in *Madame Bovary*, Lubbock writes, "If you took the dialogue, what there is of it, together with the actual things described, the people and the dresses and the dances and the banquets—took these and placed them on the stage for a theatrical performance, the peculiar effect of the occasion in the book would totally vanish."⁸¹ The issue isn't that the events are vague or nonexistent in Flaubert; indeed, "nothing could be more definite, more objective." But in the novel "it is all bathed in the climate of Emma's mood, and it is to the nature of this climate that our interest is called for the moment."⁸² Strikingly, Lubbock asserts the distinctiveness of the novel and its strengths only through a thought experiment of generic transposition. In order to test such ideas, we could look to a long history of cross-genre adaptations as well as recent examples such as *Harry Potter and the Cursed Child*, a stage play (both performed and published) that continues the series of Harry Potter novels.⁸³ Notably missing in the play are the passages of description—of Hogwarts or the Ministry of Magic, of various beasts and beings—that for many form an integral part of the pleasure of reading those books. What can such adaptations tell us about description's uses and pleasures, or as James puts it, about "representational virtue[s] . . . other than the scenic" (*LC* 2:1320)?⁸⁴ Or, moving even farther afield, how might we understand the novel in relation to new media such as video games, particularly ones that prioritize experiencing an immersive environment rather than being driven by actions or a narrative? These questions, provisional as they are, give a sense of the potential research that could be generated by placing description at the center of our thinking about the novel.

DESCRIPTION AS METHOD?

The history of description, as we saw last chapter, has been called one of "a continuous and seemingly undeserved misfortune."⁸⁵ But there are signs the tide of misfortune is shifting thanks to recent and ongoing debates over methods of reading that have brought new attention to the value of description as a critical practice. In a much-cited 2009 salvo, Stephen Best and Sharon Marcus observe that given the influence of psychoanalysis and Marxism on literary studies since the 1970s, a "symptomatic" or "suspicious" model of interpretation that takes meaning to be hidden, repressed, and deep has become virtually synonymous with critical activity itself.⁸⁶ They propose as an alternative "surface reading," ranging together an array of reading practices that looks *at* textual surfaces rather than trying to see *through* them.[87] Under this loose rubric, which has also come to be known as "postcritical reading," description has been championed as a modest way of indicating "what the text says about itself."[88] As an example of such a project, Heather Love has turned to the microsociological descriptive practices of Erving Goffman as inspiration for a mode of reading that is "close but not deep."[89] And a special issue of *Representations* in 2016 dedicated to "Description across the Disciplines" featured contributions by filmmakers, anthropologists, art historians, psychologists, and historians of science in addition to literary critics.

Strange Likeness, which focuses on literary rather than critical description, is located somewhat orthogonally to these debates, although it does aim to contribute more directly by broadening the disciplinary history of literary criticism that is usually evoked. The surface versus suspicious or symptomatic reading debate has focused on literary and cultural criticism since the 1970s. But the term *hermeneutics of suspicion* was used by Paul Ricoeur to name a chief interpretive disposition of an earlier period: the later nineteenth- and early twentieth-century convergence of Nietzsche, Marx, and Freud. Those thinkers understood the task of interpretation as being that of stripping away illusions, "a tactic of suspicion" in the "battle against masks."[90] In this framework, Ricoeur writes, the "fundamental category of consciousness is the relation hidden–shown," and hermeneutics is accordingly a demystifying activity, deciphering and unmasking the apparent to reveal the real behind it, whether it's the genealogy of morality, the material means of production, or the workings of the unconscious.[91] Ricoeur's distinction appears prominently in "Paranoid Reading or Reparative Reading," Eve Kosofsky Sedgwick's earlier anticipation of the more recent critiques of critique, but the focus of most subsequent discussion has been on later periods. Moreover, the methodological debates have centered on criticism, theory, and philosophy rather than art itself. But of course modernism, too, is part of the late nineteenth- and early twentieth-century intellectual climate described by Ricoeur, one characterized by widespread suspicion of surface appearances—indeed, some scholars have suggested that suspicion of surfaces is the dominant epistemic disposition of modernity—if not general agreement about what lay beyond them.[92] The disjunction between appearance and reality, the positing of a reality beyond appearance, and the insistence that art is the way to get to that reality—such ideas are everywhere in modernism. We have seen the way in which modernists shared this surface/depth framework with their fiercest critic, Lukács, but the terms that writers like James, Proust, Woolf, and Cather use to *reject* description—as unable to penetrate beyond the surface—are also strikingly similar to the terms used by Best and Marcus to characterize symptomatic reading and to call for a *turn* to description instead today. Turning to modernist texts thus opens up a longer historical arc for thinking about suspicion of surfaces that can put contemporary critical debates into conversation with older literary ones.

Ultimately, however, my book is distinguished from the postcritique debates by taking literary description as an *object* of analysis rather than a *method*. I am interested in how describing functions in modernist novels, but I make no claims to be doing a descriptive reading myself. Indeed, I remain unsure what exactly such a reading method would entail, since describing is always already bound up with interpretive commitments that immediately foil any attempt to posit it as an alternative. To be sure, description's advocates are by no means unaware of its inextricability from interpretative commitments, but when they state they want to "consider it on its own terms and not as a stepping-stone on the way to interpretation and critique," I am not sure how exactly that would look.[93] I am sympathetic to the desire for a truly "interdigital humanities" that balances "paranoia and generosity," as Brian Glavey puts it, but I am not especially invested in championing description as an alternative to any other kind of reading practice, nor do I want to hold it up as a critical model.[94] My goal in this book is to read *for* description, which may entail a variety of ways of reading ranging from ideology critique to phenomenology, none prescribed or precluded in advance.

What I do find unequivocally salutary about recent methodological disputes, however, is the new attention they have brought to the varieties and significance of descriptive practices, which has not only made this problem newly legible and important in literary studies but also drawn welcome connections across disciplines, some of which have been studying this topic for a long time. Thus, Lorraine Daston has shown that a transformation in the texture of descriptions of nature between 1660 and 1730—"from long accounts bristling with particulars to concise reports made deliberately bland by summary, repetition, and omission of details"—reveals a shift in what was perceived as a scientific fact "from a singular and striking event that could be replicated only with great difficulty, if at all, to a large and uniform class of events that could be produced at will."[95] And historians of art have long been forced to grapple with descriptive problems because of the inevitably intermedial nature of talking about visual images in language.[96] Whether as the foil of interpretation, causal explanation, performance, diagnosis, analysis, or experiment in disciplines ranging from anthropology, sociology, economics, and life sciences, describing has historically been invoked as the unanalytical, unintellectual, naive opposite of some other more active, more authentic, more discerning procedure. It is with good reason that Philippe Hamon calls it the methodological zero degree, an unmarked method.⁹⁷ But as the growing body of work on this topic shows, any association with neutrality and passivity, any idea that description simply transcribes the given, is no longer tenable.⁹⁸

WEAK THEORY

I noted in the introduction and throughout this chapter that description's ubiquity and its inextricability from other elements have made it inhospitable to our major schools of narrative theory in the twentieth century. If focusing on a novel's descriptions prevents us from ascending to the level of the whole, it may be the case that the best rubrics for theorizing it are those that have flown under the banner of "weak theory," especially as developed by Silvan Tomkins and adapted by Eve Kosofsky Sedgwick.⁹⁹ Strong theory, for Tomkins, is "any theory of wide generality [that] is capable of accounting for a wide spectrum of phenomena which appear to be very remote, one from the other, and from a common source. This is a commonly accepted criterion by which the explanatory power of any scientific theory can be evaluated. To the extent to which the theory can account only for 'near' phenomena, it is a weak theory, little better than a description of the phenomena which it purports to explain."¹⁰⁰ Sedgwick makes the distinction between strong and weak theories the basis for her analysis of different styles of interpretation, in particular for her claim that "paranoid reading," which characterizes Marxist and Freudian hermeneutics of suspicion, is a strong theory.

Strong theories are explanatory; they deal with causes and effects, which is to say, they deal with narration. They tell a story, they are tightly plotted, and their conclusion is often known in advance—this to Sedgwick is the chief peril of paranoid reading, which defends its position of mastery by warding off the possibility of surprise. Weak theory on the other hand, as Tomkins himself states, is "little more than description," working at the level of the local and the particular, stubbornly remaining in the weeds and inventing "nonce taxonomies" as needed.¹⁰¹ Since narrative theories seek to generalize at a broad level, it should be no surprise that they have tended to favor the elegant structures of plots over the messy particularities of description. If on the other hand weak theories are little more than descriptions of the phenomena they purport to explain—that is, unable to make the leap from particular to general—then perhaps it is also the case that descriptions themselves cannot be theorized *except* weakly. They remain local and specific, resisting subsumption to general principles not through any explicit opposition but by their sheer disparate heterogeneity. Although any argument is susceptible to counterexamples, there is something about descriptions that makes attempts to generalize about them especially fraught. In relation to narrative theory and to theories that want to and can more productively generalize about other aspects of narrative (e.g., plots, characters), perhaps the place of description is to be the unwieldy, not quite assimilable excess to any theory of narrative at all. Not only textual cysts, they may be theoretical cysts too, reminding us not to begin from a place where we assume we already know what it means to describe anything at all.

James's Airs [CHAPTER TWO]

Since literary description so often concerns setting, let us begin with a room.[1] Here is the opulent drawing room at Lancaster Gate in Henry James's *The Wings of the Dove* (1902) in which Merton Densher awaits an interview with the wealthy aunt of the penniless young woman he wishes to marry. Certain readerly expectations of visual specificity are thwarted in this passage, but we will also see that it seeks out a particular, if somewhat hazy, feature of the space, one that points toward the new likenesses sought by modernist description.

> He couldn't describe and dismiss them collectively, call them either Mid-Victorian or Early—not being certain they were rangeable under one rubric. It was only manifest they were splendid and were furthermore conclusively British. They constituted an order and abounded in rare material—precious woods, metals, stuffs, stones. He had never dreamed of anything so fringed and scalloped, so buttoned and corded, drawn everywhere so tight and curled everywhere so thick. He had never dreamed of so much gilt and glass, so much satin and plush, so much rosewood and marble and malachite. But it was above all the solid forms, the wasted finish, the misguided cost, the general attestation of morality and money, a good conscience and a big balance. (*WD* 56)

Densher cannot treat the objects in the room collectively, but James himself certainly proceeds to do so. Since they cannot be arranged under a single label, "Mid-Victorian or Early," we might expect more finely distinguished specifications. But James proceeds in the opposite direction. Although there are allusions to objects, he makes no attempt to comprehensively decorate the narrative space with particular items.[2] The preference for pluralized materials and qualities over individualized and particular objects is one of the most insistent features of this passage. So Michael Levenson attributes "the great provocation" of James's late work to "its refusal of what one may call the novelistic norm of descriptive specificity... which takes as its foundation... in J. L. Austin's phrase, 'moderate-sized specimens of dry goods.'"[3] This refusal of descriptive specificity together with his eschewal of visual concreteness is key to James's reputation for vagueness.

And yet if at the end of this description we know very little about the specific chairs, curtains, or carpets that lie within the Lancaster Gate drawing room, we are also left in little doubt about its overall effect, the impression it creates, so to speak, in the air. James's vagueness is not simply a refusal of specification altogether. Commenting on the "underdescription" of characters' bodies in *The Other House* and *The Awkward Age*, David Kurnick observes that "the attribution of some definite physical *effect* is often a means to evade positing any actual corporeal *trait*."[4] So Harold Brookenham possesses an "acuteness, difficult to trace to a source, of his smooth fair face," and his father has "a pale, cold face, marked... by a hardness of line in which, oddly, there was no significance, no accent." Meanwhile, Nanda, "whom we first encounter via the 'faded image' of a photograph, is described by Vanderbank as having 'no features'" because "'She's at the age when the whole thing—speaking of her appearance, her possible share of good looks—is still, in a manner, in a fog.'"[5] We could also compare Nanda's fogginess with a later description of the much older Adam Verver in *The Golden Bowl*. "Mr. Verver then, for a fresh full period... had been inscrutably monotonous behind an iridescent cloud. The cloud was his native envelope—the soft looseness, so to say, of his temper and tone, not directly expressive enough, no doubt, to figure an amplitude of folds, but of a quality unmistakable for sensitive feelers" (*GB* 131). In each case, the absence of defined traits—or particularized objects, to hearken back to the description of Lancaster Gate—is combined with the evocation of a strongly felt though nonlocalized effect.

How should we understand James's "underdescriptions"? To begin with, we can reframe the question by asking why we read such passages as thin or vague in the first place. That we do so reveals the extent to which we associate description with a relatively narrow idea of visualization. When we say that Lancaster Gate is underdescribed, we mean that it cannot be easily imagined as a picture, or to use Elaine Scarry's terms (discussed in the introduction), the description doesn't give us instructions for imagining a visual perception. We could say of James something similar to Walter Scott's observation of Ann Radcliffe, that if six artists tried to render the first description of the castle of Udolpho, "they would probably produce six drawings entirely dissimilar to each other, yet all of them equally authorized by the printed description."⁶ This idea of visualization, often imagined through a transmedial thought experiment like the one proposed by Scott, is often taken to be synonymous with description tout court. Accordingly, critics have proposed that Jamesian description interferes with the process of world imagining. "Reading entails an immense labor of imaginative construction," Scarry writes, but as Kurnick points out, "this process of world-imagining must feel all but effortless to function successfully."⁷ James's readers, however, are made to feel the labor involved in reconstructing the sensory scene on the basis of the descriptive information on the page: his descriptions seemed designed not to enable but rather to block perceptual mimesis.

More precisely, they block visualization. But are there other forms of perceptual mimesis that Jamesian descriptions are enabling? If we understand James's likenesses to be about something other than how things look, they turn out to be in fact quite precise, hardly underdescribed at all. In the case of Lancaster Gate, he does not give us an inventory or spatial plan of sideboards, tables, or footstools, but we know that whatever is there is made of gilt, glass, satin, plush, rosewood, marble, and malachite and that it is scalloped, fringed, buttoned, corded, gilded, drawn, and curled. James's descriptive mode remains indefinite with respect to individual objects, but it is quite specific with respect to qualities and effects. The general impression of luxurious materials and ornate aesthetics are clear even if the Balzacian inventory has disappeared. The descriptive referent has become an impression on a perceiver that is irreducible to any one of its component parts. Insofar as they issue instructions for imagining acts of perception, I propose that James's descriptions instruct us above all to imagine what it is like to feel an atmosphere.

If we pay attention to James's language throughout both the fiction and the criticism, his ethereal preoccupations are hard to miss. Air in the Jamesian world is colored and scented; it hangs (heavily, more often than not) over the proceedings or is a cool element suspended on high; it thickens with intimations, pulses with vibrations, reverberates with tones, and sounds with notes. Even the "action" tends to be described in terms of the climates in which events take place, which are also socially coded. When the Prince serves tea to Charlotte in his drawing room as they officially commence their illicit relations in *The Golden Bowl*, "the whole demonstration ... presented itself as taking place at a very high level of debate—in the cool upper air of the finer discrimination, the deeper sincerity, the larger philosophy" (*GB* 251).⁸ Individuals are also marked by the atmospheres in which they have moved, recalling ideas about the determinism of climate and character circulating since antiquity.⁹

Becoming attuned to the prominence of atmospheric concepts and vocabulary in James's writings allows us to see that what is in the air becomes an important object of description in his late novels. After a brief orienting discussion of the concept of atmosphere and a comparison with his contemporary (and another atmospheric enthusiast) Joseph Conrad, I will turn to the question of what is in the Jamesian air. It is, as we will see, above all a medium of social information filled with innuendo, subtext, and the implicit, that which has a tenuous mode of being, as when we feel the tension in a room without being able to locate it in any particular space or object or even gesture or word. By bringing this elusive dimension of experience within the scope of novelistic description, James takes seriously the idea that atmospheres have a role to play in the production of knowledge about social life.

In regarding atmospheres as sites of information, he follows a long association of air with mediation and communication, including specifically with language and print.[10] In this chapter I find a tradition for thinking about imponderable mediums of transmission in nineteenth-century ideas about the ether, when the popular notion of a pervasive ethereal medium—imagined both in scientific and occult terms—gave new currency to the idea that the air was alive with communications. And just as these (sometimes supernatural) turn-of-the-century ethereal messages required mediums with specialized powers of perception to decode, the communications in the Jamesian air, too, are perceptible only to "sensitive feelers," requiring an embodied epistemology that is differentially distributed. Being able to feel the atmosphere requires a particular mode of perceptual experience that is gendered feminine. In this regard, the characterizations of Maggie Verver, Charlotte Stant, Milly Theale, and others continue an eighteenth- and nineteenth-century tradition of associating the feminine with the atmospheric as well as the female body with a sensitive instrument.[11]

If atmospheres require sensitivity to perceive, it is because their existence seems tentative, always verging on the brink of metaphoricity, not to say fictionality. It seems clear enough that the atmosphere of the earth is a real, material phenomenon (even if an invisible and intangible one), but it is less clear whether we are referring to a material phenomenon or merely using a figure of speech when we invoke the atmosphere of a room. Air is after all the figure of ungraspability and, by extension, unreality. So in ordinary parlance building castles in the air or having one's head in the clouds indicates a loose sense of facts, which are in contrast hard and solid.[12] And in an 1899 essay, James himself calls fiction "mere unsupported and unguaranteed history, the *inexpensive* thing, written in the air, the record of what, in any particular case, has *not* been" (*LC* 1:101–2). But even as the atmosphere of a room or a party or a conversation seems figurative, the distinctiveness of James's late works lies in their insistence on the fact that such nebulous things are utterly real, capable of exerting influence and producing effects in the world. The pervasiveness of concepts and vocabulary of air in James's work thus heralds a modernist turn toward conceiving of the real as ethereal as much as ponderable, one that persists today in new iterations through ideas of the digital, the virtual, and the cloud.[13] Moreover, by making clear that what is *real* is not exhausted by what is *physical*, James gives us a form of description that is committed to realism without being a prose of things.

Finally, atmospheres are not only a prime descriptive object for James, they also provide him with the figurative grammar to describe his central preoccupation: relations. As Brad Evans observes, "the task of simply describing the externalized, temporally bedeviling, between-space of the relation is confoundingly difficult," and I propose through looking at three scenes in *The Golden Bowl* that the felt experience of spatial configurations provides a way for James to conceptualize and to figure the affective character of particular relational arrangements.[14] In so doing, he takes up and transforms the realist novel's interest in social relations. For Lukács, we recall, these could only be *narrated*. James, I want to suggest, finds a way also to *describe* them, even if they are not Marxian relations of production but rather the relations that exist at what Georg Simmel calls the "microscopic-molecular" level of sociality.[15]

Clearing the Mists

Given the slipperiness of the term *atmosphere*, compounded by the elliptical nature of James's late style, let us begin with some conceptual orientations. The term—deriving from *atmos* (vapor) and *sphere*—has always been associated etymologically with the idea of surrounding or enveloping, which is also audible in the related terms *milieu* and *ambiance*.[16] It also carries connotations of diffuse haziness and indeterminacy. According to the contemporary German philosopher Gernot Böhme, who has made the concept of atmosphere central to his aesthetics, its indeterminacy can be attributed especially to its ambiguous ontology and its unlocalizability. It is difficult to know whether atmospheres belong to "the objects or environments from which they proceed or to the subjects who experience them."[17] The atmosphere of a room cannot be said to be a property of any of the things in it, but nor is it reducible to a projection of the perceiving subject's internal psychic state, since we can come upon a serene atmosphere when we are feeling agitated and feel ourselves correspondingly affected by it. It is also difficult to say where exactly it resides, since it is diffuse and enveloping. As Böhme puts it, "[it] seem[s] to fill the space with a certain tone of feeling like a haze."[18] But even if it is vague in its ontology or location, an atmosphere can impress itself on us quite distinctly. Intangible but palpable, the concept of atmosphere does not overturn but merely torques—in a way that makes it actually more difficult to grasp than a straightforward reversal—a number of the traditional dichotomies governing modernist aesthetics: between subject and object, surface and depth, appearance and reality, and public and private. The spatiality of atmosphere—as diffuse surrounding or enveloping—differs from a surface/depth topology and the dualistic epistemology of dissimulating appearance and underlying reality that the latter underwrites. And insofar as atmospheres exist only as they are sensed by a perceiver, they seem entirely subjective and private, but they also have a kind of objective, public existence because they can be felt by multiple perceivers and are not reducible to any one person's sensation. As we will see, this liminal, suspended status makes atmospheres particularly effective for figuring the issues of sociality and epistemology onto which James's late works open. At the same time, their ambiguous ontology leads James to shift the norms of realist description.

To be sure, James was not the first to be interested in describing the atmosphere or the air. We need only think of Ann Radcliffe's gothic mists, or more immediately, the thick, miasmatic fog of Charles Dickens's *Bleak House* or the meteorological specifications of Joseph Conrad. While he draws on a gothic tradition, James is distinctive in emphasizing not what atmospheric phenomena occlude but what they reveal. And unlike Dickens's preoccupation with the literal air of London and its effects on health and sanitation, or Conrad's detailing of local as well as global climates (on which more below), James's primary concern is not with the skies outside but rather with the social climates swirling among groups of people indoors. Thus, my focus here differs from ecocritics who have studied atmosphere in terms of weather patterns and climate change as well as from scholars who have considered literary representations of atmospheric phenomena in light of historical medical-political debates about air purity, olfactory risk, and environmental injustice.[19] While drawing on this scholarship, I emphasize here the social aspects of atmospheres as they exist in closed drawing rooms and function as conduits for social relations.

As a way of delineating in broad strokes James's atmospheric interests, it is instructive to compare them with those of Conrad, his friend and contemporary. As we saw in the introduction, Conrad was intrigued as well as unsettled by the new physics' transformation of matter into vibrations, and he is far more famously an atmospheric writer than James. Indeed, in spite of Conrad's injunction that the aim of art was "before all, to make you *see*," few modernist novels are more riddled with haze, mist, and fog.[20] If Balzacian mise-en-scène reliably includes a catalog of furniture, Conradian scene setting reliably includes a weather report, a tendency that has earned him a reputation as a literary "impressionist" (a term that has been applied to James as well).[21] So as *Heart of Darkness* opens on the ship *Nellie* docked in the Thames estuary, we read, "In the offing the sea and the sky were welded together without a joint. . . . A haze rested on the low shores that ran out to sea in vanishing flatness. The air was dark above Gravesend, and further back still seemed condensed into a mournful gloom, brooding motionless over the biggest, and the greatest, town on earth."[22] Such descriptions of the diegetic environment serve to establish the mood of a place and to provide affective cues to the reader. But even as, like Monet or Whistler, Conrad sought to make nebular phenomena visible, in his novels fog, mist, and haze work persistently to impede visuality and to obstruct knowledge. In this respect Conrad shares something with popular nineteenth-century genres such as sensational or detective fiction, which thematize shrouding, obscuring hazes to indicate mystery and to generate suspense. Such are the functions of the mist through which figures pass in Wilkie Collins's *The Woman in White* (1860) or the dense fog that covers the Devonshire moors in Arthur Conan Doyle's *The Hound of the Baskervilles* (1902).[23] Conrad's novels, too, are filled with vaporous mists, as on the Congo River when the "white fog, very warm and clammy, and more blinding than the night" stands "all around you like something solid" and lifts "as a shutter lifts."[24] But in Conrad these veils serve to obscure not supernatural spirits but unspeakable horrors that are eminently human, and it is unclear to what extent the fog ever really lifts.[25]

For James, in contrast, the atmosphere is not the site of mystery or confusion but of disclosure, though not usually in the form of words spoken. Far from operating as a shutter, closing people off from the ties that bind humans to each other and to the earth, the air is teeming with hints, pulses, and revelations that bear discernable messages. In the Jamesian world, allusions to the "air" rarely refer to the air of actual diegetic environments, which are certainly not rendered with Conradian detail. James's atmospheres are primarily social rather than meteorological, and they function above all as a medium of knowledge and affective charge. Indeed, the air's role as a medium of transmission becomes most explicit at the very moment when it fails as a messenger in *The Wings of the Dove*. When Milly Theale learns that her would-be suitor, Merton Densher, is already secretly engaged to Kate Croy, Densher finds the doors of her Venetian palace suddenly closed to him. Her Italian gatekeeper Eugenio regards him silently: "Nothing had passed about his coming back, the air had made itself felt as a non-conductor of messages" (*WD* 403), echoing a moment a few pages earlier when Milly's inscrutability "made of the air breathed a virtual non-conductor" (*WD* 400). The result is rendered in the key of melodrama: as the "undue vibration" that Densher had feared comes to pass, the weather darkens and a storm passes over Venice, bringing "cold lashing rain from a low black sky ... [and] wicked wind raging through narrow passages" (*WD* 403).²⁶ Here is an instance of the pathetic fallacy that would seem straight out of a gothic novel, but the diegetic air's failure to conduct during one of the most melodramatic episodes of the novel allows James to subvert the gothic even as he avails himself of its tropes.

Feeling the Air

If atmospheres are a preeminent site of disclosure in James, what is gleaned there, and how? Put differently, what does it mean to walk into a room and feel the atmosphere?²⁷ In James's late novels, characters are constantly doing just that. Here, for instance, is Charlotte Stant in *The Golden Bowl* observing Colonel Assingham's gaze at a grand party shortly after she marries Adam Verver.

> This simplicity of his visual attention struck her, even with the other things she had to think about, as the quietest note in the whole high pitch—much in fact as if she had pressed a finger on a chord or a key and created, for the number of seconds, an arrest of vibration, a more muffled thump. The sight of him suggested indeed that Fanny would be there, though so far as opportunity went she hadn't seen her. This was about the limit of what it could suggest.
>
> The air, however, had suggestions enough—it abounded in them, many of them precisely helping to constitute those conditions with which, for our young woman, the hour was brilliantly crowned. She was herself in truth crowned, and it all hung together, melted together, in light and colour and sound. (*GB* 213-14)

Although Charlotte is struck by the colonel's gaze, her impression of it is described notably in sonic rather than visual terms "as the quietest note in the whole high pitch." Visual cues reveal limited information, but "the air, however, had suggestions enough." At this official party with "its numerosity of royalties, foreign and domestic" (*GB* 214-15), the air tells Charlotte that she is looking well, that she is a success, that with a newly acquired wealth to match her taste she has achieved the social eminence for which she has always felt herself destined.²⁸ As with Lancaster Gate, James provides few details of Charlotte's dress or "the other perfections of aspect and arrangement" beyond a brief mention of "unsurpassed diamonds" crowning her head. Nor does he describe the undoubtedly lavish setting beyond noting that glimpsing the Prince heightens Charlotte's perception of the place as more luxurious, "with its dome of lusters lifted, its ascents and descents more majestic, its marble tiers more vividly overhung ...

its symbolism of 'State' hospitality both emphasized and refined" (*GB* 214–15). Both at the party and in larger society, she and the Prince effectively become ambassadors for the Verver state, whose monarchs rule silently and out of sight. Charlotte's competence in reading the atmosphere contributes to her own skills of social diplomacy (at this party she is constantly sought after by various dignitaries) and accordingly, her value to the Ververs. Even as James omits the specifications of dress and decor that Balzac would have found essential to add, he exhibits a continuity with his predecessor's social interests, although keyed to a different aspect of the real—"it all hung together, melted together, in light and colour and sound." James's attention to the atmosphere inherits the realist novel's social hermeneutic descriptive project while shifting its focus from solid objects to things in the air.

As palpable, affective realities with an uncertain ontology, atmospheres are an especially good medium for the communication of social facts and norms, which hover in the background of any interaction and whose being is equally difficult to pin down even as they are equally forceful and efficacious. In her influential reading of the de-psychologized, nonrealistic nature of Jamesian consciousness as located not within but rather between characters, Sharon Cameron argues that in his late works, "the unsaid is not commensurate with the unheard."[29] I would add that in the air, the unsaid is not unfelt. Although forms of conversation have played a central role in analyses of sociability, and there is much to be said about Jamesian rhythms of talk, I am singling out here James's attention to the aspects of a social interaction that are intuited in more nebulous ways.[30] In particular, he homes in on what Georg Simmel calls the "microscopic-molecular" level of sociality, the innumerable "minor forms of relation and of kinds of interaction among men."[31] Although the social sciences are apt to focus on larger and more visible social formations such as "states, labor unions, priesthoods, family forms, economic systems, military organizations, guilds, communities, class formations, and industrial divisions of labor," Simmel writes, "it is really these minor forms that bring about society as we know it."[32] His characterization of these microscopic-molecular processes should resonate for a reader of James.

> That people look at one another and are jealous of one another; that they exchange letters or have dinner together; that apart from all tangible interests they strike one another as pleasant or unpleasant; that gratitude for altruistic acts makes for inseparable union; that one asks another to point out a certain street; that people dress and adorn themselves for each other—these are a few casually chosen illustrations from the whole range of relations that play between one person and another. They may be mo-

mentary or permanent, conscious or unconscious, ephemeral or of grave consequence, but they incessantly tie men together. At each moment such threads are spun, dropped, taken up again, displaced by others, interwoven with others.[33]

I will turn presently to James's own sense of "relations," similarly capacious and far reaching, comprising subtle forms of sociation whose "eternal flux and pulsation link individuals even where they do not rise to form organizations as such."[34] For now suffice it to note that just as Simmel seeks to bring these minor forms of relation within the ambit of sociology, so James highlights the atmosphere as a dimension of social interaction, bringing it within the scope of novelistic description. It is a short step from Jamesian "vibrations" to what we would today call "vibes": hard to pin down but clearly felt and information rich. James's description of this difficult-to-define yet ordinary dimension of social life, which can supplement or undercut speech and action, constitutes his contribution to the Balzacian sociological project of the novel.

The figuration of knowledge in atmospheric terms, terms that are so ontologically uncertain, also places into question the boundary between the literal and the figurative and thus the stability of the real. When later in *The Golden Bowl* Mrs. Assingham receives a summoning telegram from Maggie, she understands that Maggie has finally discovered that she knew of the Prince's intimacy with Charlotte before his marriage.

> [Mrs. Assingham] had often put it to herself in apprehension, she tried to think even in preparation, that she should recognize the approach of her doom by a consciousness akin to that of the blowing open of a window on some night of the highest wind and the lowest thermometer. It would be all in vain to have crouched so long by the fire; the glass would have been smashed, the icy air would fill the place. If the air in Maggie's room then, on her going up, wasn't as yet quite the polar blast she had expected, it was none the less perceptibly such an atmosphere as they hadn't hitherto breathed together. (GB 429)

In this scene, Mrs. Assingham imagines the apprehension of her doom in terms of a window suddenly blowing open during a blustery night and letting the cold air rush in. The low temperature is, of course, a significant feature of this analogy—her realization produces an internal chill as the cold air in the metaphor produces an external one, and this knowledge is significantly felt on the skin. In the way that, once allowed into a space, air cannot be easily contained and segmented, Mrs. Assingham fears that the revelation that she knew of Charlotte and the Prince's previous intimacy will also permeate uncontrollably, with disastrous consequences for their tight-knit ecosystem. The opening of a window introduces a disruption into the small group's established dynamics, throwing familiar patterns and habits off balance, effectively setting into motion the second half of the novel and Maggie's effort to restore the order of familial and marital relations.[35]

So far in the Jamesian scene, a change of air has been used figuratively to imagine the feeling of an intuition. But in the next sentence, it becomes transformed into the diegetically real atmosphere of the room in which Maggie actually awaits Mrs. Assingham, showing how porous the divide is between the literal and the figurative. "If the air in Maggie's room ... wasn't as yet quite the polar blast she had expected, it was none the less perceptibly such an atmosphere as they hadn't hitherto breathed together." The technique of slipping from the figurative to the literal plane is typical of James's late novels, accounting in part for our readerly confusion as we try to keep straight which rooms are imagined and which rooms real.[36] In this case, matters are further complicated by the fact that in its very lack of solidity and tangibility, air is the figure of unreality and imagination itself. The reference to the "polar blast" of air is clearly a metaphor, but the "real" atmosphere in the room, that is, its affective—and thus epistemically significant—tone, also seems metaphorical. And yet it would be wrong to read the image here as simply a metaphor for something else—the atmosphere of a room, that is, the affective one, is diegetically real in that it discloses something about what is actually going on there between the two women in their struggle over the consequences of this new disclosure. By making atmospheres central to his descriptions of spaces and encounters, James broadens the category of the real to encompass affective climates that arise only ambiguously to the level of a fact.

Moreover, as I have noted, atmospheres cannot be called objective because their experience depends on and implicates the perceiver, and yet they also cannot be reduced to subjective moods. James's interest in describing atmospheres as epistemically meaningful phenomena that are perceiver dependent while still having a public or quasi-objective existence thus serves both to dissociate something like affective tone from the subjective while simultaneously uncoupling the objective from the real. In so doing his atmospheric descriptions run counter to the subjective idealism often associated with his (and a wider modernist) interest in psychological interiority. By taking seriously the meaningfulness and efficacy of what is in the air, he does not break with the realist novel's empiricist commitments to gathering knowledge from observation and experience but rather extends its scope, showing that just as physical objects and surroundings such as dress and habitat can be carriers of social information, so, too, can atmospheres.

It is in this light that we can read one of James's most famous passages in "The Art of Fiction" (1884), one that is often taken to inaugurate the expansion of concerns with consciousness and interiority in modernist fiction.

> Experience is never limited, and it is never complete; it is an immense sensibility, a kind of huge spider-web of the finest silken threads suspended in the chamber of consciousness, and catching every air-borne particle in its tissue. It is the very atmosphere of the mind; and when the mind is imaginative—much more when it happens to be that of a man of genius—it takes to itself the faintest hints of life, it converts the very pulses of the air into revelations. (*LC* 1:52)

While the spider web is the image that has stuck, what it catches are notably vibrations in the air, which become the medium that carries the "hints of life" to those able to feel them. Throughout his career James never relinquishes the claim that fiction must be rooted in experience, and as he broadens what this term encompasses, he continually invokes the metaphorics of air, beginning with this first major programmatic statement on the novel form and continuing throughout his late fiction. "If experience consists of impressions, it may be said that impressions *are* experience, just as (have we not seen it?) they are the very air we breathe" (*LC* 1:53). James's interest in describing atmospheres is his way of expanding the domain of social interaction and relation represented in fiction, and it also constitutes an expanded, or radical, form of empiricism.[37] Like later writers such as Proust and Woolf, his experimental aesthetics do not advocate a turn away from the real world but rather suggest that the real world has been too readily conflated with the physical one.[38] To include atmospheres within the field of description is to take seriously, to include in the *données* of experience, vibrations in the air no less than the solidity of tables and chairs.

Thrilling, Vibrating

Attending to the ways in which knowledge is gleaned from the air reveals furthermore James's commitment to the body in the production of knowledge about social relations. Although less expert than Charlotte Stant and Mrs. Assingham at reading the air, Milly Theale is also deeply sensitive to it, as we see when she makes her appearance on the London social scene during her first dinner at Lancaster Gate in *The Wings of the Dove*.

> She thrilled, she consciously flushed, and all to turn pale again, with the certitude—it had never been so present—that she should find herself completely involved: the very air of the place, the pitch of the occasion, had for

her both so sharp a ring and so deep an undertone. The smallest things, the faces, the hands, the jewels of the women, the sound of words, especially of names, across the table, the shape of the forks, the arrangement of the flowers, the attitude of the servants, the walls of the room, were all touches in a picture and denotements in a play; and they marked for her moreover her alertness of vision. She had never, she might well believe, been in such a state of vibration; her sensibility was almost too sharp for her comfort. (*WD* 105)

It is hard to miss the eroticism of this passage. The quivering sensibility of Milly's "single throbbing consciousness" (*LC* 2:1298) is almost too sharp, like a tuning fork or a seismograph, an instrument so sensitive that it threatens to break down under the flux of information it cannot cease to record. For all of James's famed bloodlessness, his epistemology is an embodied one. And the kind of perceptual experience depicted here, far from being rarefied, is quite ordinary, as when we "feel" the tension in a room.

Much can be felt in the air, but impressionability is not equally distributed in the Jamesian system of characters. Specifically, its distribution is gendered. "Thrilling" and "vibrating" are how James's most sensitive characters, almost all women—Milly Theale, Fleda Vetch, Charlotte Stant, and Maggie Verver, among them—respond to their environments.[39] As their bodies register the fluctuations of the air, Milly and others could be read as inheritors of an eighteenth-century tradition of imagining instruments capable of measuring all sorts of feminine fluctuations as well as an identification of the female body itself with a sensitive instrument.[40] Notably, this kind of bodily sensitivity is also associated with authorship. Thrilling and vibrating are the very terms in which James describes the writerly ideal in "The Art of Fiction," where, as we saw, the ability to convert "the very pulses of the air into revelations" (*LC* 1:52) is said to be the mark of a writer.[41] In this way, James's own authorial position becomes feminized while his female characters become invested with authorial force. And later modernist writers who singled out James's works as "pathfinders" for their projects made more explicit the association not only of the measuring but also of the making of atmospheres with the feminine. So in *Revolving Lights*, the seventh volume of Dorothy Richardson's *Pilgrimage* cycle, Miriam Henderson reflects that women's aesthetic preeminence lies in "the art of making atmospheres. It's as big an art as any other. Most women can exercise it, for reasons, by fits and starts. The best women work at it the whole of the time. Not one man in a million is aware of it. It's like air within the air.... At its best it is absolutely life-giving. And not soft. Very hard and stern and austere in its beauty. And like mountain air."[42]

Being able to read the atmosphere is, as some sociologists might say, a matter of interactional competence.⁴³ It should come as no surprise that one of the densest characters in James's late canon, Colonel Assingham, is also the least sensitive to the air. In a conversation with his wife Fanny, when he wonders whether she suspects that Maggie knows nothing of the affair between the Prince and Charlotte, she replies,

> "It isn't my 'whole' idea. Nothing's my 'whole' idea—for I felt to-day, as I tell you, that there's so much in the air."
> "Oh in the air—!" the Colonel dryly breathed.
> "Well, what's in the air always *has*—hasn't it—to come down to the earth." (*GB* 302)

As a rare representative of straightforward masculinity, the retired soldier's rejoinder reinforces the alignment of atmospheric sensitivity—and social competence—with femininity. He dismisses what Fanny senses in the air as fictive and imagined, minimizing along with it intuitive or affective forms of knowledge, which are also associated with "women's intuition." The fact that we tend to sense atmospheres in somatic ways that are not primarily cognitive or conceptual means that it would be easy to dismiss such knowledge-laden "feelings" as fictional in ways that are gendered. But in the Jamesian world it is instead the most distinguished kind of perceiving and knowing.

There is a shift in the orientation of perceptual attention—the atmosphere that draws James's attention hovers on the edge of materiality and visibility—but even as a different order of phenomena has been made perceptible, this perceptibility is not equally distributed. James has taken a partial step toward the redistribution of the sensible, but it is not yet there in the radical way that Rancière attributes to Woolf, or for that matter to Flaubert. The Aristotelian hierarchy of souls still holds, although social distinction is rewritten in James as aesthetic distinction.⁴⁴ The uneven distribution of perceptual prowess, which is not only gendered but also class coded, is especially true in the late fiction. Whereas in *The Princess Casamassima* the upper classes are related to the lower ones whether they know it or not, and *What Maisie Knew* takes up the viewpoint of a young child and the sometimes-motley circle around her, *The Golden Bowl* leaves virtually nothing visible outside the high-bourgeois family. The comparative paucity of minor characters relative to *Mrs. Dalloway* or *Ulysses* or *In Search of Lost Time* also makes it difficult for the ones that do appear—for instance, the matrimonially minded Mrs. Rance in *The Golden Bowl*—to feel and sense with the sensitivity of a Milly or a Maggie. We could not say that in James, to use Rancière's phrase, anyone can feel anything, but what can be felt—and described—is nevertheless enlarged.

Ethereal Transmissions

If the importance of atmosphere in James has gone largely unremarked, the theme of aerial transmissions *has* been observed in a different context: the invention of wireless telegraphy and radio broadcasting in the late nineteenth century. So Mark Goble emphasizes the "circuitry" of Jamesian relations, situating James's "extravagance of mediation" as well as his dedication to "the idea of connectability" in light of his engagements with new mediums that were developing at the time, such as the telegraph.[45] But there is also another lineage of thinking about things being "in the air" in the late nineteenth and early twentieth centuries that comes from popular ideas about the ether. Imagined by the ancients as "upper" air and conceived by nineteenth-century scientists as a medium of transmission for light and heat, in the popular imagination the ether also seemed capable of transmitting thoughts between people and even communicating messages from spirits and the dead.[46] While stretching backward into the nineteenth century and earlier, ideas surrounding the ether also point forward to discoveries about electromagnetic waves that a range of twentieth-century modernist writers and artists—including Pound, Duchamp, and Boccioni—would embrace as a model for their various imagist, surrealist, and futurist aesthetics.[47] Whether conceived in terms of ethereal vibrations or fields of energy, this cluster of concepts provided a way to imagine influential environments, an unseen but potent world of forces. Thus, even as ideas about the ether seem antiquated next to the modernizing thrust of technology, it forms a surprising way of connecting James with later avant-garde figures as part of a "vibratory modernism" united by disparate forms of atmospheric interests.[48] Just as later modernists were fascinated with the vibrations suffusing the environment as "the unseen force that mediated all interactions between the interior self and the exterior environment," so for James, the interest in what can be communicated through invisible, inaudible means is a way of imagining new forms of connection and relation.[49]

Unlike some of his contemporaries, James rarely alludes explicitly to developments in physics. But he did know the work of John Tyndall, the eminent Victorian known especially for his studies of thermal radiation and atmosphere. One of the most important nineteenth-century popularizers of science, especially to artistic circles, Tyndall's writings on the ether in particular bear striking resemblances to James's own language.[50] In 1871 James reviewed Tyndall's mountaineering memoir, *Hours of Exercise in the Alps*, and in that review James praises Tyndall's mind and writing as uniting fact and imagination. In the scientist's presence, "the reader moves in an atmosphere in which the habit of a sort of heroic attention seems to maintain a glare of electric light" (*LC* 1:1357). And later in the essay James contrasts Ruskin's misty, melancholic Alpine descriptions with those of Tyndall, whose pages are said to be "pervaded by a cool contagious serenity which reminds one of high mountain air on a still day" (*LC* 1:1358–59). Whether or not James absorbed his attention to the atmosphere and air specifically from Tyndall is difficult to verify. Perhaps we can detect an echo of the Alpine mountaineer figure cut by the scientist in the scene in *The Wings of the Dove* when Milly is first introduced atop the Swiss Alps looking down at the world as at her dominion. But at any rate it is worth noting the striking resonances between Tyndall's descriptions of the ether and James's later description of atmospheres.[51] The ether, Tyndall explains, is the vehicle for the light of even the most distant visible stars, without which they would not be seen. "This all-pervading substance takes up their molecular tremors, and conveys them with inconceivable rapidity to our organs of vision. It is the transported shiver of bodies countless millions of miles distant, which translates itself in human consciousness into the splendor of the firmament at night."[52] The traffic of heat and light waves create a "ceaseless thrill . . . in the aether, which constitutes what we call the *temperature of space*. As the air of a room accommodates itself to the requirements of an orchestra, transmitting each vibration of every pipe and string, so does the inter-stellar aether accommodate itself to the requirements of light and heat."[53] The bodies described by Tyndall are in a perpetual state of vibration, the intensity of which causes the emission of heat and light, and the ether itself is just "scientifically defined as an assemblage of vibrations."[54] Ceaselessly "thrilling" and "vibrating," we can recognize in Tyndall's language for the actions of atoms that make up the universe many of the notes of James's descriptions for that which is perceived by his own sensitive feelers. Just as Tyndall conceives of the ether as bringing bodies into virtual contact, the atmosphere for James becomes a way to imagine the invisible relations filling a space. In particular, the atmospherics of different spaces form a crucial way to describe the affective qualities of particular relational arrangements.

A Likeness of Relations

It is uncontroversial to say that James's primary interest is in a relational nexus, but it remains an open question if and how these can be described. From the first, his interest in the subject has often been understood in terms of geometrical design and pictorial composition, epitomized by his own image of the figure in the carpet.[55] As Woolf wrote in an early review, in the later books one has to look not for "a plot, or a collection of characters, or a view of life, but something more abstract, more difficult to grasp, the weaving together of many themes into one theme, the making out of a design" (*E* 2:348). Woolf may have been influenced in her assessment by Roger Fry, who likens "the special pleasure" of reading James to "the counterpoint of Poussin's designs.... It's a sort of excited recognition of the aptness of formal relations like a mathematician's recognition of the validity of an equation."[56] Given the tight formal symmetry of a number of James's novels, it is not hard to see why they have been understood in geometrical terms. But there is a missing dimension to conceiving of Jamesian relations this way, one that is suggested by another early reader. What really matters for James, T. S. Eliot observes, is the "general scheme," which is "not one character, nor a group of characters in a plot or merely in a crowd. The focus is a situation, a relation, an atmosphere, to which the characters pay tribute."[57] Eliot's suggestive sentence places the three terms—a situation, a relation, an atmosphere—together appositively, multiplying terms for the "general scheme" and what he also calls the real Jamesian hero, the "social entity."[58] What does it mean to think of a situation and a relation in terms of an atmosphere?

It is, first of all, how James himself conceives of relations. The term is ubiquitous throughout his corpus, but its sense is especially clear in a passage from *The Ambassadors*, when Lambert Strether first meets Mme de Vionnet.

> He couldn't help it; it was not his fault; he had done nothing; but by a turn of the hand she had somehow made their encounter a relation. And the relation profited by a mass of things that were not, strictly, in it or of it; by the very air in which they sat, by the high, cold, delicate room, by the world outside and the little plash in the court, by the first Empire and the relics in the stiff cabinets, by matters as far off as those and by others as near as the unbroken clasp of her hands in her lap and the look her expression had of being most natural when her eyes were most fixed.[59]

To know someone, indeed, to turn one's head and look at someone, is to be in relation with them. These relations extend in all directions across space and time with no terminal point and no excluded node, each experience indelibly inflected and determined by a thousand other factors near and far. Spatially, from the air of the room in which the two characters sit the passage moves outward to the wider world, but it then travels back again to the sounds in the courtyard immediately outside. The shape traced here is accordingly not that of ever widening concentric circles but a messier set of overlapping spheres. Temporally, the first Empire bibelots in the cabinets reach back in history and connect Mme de Vionnet and her house to "some Napoleonic glamor" that dazzles the American Strether. The relation between the two is affected by everything in their environment without any way of distinguishing the discrete effects of any single element or knowing where to demarcate the boundaries of any sphere of influence.⁶⁰ Like his brother William, whose philosophy of radical empiricism placed relations rather than the substantive terms they connect at its center, for James, "really, universally, relations stop nowhere" (*LC* 2:1041).

It is here that we see a point of commonality between James and Conrad, who both in different ways evoke air and atmosphere to forge relations between sometimes distant beings. For Conrad, this is true even when the diegetic atmospheres are half a world away. Early on in *Heart of Darkness*, in a moment of meditative companionship on board the *Nellie*, we read, "The water shone pacifically; the sky, without a speck, was a benign immensity of unstained light; the very mist on the Essex marshes was like a gauzy and radiant fabric, hung from the wooded rises inland, and draping the low shores in diaphanous folds."⁶¹ By the time the setting has moved to the Belgian Congo and Marlow travels up the Congo River anticipating the prospect of meeting Kurtz, the atmosphere has turned ominously still. "Going up that river was like travelling back to the earliest beginnings of the world, when vegetation rioted on the earth and the big trees were kings. An empty stream, a great silence, an impenetrable forest. The air was warm, thick, heavy, sluggish."⁶² The atmospheric lassitude of the Congo jungle is linked to a temporal arrest, reflecting the primitivism Marlow ascribes to his surroundings. Here, the syntax has become truncated and paratactic, even elementary ("an empty stream, a great silence, an impenetrable forest") in contrast to the sinuous sentences describing the diaphanous folds of the Essex mists. But the settings are not so distant as they first appear. First, the Thames estuary in which the *Nellie* sits at the story's opening is also "a waterway leading to the uttermost ends of the earth." As Jesse Oak Taylor observes, by "conjuring the lower Thames in its global connection," London (what Conrad in a passage cited earlier calls the "biggest and greatest" city lying beneath the "mournful gloom" of smog) is placed in relation to the most distant waters and the skies.⁶³ Moreover, looking out over the opaline mist on the *Nellie* is what leads Marlow to recall the fog that descends around the ship just before they arrive at Kurtz's station. Through such instances of what Taylor calls "imaginative transference" where "one fog-shrouded landscape begets another," "the very obfuscating dynamics that make vision impossible" in Conrad also become "the substance of planetary connection."⁶⁴ Although James's airs do not index explicitly global connections in Conradian fashion, they do work to imagine unseen, unbounded, and unpredictable spheres of connection. In varied ways in modernism, atmosphere appears to be a central figure for thinking about and through relationality.

This is no accident. As Steven Connor notes, atmosphere has long "provided a name for the open milieu of human actions and relations."[65] Furthermore, sensing an atmosphere cannot be reduced to the perception of any discrete elements or limited to any one sensory mode. Instead, such perception responds to the relations between all the elements in a setting as they interact with each other in the environment created by their copresence—in the case of Milly Theale discussed above, the glittering faces of the people sitting around the table to the shape of the forks to the arrangement of flowers to the words floating in the air. As Taylor writes, "atmospheric phenomenology blends the faculties of perception, interfusing the registers of sensuous experience artificially divided by the idea of multiple discrete senses."[66] Indeed, naming something produced by the copresence of all the elements present in a space and constituted only by and through bodies affecting one another—in a certain way atmosphere is just a name for the spatialization of relationality.

With this idea in mind, we can recast James's well-known use of architectural and spatial images—most famously the "house of fiction" with its million windows, but also rooms, forges, squares, gardens, piazzas, and pagodas. These images have often been understood as metaphors for consciousness, as physical constructions figure mental ones.[67] Or else, as we saw above, the house of fiction is a figure for the art of novel writing conceived as spatial plan and geometrical design, where the narrative could be rendered as a diagram. But in fact what matters about these architectural configurations is the felt qualities of spatial inhabiting they afford.[68] In conceiving of spaces in terms of relations, James shares something with a number of influential theorists on the subject, including Henri Lefebvre's influential theory of "social space," which argues that space is not a passive locus of preexisting social relations but rather their medium and conditioning possibility, and Gaston Bachelard's phenomenological account of the ways in which the intimate space of the house is thoroughly imbued with felt qualities.[69] Especially useful for reading James is Foucault's brief but suggestive account of "heterotopias," in which he argues that space is conceived today as a "site" that is defined by the set of relations that it enables. So as a site of transportation, a train "is an extraordinary bundle of relations because it is something through which one goes, it is also something by means of which one can go from one point to another, and then it is also something that goes by."[70] This conception, like the one that emerges in James, emphasizes the way in which particular spaces enable particular relations. My focus here is not so much on space broadly construed as on the way in which the atmospheres of particular spatial configurations allow James to figure the affective qualities of relational configurations, and to fashion images that describe "situations" as a whole. James's atmospheric imaginary proves crucial to bringing relations within the ambit of description.

Relational Forms

To see how this works, I want to look at three moments of change and disturbance in *The Golden Bowl*. Here is how the first major disturbance in the novel, Maggie's marriage to the Prince, is described, focalized through her father's perspective. Before her marriage, the Ververs' union "had resembled a good deal some pleasant public square, in the heart of an old city, into which a great Palladian church, say—something with a grand architectural front—had suddenly been dropped; so that the rest of the place, the space in front, the way round, outside, to the east end, the margin of street and passage, the quantity of overarching heaven, had been temporarily compromised" (*GB* 135–36). The comparison of the Italian prince to a grand Palladian church (his face is also likened to a historic architectural front earlier in the novel) rests in no small part on his aristocratic Roman "prenatal" history, and in this respect the passage evinces *The Golden Bowl*'s pervasive tendency to turn people into objects. The intimate relation of father and daughter is transposed from the private domestic sphere into a public space ("some pleasant square") while the American Ververs also become Europeanized through the square's location "in the heart of an old city" and the reference to Palladian architecture. Significantly, an architectural style grounded on values of proportion and symmetry is here responsible for throwing something else—the atmospherics of the surrounding space—off balance, representing the first disturbance in the novel that causes a rearrangement in the nexus of relations.

For Adam Verver, the quality of his relations with his daughter is figured centrally in terms of closed or open spaces. Initially, "it was as if his son-in-law's presence, even from before his becoming his son-in-law, had somehow filled the scene and blocked the future—very richly and handsomely, when all was said, not at all inconveniently or in ways not to have been desired." Although Amerigo initially appears to Mr. Verver as a large obstacle, space and building gradually equalize in proportion as he adjusts to this new presence. "Though the Prince . . . was still pretty much the same 'big fact,' the sky had lifted, the horizon receded, the very foreground itself expanded, quite to match him, quite to keep everything in comfortable scale" (*GB* 135). The edifices do not move, but the atmosphere shifts and resettles, much in the way Tyndall described the air resettling around the sounds of an orchestra.

> The Palladian church was always there, but the piazza took care of itself. The sun stared down in his fullness, the air circulated, and the public not less; the limit stood off, the way round was easy, the east end was as fine, in its fashion, as the west, and there were also side doors of entrance be-

tween the two—large, monumental, ornamental, in *their* style—as for all proper great churches. By some such process in fine had the Prince, for his father-in-law, while remaining solidly a feature, ceased to be at all ominously a block. (GB 136)

Importantly, the essential element in this elaborate simile is the experiential character of the spatial arrangement—what it feels like to circulate in the piazza with the new, imposing presence of a Palladian church—which figures by analogy the experiential character of an arrangement, or rather a rearrangement, of a set of relations. James's spatial imagery bears a subtle relation to the process of figuration because not only the tenor but also the vehicle is actually immaterial. It is not that a set of relations is concretized through the diagrammatic description of a layout of space but rather that the whole affective-relational complex such spatial arrangements solicit and enable is invoked to describe by analogy another such affective-relational complex. Amerigo's entrance into the tight-knit lives of Adam and Maggie Verver is significant for its environmental effects, that is, for how it changes the atmosphere of the Ververs' previous relations with each other. If the "site" of the train was defined for Foucault by relations of coming and going, the site of the piazza described here is defined in terms of circulation, movement, and access. As the Ververs gradually integrate the Prince into their familial sphere, his presence is no longer felt as an obstruction. The "domestic air" eventually clears and lightens, "producing the effect . . . of wider perspectives and large waiting spaces" (*GB* 135). However, although he ceases to inconvenience access, he remains "solidly a feature." He remains a large, monumental, ornamental great church of the kind visited by wealthy Americans on grand tours, but one that is easily accessible and thus, consumable. In this way, the site of the piazza is also defined by the relations of touristic and cultural appreciation, reflecting the wealthy Ververs' acquisition of the Prince and his cultural capital. The passage thus not only describes the personal and familial relations between the trio (as father, daughter, and son-in-law) but also the social-cultural relations between collectors and objects and between the Old World and the New World. Since configurations of space are a fundamental way of shaping how we experience an environment, it should be no surprise that spatial dynamics so often furnish the terms for describing the relational dynamics of "human . . . social connexions" (*GB* 136).[71]

This spatial-atmospheric mode of figuration returns in the famous opening image of book 2, when the relations between the characters shift again. As Maggie begins to understand the truth of her marriage, her reflective process is spatialized while the object of her contemplation is turned into a monument. She feels herself circling the "situation" that had been occupying "the very center of the garden of her life," which reared itself as a "strange tall tower of ivory" or "some wonderful beautiful but outlandish pagoda," and later, "a Mahometan mosque" (*GB* 327-28). As if not trusting the reader to understand this image, James goes on to add, "the pagoda in [Maggie's] blooming garden figured the arrangement—how otherwise was it to be named?—by which, so strikingly, she had been able to marry without breaking, as she liked to put it, with her past" (*GB* 328). That past is precisely what was earlier described by the harmonious atmospherics of the piazza, whose air resettled around the Palladian church. Now, the situation becomes solidified into a series of increasingly exotic edifices. Figuring the "unnatural" relations between her husband and her stepmother, the pagoda and mosque are exoticized spaces marked by their foreignness and their out-of-place-ness in a European garden. As objects of Maggie's reflection, they are also significant for their seeming impenetrability and, in the case of the mosque, being a site of worship and pilgrimage to which one returns again and again. Although first of all intimate, James's atmospheric descriptions, as we saw clearly in the passage from *The Ambassadors*, are structured by relations that widen out in space and time, including at times fantastically.

Why does James need to explain the pagoda image after he gives it? Bill Brown suggests that the clarification "discloses his own sense of the difficulty of what he's trying to accomplish, or what his character accomplishes: not the objectification of people (a relatively easy matter, demonstrated throughout the text) but the objectification of the relations among them. A mode of sociality has become an 'outlandish edifice.'"[72] While there is no doubt that the edifice is central to figuring the situation confronting Maggie, she is importantly circling it, traversing its grounds and exploring pathways of entry. That is, even as the pagoda objectifies the mode of sociality in question, as Brown suggests, the dimension of atmospheric inhabiting nevertheless remains decisive for describing Maggie's relation to her situation. However, Brown's reading of the pagoda image raises an important question: we know the damaging consequences of objectifying people in James, but what does it mean to "objectify" *relations*?[73] For Lukács the dominance of description in the later nineteenth century pointed to modern capitalist society's growing tendency toward reification and the commodity form, where relations between people become expressed as a relation between things.[74] Is James's "objectification of relations" then an even more intensified version of commodity fetishism, or conversely its antidote, the undoing of reification?[75]

It may be hard to give an answer that would satisfy a Marxist but I would argue that insofar as James's descriptions resist hypostatization and emphasize the relations that are enabled by sites and spaces (including the objects that may be a part of those spaces), the answer is the latter. James's relational interests are keyed, as we have seen, not to the classic Marxian relations of production but to what Simmel called the microscopic-molecular level of social life, and Simmel's emphasis on the *forms* of sociality helpfully illuminates James's descriptive project. As Simmel explains, "Any social phenomenon or process is composed of two elements which in reality are inseparable: on the one hand, an interest, a purpose, or a motive; on the other, a form or mode of interaction among individuals through which, or in the shape of which, that content attains social reality."[76] The same form can be observed in quite dissimilar contents, and vice versa. So, for instance, "inner solidarity coupled with exclusiveness toward the outside" is a form that exists in both a religious community and an art school, but the "content," that is the purpose, will be different in each. And, we could add, with different effects. For Simmel, the task of sociology is to identify, order systematically, explain psychologically, and study historically "the pure forms of sociation."[77] Although he does not seek to systematize them in the same way, it is *forms* of relation that similarly interest James and for which he seeks a descriptive language. And, as we saw in the piazza image earlier, he also shows that the same form (which in that example we could call something like "inner solidarity with a desire to assimilate select outsiders") can have different content, for instance, in the context of a family or a collection.

These social relations, or "forms of sociation," that Simmel outlines are, as he puts it elsewhere, "all the with-one-another, for-one-another, in-one-another, against-one-another, and through-one-another, in state and commune, in church and economic associations, in family and clubs."[78] Combing this idea with Foucault's sites, we could say that the open vista of the piazza describes—at least from Adam Verver's perspective—a relation of against-one-another gradually becoming a relation of with-one-another. Simmel's prepositional casting of social forms recalls William James's proposal in *Principles of Psychology* that "We ought to say a feeling of *and*, a feeling of *if*, a feeling of *but*, and a feeling of *by*, quite as readily as we say a feeling of *blue* or a feeling of *cold*. Yet we do not: so inveterate has our habit become of recognizing the existence of the substantive parts alone, that language almost refuses to lend itself to any other use" (*PP* 1:245–46). The problem as William saw it was that we mistakenly dwell on the "objects" of thought, what thoughts are "about," while missing the equally important relations between them whose shadings inflect every expression.[79] James's atmospheric turn is an attempt to find a descriptive form for such transitive relations, one that resists the kind of reification that Lukács took to be inevitable to the descriptive mode. Although there are plenty of significant objects in James's corpus, these seem more often to constitute evidence of how relations, dynamic and distributed, cannot quite be objectified or fixed and encapsulated in a symbol. So the "outlandish edifice" that figures Maggie's "situation" becomes through its mutations an impossible structure, and like the golden bowl that cracks under the weight of its overdetermination, objects become symbols that undo themselves.[80] Although he does not exploit the prepositions favored by his brother William, as Stein would go on to do, James's turn to figures of air over the prose of things constitutes his own attempt to prioritize relations over substantives and to describe the forms of sociation that make up life with others.

It is easy to think of forms in terms of two-dimensional shapes, such as an enclosed circle, a hierarchical tree, or even a more sprawling network. But, as I have insisted in this chapter, it is above all the felt qualities of relational forms that James's descriptions are trying to capture.[81] By way of closing let me turn to the third moment of *The Golden Bowl*, from the novel's close, which demonstrates just how strange this mode of description can be in its effort to illuminate those affective dimensions. At this point, after Maggie has triumphed and it has been decided that Charlotte and Mr. Verver are to move back to America, all that remains is for the two couples to serve out the rest of their sentence at Fawns before the Ververs' departure. Saying nothing explicitly, the four live amid their mutual deceit, saved by the presence of visitors who show "the possible heroism of perfunctory things" and mitigate the awkwardness of more intimate intercourse.

> They learned fairly to live in the perfunctory.... It took on finally the likeness of some spacious central chamber in a haunted house, a great overarched and over-glazed rotunda where gaiety might reign, but the doors of which opened into sinister circular passages. Here they turned up for each other, as they said, with the blank faces that denied any uneasiness felt in the approach; here they closed numerous doors carefully behind them—all save the door that connected the place, as by a straight tented corridor, with the outer world, and, encouraging thus the irruption of society, imitated the aperture through which the bedizened performers of the circus are poured into the ring. (*GB* 524–25)

This is an incredibly strange image, one whose spatial plan is hard to plot out. It is in this respect not unlike the famous image of the house of fiction, whose immediate legibility is belied by the ensuing unrealism of its million windows hanging together as "mere holes in a dead wall, disconnected, perched aloft" (*LC* 2:1075). Reminding us of the "planar distortions and dimensional disjunctions" of that famous image, Anna Kornbluh argues that these "spatialize the inconsistencies of what exists and excessively mediate openings to what inexists."[82] The haunted-house-cum-circus-ring image here also spatializes what exists, namely, the feeling of living in the perfunctory, but it does so with similarly excessive mediations. What matters in this image is the atmosphere that the space creates thanks to the configuration of different chambers and the movements that this arrangement permits—the central rotunda as the place of performance, the innumerable doors opening onto empty passages that appear to lead away only to circle back, and the tent to the outside world through which society irrupts. This tent leaves some ambiguity about who the circus performers are—whether it is the foursome who perform the normal relations of marriage and family in front of their guests or whether it is the irrupting society that performs in the ring for the spectating quartet. But the "form" of the relation, which we could perhaps call appearing-to-be-with-one-another-for-others, relies on the atmospherics of the space to achieve its function of being a "likeness" of how it feels to live in the perfunctory.

In the preface to *The Golden Bowl*, written for the 1909 New York edition, James writes of the project of revision, "I have prayed that the finer air of the better form may sufficiently seem to hang about them and gild them over—at least for readers, however few, at all *curious* of questions of air and form" (*LC* 2:1337). Although many readers have been curious about questions of form, few have followed James's own linkage of form to air. And yet as I hope to have shown, taking seriously James's interest in things in the air gives us purchase on a number of key issues both in understanding his late works as well as his inheritance—and transformation—of the norms of realist description. Atmosphere is a useful concept for thinking about James's preoccupation with relations because it is irreducible to its component parts or to a single isolable feature. James's greatest compositional challenge is his inability to circumscribe a situation, to not see—and include—all the endlessly ramifying connections in an encounter. This is, incidentally, also the reason why he has such difficulty writing short works, especially later in his career when he struggles habitually to remain within the word limits imposed by exacting magazine editors. What he wants to write about essentially is the relation of anything to everything. This poses a particular challenge to description, which, in its familiar instantiation as the prose of things, is oriented toward "medium-sized specimens of dry goods" considered in their integrity. At the same time, the essential kernel of arbitrariness in description that makes it impossible to determine with any intrinsic necessity where to start and when to stop also makes it especially susceptible to the problem of proliferating relations that James faces.

Indeed, as we saw in chapter 1, the perennial problem of description for novel theorists has been that it threatens the unity of the work conceived as a whole. And I suggested that in their descriptive practice (if not in their critical rhetoric), modernist writers attempt to forge a new model of a whole through the very mode—description—that seems to undo it. Here we see the final importance of atmosphere, which has been invoked by a number of thinkers to name the singular and unifying thing that pervades—and indeed constitutes as such—a landscape or a work of art.[83] In his short but highly suggestive essay "Philosophy of Landscape" (1913), Simmel writes, "When we refer to the mood [*Stimmung*] of a person, we mean that coherent ensemble that . . . colours the entirety of his or her psychic constituents. It is not itself something discrete, and often also not an attribute of any one individual trait. All the same, it is that commonality where all these individual traits interconnect. . . . In a way that is difficult to specify, each component partakes in it, but a mood prevails which is neither external to these constituents, nor is composed of them."[84] What Simmel calls *Stimmung*, which could be translated as "atmosphere," names a particular kind of whole or totality that is different from the sum of its parts even though it arises from nothing but them. Not only an object of description (as a dimension of social experience) or a figure for particular relational forms and their affective qualities (as in the strange piazzas and rotundas of *The Golden Bowl*), atmosphere is also a figure for the kind of whole spun out of modernist description itself. At the same time that modernism is known for its tendency to fragmentation and incompleteness, it possesses a strong drive toward condensation and crystallization, summing up the whole in a single anecdote or epiphany, or what Ezra Pound called "the method of the Luminous Detail."[85] This is one way to understand Rancière's comment that for modernist writers "It is not a matter of contrasting the singular [each atom in what Woolf called the "shower of atoms," the detail] with the totality, but instead one mode of existence of the whole with another. And it is naturally a totality of an atmospheric type, a diffuse totality made up of discrete particles which are substituted for the organic model of the whole."[86] The kind of whole desired by James's airs, or, as we will see, Proust's proliferating analogies, or Woolf's *this*es and *that*s, is one that privileges relations over terms. As a way of conceptualizing the relatedness of everything to everything else and as a way of imagining a model of a whole work that would not be threatened by the sprawling nonproportionality of description, we could say that modernist description itself aspires to the condition of atmosphere.

Proust and the Effects of Analogy

[CHAPTER THREE]

According to that great monument of Enlightenment learning the *Encyclopédie,* to define something is to say what an object is in terms of its essence, *quid est*. Description, by contrast, is a "an imperfect and inexact definition." It enumerates only the accidental attributes particular to the object, "sufficient to give an idea and to distinguish it from others, but which do not develop its nature and its essence." Thus, while grammarians content themselves with descriptions, philosophers are after definitions.[1] A century and a half later, the sometime-philosopher narrator of Marcel Proust's *In Search of Lost Time* certainly seems to concur with this assessment. As we learn in the final volume, "The kind of literature which contents itself with 'describing things,' with giving of them merely a miserable abstract of lines and surfaces, is in fact, though it calls itself realist, the furthest removed from reality." Such descriptive literature "saddens us the most, because it abruptly severs all communication of our present self with the past, of which things preserve the essence, the future in which they incite us to taste them anew."[2] In the novel's own aesthetic theory, description is opposed to metaphor, which is for its part aligned with the signal Proustian invention, involuntary memory, famously embodied in a little madeleine dipped in tea that yields up the entirety of the narrator's childhood. Metaphor is said to unveil the hidden essences of things and, by connecting two experiences of the same sensation, release us from the shackles of time. Merely describing an experience, on the other hand, can only be at best an ineffective scratching at the surface and at worst a deceptive obstacle to discerning the true reality beneath. It is by now a familiar critique, and the juxtaposition of description and metaphor in the aesthetic theory of the *Recherche* corresponds to a series of value-laden binaries: not only voluntary versus involuntary memory but also appearance versus reality and surface versus depth. But as with so many of the structuring oppositions in Proust's novel, the distinction announced so clearly in theory breaks down upon a close encounter with the text, where we are confronted immediately with the simple fact that *In Search of Lost Time* is endlessly, painstakingly descriptive. Close attention to lines and surfaces—the play of sunlight, the passage of clouds, the shape of flower petals, the color of asparagus—is one of the most recognizable and distinctive features of Proust's immense phenomenology of experience. In this chapter my interest is in tracking the ostensibly discredited practice of description on the ground level of the text, as it were, rather than at the aerial level of the theory, showing that the former works to undo the binaries established by the latter. Although philosophers want definitions that have to do with a thing's essential nature, the imperfect inexactitude of description conjures up instead a series of likenesses that offer a critique of notions of identity. Finally, attending to Proustian description will also open onto contemporary debates about practices of reading and the critical possibilities of close observation of surface appearance.

But first, what is Proust's descriptive mode? If we look closely at the text, we will see that the descriptive fabric of *In Search of Lost Time* is relentlessly analogical. In some ways, this is hardly news—Proust's valorization of metaphor is well known, and as we saw, heralded by himself. Far less remarked, however, is the extent to which the Proustian text overflows with expressions that preserve the explicit comparative. We saw James turn to extended comparisons, especially spatial and architectural, in order to figure socially charged atmospheres and the affective character of particular relational arrangements. With Proust the use of analogy becomes much more pervasive, at once more ubiquitous and less highlighted, and what these analogies tend to target, as much as the individual content of each particular comparison, is the feeling of relating itself. There is perhaps no more tireless comparatist in the modernist period. Hardly a page of the *Search* goes by that does not contain a "comme," "comme si," "pareil à," or "aussi . . . que . . . ," usually several per page, often several per paragraph. The Proustian world is constructed by means of an endless chain of likes, sometimes multiplying in a cascading series, sometimes emerging in a brief flash, sometimes developed at far greater length than their ostensible subject. Hardly can anything be mentioned before it is compared to something else (and then something else and then something else) in order to be specified. Descriptive analogies are so characteristic of Proust's own style that in *The Captive*, when Albertine is eager to show the narrator how she has changed under his influence, she launches on a florid ode to ices that can only be read as a self-pastiche. They are compared to, among other things, temples, churches, obelisks, rocks, votive pillars, Monte Rosa, mountains painted by Elstir, and Japanese dwarf trees. Although the narrator is impressed at her intelligence and newfound taste, he sniffs that he himself would never use such "literary forms" in speech, and he concludes by finding her speech "a little too well expressed" (*SLT* 5:165, *RTP* 3:636).

Albertine's analogies, however, are nothing compared to the narrator's own. This is nowhere more evident than at the conclusion of *Time Regained*, when joy at the discovery of his vocation unleashes the full force of the narrator's comparative energies.

> To give some idea [of the task of writing this book], one would have to borrow from the most elevated and different of arts; for this writer ... would have to prepare his book meticulously, with perpetual regroupings of forces like an offensive, and he would have to endure his book like a form of fatigue, to accept it like a discipline, build it up like a church, follow it like a medical regime, vanquish it like an obstacle, win it like a friendship, overfeed it like a child, create it like a new world without leaving aside those mysteries whose explanation is probably only found in other worlds and the presentiment of which is the thing that moves us most deeply in life and in art. (*SLT* 6:507–8, *RTP* 4:610)

There is much to be said about each of these particular comparisons, which draw surprising connections between writing and diverse forms of activity and work. But we should also not overlook the cumulative effects of this dizzying propensity to liken, which pulls the domain of the aesthetic in so many directions. Although metaphor is valorized in the novel's own theory, *In Search of Lost Time* is in practice replete with analogies far less miraculous, ones that simply disclose particular surface appearances rather than plumb any hidden depths.[3] It is these ordinary, unmarked analogies to which I want to attend—the offhand, ubiquitous ones not deemed exceptional or miraculous that so characterize the descriptive texture of the *Recherche*. Ultimately, like Françoise working in her old age, the narrator imagines he will pin pages to each other, constructing his book, "I dare not say ambitiously like a cathedral, but quite simply like a dress" (*SLT* 6:509, *RTP* 4:610). To remain with the humbler image of the two, my inquiry into the effects of analogy in Proust is more concerned with the text's ordinary fabric than with the monumental spires with which he is more often associated. It will turn out that these unmarked, nonspecial descriptions undo the deep-seated opposition between surface and depth, reality and appearance that the narrator elsewhere insists on maintaining. At the same time, when it comes to certain domains, notably the social world where appearances circulate as currency and capital, highly precise and particularized descriptions do their critical work precisely by zooming in closely on surfaces.

In broaching the subject of Proustian description, it may seem surprising not to focus on the novel's more famous scenes of ekphrasis, such as the one detailing the eighteenth-century Hubert Robert fountain at the beginning of *Sodom and Gomorrah*. That passage has been cited to prove the analytical and narrative nature of Proust's descriptions, in other words, to prove that they are not "mere" descriptions. So Hayden White reads the scene, which "appears to be a purely descriptive pause in the main action," as instead a scene of interpretation and in fact one whose tropological structure offers a model for figuration and interpretation tout court.[4] Similarly, Gérard Genette argues that what appear to be descriptions are actually reintegrated into the narrative, typically by following the narrator's movement as he proceeds toward an object, thus narrativizing the perceptual process.[5] In fact, as Genette observes, conceits such as following the gaze of a character around a room serve to motivate or naturalize descriptions, and they were already used as early as *L'Astrée* (1607-1627). But the Balzacian novel "established a typically extratemporal descriptive canon . . . a canon where the narrator, forsaking the course of the story (or, as in *Père Goriot* or *La Recherche de l'absolu*, before arriving there), makes it his business, in his own name and solely for the information of his reader, to describe a scene that at this point in the story no one, strictly speaking, is looking at."[6] It is this particular idea of description as extratemporal, static, noninterpretive, and nonnarrative that both Genette and White—like other defenders of descriptive writers—refute.[7] As Genette sums up, "In fact, Proustian 'description' is less a description of the object contemplated than it is a narrative analysis of the perceptual activity of the character contemplating[,] . . . a contemplation highly active in truth, and containing 'a whole story.'"[8] All of this is undoubtedly right. But such approaches to description also contain an important limitation: because they restrict themselves to a traditional—and restricted—notion of the practice, the most that can be said for a description is that it is not description at all.

In this chapter, my goal is not to argue that description is actually narrative or interpretively significant. For all their merits, such arguments often have the effect of explaining—and vindicating—description by explaining it away.[9] As I outlined in chapter 1, my interest is in expanding our senses of what description can do—and what it can look like—beyond a horizon determined by narrativity. Specifying the descriptive mode particular to Proust reveals something about the coordinates of his novelistic universe, his cognitive habits and affective orientation. His inveterate habit of likening makes it so that nothing can be understood on its own terms but only with reference to something else; nothing in his world is without precedent, nothing is originary or singular, nothing bounded, nothing identical.[10] In contrast to what I called in chapter 1 an enumerative mode of description, where objects are delineated by listing their predicates and thus considered in terms of boundedness and differentiation, Proust's descriptive mode is instead overwhelmingly relational, with relations between people as likely to be linked to those between nations as they are to those between insects. Whereas James's interest in relations extended primarily to human ones, especially ones felt in the air, Proust casts a wider, and in a way more abstract, net, bringing to light isomorphic relations across a variety of phenomena. Moreover, Proust's descriptive analogies are trained both on similarities between relations and on the relation of similarity itself.

After outlining Proust's penchant for finding (and producing) likenesses and the ramifications of this practice of likening, I will turn back to his critique of description. This critique is expressed through the practice of pastiche as well as figured through the opposing visions of the camera and the X-ray, and in each case the dismissals of description are already undone in their very articulation. I will then consider in greater depth Proust's descriptive attention to the surface, especially what I call his "passing descriptions," which leads to an inquiry into the critical possibilities of closely observing surface appearances when it comes to the social world. Finally, I return to the novel's own aesthetic theory in order to see how these passing descriptions thrown away by the theory might in fact become precisely what the theory itself most prizes.

Comme, comme, comme

Citing particular examples of descriptive analogies in Proust's novel is in many ways inadequate, since what interests me is precisely their frequency and ubiquity—the way in which they are essentially constitutive of the text. But we can nevertheless begin from some general observations. To start, his analogies come from a wide variety of sources: medicine, physics, astronomy, geology, metallurgy, chemistry, optics, botany, meteorology, architecture, music, and painting, to name just a few.[11] Some fields are correlated consistently with certain phenomena (e.g., Swann's love with illness or pathology; girls with flowers), while others become more or less prominent at different moments of the novel. Some analogies are repeated, while others appear only once. Some are developed over multiple paragraphs, if not pages, while others are brief and concise, captured in a phrase or a sentence.[12] Many of these descriptive comparisons are complex and highly elaborated, making it difficult to distinguish between the tenor and the vehicle, the illustrative image and the object being described. Furthermore, the analogies are not evenly distributed. They are seldom used in dialogue, concentrated instead in the analytical excurses attributed to the narrator, suggesting that they are particular to his cognitive habit and orientation.[13]

Indeed, this habit appears to have been Proust's own, as his correspondence attests to the deliberateness with which he uses such techniques. Canvassing friends for illustrative equivalents for things he wants to describe, his typical procedure is to outline a phenomenon (often an aspect of social behavior) and then to ask his correspondent if they know of anything analogous in their field of expertise.[14] So in 1913 he asks both Max Daireaux and André Foucart about the phrase "like in a perspectival drawing of a solid, one of its faces opposed to the spectator," writing to Foucart, "Could you correct this phrase, I want to say that it does not contain any *monstrosity*."[15] This phrase later appears in *Within a Budding Grove* in a description of M. de Norpois's displeasure when the narrator asks the diplomat to mention him to Mme Swann. "I had seen . . . in his eyes that vertical, narrow, slanting look (like, in the drawing of a solid body in perspective, the receding line of one of its surfaces)" (*SLT* 2:69, *RTP* 1:470). The insatiability of Proust's analogizing habit is also revealed by his drafts. In a fragment from the *Cahiers* where, commenting on the way in which experiences in life provide the material for art, he writes, "[frivolity, laziness, sorrow] amassed themselves in me unbeknownst to me, as unknown to me as the reserve of *(put an example taken for example from legumes, wheat or something like that . . .) can be in a plant" (*RTP* 4:862–63). Indeed, he does find a long, extended analogy from botany concerning the albumen lodged in the ovaries of plants from which the plant draws nourishment to make seeds, of which we are ignorant while the plant embryo develops but which is the site of secret but very active chemical and respiratory phenomena (*RTP* 4:863). Very often, these descriptive analogies appear in parentheses, giving them the effect of being marginal asides, removable from the text without disturbing it. This is, of course, just how rhetoricians have regarded description itself, first as a decorative ornament, pleasing but superfluous to a work's structural integrity, and then later, when it began to proliferate, as a foreign element that threatened the unity of the text. But in Proust, the very expendability of such analogies (the fact that they are in parentheses) signals that they are essentially characteristic of his style, for although they are superfluous for narrative—and sometimes even for illustrative—purposes, he leaves them in, as if it is a compulsion, as if for whatever he was writing about, another *comme* always came to mind to describe it.

Although Proust himself seems to use *metaphore* and *analogie* synonymously in the *Recherche* (*comparaison* does not seem to be a term of art), I will use the broader term *analogy* here for several reasons. First, I want to avoid wading into the old debate about whether Proustian metaphor is actually metaphoric or metonymic, which entrenches an unnecessary opposition between the two.[16] Second, metaphor is closely identified with a transference in name, as Aristotle defined it in the *Poetics*, whereas I am interested instead in multipart comparisons between two sets of relationships.[17] The idea of metaphor as naming is expressed in the work of the impressionist painter Elstir, who renders seascapes in urban terms and landscapes in marine terms so that the demarcation between land and sea is suppressed. As a species of naming, metaphorizing is an Adamic act, but as I will argue at greater length in chapter 5, describing and naming are not the same. Moreover, transposed naming does not well describe the operation of Proust's own analogies, which does not transform one thing into another but rather places them alongside one another.

Although it is difficult to maintain a strict separation between metaphor and analogy, what is important for my purposes is that the latter operates by juxtaposition rather than by substitution: "x is *like* y" rather than "x *is* y." The cases I am interested in here are what we would call in English *similes*, since they preserve an explicit comparative such as *like* or *as*.[18] In the next chapter I will turn to Woolf's use of similes to describe affects, but I retain the broader term *analogy* in this chapter because what I want to single out is not so much comparisons between *things*, but rather comparisons between different sets of *relations*.[19] Indeed, Proust is distinctive not because he was the first to use descriptive analogies, nor even because it is impossible to find other writers who use them as frequently, but because his concern above all is with resemblances between relations rather than substantives.[20] Expressible in the form "A is to B as C is to D," such multipart correspondences are, according to the classical tradition, the only kind of resemblance that is properly analogical, *analogia* being the Greek word for mathematical proportion.[21] A good example of such a structure appears early in *Swann's Way*, where the narrator's experience of reading in his room is described in two analogies that are themselves in a relationship of proportional correspondence:

> The dim coolness of my room was to the broad daylight of the street what the shadow is to the sunbeam, that is to say equally luminous, and presented to my imagination the entire panorama of summer, which my senses, if I had been out walking, could have tasted and enjoyed only piecemeal; and so it was quite in harmony with my state of repose which (thanks to the enlivening adventures related in my books) sustained, like a hand reposing motionless in a stream of running water, the shock and animation of a torrent of activity. (*SLT* 1:114, *RTP* 1:82).

This paragraph as a whole is composed of a series of nested comparisons, smaller analogical units (the dimness of the room is to the sun outside as the shadow is to a ray of light) forming larger ones (the relationship of the interior to the exterior world is like the relationship of repose of reading to the adventures in the book being read). Staying in his shaded room in fact gives the narrator the full experience of being out in the summer sun, just as sitting and reading gives him the full experience of active adventuring. While the content of each pair of terms is related by inversion (the interior actually gives more of the exterior than the exterior does, for instance), the relation at stake in the analogy itself is that of resemblance (the similarity of these two counterintuitive inversions).[22] By repeatedly singling out resemblances not between things but between relations, Proust's descriptive analogies move beyond feeling the lack of determinate things, as in James's atmospheres, to taking relation itself as a determination. And by pointing out surprising homologies between seemingly disparate phenomena, multiplying particularities rather than transcending them to formulate general laws, they materialize a terrain that was not previously visible.

Analogies are customarily understood to have an illustrative function, mapping something familiar (a "source") onto something unfamiliar (a "target") in order to explain the latter or make it knowable. So for example, the Rutherford-Bohr model of the atom is called the "solar system" model because it takes the known relationship between the sun and orbiting planets and maps it onto the proposed relationship between the positively charged nucleus and the negatively charged electrons.[23] Of course, the juxtapositional energies of analogizing can also be a defamiliarizing technique, as the surrealists clearly demonstrated, deploying it as a tactic of shock, irony, and play. Although there are moments of absurdity and many more of irony in the *Recherche*, Proust's descriptive comparisons are not for the most part designed to shock. They do, however, sometimes fail to conform to the source-target model. For all that they can be arrestingly apposite, they also sometimes constitute long digressions so elaborate and cumbersome that we lose sight of the "target" altogether. So, for instance, Françoise's mixture of devotion to her family and her mistress but cruelty toward the other servants is told by way of an elaborate comparison to certain insects.

> There is a species of hymenoptera observed by Fabre, the burrowing wasp, which in order to provide a supply of fresh meat for her offspring after her own decease, calls in the science of anatomy to amplify the resources of her instinctive cruelty, and, having made a collection of weevils and spiders, proceeds with marvelous knowledge and skill to pierce the nerve-centre on which their power of locomotion (but none of their other vital

functions) depends, so that the paralysed insect, beside which she lays her eggs, will furnish the larvae, when hatched, with a docile, inoffensive quarry, incapable either of flight or of resistance, but perfectly fresh for the larder: in the same way Françoise had adopted, to minister to her unfaltering resolution to render the house uninhabitable to any other servant; a series of stratagems so cunning and so pitiless that, many years later, we discovered if we had been fed on asparagus day after day throughout that summer, it was because their smell gave the poor kitchen maid who had to prepare them such violent attacks of asthma that she was finally obliged to leave my aunt's service. (SLT 1:173, RTP 1:122)[24]

The resemblance here again concerns relations rather than things—Françoise is to her ruses to chase away servants on the sly as the hymenoptera is to its ability to wound without killing. (It's also worth noting that this same aspect of Françoise is earlier likened to monarchs whose peaceful depiction in stained glass windows belies the bloody histories of their reign.) Proust's perceptive acuity is frequently displayed in the way he conjoins behavioral, morphological, and structural observations about the natural world with the human one, illuminating analogous patterns of behavior and appearance in disparate realms. But the extended parallel in this case is intrusive, pulling us away into a second narrative about the insect so elaborate that we lose the thread of what the anecdote is meant to illustrate about Françoise—and in fact, the strain of viciousness in her nature is explained quite straightforwardly in the second part of the passage. On the most basic level, such elaborate images are a display of authorial erudition. But they also testify to the narrator's—and Proust's—propensity to understand and make sense of the world through a correlational framework, to perceive A only by perceiving that it is like B (or indeed also like C, D, and E). We can also read it as evidence of the extent of Proust's delight in likening itself: for him, the discovery of relations is as important, as much the object of a description, as the specific terms being related. Recalling William James's rejoinder that relations are as much part of experience as the terms they relate and that particular relations—disjunction, conjunction, and so forth—have their own feel, it would be fair to say that for Proust, essential to every analogy is the act of finding relations of likeness. The *feeling* of making connections, the cognitive and affective habit of relating itself, is what drives Proustian description.[25]

The Mimetic Faculty

The penchant for noticing—indeed, generating—likenesses is named by Walter Benjamin "the mimetic faculty," and Benjamin finds in Proust a passionate "cult of similarity."[26] Such resemblances, whose reach is greater than we might expect, are above all forms of "nonsensuous similarity [*unsinnliche Ähnlichkeit*]," of which Benjamin cites as an ancestral example the ancient practice of seeing correspondences between a constellation of stars and the fates of human lives.[27] For Benjamin, the mimetic faculty codetermines all of our "higher functions," but it has become increasingly fragile in modernity.[28] As glossed by Susan Buck-Morss, this attenuation of the perception of similarity occurred as the senses had to withstand the shock of overstimulation, thereby precluding affective openness.[29] In the case of Proust, the penchant for finding, indeed for generating, a series of similarities constitutes an affective orientation that could be called, after Eve Kosofsky Sedgwick, *reparative*.[30] Although his precise and granular likenesses can turn sharply, as we will see, toward the exposure of hypocrisy and the puncturing of social pretense, the larger cumulative effect of the ubiquitous analogical descriptions in the *Recherche* is the creation of a world traversed by a dense web of filiations.

Proust's orientation toward similitude was not unique in his time. It places him in what Kaja Silverman calls a countertradition in modernity—stemming from Ovid and Leonardo rather than Descartes—that "emphasizes kinship instead of separation."[31] In this tradition Silverman places Emanuel Swedenborg's *Heaven and Hell*, which found many correspondences between the natural, spiritual, and celestial worlds and which in turn influenced a number of nineteenth-century figures, including Alphonse-Louis Constant, Ralph Waldo Emerson, Charles Baudelaire, and Balzac as well as, we could add, Henry James Sr.[32] For Silverman, other nineteenth-century figures in this countertradition include Walt Whitman, a key poet of likeness ("A vast similitude interlocks all" says the speaker of "On the Beach at Night Alone"); Charles Darwin, who adopts analogy as a method of understanding in *Origin of the Species*; and Charles Fourier, whose utopian socialism took correspondences as the basis for an ideal social order.[33] In the twentieth century, Proust is a key inheritor of this analogical tradition of thinking.[34] More locally, from Baudelaire's notion of *correspondances* to the symbolists, the later nineteenth century was also the moment when analogy returned to the domain of the literary in France after its eviction during the classicism of the eighteenth century because of the danger it posed to a rationalist ideal.[35] Olivier Kachler notes that during this time it moved outside its classical home in rhetorical discourse and occupied a place among a constellation of concepts—including "*symbol, evocation, suggestion*, or even the *unnamable*"—that were at the center of efforts to rethink language and literature.[36] While an undeniably important background to Proust's analogizing habits, it is worth noting that Baudelaire's notion of *correspondance* is expressed in terms of hieroglyphs, where the artist is a kind of translator or decoder of a cryptic world of symbols.[37] This comes much closer to Proust's grand theory of metaphor than it does to the kind of passing descriptive analogies I am singling out here, which tend not to be mystical or transcendental or to offer any authentic truth or essence.[38] While Proust's turn to analogy belongs to a wider aesthetic movement, its deployment in prose description rather than poetry, and especially the offhanded descriptions I focus on here, render it far less transcendental or mystical than in Baudelaire or his symbolist inheritors.

What Proust shares with others in the countertradition of modernity is a worldview. Unlike Platonic and Christian analogies in which our world is a degraded imitation of a higher one, Silverman argues, in Ovid "every phenomenal form rhymes with many others," modeling a more reciprocal and less hierarchical structure of relation. Importantly, in such a worldview, "We also relate to *ourselves* analogically. We do not have an 'identity' because we are constantly changing, but also do not break into a million pieces because each of our 'shapes' resembles the others."[39] Proust's narrator often refers to different aspects of himself as different *personnages*, and the self at different moments becomes different people, such that falling out of love is said to be a "slow and painful suicide of the self." But the chain of resemblances woven by Proust's descriptive analogies suggests a way to imagine an alternative to self-identity that maintains openness to change without thereby shattering. An orientation toward likeness can thus bring a measure of relief when it comes to the most painful sites where issues of identity are raised, not only around the self but also around objects of desire—when they don't remain the same, when they are different than they should be, or when they are too much the same.[40] Even though Proust's plots tend toward fatalism—every love affair doomed, every person a disappointment—the mimetic faculty manifested in his descriptions constitutes a reparative instinct that stitches together the world anew.

The relief that analogy can provide in relation to self-identity does not, however, preclude it from offering a critique of identity, the very thing that, according to the *Encyclopédistes*, description fails to offer. That Proust resists an essentialist view of identity may not be a controversial point, but attention to his descriptions reveals a novel way in which his critique is mounted. Poststructuralism has taught us to resist the idea that something is stable and self-unified by appealing to internal multiplicity and difference, and certainly difference is a central engine of the drama of the final matinée in *Time Regained*, where the narrator's failure to recognize the aged guests and his inability to reconcile them with the version of themselves that he knows finally makes visible to him the passage of time. But I want to suggest that in a quieter but consistent and more thoroughgoing way throughout the novel, Proust refutes the idea that anything is only ever itself not by turning to difference but via a sustained project of likening. Such a project is able to resist identity because the very notion of similarity also contains the important fact of dissimilarity. As Jonathan Flatley writes of liking and likening in the work of a different artist, Andy Warhol, "When something is *like* something else, it means precisely that it is *not the same* as it. Things that are alike or similar are neither incommensurate nor identical; they are related and resembling, yet distinct. Similarity is thus a discrete concept aside from the same-different opposition."[41] It is precisely because analogy brings terms together on the basis of both similarity and difference that it offers an alternative to the binaries of identity elsewhere on display. By paying attention to the ways in which ubiquitous analogies make of the Proustian world a vast network of relations, we are able to move beyond the heroic binaries of identity and antithesis that the novel itself sets up: either the trauma of difference wrought by time or the redemption offered by escape from time's shackles via involuntary memory. It is not that the customary principles of identity and antithesis are not there but that in the ordinary passing descriptions that make up so much of the text, this dualistic energy is neutralized in favor of more elastic relations of likeness.[42]

In light of this sidestepping of dualism, Flatley theorizes Warhol's "commitment to liking and likeness" as a queer project, and in like manner, we could perhaps read Proust's practices of likening as his way of queering description.[43] Departing from Eve Kosofsky Sedgwick's argument in *Epistemology of the Closet* that "nothing, in Western thought, isn't categorizable and deconstructible under 'same' and 'different,'" Flatley suggests that a "roomier orientation toward likeness" should open up a whole range of problems, "including the concept of 'identity,' the constitution of collectivities, and our sense of what art is and what it does." Moreover, it can allow us to think about "attraction, affection, and attachment without relying on the homo/hetero opposition so central to modern ideas of sexual identity and desire."[44] However disparate their aesthetic practices, I would argue this applies to Proust as well (and in the next chapter we will also see Woolf's experiments with likening in regard to describing affect and sensation). In *Sodom and Gomorrah*, the coupling of the Baron de Charlus and Jupien is described through an elaborate comparison to a bee fertilizing an orchid. Understood in light of resemblance, this analogy can be read as an alternative to the logic of inversion, predicated on the binary of same/different, that was dominant during Proust's time and that governs so much of the discourse of homosexuality in the novel.[45] Although I will not be focusing on sexuality in particular here, queer theory hovers in the background of this chapter as an important resource for thinking about an orientation toward resemblance.

Description is a method of circumscribing, isolating, and identifying objects, one that, as we saw in chapter 1, has been accused of reifying. But Proust shows us a mode of describing that attempts to make its object available without thereby mortifying it. His narrator insists on the capacity of art to disclose a world, and Proust's own descriptive practices give up the need to impose a relation of identity (*x* is this or that) in favor of trusting ongoing practices of likening to disclose relations not yet cognized and to "create correspondences without instrumentalizing them toward a predetermined goal."[46]

Proust's Likes

At the risk of appearing to move backward rather than forward (however appropriate such movement may be to a discussion of Proust), before going on to look in greater detail at some of Proust's analogies, it is worth returning to the narrator's professed objections to description and its close associate, observation. These objections are crystallized in the Goncourt pastiche embedded in *Time Regained*, and a close look at the style of these passages sheds light on the place of pastiche in the novel as well as showing how its similarity to Proust's own text serves to undermine the very critique of descriptive literature that it otherwise ostensibly serves.

From the outset, the narrator is quick to disclaim his talents at observation in passages of elaborate apophasis. He first professes his lack of "l'esprit d'observation" in *Swann's Way*, blaming it for his perverse inability to remember that Gilberte's eyes are black rather than blue (*SLT* 1:198, *RTP* 1:139). A similar disclaimer is repeated much later in *Sodom and Gomorrah* during an evening with the Verdurins at La Raspelière as part of his second stay at Balbec. "I could not say today how Mme Verdurin was dressed that evening. Perhaps I was no more able to at that moment itself, since I do not have the spirit of observation" (*SLT* 4:473, *RTP* 3:339). Indeed he reports that having been absorbed in reflection, he was alone in failing to notice the derision Brichot's etymologies prompt among the other guests. If the initial profession of inadequate observational skills already seemed doubtful to a reader who has already by that point traversed minute descriptions of the experience of falling asleep and waking up, hours spent reading, the hypochondria of his Aunt Léonie, views of Combray, the contradictions of Françoise, and so on, by the time we get to *Sodom and Gomorrah*, the claim is no longer tenable in the least. Much like James's response to Walter Besant's injunction to the would-be novelist to observe everything, the notion of observation that Proust disavows here is a narrowly positivist one.[47] In Proust's case, there is an additional insistence that the perceiver actively contributes to a perception, refuting any idea of observation as impartial or objective. The antipathy to observation and its correlate, description, rests on the idea that it impedes some more penetrating faculty, figured topologically through the valorization of depth in contrast to a degraded or deceptive surface.

This critique reaches its climax in *Time Regained*, finding a foil in the pastiche of the Goncourt brothers' *Journal*, which the narrator reads while visiting Gilberte at Tansonville. Inserted into the body of Proust's own novel, the multipage "excerpt" is a fictional report of a dinner at the Verdurins' featuring the characters of the *Recherche*, and it is composed of gossipy details about the guests and minute descriptions of their attire, the food, the plates, and so on.[48] The experience of reading these pages, especially at this late point in the novel, is a strange one. Set in the same diegetic world, the pastiche presents the familiar world of the *Recherche* through "other eyes," serving to illuminate not only Goncourt's but also Proust's own style.[49] Jean Milly has cataloged the grammatical peculiarities of Goncourt that are highlighted and exaggerated in the pastiche, but I want to note that it also shows just how much analogizing is a Proustian signature.[50] In this section there is only one construction that is comparable to the rest of the novel, a moment early on when the towers of the Trocadéro are made by the gleam of dusk to "positively resemble those towers of red-currant jelly that pastry-cooks used to make" (*SLT* 6:27, *RTP* 4:287–88). We do, however, get instead several extended descriptions of the sort associated with the scorned "littérature des notations," for instance, of the vases in which Japanese chrysanthemums are displayed, and the "extraordinary cavalcade of plates" at dinner (*SLT* 6:30, *RTP* 4:289). These are often comically rendered, like the brill served on "a wonderful Chinese dish streaked with the purple rays of a sun setting above a sea upon which ludicrously sails a flotilla of large lobsters, their spiky stippling rendered with such extraordinary skill that they seem to have been moulded from living shells" (*SLT* 6:31, *RTP* 4:290).[51] In many ways, the Goncourt pastiche exemplifies exactly the kind of static descriptions of superficial sensory impressions derided not only by the narrator but also by Lukács, although for different reasons. The sense of stasis is exacerbated by stylistic tics such as the tendency to nominalize verbs and adjectives as well as the prominence of the presentative (*c'est*), which excludes human agents and effaces the "dramatic" character of the reality described. All of this leads Milly to comment, in an assessment that could have come straight from "Narrate or Describe?," "reality is thus presented as objective, cut off from human activity and from temporality, almost not even organized."[52]

Although the pastiche has been read as a cautionary tale about the perils of aestheticism, we should be cautious about taking it as a straightforward foil.[53] Rather, I would emphasize its similarities to Proust, albeit with the key difference of the lack of analogies. After all, it is not so hard to imagine such a brill being served on Chinese plates with a flotilla of lobsters at the Grand Hôtel at Balbec, where in fact the diners do turn into an aquarium in a notable scene. And the narrator waxes poetic about Odette's dresses in no less extensive a fashion than the attention "Goncourt" lavishes on Mme Verdurin's pearls. As the Pléiade editors note, in its "range, reprises, references to culture, refinement in the rendering of nuances," Proust's own style "is not without relation with that of Goncourt" (*RTP* 4:1189n3). Hannah Freed-Thall argues further that pastiche is the quintessence of Proust's style, "a rehearsal of tonal flexibility and plasticity, a practice of intimacy with a variety of styles and generic norms."[54] In this way, we can understand the Goncourt excerpt as yet another Proustian practice of finding likes, another exercise of the mimetic faculty, and thus a qualification of his indictments of description found elsewhere. We should not dismiss the Goncourt pastiche, then, as simply an example of bad style, including a bad example of descriptive literature, against which Proust articulates his superior method.[55] Although undoubtedly ironized, the *côté chez* Goncourt is adjacent to, not to say intersecting with, the *côté chez* Proust, and that proximity extends to their descriptions in spite of their seeming differences.

Surface and Depth

We have so far seen the Goncourt pastiche, by its proximity to Proust's own text, fail to serve as an altogether bad example of descriptive literature and thus undermine the critique that it initially seems to prop up. In the diegetic world of the novel, however, reading the Goncourt excerpt leads the narrator to his most direct critique of description, which is importantly figured through the opposition of two visual technologies: the camera and the new technology of the X-ray. These two instruments correspond in turn to a surface/depth dichotomy—and its correlate, appearance/reality—that is pervasive in modernist aesthetics. The articulation of this dichotomy in the *Recherche* allows us to see both how it was reinforced by the development of new visual technologies and also how the topology of these new images actually worked to undo the opposition, further undermining Proust's ostensible denigration of description and its alignment with surface appearance.

For the narrator, reading the Goncourt excerpt leaves him with an ambivalent response. On the one hand, he wonders whether literature has any truths to offer, since for all its descriptive detail and fidelity, the journal leaves something wanting; on the other hand, Goncourt's skill causes him to rue his own lack of literary talent. But he quickly reassures himself as to these doubts, leading to an epistemology figured in familiar spatial terms. First, he realizes that his observational failure is not total: "There was in me a person who did more or less know how to look, but it was an intermittent person, coming to life only in the presence of some general essence, common to multiple things, these making up its nourishment and joy" (*SLT* 6:39, *RTP* 4:296). The being who did not know how to look or listen then gives way to a savant.

> Then the personage looked and listened, but at a certain depth only, one from which observation did not benefit. Like a geometer who, stripping things of their sensible qualities, sees only the linear substratum beneath them, the stories people told escaped me, for what interested me was not what they were trying to say but the manner in which they said it and the way in which this manner revealed their character or their foibles; or rather I was interested in what had always, because it gave me specific pleasure, been more particularly the goal of my investigations: the point that was common between one being and another. (*SLT* 6:39–40, *RTP* 4:296)

This passage begins with a typical spatialization of perception that locates reality in some hidden recess. The formal relations between things that the narrator sees, like a geometer, are only visible at a profundity inaccessible to "observation." But even as the passage opposes surface to depth, it immediately reverses that spatial framing, suggesting that much more important than what people say is the *manner* in which they say it, this being more revelatory of a person's idiosyncrasies.[56] In such a hermeneutics of sociality, which we will see characterizes the narrator's depiction of society, meaning derives not from semantic decoding but close observation of surface appearances.

Staying with the stark surface/depth topology for now, it quickly becomes grafted onto competing forms of visual technology. When the discerning person who knows how to observe is awakened in the narrator, the "apparent, copiable charm" of beings escapes him because he cannot stop short there, "like a surgeon who beneath the smooth surface of a woman's belly sees the internal disease which is devouring it. If I went to a dinner-party I did not see the guests, because when I thought I was looking at them, I was in fact X-raying them" (*SLT* 6:40, *RTP* 4:296–97). First likened to the geometer who perceives the configurations of lines beneath the sensible qualities of an object, this linear outline now gives way to an internal malady ravaging a woman's organs beneath the skin, which the trained eye is instantly able to diagnose.[57] Finally, the series concludes with his transformation into a machine—an X-ray—that, unlike the camera, sees nothing of the surface.

Notably, this celebration of the penetrating gaze of radiographic vision occurs at the expense of photographic vision, which is assigned the role of superficial observer. So just before the final redemption in the last volume, the narrator compares memories recalled by will to "snapshots [*instantanés*]," such as those that he had taken at Venice, but the very word makes Venice "as boring as an exhibition of photographs" (*SLT* 6:254, *RTP* 4:444). Proust was by no means alone in associating photography with description, as we saw in the introduction, and this association was itself an extension of an older comparison of realist literature to still life, especially the scenes of everyday life in seventeenth-century Dutch painting.[58] The trope of photography is mobilized in complex ways in the *Recherche*, but there is no doubt that at numerous moments in the novel, it, especially the snapshot, is equated pejoratively with the "littérature des notations."[59]

In contrast, a different visual technology is held up as a model of insight, and in invoking the radiograph as a model of a new and authentic vision, Proust is firmly among his contemporaries. Discovered by the German physicist Wilhelm Conrad Röntgen in 1895, the X-ray was quickly embraced by a range of modernist and avant-garde movements.[60] In the visual arts it was hailed as a model by the futurist painter Umberto Boccioni, and it informed works by Marcel Duchamp, Frantisek Kupka, Man Ray, and the cubists.[61] In literature, Woolf evokes it in *To the Lighthouse* in similar ways to Proust, as penetrating bodily surfaces and laying bare emotions.[62] And in Thomas Mann's *The Magic Mountain*, the experience of having an X-ray taken at the Berghof sanatorium gives Hans Castorp pause, since no one had "taken a look into his organic interior [*Innenleben*] before."[63] Altering the matrices of perception and figuring new discontinuities between seeing and knowing, it seemed to many twentieth-century artists to offer an uncanny kind of knowledge.[64] Modernist attacks on positivism found an important symbol in radiography, as this new medium of light capable of penetrating solid matter reconfigured the boundaries of knowledge about bodily interiorities and subjectivity.[65] The X-ray, Linda Dalrymple Henderson writes, "dealt a powerful blow to the traditional sense-oriented positivism and materialism in general," hence its embrace by artists seeking to move beyond impressionism's emphasis of surface visual sensations to "the essence of form."[66] It is precisely for its ability to "see" the internal structure beneath external appearance that Proust appeals to the X-ray.

But in fact, the spatiality of the radiographic image is more complicated than it first appears. As the Hungarian artist László Moholy-Nagy points out, "[X-ray photos] give simultaneously the inside and outside, the view of an opaque solid, its outline, but also its inner structure."[67] The fact that it preserves the dimensions and shape of its object while providing a new view of the object's invisible inside means that the radiographic image generates what Akira Mizuta Lippit calls "an impossible perspective. Figure and fact, an object's exterior and interior dimensions, are superimposed in the X-ray, simultaneously evoking and complicating the metaphysics of topology in which the exterior signifies deceptive surfaces and appearances, while the interior situates truths and essences."[68] Thus, Moholy-Nagy cautions against the seeming transparency of the image: X-rays "have to be studied to reveal their meaning," requiring a hermeneutics that extends into language.[69]

This observation offers a counterpoint to Proust's seemingly straightforward valorization of authentic vision and its association with a particular literary style.

> We can describe a scene by describing indefinitely one after another the innumerable objects which at a given moment were present at a particular place, but truth will be attained only when we take two different objects, state the relation between them, a relation analogous in the world of art to the unique relation which in the world of science is provided by the law of causality—and encloses them in the necessary links of a beautiful style; truth—and life too—can be attained by us only when, by comparing a quality common to two sensations, we succeed in extracting their common essence and in reuniting them to each other, liberated from the contingencies of time, within a metaphor. (*SLT* 6:290, *RTP* 4:468).

While description is the stylistic correlate of a degraded cinematographic vision in which impressions parade by, voluntary and impotent, metaphor is the correlate of involuntary memory, functioning much like an X-ray to reveal the internal structure beneath the sensible form. But this idea is itself notably elucidated by an analogy between the artist and the scientist, and immediately afterward, by appeal also to nature, which the narrator attributes to making him aware of "the beauty of one thing only in another thing" (*SLT* 6:290, *RTP* 4:468). Recalling Moholy-Nagy's point that the X-ray, promising to pass through appearance to the truth underneath, in fact only results in another image, this passage promises the way to an ultimate essence only by way of analogy, appealing to another example in the set, another likeness.

In fact, in one of the very few other invocations of radiography in the *Recherche*, the narrator comes close to Moholy-Nagy, revealing a new perspective on the importance of adopting an analogical perspective. Having earlier invoked radiographic vision uncomplicatedly as a model of insight, he now issues an explicit warning about taking the X-ray, as it were, at face value.

I had seen everybody believe, during the Dreyfus Affair or during the war, and in medicine too, that truth is a certain fact which cabinet ministers and doctors possess, a Yes or No which requires no interpretation, thanks to the possession of which the men in power *knew* whether Dreyfus was guilty or not and *knew*, without having to send Roques to make an inquiry on the spot, whether Sarrail in Salonika had or had not the resources to launch an offensive at the same time as the Russians, in the same way that an X-ray photograph is supposed to indicate without any need for interpretation the exact nature of a disease. (*SLT* 6:327–28, *RTP* 4:493)

This caution against certainty comes at the end of a section where the narrator has drawn analogies between the successive loves of an individual, the reversals that can take place in social status, and national opinions that shift with political fashions. Each betrays the distance between subjective perception and external reality, and the narrator's realization that his perception of Albertine or Charlus's perception of Morel differs wildly from the way others perceive them helps him to understand that the same gap can exist in collective perceptions. So although France's current revulsion for Germany seems to arise out of some quality intrinsic to the object, "just as I as an individual had had successive loves and at the end of each one its object had appeared to me valueless, so I had already seen in my country successive hates" (*SLT* 6:325, *RTP* 4:491–92). Proust could be seen here as rather cynically refusing to make any political commitments, equating all stances as so many passing fashionable opinions, much like a parade of passing love objects in an individual's life. Certainly he has often been read as a nostalgic and largely apolitical writer if not a downright reactionary one, and his more distanced or ironized portrayal of the Dreyfus Affair in the *Recherche* departs from the impassioned sincerity of his defense of the soldier in the earlier *Jean Santeuil*.[70] But more than a refusal of commitment, this passage betrays Proust's allergy to *doxa* and pieties of whatever political stripe. Importantly, it also betrays his scorn for the unthinking certainty of a perspective that does not draw analogies. Such a perspective, it turns out, is also ahistorical because it fails to connect current beliefs to past ones, and it fails to see the parallels across scales, such as between an individual life and the life of a nation. In this way, the orientation toward likening betrayed in Proust's descriptions belongs to a larger historical, comparative perspective that is capable of generating new understanding by seeing likenesses across cases.[71]

What is also worth noting is the way in which new technologies of vision feature in this passage. In a significant earlier scene where the narrator sees his grandmother without her being aware of his presence, the mechanical apparatus, there the camera, functioned as a neutral record showing the falsehoods of human perception woven by desire and habit.[72] In contrast, here it is the deceptive allure of the transparent and self-evident truth of the mechanical image, this time the X-ray, against which one has to be on guard. But rather than the stark contrast between radio and photographic vision set up elsewhere—with its attendant literary stylistic correlates, metaphor and description—both are implicated here in a more complicated interplay of appearance, knowledge, and certainty.

Passing Descriptions

We have seen how Proust's disavowals of description in the novel's own aesthetic theory is already unraveled on its own terms. I want now to look at how his descriptive analogies work in practice, particularly how they allow him to pinpoint and bring to light nuances of relations and appearances in the most ordinary of phenomena. For in spite of the narrator's disclaimers, Proust's own readers have often singled out how much and how thoroughly he notices. In Benjamin's words, "There has never been anyone else with [his] ability to show us things; Proust's pointing finger is unequaled."[73] And it is his descriptive analogies above all that allow him to point the finger.

As Barbara Stafford notes, "All of analogy's simile-generating figures are ... incarnational. They materialize, display, and disseminate an enigma that escapes words."[74] Stafford alerts us to analogy's materializing abilities, but if "enigma" applies to experiences like the madeleine or the steeples of Martinville that so fascinate the Proustian narrator, it does not quite fit the kinds of ordinary, throwaway descriptions that are much more pervasive in the text. These nonsignal descriptions tend to target highly specific features of how a phenomenon appears and particular aspects of behavior and being-in-the-world. Sometimes it will turn out later that some seemingly trivial descriptively specified phenomenon is significant (so, for instance, the way Legrandin bows, which strikes the young narrator in Combray and is later realized to have been a sign of his homosexuality), but many such moments are not laden with latent meaning. While Proust is well known for his tendency to leap from a particular observation to the abstraction of a general "law," as often as not particular details do not ascend to any more general level. The text is filled with unimportant descriptions that simply pass by and which it would be easy to pass over. So during his childhood walks along the Méséglise way, the narrator observes, "Sometimes in the afternoon sky the moon would pass white as a cloud, furtive, without light, like an actress whose call time has not arrived and who, in the hall, in her street clothes, watches her fellow actors, withdrawing into the background, not wanting anyone to pay attention to her" (*SLT* 1:205–6, *RTP* 1:144). The pleasure of observing the play of surfaces is in evidence again a little later when the narrator delights in walking along the Vivonne. He sees first a water lily that is carried along on a current and perpetually moving: "like a mechanically operated ferryboat[,] as soon as it reached one bank it would return to the other where it had come from, eternally making the double crossing" (*SLT* 1:238, *RTP* 1:166). Farther on, as the current slows, little pools turn the river into a flowering garden, which is described through a variety of comparatives and hypotheticals. "Here and there on the surface, blushing like a strawberry, floated a water-lily flower with a scarlet center and white edges. . . . Elsewhere a corner seemed to be reserved for the commoner kinds of lily . . . washed clean like porcelain with housewifely care" (*SLT* 1:239, *RTP* 1:167). This description of flowers floating on the Vivonne goes on for quite some time longer in a similar vein. Such detailed evocations are also representative of the way descriptive analogies continually fill out the text, swelling it with specifying (for some, excessive) detail. The air, the moon, and the sun all loom large in the novel, since for the narrator the ambient surroundings that mark any epoch are essential to it. And certainly flowers are a persistent theme throughout the novel, although unlike hawthorns, water lilies do not seem to bear special significance. But in the above passages none of these things appear to be indicators of a higher law.

The moon floating across the sky and the flowers floating by on the water: these are not only descriptions of passing surfaces, they are themselves passing descriptions in the flow of the text, offhand analogies seeming to reveal nothing more significant than the perception of a particular, momentary appearance.[75] Indeed, what they seem to reveal most is the narrator's analogizing habit of mind, the pleasure he takes not only in attending to the phenomenal world around him but more specifically in likening as a way of making sense of the world. In this way, describing by analogy is both a cognitive mode of comprehension and an affective orientation that delights in finding resemblances and connections and in seeing "the beauty of one thing only in another thing."

Social Work

What is passing are surface appearances, and that is one way to understand the *Encyclopédie*'s definition of description's failure to say what an object is in terms of its essence. But in at least one realm, appearances *are* essential, constituting the very currency of exchange and the measure of value. Not only applied to flowers on the Vivonne, analogies continually appear in an offhand, ordinary way in Proust's descriptions of both aristocratic and bourgeois society. In so doing, they play a crucial role in generating his caustic commentary on the politics of class snobbery and social life even as the narrator is, for much of the novel, ostensibly an apprentice in the ways of *la vie mondaine*. Just as James retains a commitment to the social hermeneutic project of the realist novel even though his mode of description departs from the Balzacian path approved of by Lukács, so, too, Proust shows a different way of revealing the truth of social relations not by turning to atmospheres but by zooming in even closer on surface appearances. This attention to social appearances suggests a way to negotiate the relationship between description and critique that has occupied recent methodological debates about practices of reading. Moreover, it calls attention to the gendering of appearance that attends traditional critiques of description, insisting on their value in the social world that the novel depicts.

Again, what is so distinctive about *In Search of Lost Time* is the ubiquity of such descriptions, but let me offer two examples to illustrate what I mean, both from the "Swann in Love" section of *Swann's Way*. The first example concerns Mme Verdurin's "little clan," the bourgeois salon that Swann, who hobnobs with princes, joins while pursuing Odette. One of the clan's "faithfuls" is the socially tone-deaf Dr. Cottard, who, because he is always unsure of whether people are speaking in jest or sincerely, hedges his bets by maintaining a constant expression of half irony. During the first evening that the refined aesthete Swann visits the Verdurin salon, the guests all heap praise on a performance of Vinteuil's sonata, which has left Dr. Cottard and his wife, aesthetic naïfs, mostly baffled. But he fears being left out, so after the regulars disperse, "the doctor felt this was a favorable opportunity, and while Mme Verdurin was saying a last word about Vinteuil's sonata, like a beginning swimmer who throws himself into the water in order to learn, but chooses a moment when there are not too many people to see him: 'Now, this is what one calls a musician *di primo cartello!*' he exclaimed with sudden determination" (SLT 1:301, RTP 1:210). What is being singled out in this highly specific comparison is the manner in which Cottard tentatively tries out an aesthetic judgment aimed at ensuring inclusion within the group. It is no accident that the criterion of belonging here is aesthetic taste. As the sociologist Catherine Bidou-Zachariasen has argued, in the late nineteenth century the grounds on which the ascendant bourgeoisie fought the aristocracy were precisely those of culture, from which the aristocracy, so long centered entirely around courtly intrigues, remained removed after the fall of the monarchy.[76] Cottard's clumsy attempt to demonstrate this crucial criterion of membership to the Verdurin salon is evoked by being likened to the desperate manner in which a novice swimmer throws himself into the water in order to learn. More specifically, the riskiness of making the wrong judgment and the importance of saving face is made clear by the way in which the novice swimmer takes care to choose a moment when no one is looking so as to minimize embarrassment. The sharp, sometimes downright absurd nature of social descriptions like these accounts in no small part for the sardonic humor in Proust's writing (even as lengthy explications of them such as the one I have just given no doubt kill the joke). What we are left to understand clearly is both the importance of taste to social belonging in this milieu and also how little it has to do with any actual aesthetic appreciation.[77] An extraordinary amount of information is conveyed in this descriptive analogy, which functions not only to render its object with precision but also to demonstrate the knowingness of the narrator.

Proust has a reputation as a snob, but the Faubourg Saint-Germain is by no means immune to his gimlet eye, and there, too, the intricacies, hypocrisies, and self-deceptions of group membership are described with microscopic attention.[78] At an aristocratic party given by the Marquise de Saint-Euverte a little later on in "Swann in Love," a lesser Guermantes cousin, the Marquise de Gallardon, is pained by the fact that she is unable to outwardly broadcast her kinship with this prestigious family. This kinship is the source of her great pride but also secret shame, since the Guermantes keep her at a distance. Reflecting on the slight she has suffered by not having been invited to one of their parties, she ends up convincing herself that it was in fact she who chose not to go. The snubs she had received, we read, had straightened her up "like those trees which, born in an unlucky position at the brink of a precipice, are forced to grow backward to keep their balance" (*SLT* 1:468, *RTP* 1:324). The resemblance here concerns the parallel relationship between one's bearing and one's environment, be it social or natural. In Mme de Gallardon's case, the adverse conditions she faced "had ended by shaping her body and by giving her an imposing sort of presence that passed in the eyes of bourgeois women for a sign of breeding and sometimes even kindled a spark of fleeting desire in the clubmen's weary glances" (*SLT* 1:468–69, *RTP* 1:324). The fact that her upright posture, adopted to compensate for her harsh surroundings, is sufficient to appear imposing (and even to generate desire, however fleeting) also serves to denature the social world, showing the value and the power of appearances. In both cases, what is described is not simply Cottard or Mme Gallardon as object but rather a cosmology, a whole set of relations and rules, or what Vincent Descombes, following Mary Douglas, calls "the world-system of a social group," which orients its members and gives meaning to their actions and gestures.[79] Much as in the sciences, where analogies function as an instrument of discovery, here, too, they function to extend knowledge.[80]

Microanalogies such as these are found everywhere in the text, making evident highly particularized aspects of even the most minor characters. Although the narrator fetishizes the Faubourg Saint-Germain, Proust's common descriptive treatment of a range of society undermines the gulf between the vulgar and the refined that the narrator and the other characters underscore, making clear instead the resemblances between social worlds—Vinteuil and Guermantes, bourgeois and aristocratic—that the narrator believes to be entirely separate. This has particular trenchancy in the earlier volumes of the *Recherche* both because it is set during a time when social-class barriers are at their most fixed and because the novel's depiction of the Vinteuil salon is at its most merciless early on, a fact that contributed to the idea (common among early readers) that Proust idolized the aristocracy. In fact, it is with good reason that Benjamin singles out Proust's great achievement as the depiction of social snobbery. As Roland Barthes put it, "Proust's work is much more sociological than is thought; it describes with exactitude the grammar of promotion and of class mobility."[81] Importantly, this sociological descriptive exactitude, which lays bare the operations of implicit codes and unspoken laws—notably their cruelty and hypocrisy—is accomplished simply by recording with precision exactly how things appear.

A link between sociology and description has featured prominently in recent methodological debates in literary studies. Heather Love, for instance, takes the descriptive practices of Erving Goffman's microsociology as a model of reading that is "close but not deep": a kind of neutral observation of "surfaces, operations, and interactions" without speculating about underlying motivations, essences, or drives.[82] As discussed in chapter 1, the appeal to description in recent methodological debates typically presents it as an alternative to "critique," with an attendant revaluation of surface over depth.[83] Proust's descriptive practices are not like the sociological ones Love advocates; attended always by an ironic, sometimes mocking edge, they are hardly the neutral observations of Goffman. However, I would argue that Proust offers a way of satirizing, indeed critiquing, through detailing with microprecision exactly how things seem on the surface. But this procedure need not be opposed to a depth-focused hermeneutics, whether that is called critique, symptomatic reading, or something else. Instead, I would emphasize the continuity, indeed the imbrication, between these practices, much as the promise of depth and transparency over surface in the X-ray image was already undone by its impossible spatiality. Proust's descriptions disclose some social or psychological truth by doubling down on recording surface appearances, but in order to understand them, we also need to be able to see the entrenched hierarchies and subtle games of power, the rules of the social group's worldsystem, that they are disclosing.[84] In this respect it may be more helpful to think of the spatial topology not in terms of layers laid over one another but rather in terms of expansion and unfolding, one space opening outward onto another.

It is also the fine-grained closeness of Proust's descriptions of society that distinguishes them from those of Balzac, who tends to paint with a broader brush, rarely focusing on such particularized microaspects of behavior and appearance. For Lukács it was the fact that Balzac's descriptions served his narration that rescued them from the reification that befell Flaubert and Zola's works after him. According to Lukács, narration alone— the story of historical becoming and the rise and fall of a protagonist's fortunes embedded within social change—is capable of elucidating the truth of social relations. Of course Proust's novel does contain such a narrative of social transformation. It traces a trajectory roughly from the 1880s to the 1920s by the end of which the arch representatives of the bourgeoisie and even the demimonde, Mme Verdurin and Odette de Crecy, end up at the very top of the Faubourg Saint-Germain. The question is what role description plays in all of this.

The answer turns on the long-standing connection between description and appearance, which has to take into account the gendered dimensions of the value of appearances. As Bidou-Zachariasen notes, since it was through skillful management of their symbolic capital that the aristocracy had up until that point maintained the "naturalness" of their superiority, in the late nineteenth and early twentieth centuries, the ascendant bourgeois classes parried similarly with games at the level of the symbolic, creating new values and new forms of currency.[85] Notably it was women who were at the forefront of this kind of "travail de salon," and it is this salon work that is central to the social relations depicted in the *Recherche*, whether those orchestrated and managed by the Duchesse de Guermantes, Mme Verdurin, or any of the other countless hostesses in the novel. Such work, we should note, is related to women's "art of making atmospheres" that Dorothy Richardson insisted, as mentioned in chapter 2, was "as big an art as any other."[86] It is also connected to the party-giving that Clarissa Dalloway feels to be her only skill—work that she feels is world making even as it earns her Peter Walsh's scorn ("the perfect hostess, he said" [*MD* 7]).

For Proust, the highly gendered "espace mondain," the space of society (as in "society life"), is the terrain of experimentation and demonstration of his social theory, something that sets him apart from other writers. Emphasizing the importance he accords to this gendered space, Bidou-Zachariasen writes, "As opposed to the Balzacian novel, which describes with precision how to amass fortune, how to build a political career, how to realize an ambition, Proust deliberately leaves aside the worlds constituted by other types of capital, such as economic strength or political power, that are predominantly masculine." Indeed, she goes so far as to argue that "the important characters in the *Recherche* are consequently nearly all women. It is through them that events will arise."[87] Bidou-Zachariasen's point here is to underscore the extent to which women are the social agents and actors in *In Search of Lost Time*. This resists the idea that nineteenth-century women were simply dominated, restricted to the domestic world, and did not intervene in any sphere of power, an assessment that only holds when we limit ourselves to the most visible and most public social worlds, such as the world of affairs or that of politics. "In the space of society, where women are the major protagonists, the stakes of power are not small."[88] Much like Rancière's idea of the division of the sensible, Bidou-Zachariasen characterizes the work of the salon as "cognitive battles having for a goal to impose or to transform images, visions, and divisions of the world."[89] While we could certainly point to the counterexamples of Swann, Charlus, and Morel, what she highlights is both the active, agential nature of women in the *Recherche* as well as the modality of their importance. They are the creators and arbiters of social capital, and Proust's prioritization of *l'espace mondaine* over other masculine-coded political or public domains in portraying the social world constitutes a shift in the locus of importance.

In her classic *Reading in Detail*, Naomi Schor shows the gendered double devaluation of the detail (which is itself closely related to description) in terms of the domestic on the one hand and the ornamental on the other.[90] In similar fashion, we can see that the devaluation of description is gendered in its dismissal of the realm of appearance, which in Proust's case is associated with society and the world of the salon rather than the domestic sphere. Lukács's idea that description's concern with the surfaces of the phenomenal world leads inevitably to reification fails to appreciate the importance of appearance in domains not considered public or indeed historical. It fails, accordingly, to appreciate the way in which closely describing appearances can in fact be a way to disclose the truth of social relations. James, Proust, and in her own way Woolf all turn their descriptive—and sociological—gaze on a sphere coded as feminine. Revaluing the place of description in Proust, and more generally in the novel, can thus also be a way to recognize the feminine labor involved in shaping social relations outside the domains recognized as overtly political.

The Exact Curve of the Thing

Proust's descriptions, as we have seen, gain their power and do their work through their precision and the microscale of their attention. As Barthes put it above, his work "describes with exactitude the grammar of promotion and of class mobility." The exactitude of Proust's descriptive grammar, not only in the social realm but across the *Recherche*, was an ideal he himself held, and it places him amid a wider ideal of precision in language evident in modernist aesthetics in which analogy functioned as an important resource. Proust expressed this ideal sometimes as the closeness of fit between an image and its object, or its "inevitability." So in his preface to Paul Morand's *Tendres Stocks*, a collection of short stories published in 1921 and later translated into English by Ezra Pound, Proust reproaches Morand for including "images that are not inevitable. Now, all approximate images do not count. Water . . . boils at 100 degrees. At 98° or 99°, it doesn't work. In that case, it would be better to have no images."[91] This sentiment, shared among Proust's contemporaries, is found more prominently in poetics than in discussions of the novel. T. E. Hulme, an influential figure who was also the English translator of Bergson, similarly condemns any excess or ill fit in an image expressing a thought, thus championing analogy as the method by which a new poetry could rejuvenate language and achieve such a precision. "When the whole of the analogy is necessary to get out the exact curve of the feeling or thing you want to express—there you seem to me to have the highest verse, even though the subject be trivial and the emotions of the infinite far away."[92] And echoing Proust a few decades later, Wallace Stevens writes that the effect of analogy is "the effect of the degree of appositeness . . . as if in the vast association of ideas there existed for every object its appointed objectification."[93] (In chapter 5, we will see the culmination of this ideal of precision in the turn to deictics, words that are the most precise precisely by saying the least.)

The poetic or aesthetic notion of exactitude, inevitability, or necessity of the descriptive image at work in all these elaborations is one that I will explore in the next chapter under the rubric of *matching*. For now, let us note that Proust revises standard expectations of these concepts in several ways. First, we might expect descriptive precision and exactitude to entail directness and getting as close as possible to its object. But Proust's descriptive practice is oblique—as Beckett put it, "the indirect and comparative expression of indirect and comparative perception."[94] An analogy describes its object only by moving away from it, specifying its object by referring to some other thing while holding in view the relation of similarity. Second, the Proustian descriptive image breaks with the presumption of a universal or objective standard that seems contained in the notion of inevitability or necessity. As critics have pointed out, the associations set up between terms in his work are often contingent and accidental rather than necessary or inevitable. The vehicle is chosen because of some accident of circumstance—they happen to be next to each other, for instance—rather than because of an essential connection between the two.[95] The selection of analogies will thus always be idiosyncratic, drawing on the accidental connections that cause one association to be recalled instead of another. This itself recalls the classical definition of description given in the *Encyclopédie*, where it could only reveal the accidental, never the essential. But in Proust nothing is more essential than accident and contingency.[96]

The intensely correlational structure of the Proustian universe accounts in important ways for the novel's refusal to cohere and its flaws of structure and design. In a 1929 appraisal of the *Recherche* in which Woolf celebrates Proust's powers of observation, she also points out the pitfalls of his inability to stop making connections.

> In Proust, the accumulation of objects which surround any central point is so vast and they are often so remote, so difficult of approach and of apprehension that this drawing-together process is gradual, tortuous, and the final relation difficult in the extreme. There is so much more to think about them than one had supposed. One's relations are not only with another person but with the weather, food, clothes, smells, with art and religion and science and history and a thousand other influences. (*E* 5:67)

He amplifies, he digresses, he is impossible to hold together. Since consciousness "is stirred by thousands of small irrelevant ideas stuffed with odds and ends of knowledge," when "we come to say something so usual as 'I kissed her,' we may well have to explain also how a girl jumped over a man in a deck chair on the beach before we come tortuously and gradually to the difficult process of describing what a kiss means" (*E* 5:67). The problem identified by Woolf here is the one James faced of circumscribing in art the proliferating links of experience. "Really, universally, relations stop nowhere, and the exquisite problem of the artist is eternally but to draw, by a geometry of his own, the circle within which they shall happily *appear* to do so" (*LC* 2:1041). As Rancière has argued, modern novelists were plagued by the difficulty of finding such a geometry. Proust occupies a strange place in the modernist response to this problem. He is considered on the one hand a totalizing, encyclopedic writer alongside Joyce, Mann, and Musil and on the other hand a writer whose incomplete monumental project testifies to the impossibility of totality in modernity. In her study of association as a basis for thought in Proust, Christie McDonald argues that the *Recherche* "straddles the dominant thinking patterns of two centuries: the nineteenth century, in which the association of fragmentary thought was to be subsumed into the notion of a totality; and the twentieth century, in which the notion of associative thinking was to move toward an infinite process of referral and interpretation."[97] Both tendencies are undoubtedly present in his work, but what I want to highlight here is that although the deviations and digressions of his endless analogies prevent the achievement of a certain kind of classical, unified whole, Proust's mode of relational description becomes the very means by which a new kind of whole is fashioned, one that is left undetermined by the openness of its associations. If the arc of *In Search of Lost Time*'s plot could in fact be said to narrate as a totality French society undergoing transformational changes in the early decades of the twentieth century, the novel's descriptions form a kind of shadow whole that attends the narrative, one with loose threads and contingent nodes but whose correlational structure nevertheless searches for connection.

The idea of the novel's descriptive fabric as weaving a dense net of contingent associations brings us back around to Proust's own aesthetic theory. It is perhaps not too controversial to say that Proust is not someone whom we read for the plot. Events are difficult to piece together into a coherent chronology and impossible to hold in mind all at once. Moreover, they unfold according to laws and patterns established early on, quickly becoming predictable and repetitive—one need not read far into the novel to know how every love affair will end, and we soon stop being surprised by the disclosure of yet another character's sexual tastes. But on the level of description, in the disclosure of a world, the reader continually meets with surprise and a sense of plenitude.[98] As Rilke wrote in a 1922 letter of being one of Proust's first readers, "It is simply not yet possible to foresee *all* that has been opened to us and those to come with these books, they are crammed so full of a wealth of discovery, and the strangest thing is the use, already so natural and in its way quiet, of the boldest and often most unheard-of."[99] A century later, Eve Kosofsky Sedgwick, too, refers to the "psychology of surprise and refreshment" that readers continue to find in his work.[100] The work of art, according to the *Recherche* itself, is a place that harbors the possibility of contingency and surprise, one that, to a reader willing to internalize and interpret its impressions, may yield truths of her own. In the novel, the madeleine, the steeples, and the uneven paving stones are miracles of analogy that are already faits accomplis. The hard-won truths extracted from them and celebrated have already been illuminated and revealed. Thus, according to the work's own logic, they are less likely to be appropriated and recreated by a reader. But the unmarked analogies, the offhanded, ordinary, endless descriptions of variegated shades of experience, which in the end don't turn out to be significant, reveal no higher-order law and offer no transcendence—these "déchets" of experience may nevertheless furnish something that solicits a reader's attention, reminds her of something she didn't know she had forgotten, triggers some surprising association, relates some far-flung experiences, and perhaps opens up an unknown world. We might even call them involuntary descriptions. Disowned by the narrator within the theory but bearing witness to his essential temperament, for the reader it is the descriptive texture of the novel that holds the truest possibility of an encounter with the Proustian real.

Feeling with Woolf [CHAPTER FOUR]

Who among us has not stumbled in trying to describe a feeling? This struggle is felt keenly by Woolf's characters. As Bernard puts it in *The Waves* when all six characters gather for Percival's farewell dinner, "We are drawn into this communion by some deep, some common emotion. Shall we call it, conveniently, 'love'? Shall we say 'love of Percival' because Percival is going to India? No, that is too small, too particular a name. We cannot attach the width and spread of our feelings to so small a mark" (*W* 126-27). In a late radio address titled "Craftsmanship" (1937), she attributes this difficulty to the nature of words, which are "the wildest, freest, most irresponsible, most unteachable of all things." If we want proof of this, "consider how often in moments of emotion when we most need words we find none" (*E* 6:96).

And yet the search for marks capable of encompassing the width and spread of our feelings is an ongoing project for Woolf, one that forms the central concern of this chapter. Like James, she takes on the challenge of describing what is not material or visible, and like Proust, her descriptive strategies are primarily comparative, but she directs them toward the problem of limning affects and sensations. Affect has received a great deal of attention within the humanities in recent years, but the precise contours of its formal expression in literature are not always clear.[1] Further, much of contemporary theorizing on the subject emphasizes the way in which affect, sometimes in distinction to emotion, escapes representation and linguistic capture, thus raising the question of how it is possible to describe affective states or qualities at all.[2] I argue that Woolf's work stages this very conundrum, finding both distinctive ways to express feeling and, as we will see in the following chapter, ways to foreground the impossibility of complete success in any such endeavor.

To begin with, it may be surprising to assert that Woolf was interested in description at all, since she is one of its most vocal early twentieth-century critics. And yet a quick survey of her critique in some landmark essays reveals the narrow and constrained way in which she understood the term, bringing us back to the issue of scale. In her most famous manifestoes on the modernist novel—"Modern Fiction" (1925) and "Mr. Bennett and Mrs. Brown" (1924)—Woolf dismisses description in no uncertain terms as a mechanistic "tool" ranged on the side of the obsolete, "materialist" Edwardians against whom the newer generation of "spiritualist" Georgians (represented by Forster and Joyce, among others) are struggling to fashion a new novel.[3] In minutely sketching the villas in which they live and the buttons on their coats, she charges, her predecessors have confused a plethora of detail for the reality of character. Citing a long passage from *Hilda Lessways* in which Arnold Bennett "begins to describe, not even Hilda herself, but the view from her bedroom window," Woolf writes dismissively, "One line of insight would have done more than all those lines of description" (*E* 3:429). What she prescribes instead is well known. The novelist should "examine an ordinary mind on an ordinary day," recording the "incessant shower of innumerable atoms" as they fall and "shape themselves into the life of Monday or Tuesday" (*E* 4:160). In this shower of atoms, it would seem, description has no place. But in spite of her polemics against that "ugly, clumsy, incongruous tool," even the most cursory reading of Woolf's novels reveals that the tool of description is far from eliminated. Her explicit pronouncements on the subject do not match what she does with it in practice, and this chapter aims to construct a Woolfian theory of description based on what she does rather than what she says.

There are two sources of confusion in her comments on the subject that should be clarified immediately. The first returns us to a problem discussed in chapter 1: the fact that the status and meaning of description alters according to the scale at which we consider the work. At the level of the whole, it is possible to isolate largely descriptive passages from largely narrative ones and to subordinate the former to the latter or to fault the absence of such subordination. But at the level of the sentence, it is difficult to find anything that is *not* in some way descriptive, since even verbs—words of action, that preeminent concern of narrative—inevitably contain descriptive connotations. When Woolf censures Bennett for trying to make us believe in the reality of Hilda Lessways "by describing accurately and minutely the sort of house Hilda lived in, and the sort of house she saw from the window" (*E* 3:431), she is objecting not only to what she sees as a mistaken identification of person and domicile but also to the separation of narration and description at larger-scale units in the composition of the work as a whole. Specifically, she objects to what Genette called "extratemporal" descriptions, or what we could further call preparatory descriptions, those semiautonomous passages of mise-en-scène or portraiture that frequently appear in realist fiction at the beginning of a chapter or whenever a new setting or character is introduced.[4] Woolf's critique operates at the standard macrolevel understanding of description, and her experiments with the descriptive in her own works do sometimes function at the macrolevel as well. However, her innovations occur more at the microlevel, at the level of the passage, the sentence, and, as we will see in the next chapter, at the level of the word.

Woolf's experiments involve shifting the balance of description in two divergent directions. On the one hand, she *increases* the separation of description from the rest of the narrative by splitting off—often typographically—the passages that could be read as mise-en-scène, as happens in varied ways in the "Time Passes" section of *To the Lighthouse*, the seascape interludes of *The Waves*, and the opening vignettes of each chronological section of *The Years*. These moments, which attain their significance when viewed at the level of the whole, do not abandon but rather intensify realist conventions, isolating descriptive passages even more from the rest of the text while estranging them by making them less subordinate to the human characters ostensibly at the heart of a novel. The most extreme example of this strategy is the "Time Passes" section of *To the Lighthouse*, where the Ramsays' house is the focus of descriptive attention while major life events among the Ramsays themselves are relegated to brief parenthetical appearances. On the other hand, at the more local scales of the paragraph and the sentence, where my focus in this and the next chapter will be primarily directed, description and narration become braided together so tightly that they cannot be extricated.[5]

The second source of confusion or discrepancy between Woolf's comments on description and her own novelistic practice has to do with her willful confinement of this mode of writing to material objects in her critical pronouncements. It is certainly not the case that she does not describe concrete things, nor that these are without significance in her novels—we need only think of a piece of green glass found on a beach, a mark on the wall that turns out to be a snail, Minta Doyle's lost brooch, Peter Dalloway's pocket knife, or the broken gramophone in *Between the Acts*, to name just a few. But my primary concern here is not with "solid objects in a solid universe" (*E* 5:43). As discussed in the introduction, since nineteenth-century realism description has become synonymous with the prose of things, but the latter does not exhaust the former. In Woolf's hands, description might be better called a prose of sensations directed toward affect attunement.[6] If there appears something contradictory about the idea of a *prose* of sensations, Woolf herself was aware of this fact, working through the problem in her essays as questions of genre (novel vs. poetry) and medium (visual art vs. literature).[7]

Woolf's critique of description is closely tied up with her polemicizing response to an older generation of writers, and she fails to recognize the place of description in her own project. She chafes at "the powerful, unscrupulous tyrant" who commands the writer "to provide plot, to provide comedy, tragedy, love interest, and an air of probability embalming the whole" (*E* 4:160), but in these very critiques there is also something of a paradox, one that suggests how her affective descriptions may be working at odds with her stated aims. In "Modern Fiction" Woolf denounces the "materialists" for writing of "unimportant things," spending immense skill and industry "making the trivial and the transitory appear the true and the enduring" (*E* 4:159). In spite of this labor, they fail to capture "life or spirit, truth or reality," which, she says, is not "like this." What then is life like? The answer, as we saw, is an incessant shower of atoms, "myriad impressions—trivial, fantastic, evanescent, or engraved with the sharpness of steel" (*E* 4:160). But what is the difference, as Rancière very reasonably asks, between "the trivial and the transitory" things of the (bad) materialists and the "trivial ... evanescent" impressions of the (good) spiritualists? There are after all plenty of ordinary, everyday details in even the most "poetic" of Woolf's novels, *The Waves*, which is filled with eating, drinking, walking, bread baking, train riding, and flower admiring, among other activities. The difference cannot lie in "the intrinsic quality of the things that are described or the events that are told," Rancière concludes, but rather "the mode of their linkage, or, in Woolf's terms, their *way* of making the trivial true and the transitory enduring."[8]

This point has to do with the structure of the work, how we get from next to next, but Rancière also makes a suggestive proposal for understanding Woolf's opposition of "spiritual" to "material" that de-psychologizes her affective descriptions and puts them at odds with what she remained committed to as the chief aim of the novel: character. What could not be captured by the tyranny of having to get on from lunch to dinner was not the inner sentimental world of the heroes but "the impersonal and universal soul that does not know the opposition between consciousness and reality, the soul that is made of a multitude of microsensory events through which thought and matter, activity and passivity become indiscernible."[9] In other words, not more interiority, as is commonly supposed of modernist fiction, but the breakdown of a clear distinction between interior and exterior; not the exclusion of material details, but "the erasure of the very border separating the material from the spiritual, the liberation of sensory events from scenarios based on that separation: scenarios of the mind imposing its will in the material world."[10] The liberation of sensory events finds a formal correlate, I argue, in the form of descriptive similes, hearkening back to the epic simile, that continually pull the reader away from the thread of the plot. Even as Woolf is often hailed for the acuity of her depictions of psychological states, it will turn out that her descriptions of feeling often float free of the individuals to whom they ostensibly belong, unable to be folded into a causal narrative of individual development (in the form of backstory) or personality (as motivation or explanation). The prose of sensations thus constitutes a counterthread to the prevailing understanding of Woolf's status as a preeminent writer of individual psychological interiority.

In what follows, I begin with Woolf's remarks on painting and film, for it is with the aid of these visual media that she worked through the problem of how to convey in language what does not look like anything at all. I argue that through her thinking about "likeness" in "The Cinema" and elsewhere, she finds a way to describe affective states through strategies of displacement and transposition. To elucidate how these mechanisms work, I turn to the work of psychoanalyst and developmental psychologist Daniel Stern on "affect attunement." Stern's model provides not only a robust and precise way to understand how it is that affective states can be described at all, it also suggests ways of thinking about the work that is accomplished by such descriptions, work that is distinct from supplementing narrative. Finally, I conclude by turning to two recent accounts of the modern novel, Rancière's and Jameson's, in order to consider the implications of descriptive temporality when it is oriented toward affect. Description has long been accused of stasis and interrupting narrative flow, but the affective similes that pull away from both character and narrative in Woolf constitute a resistance to the progressive view of history implicit in the forward movement of narration.

Moving Pictures

Late in *To the Lighthouse*, as James and Cam Ramsay finally make the long-awaited journey with their father, James confusedly searches for ways to describe the complex feelings—murderous, sympathetic, and ones more difficult to name—provoked by his father. "Turning back among the many leaves which the past had folded in him, peering into the heart of that forest where light and shade so chequer each other that all shape is distorted, and one blunders, now with the sun in one's eyes, now with a dark shadow, he sought an image to cool and detach and round off his feeling in a concrete shape" (*TL* 185). What kind of "image" could this be? In what way can it round off feelings and give them concrete shape? Literary description has long been considered to bear a close proximity to the visual, and if feelings and sensations pose a challenge to prose, it is in no small part because of the banal fact that they don't look like anything at all. Presenting no physical parts to detail, the modes required to figure them must depart from the visual morphology that structures so much of realist description. We saw in chapter 2 how James blocked visualization by refusing to particularize objects at the same time that he sought to render the affective qualities of relations through a metaphorics of atmospheres and spatial inhabiting, albeit in spaces that were often impossible. Woolf, turning squarely to the challenge of describing affect, forges highly specific, vivid images that work through what I will call "matching" rather than representation. To understand how this works, it is useful to turn to Woolf's remarks on painting and cinema—admiring, resistant, competitive by turns—because it is paradoxically through these visual mediums that she works through the problem of describing what does not present itself to the eye. What I am interested in here are not so much the sensory impressions of light and color and intense visual perceptions of the natural world for which Woolf is so well known.[11] Instead, I mean to emphasize something a little different: the ways in which visual images can have figurative power without operating as a representational portrait.[12]

Woolf's relationship to the visual arts has often been noted. Her inner circle included numerous art critics and artists, including her sister Vanessa Bell, her sister's husband Clive Bell, and Roger Fry, who was instrumental in bringing postimpressionist painting to England.[13] And her remarks on the cinema have become an important document of the relationship between literary modernism and film.[14] Although "The Cinema" (1926) is her most developed and best-known statement on the subject, an earlier essay, "Pictures" (1925), comments directly on description through linking it to painting. In that essay, she sounds like a latter-day Lessing, arguing that whereas sculpture influenced Greek literature, music influenced Elizabethan drama, and eighteenth-century letters drew inspiration from architecture, the present literary moment labors under the dominion of painting, which manifests as a proliferation of description. The literary world is currently full of writers who are incapable of using their medium for its intended purpose, instead painting "apples, roses, china, pomegranates, tamarinds, and glass jars as well as words can paint them, which is, of course, not very well" (*E* 4:243). But even though Woolf echoes Lessing's insistence on the medium specificity of paint and words, the essay itself evinces a constant movement of assertion and qualification that belies such clear distinctions, while the plethora of highly evocative images in the essay enacts the susceptibility to visuality to which she describes the writer as being prey.

Indeed, the problem seems more to be one of degree than kind; the presence of pictures can be invigorating rather than "crippling" in "complete" writers because in their works it is hard "to put one's finger on the precise spot where paint makes itself felt" (*E* 4:243). Here already we can see the strange form of Woolf's understanding of textual visuality—when absorbed, paint in writing is not seen but *felt*. A problem seems to arise only when the romance of attraction becomes a case of mistaken identity; in contrast, visually descriptive writers that she approves of (Proust, Hardy, Flaubert, and Conrad are named) do not let their eyes impede their pens.

> Moors and woods, tropical seas, ships, harbours, streets, drawing-rooms, flowers, clothes, attitudes, effects of light and shade—all this they have given us with an accuracy and a subtlety that makes us exclaim that now at last writers have begun to use their eyes. Not, indeed, that any of these great writers stops for a moment to describe a crystal jar as if that were an end in itself; the jars on their mantelpieces are always seen through the eyes of women in the room. The whole scene, however solidly and pictorially built up, is always dominated by an emotion which has nothing to do with the eye. But it is the eye that has fertilized their thought; it is the eye, in Proust above all, that has come to the help of thought. (*E* 4:243–44)

It is not that Proust and Flaubert have rejected the influence of painting but that they have learned it so well that it has been sublimated. Note the capaciousness of items Woolf lists as being indifferently susceptible to description: familiar items such as natural landscapes (moors, woods, tropical seas), settings (harbors, streets, drawing rooms), and material objects (ships, clothes), but also "attitudes" and "effects of light and shade." Whereas she calls for the elimination of description in "Mr. Bennett and Mrs. Brown," it is clear here that she is really after an expansion of its domain, which will also present new representational challenges. In the end, painting is important to Woolf insofar as it can be a resource for fiction and a spur for language. So one of Cézanne's rocky silent landscapes "stirs words in us where we thought none to exist; suggests forms where we had never seen anything but thin air" (*E* 4:245), and a still life of red-hot pokers "is to us what a beefsteak is to an invalid—an orgy of blood and nourishment, so starved we are on our diet of thin black print. . . . We carry those roses and red-hot pokers about with us for days, working them over again in words" (*E* 4:245). For all her insistence on medium specificity, a model of intermedial inspiration is more prominent in Woolf's writings on the visual arts.

The inspiration she draws from the visual medium of film in particular is a paradoxical one. We might expect her investment in the specificity of language to lead her to turn away from attempting in language what could be (better) represented visually. This was, as we saw in the introduction, the path counseled by Valéry and Breton in relation to photography. But even as Woolf does turn her attention to immaterial, invisible things, specifically affective states, she does so only by taking inspiration from the ways in which film itself evokes what is not visible. In "The Cinema," first published in 1926 but which she worked on throughout the late teens and early twenties, Woolf urges the younger art to explore its capacity to express emotions through a new language of shapes belonging to it alone.[15] She catches a glimpse of this promise in a wiggling black mark, initially thought to be a tadpole, that she sees on the screen at a showing of *The Cabinet of Doctor Caligari*. "For a moment it seemed as if thought could be conveyed by shape more effectively than by words. The monstrous, quivering tadpole seemed to be fear itself, and not the statement, 'I am afraid'" (*E* 4:593–94). The mark is later identified as likely a scratch on the material medium of the film itself, but it makes clear that "the cinema has within its grasp innumerable symbols for emotions that have so far failed to find expression. Terror has, besides its ordinary forms, the shape of a tadpole; it burgeons, bulges, quivers, disappears. Anger is not merely rant and rhetoric, red faces and clenched fists. It is perhaps a black line wriggling upon a white sheet" (*E* 4:594). Woolf's ideas here about the expression of emotion in a visual medium—anger as a wriggling black line, terror as a quivering tadpole—find a direct parallel, as we will see momentarily, in the nonrepresentational or nonmimetic way in which she describes affective states in language.

The idea that film could explore emotion through the language of shapes not only provided Woolf with a model for a nonrepresentational language of description, it also provided a way for her to think about the idea of emotion as separate from individual personality and thus closer to what critics today are more likely to call affect. Modernism is famously governed by an ideal of impersonality, understood classically as the desire (represented especially by Eliot and Pound) to escape the lyrical self-expression of Romanticism.[16] But in recent reconsiderations of the varieties of modernist impersonality, critics have notably turned to contemporary discourses on affect, which is similarly interested in forms of experience that exceed or bypass the bounds of the individual.[17] Although Woolf championed forays into psychology in essays written earlier in the 1920s, in "Poetry, Fiction, and the Future" (1927), written around the time she started to work on *The Waves*, she argues that "the psychological novelist has been too prone to limit psychology to the psychology of personal intercourse; we long sometimes to escape from the incessant, the remorseless analysis of falling into love and falling out of love, of what Tom feels for Judith and Judith does or does not altogether feel for Tom. We long for some more impersonal relationship" (*E* 4:435-36).

Woolf's thinking about the impersonality of emotion is especially clear from her notes and drafts of her writings on film aesthetics. In an early draft of what would become "The Cinema," she associates emotion with sensory impressions like a feather pirouetting in the wind, an unexpected shadow, the clang of the city heard through a doorway.

> Idly dreaming [ ] in a garden lawn the wind blows a feather pirouetting before us <instantly>. A new sensation instantly tightens our nerves—something terrifying & unknown has happened & exciting & inexplicable has happened. or again So, perhaps a horse feels at the sight of a motor car... something that has never been tamed & familiarized by the genius of man. Or it may be simply the sudden [ ] emergence of an unexpected shadow. <wh. Stalks & swells>.[18]

Similar moments can be found especially in *The Waves*, and especially with Rhoda, the least psychologically integrated character, whose impressions are intensely cinematic: "alone I should stand on the empty grass and say, Rooks fly; somebody passes with a bag; there is a gardener with a wheelbarrow" (*W* 161). The simple recording of these scenes accords with Woolf's special interest in nonfiction films—the newsreels, travel footage, and topical *actualités* that would have made up a quarter of the film programs of her day—which presented scenes of accidental and ordinary sights that she found "delightful."[19] Pirouetting feathers and passing rooks, fleeting microsensory events, often give rise to greater affective intensities in Woolf than the "events"—falling in and out of love, births, marriages, deaths—that we would ordinarily associate with swells of passion.[20]

Although Woolf is ostensibly addressing the specific power of the cinema in her essay on that topic, it is clear that, as in "Pictures," she really has literature in mind, evident from the fact that all her references are literary (e.g., Shakespeare and Robert Burns) while her cinematic examples are largely made up.[21] The lesson Woolf absorbed most from film was that conveying emotions required a certain act of displacement, and we can "feel" this lesson in *Mrs. Dalloway*, the novel published around the same time as "The Cinema." When she wonders in her essay, "is there ... some secret language which we feel and see, but never speak, and, if so, could this be made visible to the eye?," she observes that especially in moments of emotion, thought has "the picture-making power, the need to lift its burden to another bearer; to let an image run side by side along with it. The likeness of the thought is for some reason more beautiful, more comprehensible, more available, than the thought itself" (*E* 4:594). She is also adamant that there is an image-making power specific "to words and to words alone," of which the visual is only one part.[22] Nevertheless, "the likeness of the thought" becomes a key part of her poetics, and what her encounter with film shows her is the emotional power of images to "run alongside" that which has no material form.[23] While film is counseled to sidestep narrative fiction in order to discover its unique capacities, the novel finds *its* purpose in conveying things that "are not in words and not in writing and not in shape" but that can only be done paradoxically by finding appropriate "images."[24] This complex attraction and repulsion of mediums ultimately results in a dialectical movement of one working through the other via a logic of sublimation and displacement.

"The Likeness of the Thought"

When Woolf suggests that thought has a "picture-making power" and a tendency to lift its burden onto another bearer, she is in effect describing a strategy we know familiarly as simile. This, I propose, is a key strategy in her response to the challenge of describing feelings that present nothing to visualize, and the result is a notion of likeness based on what I will call "matching" rather than imitation. The *Princeton Encyclopedia of Poetry and Poetics* tells us that *simile* refers to "A comparison of one thing with another, explicitly announced by the word 'like' or 'as.'"[25] Although *simile* is sometimes merged with *metaphor*, as we saw last chapter, it was deemed by Aristotle—and the tradition after him—the weaker and inferior term. And yet that explicit acknowledgment of its untruth alongside its truth—*like*, not *is*—is precisely what makes it attractive to Woolf, who finds in it both a means of writing affect as well as the formal expression of an ethical demand.

To see how this works, I want to turn to an example from early on in *Mrs. Dalloway* when Clarissa returns home from buying flowers. "The hall of the house was cool as a vault. Mrs. Dalloway raised her hand to her eyes, and, as the maid shut the door to, and she heard the swish of Lucy's skirts, she felt like a nun who has left the world and feels fold round her the familiar veils and the response to old devotions" (*MD* 29). The ratio of material information about the house and information about Clarissa's sensations has markedly tilted in the latter direction. Unlike an ekphrastic representation, Woolf's descriptive process conveys sensations and emotions by means of experiential homologies. These descriptions are, to recall terms discussed in the introduction, instructions for affective mimesis, that is, instructions for imagining feeling. Both the tenors and vehicles of Woolf's similes tend to be highly specific, as we see a little later in this scene when Clarissa learns that Lady Bruton has invited Richard Dalloway to lunch without her, and the shock of the snub "made the moment in which she had stood shiver, as a plant on the river-bed feels the shock of a passing oar and shivers: so she rocked: so she shivered" (*MD* 30). If the earlier figure of the nun was more obviously laden with allegorical meaning, symbolizing Clarissa's withdrawal from life and retreat into a second virginity, the plant on the riverbed is less susceptible to such readings.[26]

The aqueous motif continues in the next paragraph as Clarissa contemplates her share of life dwindling with age, feeling how little capable the remaining margin is

> of stretching, of absorbing, as in the youthful years, the colours, salts, tones of existence, so that she filled the room she entered, and felt often as she stood hesitating one moment on the threshold of her drawing-room, an exquisite suspense, such as might stay a diver before plunging while the sea darkens and brightens beneath him, and the waves which threaten to break, but only gently split their surface, roll and conceal and encrust as they just turn over the weeds with pearl. (*MD* 30)

This passage is typically Woolfian in its combination of narrative information (Clarissa feels snubbed by Lady Bruton), philosophical meditation (on aging), and highly specific descriptive images (the diver pausing before plunging into the waves). Descriptions, as we have seen, have typically been understood to pause narrative time and momentum in order to expand into space. It is certainly true that the diver image briefly suspends the story, which resumes in the next paragraph by following Clarissa up the stairs to her room. But rather than expanding spatially into the diegetic environment and thus working to supplement the narrative, Woolf's descriptions pull us away from the story by their persistent tendency to liken a character to an unspecific, hypothetical figure marked by the indefinite pronoun. The diver image in this case stretches the thread of the narrative away from the prosaic situation and concrete individual at hand—Clarissa sitting in her house stung by social rejection—and connects it to a more lyrical and abstract register with the bridge of "such as," which moves us to a hypothetical, indefinite realm. The comparison is to *a* diver, unspecified and anonymous except for the transposition of gender, which enacts here in miniature the gender fluidity that *Orlando* performs at the level of plot. If it is relatively clear what the connection is between Clarissa's pause of delighted anticipation and a diver's moment of suspension, the rest of the passage that lingers with the waves splitting and rolling seems to become completely separated from *Mrs. Dalloway*'s story. Since it is an extensive strategy rather than the intensive one of metaphor, expanding rather than condensing, similes are especially liable to go on a little longer than expected.[27] Accordingly, the more descriptive asides there are, the harder it is to hold on to the thread of the main story.[28] The extensiveness of simile in narrative thus contrasts with the extreme compression of a poem like "In a Station of the Metro" even though imagism also works with comparative techniques.

As with James, length is often a crucial factor in what makes Woolf's descriptive images come unmoored from the characters and scenarios that gave them their initial impetus. In Woolf's case they also interrupt the intimacy with a character's thoughts and perceptions that is established by the use of free indirect discourse.[29] "Millicent Bruton, whose lunch parties were said to be extraordinarily amusing, had not asked her. No vulgar jealousy could separate her from Richard" (*MD* 30). These lines, found in between the two passages I have quoted above, are representations of Clarissa's own thought. "But she feared time itself, and read on Lady Bruton's face, as if it had been a dial cut in impassive stone, the dwindling of life; how year by year her share was sliced; how little the margin that remained was capable any longer of stretching, of absorbing" (*MD* 30). Even if the initial image of Lady Bruton's face as a sundial could be ascribed to Clarissa's consciousness, as the passage continues with the diver image discussed above, that assumption is increasingly harder to maintain. The descriptive simile belongs not to Clarissa but to the narrative voice, drawing us not only away from the plot but also in a certain sense away from character itself, or at least her point of view. Embedded amid moments of great intimacy with a character is the impersonal force more obviously present in *Mrs. Dalloway* in the passages referencing prehistoric and Roman London and later in the "Time Passes" section of *To the Lighthouse* and the interludes in *The Waves*.

The image of a diver pausing in a moment of "exquisite suspense" before plunging underscores the traditional understanding of a descriptive aside as a narrative pause. It recalls as well Clarissa's pause before entering her party, much as Mrs. Ramsay pauses before going in to dinner in *To the Lighthouse* and Jinny pauses in *The Waves* before stepping out into the promises of the night. The entrance into the social in Woolf is often preceded by moments of hesitation and suspension that allow characters to collect their selves and to "assemble."[30] But the idea that this is a pause in the narrative requires some modification. For one thing, the suspension is not a static dilation because this simile is highly dynamic, taking us into another story entirely, that of the waves rolling and turning. Indeed,

Feeling with Woolf 129

the absence of a visually mimetic connection in Woolf's similes is usually coupled with their dynamism; the criticisms that compared description to still life painting are difficult to sustain here. There is not so much a pause in narrative momentum as the introduction of a new, hypothetical temporality.

At times, Woolf's descriptive dynamism also accomplishes the work of narrative itself, which we can see especially in moments that allude to an older, classical tradition. Epic similes, also known as Homeric similes, are "based on the juxtaposition of two passages describing objects, persons, or events connected by the words 'like' or 'as,' in which the subject of the simile may be developed as an independent picture."[31] Rather than "mere static descriptions of objects," epic similes are "long digressions," but "each digressive interruption is in motion," possessed of its own beginning, middle and end.[32] They are lengthy comparisons of "*composite* actions or relations" (my emphasis), and the simile's digressive and diffusive tendency stands opposed to the principle of condensation and compression governing metaphor.[33] Usually made up of both descriptive and narrative elements, the digressions become stories within the story, causing it to move along its path effectively through a series of epicycles, a structure also exhibited in Proust.

The novel, Lukács famously argued, is the genre of a constitutively alienated modern world in which the totalized harmony of epic is no longer possible. But of course modernists also persistently turned to an epic past for poetic forms and archetypes even if these were only available in shards and splinters.[34] *Mrs. Dalloway* provides the best examples of similes that are epic both in structure and in the subject matter of the comparison, and scholars have argued that the novel contains both allusions to and parodies of a Homeric tradition that includes Joyce's rewritings of *Ulysses*.[35] During the scene of Clarissa and Peter Walsh's first reunion, for instance, we read, "So before a battle begins, the horses paw the ground; toss their heads; the light shines on their flanks; their necks curve. So Peter Walsh and Clarissa, sitting side by side on the blue sofa, challenged each other" (*MD* 44).[36] If this equine transformation of the two former suitors is liable to be called mock heroic, that term is less clearly applied to other extended similes, as when Clarissa accidentally alludes to Peter's old desire to marry her.

> Of course I did, thought Peter; it almost broke my heart too, he thought; and was overcome with his own grief, which rose like a moon looked at from a terrace, ghastly beautiful with light from the sunken day. . . . And as if in truth he were sitting there on the terrace he edged a little towards

> Clarissa; put his hand out; raised it; let it fall. There above them it hung, that moon. She too seemed to be sitting with him on the terrace, in the moonlight. (*MD* 42)

Here, as is often the case in extended comparisons, concrete events within the narrative are likened to something more lyrical and visionary, "that queer amalgamation of dream and reality, that perpetual marriage of granite and rainbow" (*E* 4:478). In this passage, the description of Peter's grief as rising like a moon seen from a terrace becomes incorporated into the movement of the narrative itself. He enters the dream "as if in truth" he were sitting there on the terrace, where Clarissa joins him. In the realm of feeling, it is the truth, they are sitting there together. What makes the "as if" here strange is that it is also true in the "actual," that is, diegetic, world, where they *are* in fact also sitting together, albeit in her parlor.

This long simile goes on to extend over the rest of the scene, its borders becoming entirely porous with the actual narrative events.[37] "Then, just as happens on a terrace in the moonlight, when one person begins to feel ashamed that he is already bored, and yet as the other sits silent, very quiet, sadly looking at the moon, does not like to speak, moves his foot, clears his throat, notices some iron scroll on a table leg, stirs a leaf, but says nothing—so Peter Walsh did now" (*MD* 42). Like the epic simile in length and the independent development of the vehicle, it is not, however, a digression that "temporarily obscur[es] the main thread of the narrative."[38] The substance of this detailed simile is in fact precisely the narration of the actual events. What actually *happens* here? Growing bored as they sit together, Peter fidgets a little uncomfortably but does not move because he fears disturbing Clarissa, who is still absorbed in reverie. These are the diegetic events recounted, but they are not presented as actually happening. Instead, they are presented as the *type* of thing ("just as") that happens in such situations, which, as it happens ("so"), is happening precisely at this moment. Both sitting on this figural terrace with the moon rising, Peter and Clarissa share a kind of collective vision, suggesting the strength of the understanding between them that still persists despite the years. Just as, thematically, their streams of thought seem to have merged, "they went in and out of each other's minds without any effort" (*MD* 63), so the descriptive and the narrative have become formally knitted together in a single fabric. The analogy of sitting on a terrace looking at a moon, first introduced as a metaphorical description of Peter Walsh's grief, is progressively woven into the diegetic plane of events until the two become indistinguishable. We have seen how descriptive similes can pull us away from the thread of narrative, but it can also become a way to interweave more closely description and narration, making the traditional binary impossible to maintain.

Matching, Attuning

The images discussed so far do not "picture" anything but instead operate by appeal to some congruence or correspondence of felt qualities, some likeness, between one experience and another. In order to clarify and make more precise how similes can function to describe feeling, I want now to turn to the work of the psychoanalyst and developmental psychologist Daniel Stern on "affect attunement," or the ways in which affective states can be shared.[39] His elucidation of the mechanisms of attunement gives us a robust theory of affective description and shows how Woolf's descriptive practices move toward a nonmimetic mode of correspondence.

The importance of Stern's work for our purposes begins with his insight that in order to let others know that we are feeling something very like what they are feeling, that we are "in tune" with them, imitation is insufficient. A mother imitating the cry or gesture of her infant would only let the infant know that she understood what he *did*, not necessarily that she knew what he *felt*. For that, some other kind of correspondence is required.[40] In one of Stern's examples, a nine-month-old girl becomes excited about a toy and reaches for it, letting out an exuberant cry of "aaaah!" in the process. In response, her mother scrunches up her shoulders and "performs a terrific shimmy of her upper body" that lasts the same amount of time as her daughter's "aaaah!" and is "equally excited, joyful, and intense."[41] In another instance, a boy bangs his hand on a soft toy, "first in some anger but gradually with pleasure, exuberance, and humor," setting up a steady rhythm. His mother falls into this rhythm and says "kaaaaa-*bam*, kaaaaa-*bam*," the "kaaaaa" riding with the preparatory upswing and the suspenseful holding of his arm aloft before it falls, while the "*bam*" coincides with the fall of the arm.[42] In each case, the parent does not repeat the child's cry or gesture but instead transposes it into some other behavior that expresses the same affect in a different way. In attunement, no faithful rendering of overt behaviors takes place, "but some form of matching is going on."[43] In practice the two exist on a spectrum rather than as an actual dichotomy, but there is a real difference: "imitation renders form, attunement renders feeling."[44]

A crucial feature of this matching is that it usually takes place across sensory modes. In the first example above, the intensity level and duration of the girl's vocalization are matched by the mother's shoulder shimmy, but there is a transposition from sound to movement. And in the second example, it is the rhythm and shape (rising and falling) that are matched. Such transpositions are made possible by the fact that certain qualities (those that philosophers call "primary qualities") are perceptible across a range of perceptual modalities. Properties such as intensity, timing, and shape can be understood and felt regardless of whether they appear in the form of sound, color, movement, or gesture. Thus, intensity can be matched across the vividness and saturation of a particular hue, the brightness of a light, and the force of a swing of the arm; alternately, the same shape can be perceived in a cry's change in pitch or in the kinetic shape of a jump. For Stern these three properties—intensity, timing, and shape—form the basic features that allow for affects to be matched, and they can be further broken down into six more specific categories: absolute intensity, intensity contour (i.e., change in intensity over time), temporal beat, rhythm, duration, and shape.[45]

Stern's analysis of affect attunement provides a way to think about matching that is neither mimetic nor representational but that relies instead on the correspondences afforded by amodal qualities perceptible across a range of forms. This model illuminates the ways in which Woolf's descriptive similes work to convey affects without naming or representing them. In the case of the diver image discussed above, the basis for comparison is the timing-intensity contour, that is, the affective quality of suspension before plunging matches the pause before entering a room. Very often, the point of correspondence in Woolfian descriptions hinges on shape. Take Elizabeth Dalloway descending an omnibus, freed temporarily from the confines of her patrician life in Westminster. Inspired by the bustle of the Strand to feel "quite determined, whatever her mother might say, to become either a farmer or a doctor" (*MD* 137), no sooner does she have the thought than she hesitates.

> It seemed so silly. It was the sort of thing that did sometimes happen, when one was alone—buildings without architects' names, crowds of people coming back from the city having more power than single clergymen in Kensington, than any of the books Miss Kilman had lent her, to stimulate what lay slumberous, clumsy, and shy on the mind's sandy floor to break surface, as a child suddenly stretches its arms; it was just that, perhaps, a sigh, a stretch of the arms, an impulse, a revelation, which has its effects for ever, and then down again it went to the sandy floor. (*MD* 137)[46]

The figure of the child underscores Elizabeth's youth and makes of her ambition to work a juvenile idea, cast aside as she is reminded of her duty to attend her mother's party and the life she will likely lead instead as an upper-middle-class young woman. But another important feature of the simile, one that figures not the meaning but the feeling, is its shape—a burst or sudden eruption before falling that could be graphed as a line with a spike—which allows the child's sudden outstretched arms to figure the impulsiveness of Elizabeth's thought.[47]

We can also see cross-modal matching via shape clearly in a striking simile that occurs just after Peter Walsh leaves Clarissa after their reunion, one that makes a further connection to memory as another mode of looking for likenesses. He hears the bell of St. Margaret's toll as he walks down Victoria Street and experiences "an extraordinarily clear, yet puzzling, recollection of her, as if this bell had come into the room years ago, where they sat at some moment of great intimacy, and had gone from one to the other and had left, like a bee with honey, laden with the moment" (*MD* 50). This description depends on shape and rhythm to achieve its work of matching not only in the content of the image (the bee going back and forth) but also in the rhythm of the sentence itself, with its divided clauses and intervals of its commas. The affective quality that the description targets is the feeling of déjà vu when a past moment seems to be overlaid on a present one. But unlike Proustian involuntary memory, which collapses past and present time, the distance traveled between the two moments is here delicately preserved in the flight of the bee. Indeed, the model of cross-modal matching at work in Woolf's affective similes evokes Proust's varied practices of finding likes, including pastiche, a different form of transposed correspondence.[48]

There are of course important differences in the problem of literary description and the cases of affect attunement through spontaneous behavior discussed by Stern. For one thing, focused as it is on the preverbal child, Stern's study is concerned with how interaffectivity can be expressed without words.[49] This would seem to be precisely the opposite of the problem facing the writer, for whom words are her medium. And yet the reason that the affects and emotions remain such a descriptive challenge, as Woolf makes clear, is that they so often render us dumb—as Lily Briscoe wonders, "how could one express in words these emotions of the body?" (*TL* 178). If construed as something like a correspondence theory of truth, the idea of "matching" sounds hopelessly nostalgic and naive, indicating an impossible prelapsarian dream of identity between word and world. But, as we see in her similes, what Woolf is after is not identity but likeness, not imitation but attunement.

This is something that she recognized most clearly in her writings on the cinema, as we began to see above, but which we can now appreciate more fully. When she writes of the black wiggling mark in *Doctor Caligari* that "the monstrous, quivering tadpole seemed to be fear itself, and not the statement 'I am afraid'" (*E* 4:594), she is expressing the desire to find a way to describe emotion without recourse to allegory or symbol. In the way that anger is not merely "red faces and clenched fists" but "perhaps a black line wriggling upon a white sheet" (*E* 4:595), the feeling of youth relishing an experience about to happen, whose anticipation is made pleasurable by the certainty of its arrival—that entire feeling complex is made available through the likeness of the diver preparing to break through the waves. Recalling the penchant of thought (which for Woolf is never separate from feeling) to shift its burden onto an image that runs alongside it, the dynamic, complex, precise similes that describe specific affective states are the likenesses of thinking and feeling that bear the burden of their expression, but *in* language. And they derive this capacity through the cross-modal transpositions that allow affects to be matched.

Like and Like and Like

The simile displays a certain shyness in its very construction, unlike the assurance and directness of metaphor, which does not hesitate to say confidently "is."[50] After all, we say something is *like* something else when we mean that it is only approximate to that thing and thus not quite like it either. In these imperfect likenesses, to borrow Roland Barthes's words from a different context, "even the copula would seem excessive, a kind of remorse for a forbidden . . . definition, forever kept at bay."[51] The provisionality of simile and other analogical strategies is key in allowing relational modernists to maintain descriptive fidelity to their object while also opening up the possibility for things to be otherwise. These writers were not looking for new names for objects but rather the space provided by the "like" or the "as," each likeness always partial and subject to continual modification.[52] As Stephanie Burt observes in a "speculative essay" on simile, it "does justice to a mind in motion, tightening screws, or bracing itself for the worst, or calmly adjusting its focus in order to get closer and closer (though it can never get close enough) to the real: 'like bits of mirror—no, more blue than that: / like tatters of the Morpho butterfly' (Elizabeth Bishop)."[53]

Comparison is not metamorphosis, as we saw last chapter, and like Proust, there is also an implicit argument about the problem of identity in Woolf's descriptions that opens onto larger relations between the self and others. Since analogical descriptive strategies insist that something cannot be known except by way of knowing what it is like, the argument is not only that any likeness is provisional but also that identity cannot be understood in terms of enclosure and integrity but instead requires the thinking of relations. Perhaps another way of making this point would be to say that "likeness" has something queer about it. Last chapter we saw this idea introduced via Jonathan Flatley's reading of Andy Warhol's commitment to generating similarities in which Flatley argues that an orientation toward liking and likeness offers a roomier alternative than the "same/different" binary that structures ideas of identity as well as the constitution of collectivities.[54] Finding things to be like other things is precisely to say they are not the same and so to keep them apart, but it is also to trace the outline of one only by drawing it against the outline of the other. An other, however, that is alike. As Burt observes, *like* is the only word in English that is both a preposition and an active verb. "This is like that," but also "I like that."[55] Or, as Woolf imagines reading in *A Room of One's Own*, "Chloe liked Olivia."[56]

But this is not to say likeness is always a harmonious matter. Aristotle famously deemed the ability to perceive similarity in dissimilarity a sign of genius, but sometimes the perception of identity can be too much to bear. In *Mrs. Dalloway*, metaphor becomes associated with madness in the figure of Septimus Smith, the shell-shocked solider whose inability to remain anchored to reality expresses itself in visions where the bridge of likening collapses into identity. As Septimus and his wife Lucrezia sit in Regent's Park soon after they are introduced in the novel, he struggles to remain present in the world. The sight of a terrier causes "an agony of fear. It was turning into a man!" (*MD* 68), leading to a continual series of hallucinations. "His body was macerated until only the nerve fibres were left. It was spread like a veil upon a rock," "Red flowers grew through his flesh; their stiff leaves rustled by his head" (*MD* 68). Septimus is the character who suffers for the world's sins, and his visions, which allow for the expansion of Woolf's lyricism, are also subtended by a danger. Clarissa is equally sensitive to feeling experience in terms of physical sensations ("always her body went through it first," she thinks when she hears of the young man's death late in the novel [*MD* 184]). But witness the difference when the feeling is rendered as assertion in the form of metaphor, "his body *was* macerated until only the nerve fibres were left" as opposed to in the form of simile, "it was *as if* his body was macerated until only the nerve fibres were left." It is effectively the difference between a thought that belongs to Septimus and one that belongs to Clarissa. The line between madness and sanity is thin—that is of course the point of the two characters serving as doubles—and it is expressed formally in the text with the difference between being and being like.

I do not mean to suggest that no similes appear in descriptions of Septimus's experience, but metaphors dominate in rendering his perception of the world in a way that is distinct from other characters, and they are more liable to turn into cases of mistaken identity. These are very often violent, but in the same scene in Regent's Park, the only extended simile (of the kind that characterizes so much of the book) appears quite differently.

> I leant over the edge of the boat and fell down, he thought. I went under the sea. I have been dead, and yet am now alive, but let me rest still; he begged (he was talking to himself again—it was awful, awful!); and as, before waking, the voices of birds and the sound of wheels chime and chatter in a queer harmony, grow louder and louder and the sleeper feels himself drawing to the shores of life, so he felt himself drawing towards life, the sun growing hotter, cries sounding louder, something tremendous about to happen. (*MD* 69)

Having felt himself go under the sea in the confusion of what is real and what is not, Septimus experiences a return to consciousness that echoes the Proustian narrator's various scenes of awakening from slumbers. Here, as the sounds of birds and passing wheels draw the sleeper back to life, the simile is the thread that allows for Septimus to regain a tenuous hold on reality.

Other characters express impatience with simile's approximations. "'Like' and 'like' and 'like'—but what is the thing that lies beneath the semblance of the thing?" Rhoda asks in *The Waves* soon after learning of Percival's death (*W* 163). This comes after a series of quasi-grotesque comparatives about a crowded scene in Oxford Street: "I should stand in a queue and smell sweat, and scent as horrible as sweat; and be hung with other people like a joint of meat among other joints of meat" (*W* 161-62); "therefore we cluster like maggots on the back of something that will carry us on" (*W* 162); "we settle down, like walruses stranded on rocks, like heavy bodies incapable of waddling to the sea" (*W* 162). The term *semblance* suggests there is some authentic truth beneath facades that are false, but Rhoda, like Septimus, is a visionary character who suffers a similar end, suggesting the danger of discarding semblances in pursuit of some authentic truth. Even when, in the same passage, she feels Percival's death to have bestowed the gift of "let[ting] me see the thing. There is a square; there is an oblong." The thing beneath the semblances is just shapes, perceptible in a myriad of ways. (Between these two sentences she effectively moves from the vision of Septimus Smith to that of Lily Briscoe.) But even as Rhoda hungers for the thing itself, it is the approximate series of likes that enables an escape from the rigidity of a single, fixing definition.

In and Out of Tune

The most extreme instance of the capacity to perceive similarities across perceptual modes is synesthesia, encapsulated in poetic form by Baudelaire's "Correspondances," elevated to a poetic principle by later symbolists, and reaching epidemic proportions in fin-de-siècle Europe. Synesthetic experiments abounded in the early twentieth century, including symphonic light shows and color organs (devices intended to represent sound visually), while the advent of sound film also made available new possibilities for integrating sound and vision that fascinated early filmmakers such as Sergei Eisenstein.[57] But this condition only makes more extreme something that most of us understand intuitively and that is registered in many expressions of ordinary speech. Stern gives the example of an imagined therapeutic scenario. "When a patient says, 'I was so anxious and uptight about how she would greet me, but as soon as she spoke it was like the sun came out—I melted,' we understand directly."[58] Or as we read in a similar moment in *To the Lighthouse*, "as sometimes happens when a cloud falls on a green hillside and gravity descends and there among all the surrounding hills is gloom and sorrow... so Cam now felt herself overcast (*TL* 168)." The ability to understand such descriptions of feeling may be of particular importance to the analyst or the poet, but the assumption of cross-modal legibility underlies our capacities for ordinary affective interchange. In identifying "metaphor and analogue" as central vehicles of transfer enabling the sharing of feeling, Stern makes clear that there is something literary about one of our most basic forms of intersubjective experience.[59]

The fact that artful forms of language exploit the legibility of cross-modal affect expression that we take for granted in everyday life suggests something most readers already know, that these discursive forms, no less than our ordinary affect behaviors, are capable of producing experiences of affect attunement.[60] Woolf herself was keenly aware of our capacity to be attuned to and by texts. This is abundantly evident from her accounts of reading, which frequently center on its effects on bodily sensation and attention. So she writes, "The impact of poetry is so hard and direct that for the moment there is no other sensation except that of the poem itself" (*E* 5:578), while certain passages of *Tristram Shandy* bring "by the curious rhythm of their phrasing, by a touch on the visual sense, an alteration in the movement of the mind which makes it pause and widen its gaze and slightly change its attention" (*E* 5:76). Of course, all elements of a text may work toward generating affective responses (suspense, for instance, is famously the province of plotting), but I would suggest that descriptions of feeling play a particular privileged role in enabling experiences of attunement.

From the vantage point of production (i.e., writing), the task of describing is to find a likeness that matches a feeling, but from the vantage point of reception (i.e., reading), descriptions are likenesses in search of feelings that match. Woolf used the term herself in "Mr. Bennett and Mrs. Brown." The "appalling effort of saying what I meant" demands she "experiment with one thing and another; to try this sentence and that, referring each word to my vision, matching it as exactly as possible, and knowing that somehow I had to find a common ground between us, a convention which would not seem to you too odd, unreal, and far-fetched to believe in" (*E* 3:432). Writing is imagined here as a process of calibration. It needs to hew as closely as possible to the writer's vision while retaining enough "common ground" to be understood by the reader.[61] Importantly, the notion of matching does not institute a relation of priority and originality between two terms. A match is only accomplished, in fact, by the second term, or more precisely by the relationship between the terms, thereby avoiding the hierarchy of an original and a copy. This means that it can be capable of creating a community of feeling with no test for correctness, as we will see even more clearly in the next chapter when we get to "small marks" that are the ultimate match. There is no universally applicable formula, but when we as readers encounter descriptions that strike or move us, the experience is one of simultaneous recognition and surprise: meeting with something familiar but which we didn't even know we knew or had never known in quite that way. Such experiences can produce a sense of "feeling-with" another, which accounts for the sense of accompaniment that readers often feel even during the ostensibly solitary experience of reading.[62] It would make sense, finally, that the pleasure, or more minimally the sustainment of ongoing being gained through experiences of affect attunement, plays a role in the attachments that readers form toward books, which can be so oddly similar to the attachments we feel toward people.[63]

What I characterized as accompaniment in the phenomenology of reading is more frequently understood in terms of empathy and identification, psychic dynamics that often underlie our judgments about characters and stories. But Stern argues that although affect attunement and empathy are related and share the initial spark of emotional resonance, "attunement takes the experience of emotional resonance and automatically recasts that experience into another form of expression. Attunement thus need not proceed towards empathic knowledge or response."[64] Hence I use the term *accompaniment*, which has the connotation of togetherness but without the collapse of distance implied by identification. What is at stake in such acts is minimally just a sharing of affective states, or as Stern puts it, communion rather than communication.[65] These feelings need not even be personalized; that is, they need not be tied to a notion of the subject, separate as they are from questions of intentions and motivations. The experience of being-with is distinct from identification or projection and is thus distinct from sympathy. In order for a description of a feeling state to produce a sense of attunement, we need not identify with a particular character conceived of as a discrete individual or a consolidated entity (precisely the problem that gives Woolf's characters so much trouble) but as something more diffuse and discontinuous, a mere "structure of sensations."[66]

To be sure, the conditions of shared feeling are not always idyllic. A harmonious sense of feeling with others is, in social experience, usually dependent on there being some who are out of tune with the group. Taking up Stern's brief discussion of "misattunement" as a way of modifying affective states and behaviors, Sara Ahmed cautions against moments when "affective description can become prescription," which she links especially to prescribed national feelings.[67] Such a moment occurs early on in *Mrs. Dalloway*, when the car passing down Bond Street unites a range of Londoners in a moment of communal experience.

> For thirty seconds all heads were inclined the same way—to the window... in all the hat shops and tailors' shops strangers looked at each other and thought of the dead; of the flag; of Empire. In a public house in a back street a Colonial insulted the House of Windsor which led to words, broken beer glasses, and a general shindy, which echoed strangely across the way in the ears of girls buying white underlinen threaded with pure white ribbon for their weddings. For the surface agitation of the passing car as it sunk grazed something very profound. (*MD* 17-18)

The disruption of fellow feeling here is caused by one whose thoughts of "the dead; of the flag; of Empire" do not accord with the "vibration," that Jamesian word, indiscernible to mathematical instruments capable of transmitting shocks in China yet "in its fulness rather formidable and in its common appeal emotional" (*MD* 18). This vibration ripples out behind the car's wake, "tuning" the citizens in the street around it. Similarly, the misattunement of the colonial subject in the heart of Empire is transposed into sound, a verbal fracas, shattered glass, and a general "shindy," which in turn "echoed strangely" in the ears of virginal girls preparing for their entry into the institutions that uphold this national structure. Woolf's language here is itself notably not discordant—the moment of misattuned feeling is not set off from the rest of the passage but harmonizes and blends in with it, and the soft unvoiced fricative in "shindy" is hardly cacophonous. This could be read as a denial or erasure of those who are out of tune with the socially prescribed feeling, but I would argue that the immediate and intimate connection drawn between the discordant sound and the girls (it echoes *in* their ears), whose trousseau buying also serves to link nationalism with patriarchy, instead highlights the bad or wrong feelings whose punishment or exclusion is constitutive of normative forms of social affective communion.

Being and Time

My claim is not that this is the first time that descriptions oriented toward affect attunement appear in the history of the novel. Indeed, affect attunement is an essential part of the work of literature as it is of dance, music, or cinema, although their methods and the affects attuned to vary across time. But the new attention to registering sensory impressions and the emphasis on the *felt* nature of perception results in their gaining a new dominance in modernist works. In this respect, my argument chimes with two influential recent accounts of the modern novel discussed earlier, Jacques Rancière's and Fredric Jameson's, which contain striking and little-noticed resonances between them.[68] In particular, I want to highlight the temporality that is directly or indirectly ascribed to description and propose an alternative understanding of it via Woolf.

In *Antinomies of Realism*, which in many ways rewrites and extends Lukács's "Narrate or Describe?," Jameson proposes that realism entails an irresolvable struggle between two forces. On the one hand, the storytelling impulse of the *récit*, which has the temporality of past-present-future, and on the other hand, everything that impedes this forward-moving progress in favor of an extended, dilatory, "eternal," or "perpetual" present, but a present that does not belong to the order of before-and-after characteristic of the *récit*. This latter impulse, which is identified with the descriptive and the scenic, he names the "affective."[69] Historically, he locates the rise of the affective pole in the European novel from the mid-nineteenth century on, when there emerges a new attention to the lived experience of the body that cannot be contained by the old feudal classifications of named emotions. As generalized sensations of the body move into visibility in the field of literature, these call for different modes of representation.[70] One of these modes, I have suggested, is the pervasive use of simile, sometimes extended or epic, which introduces motion and dynamism into descriptions and also expresses states of feeling that are not subsumable under named emotions or comprehensible in terms of individual psychological depth.

Jameson's account converges with Rancière's around the issue of temporality, which allows us to see a final significance of Woolfian descriptions. For Jameson, the affective/descriptive pole belongs to the order of an expansive "eternal present," one that leads eventually to the congealed, ahistorical temporality of postmodernism.[71] For his part, Rancière identifies a "devastating force of inertia" in the nineteenth-century novel that thwarts its "big plot" to make "the plans of individual characters coincide with the revelation of the laws of society."[72] Rancière's chief exemplars of the inertial force that afflicts the willed actions of heroes are moments when characters are held in thrall by microsensory events, as in Balzac's *History of the Thirteen*, which ends with the chief of the intriguers, Ferragus, inertly observing a game of bowls. In his preface to that novel, Balzac ascribed the failure of the thirteen adventurers "to action itself, to the mere opposition of doing to being." This amounts, Rancière argues, to a "nihilist denunciation of the vanity of will and action" that arises at the same moment "as the great narrative of the transformation of society by science and by rational willful action." The result is the expansion of the lyrical in the field of prose and prosaic life such that the new conquering genre of the novel appears "to host the force that is bound to devour it from the inside," the prose poem.[73]

Although Rancière does not put it this way, the force of inertia that thwarts the pursuit of ends belongs to the mode of description, which creates a kind of durational lassitude that is distinct from the transit from one event to the next that makes up the temporality of causes and effects. This idea shares something with Lukács's assessment of description as stasis and with Jameson's notion of the eternal present.[74]

Being is aligned with the force of inertia afflicting the inaugurating heroes of modern fiction, and it is in opposition to *doing*, which is on the side of history, action, will, and event. Moments of being can quickly become a refusal of historicity, but Woolf expresses some skepticism about what action, and by extension history, includes and what it does not. These positions are expressed most directly in her critique of the patriarchal nature of fascism in *Three Guineas* (1938) and other political writings of the 1930s, but they are already evident in earlier novels. We see it in *Mrs. Dalloway*'s Dr. Bradshaw, worshipper of "proportion" and perhaps the closest thing we get to an unambiguous villain in Woolf. And it is already there as early as *Jacob's Room* (1922), where the nonchalant deaths of young men at war ("Like blocks of tin soldiers the army covers the cornfield, moves up the hillside ... and falls flat, save that ... one or two pieces still agitate up and down like fragments of broken match-stick") is directly linked to the gears of society grinding at home (*JR* 164). "These actions, together with the incessant commerce of banks, laboratories, chancelleries, and houses of business, are the strokes which oar the world forward, they say" (*JR* 164). This passage goes on to conjure an image of an "impassive policeman at Ludgate Circus" whose face "is stiff from force of will, and lean from the effort of keeping it so," and, when he raises his arm, "not an ounce [of force] is diverted into sudden impulses, sentimental regrets, wire-drawn distinctions. The buses punctually stop" (*JR* 164). We have here effectively a Weberian critique of rationality, efficiency, and progress, one that also draws futurist and vorticist ideals of force and will within its compass.

Belonging to the temporality of being, description constitutes thus a countermovement to the force of rationalization, speed, and progress that are keywords of modernity. "In a world which contains the present moment," Neville says in *The Waves*, "why discriminate? Nothing should be named lest by so doing we change it. Let it exist, this bank, this beauty, and I, for one instant, steeped in pleasure" (*W* 81). He follows this notably with plain observations of what is happening around him in short declarative sentences. "The sun is hot. I see the river. I see trees specked and burnt in the autumn sunlight. Boats float past, through the red, through the green" (*W* 81). Woolf returned to the idea of dwelling in the presence of what is in a diary entry from 1932 while working on *The Years*: "If one does not lie back & sum up & say to the moment, this very moment, stay you are so fair, what will be one's gain, dying? No: stay, this moment. No one ever says that enough" (*D* 4:135). As easily as this sentiment can be read as an aestheticist or quietist retreat from the world, in light of the devastation wrought by a catastrophic world war and the instability of financial collapse as well as the impending forces of fascism already gathering in Britain and in Europe, dwelling in the presence of things was not to be taken for granted.

Woolf's skepticism toward a model of unbridled forward action whose formal correlate is propulsive narrative is reinforced by her involvement in feminist movements supporting antifascism, internationalism, and pacifism. Jessica Berman has documented the different responses of Woolf and Oswald Mosley's New Party (which was initially supported by a number of left-leaning intellectuals) to the political and economic crisis following the Great Depression.[75] In the first issue of the New Party's organ, *Action*, launched in 1931 and coedited by Harold Nicolson, Vita Sackville-West's husband, Mosley presents the nation as lethargic and in need of a movement to restore them to vitality and power, hence the name of the journal.[76] In contrast, while Woolf was similarly responsive to the political and historical crisis of this turbulent period, she critiqued the valorization of aggressive action in the service of "dynamic progress" and "iron decision, resolution and reality . . . which cuts like a sword through the knot of the past to the winning of the modern state."[77]

If for Lukács the descriptive mode meant a refusal of history, it was not clear to Woolf that history had a place for all actors. By identifying it with coercive patriarchal aggression and violence, she brings to light the masculinist assumptions underlying Lukács's critique of description and his coded identification of it with sexual difference. A related point has also been made more recently by postcolonial scholars who have connected "the central and largely unshakeable binary of narratology" to questions of historical agency and discursive violence. As Toral Gajarawala writes, "the native is subject to a regime of ekphrasis—'still life,' in effect—while the settler is associated with the 'epic' and the 'odyssey.'"[78] We can also recall here Rancière's argument (discussed in chapter 1) that the disproportions introduced by the growth of description and its proliferation of details, which Lukács deplored as nullifying any hierarchy of significance or organic whole, overturned classical narrative hierarchies (and the social hierarchies subtending them), resulting in a kind of radical egalitarianism.

The affective descriptions that I have focused on in this chapter, which often pull us away from the narrative and away even sometimes from character, would seem to be prime examples of the eternal present or a refusal of historicity. In earlier sections I have highlighted the work that such descriptions accomplish outside of the terms of narrativity, specifically in terms of affect attunement and the nonimitative model of matching that it presupposes, which opens onto the possibility of matches not established in advance. Now, we see that within the terms of the narrate/describe binary, the very temporality that consigns description to ahistoricity also challenges the masculinist ideas of history as doing and action that underlie this opposition. Reframed in this way, description moves from being a mode that refuses historicity to one that places into question what history—the unseizable force oaring us forward—itself refuses.

The Ends of Description [CHAPTER FIVE]

Are there limits to what can be described? And if so, with what consequences? Throughout this book I have been tracing some of the ways in which James, Proust, and Woolf bring subtle, elusive aspects of perceptual, social, and affective experience within the descriptive scope of the novel. Now the end (in all of its senses) of this enterprise takes center stage. Whereas the last chapter suggested that Woolf's affective descriptions are capable of producing the possibility of feeling-with or affective communion, this chapter is in many ways its negative counterpart, tracking what happens when a descriptive limit is encountered. As we will see, the problem of what cannot be described is part of a larger preoccupation with the incommunicability of experience in the early twentieth century, but the very novelistic forms that register this limit also offer new possibilities for the establishment of nondetermined relations.

The predicament of indescribability is made clear by the artist Lily Briscoe, who is introduced to us at the beginning of *To the Lighthouse* standing in front of her easel on the lawn of the Ramsays' house.

> She could see it all so clearly, so commandingly, when she looked: it was when she took her brush in hand that the whole thing changed. It was in that moment's flight between the picture and her canvas that the demons set on her who often brought her to the verge of tears and made this passage from conception to work as dreadful as any down a dark passage for a child. Such she often felt herself—struggling against terrific odds to maintain her courage; to say: 'But this is what I see; this is what I see,' and so to clasp some miserable remnant of her vision to her breast, which a thousand forces did their best to pluck from her. (*TL* 19)

Lily Briscoe's inability to materialize the vision she sees so clearly in the privacy of her mind onto the external canvas foregrounds the thematic problem of artistic expression, but it is also a version of an ordinary experience that may be familiar to many of us when we try to describe something that we ourselves know quite well. The scene in front of the canvas also presents the question of representing this failure in the novel itself—how describe the failure of description? It cannot be conveyed by the standard means of enumerating an object's qualities, since it registers precisely the limit of any such enterprise. Nor is it adequately expressed by simply attributing indescribability to the object, since what is at issue here is not the object's incomprehensibility but rather the feeling of being unable to communicate something one knows oneself quite well.

Notably, Lily Briscoe is not confronting a strange, foreign vista but a perfectly familiar landscape, not a sublime beyond cognitive comprehension but something with which she is intimately acquainted. It is a peculiar fact that what is most indescribable is often also what we know best, the feelings, sensations, and impressions that make up our individual experience in the course of "the life of Monday or Tuesday." Latter-day philosophers call these "qualia," which can range "from hard-edged pains to the elusive experience of thoughts on the tip of one's tongue; from mundane sounds and smells to the encompassing grandeur of musical experience; from the triviality of a nagging itch to the weight of a deep existential angst; from the specificity of the taste of peppermint to the generality of one's experience of selfhood."[1] Put most simply, it is just *"the way things seem to us."*[2] But even as these experiential textures make up what is most ordinary and intimate, they can also give us the greatest difficulties when we try to convey them to others.

This difficulty is in no small part a problem of language, as Proust makes clear in *The Captive*. There the narrator privileges music over literature because it is better able to express "that interior and extreme point of sensations" that, "when we say 'What beautiful weather!' 'What beautiful sun!' we fail to make known in the slightest to another, in whom the same sun and the same weather arouse quite different vibrations" (*SLT* 5:504, *RTP* 3:876). The same conditions create different sensations in each individual, but we cannot make the particularities of our own sensations known to another by words that can be commonly understood because such words designate only what is shared. It is for this reason that in 1911 T. E. Hulme calls for a new "classical" poetry that has as its aim "accurate, precise and definite description." Such an endeavor is extraordinarily difficult, Hulme notes, because "you have to use language, and language is by its very nature a communal thing; that is, it expresses never the exact thing but a compromise—that which is common to you, me and everybody. But each man sees a little differently, and to get out clearly and exactly what he does see, he must have a terrific struggle with language."[3]

An answer to the question of how to describe the inability to describe is suggested in Woolf's passage itself. Failing to paint with her brush what she sees so clearly with her eyes, Lily's frustration with her communicative failure articulates itself in a single word: the demonstrative *this*. Her thought "but this is what I see; this is what I see" is akin to a sweep of the arm across the landscape in front of her, *pointing* to something that she has no other way of conveying. It is at once a cry of defiance (she clutches her vision to her breast, refusing to give it up) and an imploring plea (How can I make you understand? *This* is what I see). Here, the demonstrative does not only refer to the content of Lily's vision, *what* it is she sees, it also indicates the vision's indescribability, *that* she cannot express it. A semantically slight *this* is all that can be said when there is no way of describing the *what*. Woolf finds the linguistic resources to represent the limits of description in words that, in fact, do not describe at all. Such words—above all demonstratives, supplemented by personal pronouns and proper names—are thus uniquely able to register the limits of linguistic expression.[4] Moreover, Woolf is not alone among her contemporaries in noting the peculiarities of demonstratives and their connection to the "intimate epistemic relation" we have to our own experience.[5] In the introduction we saw the physicist Hermann Helmholtz observe the differences between how we know our own experience and how we know the experiences of others. This chapter will focus on two of the most prominent Anglophone philosophers of the late nineteenth and early twentieth centuries, William James and Bertrand Russell, who, in spite of their differences, both attribute a special role to the demonstrative in their meditations on different modes of knowing and relating to our experience and to the external world.

The challenge posed by describing subjective phenomena opens onto widespread modernist concerns about the shareability and communicability of experience during a period of social fracture and epistemological uncertainty.[6] Both the desire for and the difficulty of describing experience in language belong to a larger preoccupation with the gap between knowledge about the self and knowledge about others. Woolf was keenly aware of what William James called the most fundamental breach in nature, the one between two minds (*PP* 1:226). Indeed, it is a central preoccupation throughout her novels, expressed most concisely in what E. M. Forster would call the summation of her message insofar as her novels contain one: Clarissa Dalloway's conclusion, as she observes through her window the old lady in the house opposite, that "the supreme mystery ... was simply this: here was one room; there another" (*MD* 127).[7] Whatever its limits may be, descriptions of what we see and what we feel thus respond to a need. "Did religion solve that, or love?" (*MD* 127) is the question that follows the supreme mystery of separate rooms, and the implied answer, of course, is no.[8] In the early twentieth century, Woolf, like Proust and a number of other contemporaries, turned to art as a way of ensuring intersubjectivity even as she also thematized the unknowability of other people in her works. Thus, while demonstratives mark the junctures where the art of describing can go no further, they also call it forth ever more urgently. Description is crucial to establishing a common reality, and for both James and Russell, it also accomplished the crucial work of extending knowledge beyond the limited constraints of first-person experience into a shared and public realm, thus epistemologically securing the social. For none of these thinkers does encountering the limits of description lead to solipsism or a retreat away from the external world into private knowledge of the self. Rather, a desire for shared feeling and knowing is registered by the very words that mark the limits of any such possibility. In fact, such words, which seem at first so referentially exclusive, turn out to be capable of creating new forms of linguistic community whose social analogue is a form of nondetermined relationality.

Before going on, a word is due about the selection of this trio of thinkers. In bringing together these three figures, I want to trace some parallel histories of a shared preoccupation while highlighting a less recognized matrix of modernism.[9] Russell maintained ties to a number of key modernist figures: he was prominent among the Cambridge Apostles—the intellectual society that included many of the male members of Bloomsbury, including Roger Fry, Leonard Woolf, and Lytton Strachey—and he was a close friend of T. S. Eliot during the latter's early years in England.[10] Ann Banfield has thoroughly and persuasively established Russell's importance for Woolf's intellectual formation and aesthetics in *The Phantom Table*, but in general early analytic philosophy still remains a neglected corpus among literary critics.[11] And yet in the modernist period, Russell was a widely known public intellectual grappling with questions about how we know the world and how language attaches to reality that were not far from the preoccupations of writers and artists even if they elaborated their concerns very differently. William James is no doubt more familiar to literary critics, but because of the disciplinary tendency to divide fields along national lines, he tends to figure primarily in discussions of American rather than British or European modernism. And while James and Russell diverge greatly and undeniably in temperament and method, these differences have tended to obscure the aspects of their thought that are shared. By situating literary modernism within wider networks of discourses, we gain a more complete sense of its place within an intellectual historical trajectory. At the same time, my aim is to work across disciplines without relying either on a model of influence or a "lens." Instead, I hope to uncover how literature and philosophy can be concerned with similar problems and how they develop these problems in their own distinct ways.

Simply This

With Lily Briscoe, we have already met the paradigmatic nondescriptive word. Before turning to an account of its peculiar nature, let us look at a few more examples of the demonstrative's appearance in Woolf. *Mrs. Dalloway* furnishes particularly numerous cases. Leaving Clarissa's house after their first meeting of many years, we find Peter Walsh deep in reflection as he walks across London: "The compensation of growing old, Peter Walsh thought, coming out of Regent's Park, and holding his hat in hand, was simply this; that the passions remain as strong as ever, but one has gained—at last!—the power which adds the supreme flavour to existence,—the power of taking hold of experience, of turning it round, slowly, in the light" (*MD* 79). Before being elaborated, the compensation of age is notably introduced first as "this." Such a syntactic construction, with the intervention of the little demonstrative before its explication, signals the intimacy with which we are ensconced in Peter Walsh's consciousness. The passage is in free indirect discourse, representing the thought in Peter's mind directly as he is thinking it rather than as reported externally by a narrator. In his own thoughts, *this* indicates Peter Walsh's mental pointing at an object known to him, which must be further described, however, in order to be made clear to the reader. Moreover, it signals the fact that he is *aware* of his thinking. If the demonstrative were omitted: "the compensation of growing old, Peter Walsh thought . . . was simply that the passions remain as strong as ever," we would still understand the sentence as representing a thought in his mind, but the presence of *this* reinforces the sense that he is thinking the thought *self-consciously*; that is, he is both reflecting to himself and aware that he is reflecting. In this way, the content of the sentence is mirrored in its very syntax. Peter Walsh feels that age graces one with the ability to experience intensely while being able to reflect self-consciously on that experience at the same time, and this sentiment is conveyed in a sentence that indicates by its form that he is self-consciously reflecting on this very sentiment.

A similar structure is exhibited in the representation of Richard Dalloway's thoughts a little later in the novel during his walk home after lunch at Lady Bruton's. At lunch, Richard finds himself thinking of Clarissa, feeling it a miracle that they should have had their life together, and immediately resolves to tell her of his love "in so many words, when he came into the room" (*MD* 116). Filled with a sense of pride and well-being, he strides through London. "His own life was a miracle; let him make no mistake about it; here he was, in the prime of life, walking to his house in Westminster to tell Clarissa that he loved her. Happiness is this, he thought. It is this, he said, as he entered Dean's Yard" (*MD* 117). Like Peter Walsh, Richard is both happy and aware that he is happy, and in reflecting on his happiness he too characterizes the feeling as simply "this."

The upsurge of emotion is checked upon his arrival at home when he finds himself suddenly unable to tell Clarissa he loves her as he had intended. Instead, husband and wife recount to each other the events of the day, but the phrase continues to repeat in Richard's thoughts, forming a kind of refrain throughout the scene. "(But he could not tell her he loved her. He held her hand. Happiness is this, he thought)," and again a few lines later, "He had not said 'I love you'; but he held her hand. Happiness is this, is this, he thought" (*MD* 119). There are myriad reasons why Richard Dalloway cannot tell Clarissa he loves her—sociohistorical customs of time and place, the expectations of his class and upbringing, and his diffidence and reserve, to name a few. Regardless of the cause of his communicative failure, it is notably accompanied each time by the thought, "happiness is this." Unlike Lily Briscoe, Richard finds nonverbal ways to communicate his feeling, trusting Clarissa to understand the flowers he brings and his gesture of holding her hand. Nevertheless, his quietly contented "happiness is this" bears a certain echo of Lily's more plaintive cry.

This belongs to a class of words that has received attention from a variety of thinkers interested in language, including philosophers and linguists. Sometimes called *indexicals* or *deictics*, this class includes, among others, demonstratives (this, that), the first- and second-person pronouns, a set of adverbs of time (now, today, tomorrow), and a set of locatives (here, there). As the etymologies of *demonstrative, deictic,* and *indexical* suggest, these words can be understood as a kind of linguistic pointing. In contrast to ordinary nouns such as *tree* or *dog*, whose meanings do not shift, indexicals such as *here* and *now* derive their referent each time from the context of their use, hence Roman Jakobson's term for them, "shifters."[12] As Émile Benveniste writes, "*This* will be the object designated by ostension simultaneously with the present instance of discourse, the reference implicit in the form (e.g., *hic* as opposed to *iste*) associating it with *I* or *you*."[13]

The frequency with which indexicals appear in Woolf's novels is difficult to ignore, and it is explicable in no small part by the fact that they are a central feature of free indirect discourse, the grammatical form in which the vast majority of her novelistic sentences are written.[14] Literary criticism is by now familiar with the remarks of Benveniste and Jakobson on the peculiar features of this class of words, but it is far less so with

Russell's comments on the subject. Yet Russell's analyses—many of which are, moreover, already implicit in William James—elucidate an important function of the demonstrative in Woolf's novels: to signal the limits of what can be described in words. Moreover, even as they note its limits, for both Russell and James description is a crucial way to proceed to common knowledge, and via a triangulation with Woolf, we will also see Russell intersect in surprising ways with Lukács.

Making Acquaintance

Russell's remarks on the demonstrative arise in the context of a distinction between two modes of knowing: inferential, indirect "knowledge by description," and immediate, direct "knowledge by acquaintance." He first introduces these terms in his seminal 1911 paper "Knowledge by Acquaintance and Knowledge by Description," read to the Aristotelian Society, a philosophical club founded in Bloomsbury in 1880. But the term *acquaintance* had in fact also appeared a few decades earlier in another paper delivered to the Aristotelian Society in 1884 by William James, and it is to this earlier discussion that I want to turn first. James suggested that there is a particular way in which we know a "feeling of q" when we experience it ourselves, which is different from the way we know everything outside our own experience. "Let the q be fragrance, let it be toothache, or let it be a more complex kind of feeling, like that of the full-moon swimming in her blue abyss, it must first come in that simple shape ... before any knowledge *about* it can be attained."[15] As James would write later in *The Principles of Psychology*, we are first of all acquainted with immediately present "feelings," that is, "the *emotions*, and the *sensations* we get from skin, muscle, viscus, eye, ear, nose, and palate" (*PP* 1:222). Beyond the sensory data of the present moment, we are also acquainted with memories of "our own past states of mind," which "appear to us endowed with a sort of warmth and intimacy" (*PP* 1:223). We are limited in such direct apprehension, however, by the bounds of our own experience. "Our senses only give us acquaintance with the facts of body.... Of the mental states of other persons we only have conceptual knowledge" (*PP* 1:222–23).

Such immediate, intuitive knowledge is utterly certain, James asserts, but precisely by that token it remains incapable of verbalization.

> I know the color blue when I see it, and the flavor of a pear when I taste it; I know an inch when I move my finger through it; a second of time, when I feel it pass; an effort of attention when I make it; a difference between two things when I notice it; but *about* the inner nature of these facts or what makes them what they are, I can say nothing at all. I cannot impart acquain-

tance with them to any one who has not already made it himself. I cannot *describe* them, make a blind man guess what blue is like. . . . At most, I can say to my friends, Go to certain places and act in certain ways, and these objects will probably come. (*PP* 1:221)

Since the way in which I know my experience of the color blue or the flavor of the pear cannot, by definition, be described, James calls it a "dumb" way of knowing (*PP* 1:221). To have acquaintance with something is thus only "a very minimum of knowledge," and although our own sensory experience remains the ground of all knowledge for the empiricist James, cognition proceeds outwards from acquaintance to knowledge-about like the "germ" to the "developed tree."[16]

When Russell introduces the notion of acquaintance again a few decades later, his account shares many features with James's. Russell also calls it "a direct cognitive relation," writing simply, "we shall say we have *acquaintance* of anything with which we are directly aware" (*PPH* 46). And like James, Russell identifies as first among our acquaintance our own "sense-data," the immediately present information given to us by our senses. This includes everything "of which I am immediately conscious when I am seeing and touching my table," its "colour, shape, hardness, smoothness etc.," all that makes up the appearance of the table to me (*PPH* 46). If acquaintance were restricted solely to immediate sensory information, however, "the experience of each moment" would be "a prison for the knowledge of that moment," and its boundaries would be "the boundaries of our present world."[17] Accordingly, the first extension beyond sense-data that both Russell and James identify is acquaintance by memory, through which we are still immediately aware of what we have seen or heard "in spite of the fact that it appears as past and not as present" (*PPH* 48-49). The next extension is acquaintance by introspection, through which we are not only aware of things but aware of our awareness. "When I desire food, I may be aware of my desire for food; thus 'my desiring food' is an object with which I am acquainted" (*PPH* 49).[18] Importantly, acquaintance is an absolutely certain form of knowing, but for Russell it yields no knowledge of *truths*, or in James's terms, it tell us nothing *about* the table, not even that it is "a table." It is rather the name both thinkers use for our distinctive relation to our qualia, the patch of brown in my vision, the hard texture at my fingertips, the sound the table makes when I knock it, and so on, the felt qualities of our everyday experience that we know, in terms used by both, with a particular "warmth and intimacy."

In contrast to this simple, direct way of knowing, my knowledge of the table as a physical object is "knowledge by description." More rigidly or minimally defined than our usual use of the term, a Russellian description is "any phrase of the form 'a so-and-so' or 'the so-and-so,'" for instance, "a man" or "the man with the iron mask" (*PPH* 52).[19] When something is described, it is no longer directly apprehended but instead is characterized through inferences and generalizations. "The table is 'the physical object which causes such-and-such sense-data.' This *describes* the table by means of the sense-data" (*PPH* 47). As is clear, talking about what we know by acquaintance without in some way describing it—and thus generalizing, inferring, losing something of its particularity—is extremely difficult, not to say impossible, hence James's conclusion that such knowledge is unverbalizable.

For both thinkers, our immediate awareness of our own sensations, memories, and thoughts is the departure point for knowledge of the external world, but it is only a departure point. Only through descriptive inferences and generalizations can we then move from a statement like "I see this" (referring to a pattern of colors occurring in my vision) to "I see a chair," which can be publicly understood and thus capable of being true or false. "In view of the very narrow range of our immediate experience," Russell writes, the "chief importance" and "vital result" of description "is that it enables us to pass beyond the limits of private experience" (*PPH* 59). Indeed, description is the crucial means by which we come to know everything outside our own minds and bodies, including, notably, "other people's minds." What is at stake in description then is a move from the private bounds of the self into the wider public world. This is also in many ways what novels seem to promise: the experience of the other, but rendered intimately as if experienced by the self; put otherwise, descriptions that aspire to the condition of acquaintance.

But however elemental and quickly surpassed, for both thinkers acquaintance names the inexorable, irreducible way in which we know our own experience. It names that which remains continually fugitive to language when I try to describe what I see or feel, however finely I qualify the description—everything that escapes, as the Proustian narrator lamented, in a paltry phrase like "what a beautiful day!" This form of epistemic intimacy interests the philosophers insofar as it belongs to a theory of knowledge, but it is also of concern to the writer attempting to represent "an ordinary mind on an ordinary day" (*E* 4:160).[20] Extending James's atmospheres and Proust's analogical relations, Woolf takes description to its limit, bearing witness both to the descriptive impulse and to the constant encounter with the indescribable.

To be sure, the possibility of direct, prelinguistic knowledge has been subject to much critique. Against the idea that knowledge preexists expression, Russell's onetime student Ludwig Wittgenstein wrote, "The words are not a translation of something else that was there before they were."[21]

This argument is later echoed in Wilfred Sellars's critique of the "myth of the given," and it is also mounted from a different angle in antifoundationalist works of poststructuralism and deconstruction.[22] Skepticism about immediate knowledge—indeed, any notion of unmediated experience—has become itself a given in literary studies today, but the fact remains that the question of acquaintance was a significant philosophical problem in the early twentieth century. My concern here is not with vindicating it as an epistemological theory but with highlighting the problem it raises of describing first-person experience in language, which can certainly feel real even if debunked in theory, and which has important consequences for the modernist novel.[23] Russell identifies a set of words that register this difficulty, terms whose peculiar features Woolf exploits to foreground the limits of description. If the philosophers make acquaintance the beginning of knowledge, the novelist shows it is also the end of description.

The Sharp Point

The distinction between direct and indirect knowledge has a long philosophical heritage, but Russell was the first to suggest that these correspond to two distinct functions of *language*: describing and naming.[24] The language of acquaintance comprises "logically proper names" that "merely designate an object without in any degree describing it."[25] In contrast, the basic form of a description is "the table" or "a chair," but these can be infinitely enriched: "the perfect hostess" (*MD* 7), "the charming woman... [with] a touch of the bird about her" (*MD* 4), or "one of the most thoroughgoing skeptics he had ever met" (*MD* 77). Describing is perforce mediated, comprising inferences and generalizations about an object's properties, and Russell conceived of it as casting a qualitative net under which an object falls if it has the appropriate properties. A logically proper name, on the other hand, seizes its object directly, referring to it without recourse to its qualities or saying anything further about *what* the thing is.

If the semantic wealth of nouns and adjectives belongs to the "what" of description, language furnishes very few such words capable of referring to things known by acquaintance. Russell dismisses the vast majority of what appear to be names, including ordinary proper names, as disguised or abbreviated descriptions.[26] In his later writings he speculates that there may in fact only be one true, *logically* proper name: "this."[27] The demonstrative is possessed of several peculiar characteristics, as we have already seen. There is first of all, to paraphrase Jakobson, its shiftiness in continually changing referents. But not only does it "seldom mean... the same thing two moments running," Russell observes, it also "does not mean the same thing to the speaker and to the hearer." Not only is the referent of the demonstrative continually changing, but my "this" is also never the same as yours. The only name that is proper in the logical sense is thus also ambiguous. Strictly speaking, when used to denote an object of acquaintance such as a sensation, each individual "this" is mutually unintelligible, because no one can be acquainted with another's sensations. If I say "this is white" while holding up a piece of chalk, and you agree, "meaning the 'this' that you see, you are using 'this' as a proper name. But if you try to apprehend the proposition that I am expressing when *I* say 'This is white,' you cannot do it."[28]

It is for this reason that the complete and impersonal description of the external world sought by science is expunged of all "egocentric" words. But logically proper names mark "the sharp point, in language, of the essential privacy of each individual's experience."[29] So it is that, yearning to know Mrs. Ramsay as she sits by her knee, Lily Briscoe "imagined how in the chambers of the mind and heart of the woman who was, physically, touching her, were stood, like the treasures in the tombs of kings, tablets bearing sacred inscriptions, which if one could spell them out, would teach one everything, but they would never be offered openly, never made public" (*TL* 51). The inscriptions in an individual's sealed chamber may remain illegible, but what they spell out is just each person's "this." To be expressed in their completeness and particularity, the qualitative feels of experience cannot be described but only named by a name that is truly proper. The vocabulary of acquaintance is limited and primitive, but it is capable of the most precise description precisely because it remains utterly undescriptive. In the occurrence of a certain pattern of colors when I see a chair, "no words exist for describing the actual occurrence in all its particularity.... When you translate the occurrence into words, you are making generalizations and inferences, just as you are when you say 'there is a chair.'"[30] It is a curiosity of language that the only words capable of expressing the full particularity of individual experience are precisely the ones that indicate the limits of linguistic expressibility. This limit, this "sharp point," is what the demonstrative signals in Woolf's novels.

Here then is one reason for the importance of marking the representations of a character's thought as self-reflective: only thus—in the thoughts of someone aware of his thinking—do these words attain their proper sense. When we use the demonstrative in our thoughts to refer to the events in our minds and the sensations in our bodies, we understand it perfectly well. We understand *this* better than any other word, in fact, for it names the things we know most intimately. In Richard Dalloway's own thoughts, *this* is the most comprehensive and precise way of referring to his feeling of happiness even if it cannot in a strict sense be communicated to anyone else. And yet, of course, we are confronted with the fact almost too banal to state that we are speaking of a novel and that Richard Dalloway does not exist, so we cannot possibly be acquainted with his thoughts. How, then, can we understand such a statement? Although Wittgenstein would famously attack the possibility of a private language, in Woolf's work demonstratives constitute not so much a private as an *intimate* language. As we will see, it is, furthermore, an intimacy that is extended to the reader, who can be conscripted within its sphere of reference and thus brought within a community that remains conceptually undetermined precisely because the demonstrative is not content dependent.

Descriptive Dialectics

When described in words that are general, something of the particularity of a qualitative feel is inevitably lost. But of course, even as the demonstrative perfectly captures its referent, it cannot be understood by anyone else. So far I have been emphasizing the limit of description, but that limit does not render the descriptive enterprise unimportant or futile. Words are general, Russell argues, because language is essentially social. Even if, "when we come to knowledge expressed in words, we seem inevitably to lose something of the particularity of the experience that we seek to describe," in order to serve its chief purpose of communication, language "must be public, not a private dialect invented by the speaker."[31] The privacy of the sharp points is thus what also necessitates their descriptive elaboration—idiolect must become dialect if we wish to avoid imprisonment within our own rooms. Simultaneously empty and full, demonstratives give rise to other words that say more by saying less. The feeling Richard Dalloway knows with warmth and intimacy that is perfectly crystallized in his own thoughts in *this*, must be described in the novel itself for the reader. So we can surmise it is a renewed sense of love for his wife and gratitude for his blessings; or, if we are less charitable, we might chalk it up to the self-satisfaction of his "public-spirited, British Empire, tariff-reform, governing-class spirit" (*MD* 76).

Although the promise of novels is to allow entrance into another's mind, we can never actually be acquainted with what we find there. To create the *fiction* that we are within a character's perspective, the novel must represent the intimacy with which we are acquainted with our *own* feelings and sensations (happiness is this). At the same time, in the novel's own construction this fiction must be set aside and those feelings further elaborated (happiness is etc., etc.), even as we are simultaneously invited to fill the empty demonstrative with our own sense of what happiness is like (a point to which I will return). Woolf's representation of consciousness reaffirms the breach between minds in the same breath that it promises to draw a bridge across it. This dual movement forms the dialectical principle of her novels: as the sentences in free indirect discourse allow the reader to inhabit fluidly shifting points of view, her characters are constantly preoccupied with the problem of how we can know another. A major thematic concern throughout Woolf's corpus is thus also registered on a linguistic level in the perpetual movement between describing and naming: adjectives and nouns must fill out and shade in what is *completely* but *merely* named.

Hence, we see a frequent structure of demonstrative designation accompanied by descriptive enumeration, as when Peter imagines the emotions provoked in Clarissa by his surprise visit. "She had felt a great deal; had for a moment, when she kissed his hand, regretted, envied him even, remembered possibly (for he saw her look it) something he had said—how they would change the world if she married him perhaps; whereas, it was *this*; it was middle age; it was mediocrity" (*MD* 155, my emphasis). Not only the proximal but also the distal demonstrative functions in this way of punctuation and summation, the distal form suggesting the thinker's desire to distance herself from the referent of *that* as opposed to *this*.[32] When Clarissa sees Peter at her party, she marvels, "It was extraordinary how Peter put her into these states just by coming and standing in a corner.... But why did he come, then, merely to criticise? ... There he was wandering off, and she must speak to him. But she would not get the chance. Life was *that*—humiliation, renunciation" (*MD* 168, my emphasis). And in the same scene, when she unexpectedly sees an old friend with whom she had been in love as a girl, Clarissa thinks, "It was Sally Seton! Sally Seton! after all these years! She loomed through a mist. For she hadn't looked like *that*, Sally Seton, when Clarissa grasped the hot water can, to think of her under this roof, under this roof! Not like that! ... The lustre had gone out of her. Yet it was extraordinary to see her again, older, happier, less lovely" (*MD* 171, emphasis in original). Older, happier, less lovely, yes, but we have the sense that these adjectives do not exhaust the "that!" of Sally Seton's appearance to Clarissa at their reunion after so many years. The distal demonstrative here serves not only to emphasize the differences in Sally wrought by time but also effectively distances Clarissa's current self from a former, youthful one more open to love outside the bounds of heterosexuality and marriage.

Demonstratives used in this way often serve to name complex wholes, none more exemplary than *life itself*, as in the first two passages cited above. Since any descriptive qualification of this all-encompassing term must be partial (middle age, mediocrity, humiliation, renunciation), it is as if *this* and *that* are first required to sum it up, distilled in its complex entirety, before it can then be specified and elaborated. And if they are markers of a limit reached in the descriptive powers of language, it is no coincidence that such words are found above all during moments of intensified emotion, as in this scene during Peter and Clarissa's first meeting, when a childhood memory becomes a present vision.

> For she was a child, throwing bread to the ducks, between her parents, and at the same time a grown woman coming to her parents who stood by the lake, holding her life in her arms which, as she neared them, grew larger and larger in her arms, until it became a whole life, a complete life, which she put down by them and said, 'This is what I have made of it! This!' And what had she made of it? What, indeed? (*MD* 43)

Bowled over by the feeling produced by her vision, the emphatic, demonstrative "This!" is the only word Clarissa finds appropriate to its subject, the "whole life, a complete life" that she wishes to lay at her parents' feet. We can give close approximations of what these words designate by listing qualities, but such descriptive inventories will always, at some point, fall short. So Woolf records one of her earliest memories, of "hearing the blind draw its little acorn across the floor as the wind blew the blind out," and despairs that she could spend hours trying to "write that as it should be written" but would still fail.[33] Like a throwing up of hands in a gesture of defeat, the mute finger of the demonstrative pronoun points not only at its object but also simultaneously to the stumbling of description.

The semantic value of the demonstrative in itself is slight, but what it communicates, not by its meaning but by its very presence, is precisely the feeling of something being, in a strict sense, indescribable. In the modernist period, as we have seen, a variety of thinkers observe that words, being general by nature, cannot fully convey the particularity of individual experiences. Hulme advocated analogy as a poetic solution, Proust turned to music as a model, and Woolf, looking to cinema, wondered whether there was "some secret language which we feel and see, but never speak" (*E* 4:350). In addition to images, a secret language seems furnished by words that speak without saying anything. Unlike a Romantic sublime beyond comprehension, the ineffable in modernism is what we know *too* well for words.

There We Are

The unique way in which demonstratives name our sensations and feelings is explicitly elaborated by Russell, but this insight is also evident, albeit implicitly, in James's remarks, which reveal a further dimension of their function. Since being unverbalizable is definitional of our elemental way of knowing, James observes, it follows that "the minimum of grammatical subject, of objective presence, of reality known about, the mere beginning of knowledge must be named by the word that says the least. Such a word is the interjection as *lo! there! ecco! voilà!* Or the article or demonstrative pronoun introducing the sentence, *the, it, that*" (PP 1:222). Whereas for Russell, what is essential about the demonstrative is its ability to refer to a *private* meaning, for James, the demonstrative's importance lies rather in the fact that it is *nonqualitative*. Referring without predicating, *lo! there! ecco! voilà!* are the barest of words, uniquely suited to expressing our most primitive forms of knowledge. These interjections have the force of pointing, offering up their referent in a way that is irreplaceable by any description, which, as soon as substituted, would prove itself to miss the point. The demonstrative is thus not only punctuation and summation but also an imperative, issuing the command that Bernard hears in *The Waves*, "Look! Take note of that!" (*W* 115).

James does not accord ultimate privilege to any single term in Russell's manner, but the just-cited passage alerts us to another important demonstrative in Woolf, one that is central to the enigmatic conclusion of *Mrs. Dalloway*: *there*. At the end of Clarissa's party, Peter Walsh and Sally Seton are waiting for her to finish her social duties so she can speak to them at last (unbeknownst to them she has in fact retreated to reflect on the news she has just heard about an unknown young man's suicide). Compelled by the lateness of the hour, Sally finally gets up to leave.

> "I will come," said Peter, but he sat on for a moment. What is this terror? what is this ecstasy? he thought to himself. What is it that fills me with extraordinary excitement?
>
> It is Clarissa, he said.
>
> For there she was. (*MD* 194)

The distal form of the final demonstrative—"*there* she was," not "*here* she was"—maintains a distance between Peter and Clarissa, but his assertion of her presence is also not without a note of joy. In her diaries, Woolf records her own excitement as she approaches the novel's completion, outlining a plan that will "knit . . . together everything," ending "on three notes, at different stages of the staircase, each saying something to sum up Clarissa. Who shall say these things? Peter, Richard, and Sally Seton perhaps: but I don't want to tie myself down to that yet. Now I do think this might be the best of my endings and come off, perhaps" (*D* 2:312). We know her decision on the score of the last speaker, and a month later, she records "that astounding fact—the last words of the last page of *Mrs. Dalloway* . . . 'For there she was'" (*D* 2:316).

In fact, "there she was" forms a refrain in Peter's thoughts of Clarissa throughout the novel. Earlier on he thinks, "She came into a room; she stood, as he had often seen her, in a doorway with lots of people round her. But it was Clarissa one remembered. Not that she was striking; not beautiful at all; there was nothing picturesque about her; she never said anything specially clever; there she was, however; there she was" (*MD* 76). Mrs. Dalloway, it would seem, is the woman without qualities. These lines appear at the end of a paragraph in which Peter turns over thoughts and memories of Clarissa, trying out various descriptions of her, none of which seem to sum her up, to capture what it is that makes her *her*. Just as Peter Walsh's feelings for her do not proceed from any of her qualities—she is not striking, not picturesque, not beautiful, not clever—her appearance to him, the cause of his extraordinary excitement, ecstasy, and terror cannot be adequately described with reference to her properties.

Woolf faces a similar quandary when describing her father much later in "A Sketch of the Past": "if one points to his obvious qualities—his honesty, his unworldliness, his lovableness, his perfect sincerity—one is singling out from a whole single qualities which were part of that whole; and the whole was different from the qualities of which it was made."[34] The issue here is the problem of a whole that resists decomposition into parts, which results from enumerating qualities, or indeed, any procedure of qualification. Whereas Russell conceives of description as casting a qualitative net under which an object falls if it has the appropriate traits, the equation of a person with a list of properties is precisely what Woolf is resisting. As Roland Barthes states the problem in *A Lover's Discourse*, "By a singular logic, the amorous subject perceives the other as a Whole.... He imagines that the other wants to be loved, as he himself would want to be loved, not for one or another of his qualities, but for *everything*, and this *everything* he bestows upon the other in the form of a blank word, for the Whole cannot be inventoried without being diminished."[35] Barthes's amorous subject, Peter Walsh, and Woolf herself writing of her father—these figures all bring out not only the challenges but also the desire that animates any project of description, which only gets off the ground because of a wish to say how something or someone is.[36]

Woolf is keenly aware of the impossibility of inventory without diminishment, and the last line of *Mrs. Dalloway* is an attempt, to borrow a phrase from Faulkner, "to put it all, if possible, on one pinhead."[37] Pointing to what is before it, the demonstrative injunction yields a counterintuitive understanding of what we could call the hyperrealism of modernist aesthetics, the insistence on hewing more closely to the likeness of life. Extended to its limit, realist verisimilitude tends not toward greater detail (the ever-proliferating catalog) but toward the austerity of ostension, this being in fact the most precise way of describing. Here is one version of the modernist ideal of poetic exactitude that we began to see in chapter 3: the urge to capture "the exact curve of the feeling or thing" culminates in the form of a blank word.[38]

But "there she was" is not only an attempt to capture a whole without qualification, it is also an assertion of presence. The demonstrative statement insists on the presence and reality of the pronoun's referent—*there she is*, it says, *right there before us*. More accurately, it conjures up its referent by the very act of pointing toward her. We cannot describe to a blind man what blue is like, James suggested, because we cannot "impart acquaintance" to another; the most we can do is to tell him where to go to and hope he will experience it for himself. But "there she was" is just the novel's attempt to impart acquaintance in the most proper means available to language. It is the baldest instantiation of William Gass's observation that "there are no descriptions in fiction, there are only constructions."[39] Belonging to the mode of acquaintance, in a certain way Woolf's *this*es and *there*s mark the end of the novel's tarrying with description at all. But in another way, they underscore that the world of fiction is *purely* a matter of description, because there is no acquaintance with it otherwise. When we read of Clarissa Dalloway "there she was," this is not a statement that can be tested with regard to any empirical fact. But the novel has predicated her existence nevertheless, demonstrating the paradox of what description has become: that which is known without reference to acquaintance.

Because of the fact that the novel is a fiction and thus deals with people and situations with which we can never actually be acquainted, Woolf transforms Russellian acquaintance into description, albeit a strange one that avoids the pitfalls of qualitative inventory—and by extension, one that avoids the kind of representation liable to fall into reification. We can in this way read Russell and Woolf together with Lukács.[40] For the latter, the way to generate social legibility was through narration, whereas description (as a literary mode) led toward fragmentation into private subjective perspectives, especially with modernism's privileging of point of view. But for Russell, as for James before him, whereas acquaintance is more certain and more intimate, it is description (as an epistemic mode) that gets us to the possibility of public knowledge and communicability across minds. It is description that provides the way to epistemically secure the social, performing the mediating work of moving from the privately available *this* to the publicly available *table*.

At the risk of confusion by multiplying frameworks, description's work of mediation between the individual and the social is made clear in Raymond Williams's characterization of art as an integration of "personal vision" and "social communication" and an active response to both the material and the perceptual worlds. "Reality . . . is that which human beings make common, by work or language," Williams writes. "Thus, in the very acts of perception and communication, this practical interaction of what is personally seen, interpreted and organized and what can be socially recognized, known and formed is richly and subtly manifested."[41] Modernist writers did not take the path of Balzac, Eliot, Tolstoy, and other realists favored by Williams or Lukács, but they, too, were engaged in the task of establishing a common reality—as an interaction of what is personally seen and what is socially recognized—via description. If much of the pathos in Woolf's novels comes from the desire for communion or the ability to share a personal vision, her use of demonstratives constitutes its logical endpoint: through words such as *this*, *here*, and *there*, she achieves a sort of ultimate communion, one that is total but purely formal, empty, and contentless. At the same time, it is the final step in responding to the problem of mediating a shared understanding of subjective experience.

This is not to suggest that the demonstrative always functions to connect. In James, characters' elliptical statements of "there we are" usually serve to remind the reader of what we don't know, and in Proust deictics often work to determine the boundaries of who is in and who is out among the characters navigating salon life. But Woolf's sensibility is different. In her novels, these shifting, contentless words offer an invitation to the reader to participate in the process of meaning making. The sharp points of language mark a limit of representation—in many ways they fail to tell us *what* exactly life or happiness or Lily's vision are like—but by that token, they also escape being determined by particular conceptual content. Our usual understanding of descriptive representation entails something like a correspondence theory of truth, where we might ask how much Balzac's Paris or Dickens's London or indeed Joyce's Dublin is *actually* like those real places. But when we read a statement like "there she was," we are invited to understand it without reference to some predetermined notion to which it must correspond. It works instead through a form of matching, to use the term from last chapter, that is undetermined with regard to its whatness and so in a certain way is potentially comprehensible to anyone. Indexicals register the limits of communicability, since no one can have certain and complete access to another's *this*, but the very unverifiability of such words also allows readers to fill in, making meaning a matter of continual, plural-collective adjudication. In this way, they hold the possibility of creating a community of understanding not based on verification and correspondence whose social analogue is a form of relationality not determined by preestablished criteria.

Point of View

The bare gesture of pointing offered by the demonstrative at once affirms the absolute privacy of experience (the individual, monadic subject locked in its room) and simultaneously undoes that privacy by emptying it of content and conscripting the reader into its sphere of reference. This also has ramifications at the larger level of point of view, where the demonstrative turns out to be both the apex and dissolution of the modernist atomization of perspectives. Discussing description in Zola, Mieke Bal draws attention to the fading away of clear diegetic focalization at the ending of both *Nana* and *The Belly of Paris*. The presence of focalization raises for her the question of whether description and voyeurism "hang together 'naturally,'" which is exacerbated in the case of Nana by the foregrounding of her sexual objectification. "Whereas in the description of Nana's glorious entry on stage the theater is full of life-sustaining admirers, the final description pushes the devastation of its detailed object to utter isolation. The framing gaze moves away so that the reader alone remains, unable to offer comfort to the dying woman if he or she should wish to do so."[42] Similarly in *The Belly of Paris*, Florent's expulsion from the community of Les Halles after his failed coup is mirrored by his expulsion from diegetic focalization, although now the reasons are political rather than sexual. "Clearly," Bal concludes, "description can be more than just an accompaniment to the closing scene or event; in these two cases, by withdrawing companionship it *constitutes* that ending."[43] Indeed, she adds, "the withdrawal of the focalizing agent is the narrative-descriptive enactment of abandonment." In Nana's case, this abandonment is more descriptive than narrative, since in the final descriptive scene, introduced by the statement "Nana restait seule," "the verb's tense, the durative imperfect, insists that the description is definitive and thus, that this is the final image."[44]

This intriguing idea of focalization as a form of companionship within a description raises especially interesting questions for Woolf, whose work is heavily focalized and who uses free indirect discourse to create differing, multilayered levels of intimacy between character, narrator, and reader. "Nana restait seule" (Nana was left alone) is, I would argue, the opposite of "there she was," but not because the latter has a clear focal perspective whereas the former does not. Although it is Peter who speaks the penultimate line, "It is Clarissa, he said," and it would seem the final "for there she was" is narrated from his perspective as well, the last line is a represented thought or perception rather than a piece of dialogue with a clear speaker, and it is notably placed after a line break. Both of these facts create some ambiguity about whose perspective the narrative is actually focalized through in that final line. If, as I have suggested, "there she was" posits Clarissa without descriptive inventory and in so doing creates a community of understanding that functions without reference to a particular concept, then we could also read this line as entailing a form of focalization that moves beyond any particular character without thereby simply "withdrawing companionship." The unoccupied (because left open) focal perspective of "there she was" is one that Ann Banfield calls "subjective yet subjectless": subjective because the demonstrative *there* is a form of language that only has meaning in reference to a speaker and an utterance, but subjectless because it is not clear that it belongs to any actual character.[45] In this respect the progression here of Peter Walsh's perspective to something more anonymous is also continuous with the affective descriptions we saw last chapter that began by being anchored to a character before becoming unmoored as it went on.

The ambiguous focalization of "For there she was" therefore constitutes a minimal form of companionship without recourse to the mechanisms of identification or sympathy entailed by the ideology of point of view. Recall Jameson's contrast between Balzac's lustful description of the Cormon house in *La vieille fille* and Dreiser's description of Carrie's taste for luxuries in *Sister Carrie* discussed in the introduction. Whereas the Balzacian passage created an anonymous, generalized state of desire, Carrie's attraction to fine goods "is represented as a private wish or longing to which we relate ourselves as readers by the mechanisms of identification and projection" or alternately by a stance that is moralizing or ironic. Carrie has become merely a "point of view," which is "the textual institution or determinant that expresses and reproduces the newly centered subject of the age of reification," a subject constituted as "a closed monad, henceforth governed by the laws of 'psychology.'"[46] Although the demonstrative statement in Woolf is focalized, its undetermined nature disrupts the very bourgeois monadic subjectivity that it enshrines, not by denying the representation of private feeling but by describing it with perfect precision. At the same time, it ultimately resists (even as it invites) relations of identification with a focal character by making its propositional content at some level unintelligible, not only because of the demonstrative but also because "there she was" is such a minimal assertion of presence. In this way, Woolf is able to register "the scars and marks of social fragmentation and monadization, and . . . the gradual separation of the public from the private" that the growing dominance of focalization in early twentieth century fiction symptomizes without simply affirming the "atomization of all hitherto existing forms of community or collective life."[47] Or more precisely, she is able to acknowledge this atomization ("did religion solve that, or love?") while imagining an alternate basis for collectivity.

What we glimpse here is a way of understanding the politics of description that does not appeal, as is standard, to its referential content. Viewed from a referential perspective, naturalist description (indeed, much realist description) is to be praised for its representation of realities and experiences previously considered outside the realm of the aesthetic, while high modernists are to be faulted for the narrow social scope of their work. The expanded social descriptions of naturalist fiction are undoubtedly crucial and necessary (and critics like Jennifer Fleissner have shown their formal sophistication and significance), but the foregoing offers another way to understand the possibilities of descriptive form.[48] Even as authors like James, Proust, and Woolf can be taken to task for failing to depict wider milieus than the narrow circle of the high bourgeoisie, their descriptions seek to imagine the possibility of nonalienated social relations that are not predetermined in advance. The bare gesture of "there she was" attempts to access reality by baldly asserting a presence and thereby provoke some relational possibility beyond those that are already encrusted and sedimented in a capitalist modernity. This is all the more remarkable given description's susceptibility to reification—as Lukács pointed out, it seems to be the most referential, most determined of forms. But as Robert Kaufman reminds us, for Marx the problem with reification is not only that social relations are expressed as relations of production but just as importantly that it forecloses the possibility of any alternative forms of relation or judgments of value that are not predetermined in advance. What Marx called for was the ability to determine value freely, a process to which aesthetic judgment—characterized since Kant precisely by nondetermined conceptuality or purposiveness without purpose—opened the way.[49] My suggestion here is that modernist descriptions achieve something Lukács thought was impossible for this narrative mode, a way of imagining nonreified forms of relation.

"Merely to Be Themselves"

Woolf conceived of the last lines of *Mrs. Dalloway* in her diaries as "summing up" Clarissa, something that characters often seek—and fail—to do in her novels. Having wrestled with the problem of how to describe atmospheres, relations between relations, affects, and qualia, the problem of description takes on an ethical dimension when it comes to the question of how to describe others. In particular, as we began to see with her attempt to describe her father without the diminishment of inventory, how to do so without imposition? Last chapter I suggested that the alignment of descriptive temporality with being over doing evinced an instinct to bear witness to what is, an instinct that is a reaction to the destruction of World War I as well as a critique of masculinist notions of history and progress associated with action. When it comes to describing others, the element of bearing witness shades more strongly into an ethical imperative to let be.

In "Mr. Bennett and Mrs. Brown," Woolf chided her elders' interest in real estate, and in her novels she also questions the impulse to render another kind of facade that has long served to index social status and moral character. Skepticism about the trustworthiness of physiognomic description is already evident in James, as our first introduction to Merton Densher in *The Wings of the Dove* makes clear: "He was a longish, leanish, fairish young Englishman, not unamenable, on certain sides, to classification—as for instance by being a gentleman, by being rather specifically one of the educated, one of the generally sound and generally civil; yet, though to that degree neither extraordinary nor abnormal, he would have failed to play straight into an observer's hands" (*WD* 33). Densher's nondescriptness is a function of the indeterminacy of his traits (long*ish*, lean*ish*, fair*ish*), but ultimately in James, the fact that Densher cannot be classified signals his exceptionality more than it does the futility of the classificatory endeavor, whose principles of social hermeneutics remain intact. By the time we arrive at the following sketch of Septimus Warren Smith, such an undertaking has become altogether hopeless.

> To look at, he might have been a clerk, but of the better sort; for he wore brown boots; his hands were educated; so, too, his profile—his angular, big-nosed, intelligent, sensitive profile; but not his lips altogether, for they were loose; and his eyes (as eyes tend to be), eyes merely; hazel, large; so that he was, on the whole, a border case, neither one thing nor the other, might end with a house at Purley and a motor car, or continue renting apartments in back streets all his life. (*MD* 84).

Rather than clear indexes of moral traits or socioeconomic standing, physical features here become autoreferential, yielding no hidden meaning. Eyes, traditionally the most significant feature of a face, are not windows into the soul but, "(as eyes tend to be), eyes merely." Along with houses and clothing, physiognomy, too, loses its reliability as indications of profession, rank, and character. In this regard, it is of course no coincidence that *Mrs. Dalloway* is set in post–World War I London and that the young man of indeterminate station is a returned soldier, the war having shaken the rigidity of social hierarchies even if class snobbery remains alive and well in the novel.[50]

Already in *Jacob's Room* (1922), Woolf's first full-length experimental novel, she was foregrounding the unreliability of classification via description, or the futility of "cataloguing features" (*JR* 71). At the same time, her continual staging of the attempt to do so testifies to the indispensability of description as a means of social knowing. *Jacob's Room* dramatizes a scenario that is repeated in "Mr. Bennett and Mrs. Brown," a stranger being observed on a train, although this time it is the observer who is the old woman, a Mrs. Norman, while the observed is Jacob, the young man who will eventually die in Flanders and whose unknowability constitutes a void at the center of the novel. In this scene, Mrs. Norman—a character who appears here for the first and last time, seemingly introduced for the sole purpose of recording observations about Jacob—is on her way to Cambridge to see her son. In the first sentence, when Jacob enters her train carriage, he is described only as a "powerfully built young man" who causes her to fear for her safety. Mrs. Norman's attempt to see or to read Jacob in familiar typological terms is rendered self-consciously.

> She read half a column of her newspaper; then stealthily looked over the edge to decide the question of safety by the infallible test of appearance....
> Taking note of socks (loose), of tie (shabby), she once more reached his face. She dwelt upon his mouth. The lips were shut. The eyes bent down, since he was reading. All was firm, yet youthful, indifferent, unconscious—as for knocking one down! No, no, no! (*JR* 28)

Now she revises her initial assessment of the danger Jacob poses, smiling at the foolishness of her initial misreading and taming this once-threatening stranger by assimilating him to a familial archetype: "But since, even at her age, she noted his indifference, presumably he was in some way or other—to her at least—nice, handsome, interesting, distinguished, well built, like her own boy?" (*JR* 29). Mrs. Norman's revision of his status is notably based on his likeness to her own son, dependent not only on the qualities named here, "nice, handsome, interesting, distinguished, well built," but also implicitly on similarities of nationality and class. Although I have been stressing the ways in which likeness in modernist descriptions work in nonmimetic, nondetermined ways, I do not mean to deny the more familiar ways in which likeness between people serves to draw lines of inclusion and exclusion. Nor do I mean to suggest that social distinctions disappear in modernism or in Woolf, or that they are physically unmarked. As scholars have noted, in order to represent the truths of character that Woolf claimed would always elude Bennett's powers of visual description, she, too, often relies on stereotyped images.[51] Nevertheless, scenes of failed descriptive classification mark an entrenched skepticism toward any continuity between seeing and knowing in an age of new social mobility, especially in major European cities and after the war. "Nobody sees anyone as he is," the narrator of *Jacob's Room* continues in the scene discussed above, "let alone an elderly lady sitting opposite a strange young man in a railway carriage. They see a whole—they see all sorts of things—they see themselves . . ." (*JR* 29, original ellipsis). The dizzying turns of the social kaleidoscope portrayed by Proust lead to the indeterminate figures cut by Jacob Flanders and Septimus Smith.

And yet, even as Woolf critiques character taxonomies and accordingly classificatory description, she simultaneously recognizes that it is impossible to do without them—the "test of appearance" may not be infallible, but it seems to remain an initial and inevitable yardstick.[52] Everyone "is a judge of character," she writes in "Character in Fiction." "Indeed it would be impossible to live for a year without disaster unless one practiced character-reading and had some skill in the art" (*E* 3:421). Types function as a kind of necessary but not sufficient shorthand, an initial way of tracing a circumference around a shape. But in order to be faithful, these shapes also require views from multiple perspectives, reflecting the near-universal structure of Woolf's novels, in which characters are built up not only from the glimpses we have of their interior worlds of thinking and feeling but also, just as importantly, from others' impressions of them. In this regard, Woolf's use of free indirect discourse is crucial, allowing her descriptions to acknowledge the way in which everyone sums each other up without necessarily intervening to set it straight by correcting others' mistaken perceptions in an authoritative narrative voice.[53] Thus, even as Mrs. Norman's typologizing is said to be futile, it nevertheless allows us to understand something about how Jacob appears to others, a technique that is taken to its apex in the party scenes that so often form culminations in Woolf's books—Clarissa Dalloway's party, Mrs. Ramsay's dinner, the party that brings together the Pargiters in *The Years*, and in its own way, the pageant in *Between the Acts*. It would be a mistake to think that her skepticism about the ability to describe others is simply an affirmation of an individuality knowable only to the self or a view of identity that is divorced from social matrices within which others' character reading occurs. Whatever the real limitations imposed by her own social coordinates, Woolf does not posit inside and outside views as being separate from one another or as unequivocally arranged in a hierarchy. Any notion of identity is for her fundamentally relational, constituted through interaction with external views of the self, and her shifts between perspectives give the lie to the idea that our own self-understanding is the locus of authenticity or authority.

In staging scenes where the attempt to know and to classify others breaks down, Woolf is objecting to the element of imposition in any project of description. This is another version of the Proustian critique of an identitarian descriptive logic that tries to fix what things are, especially when they are not as they should be. No one represents this latter position more than *Mrs. Dalloway*'s Dr. Bradshaw, a representative of the ossified

Edwardian social order who works diligently to eliminate all idiosyncrasy and difference, most disastrously in the case of Septimus. "[They] saw nothing clear, yet ruled, yet inflicted. 'Must' they said" (*MD* 148), and just before his suicide, Septimus thinks, "'Must,' 'must,' why 'must'? What power had Bradshaw over him? 'What right has Bradshaw to say "must" to me?' he demanded" (*MD* 147).[54] In contrast to the imperial "must," Clarissa prefers the optative *let*, as we see clearly in the scene during which she realizes the "supreme mystery" of "here was one room; there another" prompted by glimpsing the old woman in the house across from hers. "Let her climb upstairs if she wanted to; let her stop; then let her, as Clarissa had often seen her, gain her bedroom, part her curtains, and disappear again into the background" (*MD* 126). The optative mode of *let* is continuous with Woolf's use of the demonstrative, which evokes its referent—be it a feeling, a thing or a person—just as it is, without any qualifications. Both promulgate what we could call an ethics of nonimposition similar to Roland Barthes's notion of "the neutral."[55] In particular, they are attempts to avoid the imposition that is inevitable with any qualitative description, which refers to an individual through their attributes and qualities. According to the logic implicit in such a mode of reference, any two people who possess the same inventory of properties could be substituted for one another. It is not difficult to see how this logic could lead to a kind of utilitarianism that converts individuals and the lived experience of social interactions into abstract measures where each person is infinitely fungible because they are reduced to a set of attributes or functions that could be exhibited or fulfilled by anyone.

Although "summing up" a person is condemned in *Jacob's Room* as futile, a different kind of summation seems operative in a statement like "there she was," one that does not fix an individual with a particular description of them but that simply names her as she is and lets her be. "Had she ever tried to convert any one herself?" Clarissa thinks indignantly as she feels the weight of their imposition bearing down on her; "Did she not wish everybody merely to be themselves?" (*MD* 126). The desire for people to be "themselves" without demanding they be any particular way entails a resistance to the attributions of qualitative description in favor of the neutrality and indeterminacy of the name and the pronoun. It is difficult, not to say impossible, to avoid the element of imposition in any description, and Woolf's turn to the most minimal forms of reference constitutes an attempt to render character nondescriptively. An ethos of bearing witness to what is can always be susceptible to charges of quietism, but for Woolf, the valorizing of being and presence amounts to a noninterventionist capacity to let things—including people—be as they are without demanding that they be more to our own liking. In this respect her work finds affiliations with more actively obstructionist forms of passivity, such as Bartleby's "I would prefer not to."[56]

In Other Words

Throughout this book, I have been tracing various strategies of comparison and likeness that attempt to describe how things are without reifying them. What happens, however, when we reach something incomparable, for which nothing may be substituted? The question is posed by the dedication in one of Woolf's earliest novels, *Night and Day* (1919), to her sister. "To Vanessa Bell. But looking for a phrase I found none to stand beside your name." There is, as Barthes put it, no inventory without diminishment—as soon as we begin listing particular attributes, we lose the whole in its entirety. It can thus only be marked by a zero degree, a blank space, a marker of absence where something singular (*this* person, *this* desire) has eluded linguistic capture. In Latin, Barthes writes, the trace of this escape is registered in the word *ipse*, "it is the self, himself, herself in person. . . . From word to word, I struggle to put 'into other words' [dire autrement] the ipseity of my Image, to express improperly the propriety of my desire: a journey at whose end my final philosophy can only be to recognize—and to practice—tautology."[57] Love, according to Barthes, is not a question of *quidditas* but of *ipseitas*, not of whatness but of itselfness, but this is also more generally a problem of description, which is a continual act of translation, *dire autrement*, saying otherwise.

Barthes is the great twentieth century theorist of the possibility of nonimpositional language (framed here in terms of the lover but which he also theorizes under a variety of other rubrics, including the neutral), but it is a problem he inherits from modernism, and his conclusion is already anticipated in Woolf. When no way of saying otherwise can be found, the result is tautology. As Neville says of Percival, the absent center in *The Waves*, "You are you. That is what consoles me for the lack of many things" (*W* 181). Or in the formulation of Jacob's "obstinate irrepressible conviction which makes youth so intolerably disagreeable," "I am what I am, and intend to be it" (*JR* 34). Faced with the incomparable, in the absence of any adequate substitution, no word will do but the repetition of a pronoun. "When I say to myself, 'Bernard,' who comes? A faithful, sardonic man, disillusioned, but not embittered. A man of no particular age or calling. Myself, merely" (*W* 81). After a string of adjectives, Bernard arrives in the end at something that eludes inventory. The tautological expression of identity does not result so much from an expressive failure as from having reached something whose final description can only be itself. Or, if it is a failure, it is achieved only with difficulty, for it is also the affirmation of something for which there is nothing equivalent.

The tautology communicates something not by means of its content, which is held to be one of the most basic laws of logic and thus entirely self-evident, but, like the demonstrative, by its very presence. And what it announces is that a limit has been reached. Without synonyms, not susceptible to substitution, what can only be said tautologically cannot be put into other words. Whereas Proust tried to get around the problem of saying what something is by proliferating analogies, ultimately Woolf finds another solution. In the strictest sense, the question "who is she?" cannot be appropriately answered by any description: "she is the wife of a member of parliament," "she is a thoroughgoing skeptic," and so forth, but only with semantically impoverished words emancipated from the constraints of predication and definition to which nouns and adjectives are beholden. Woolf shows that the only precise answer to the question "who is she?" is "she is who she is" or "she is herself." This should not be understood as a heroic celebration of liberal humanist individuality but something far more austere. An instantaneous comprehensiveness within language can be achieved only at the expense of all determinate content, an absolute plenitude that is merely the flip side of emptiness.[58] And although a statement like "it is what it is" can be seen as a form of resignation, sometimes a tautological description that simply reasserts how things are can be the clearest form of indictment. In this way, we can trace a line between Woolf's ethics of nonimposition and the moral critique contained in something like Pablo Neruda's antisimile in his Spanish Civil War poem: "and the blood of children ran through the streets / without fuss, like children's blood."[59]

The plethora of carefully wrought, richly evocative, finely shaded descriptions in Woolf's novels is ample evidence that she does not entirely accede to the Barthesian dream of "a language without adjectives."[60] But the counterpoints to her lyricism are the words, at once sharp and obtuse, that mark an encounter with a limit. Nor are such formulations by any means isolated across the modernist landscape. As Michael Levenson has noted, "One of the most distinctive mannerisms in James's dialogues is the short almost tautological utterance, composed of personal pronouns, the verb 'to be' and a demonstrative adverb: 'there he is'; 'you're not where you were'; 'here I am'; 'then there we are.'"[61] Among these expressions Levenson singles out the prominence of the idiom "being like that." To recognize something as being "like that" is "neither theoretical nor figural knowledge; the recognition depends on a direct encounter, a felt acquaintance, and often manifests itself in definitive judgment—as in Kate Croy's verdict upon Milly Theale, 'She's *like* that.' If intimacy is *like* that and Milly is *like* that, then there can be no further appeal. We have arrived at a crux, an integrity, a final truth that cannot be paraphrased."[62] We find an explicit acknowledgment of the demonstrative as final appeal in *The Golden Bowl* when, uncertain as to her next course of action after the eponymous object furnishes proof of her husband's infidelity, Maggie Verver cries, "How do I know? With *this*!" Maggie's statement causes her interlocutor, Mrs. Assingham, to marvel at "the way the little word representing it seemed to express and include for her the whole of her situation" (*GB* 439). If such expressions, at once so empty and so full, impart no theoretical or figural knowledge, they can only be understood by already being in the know. They thus also set up a complicity between the characters who understand each other perfectly—so the greatest sign of intimacy in James is when two characters know "where they are"—and others who don't. And what of the reader? Are we excluded from understanding, or are we brought into the circle? I have suggested that at least in Woolf's case, it is the latter (though not through an understanding of semantic content), but such expressions no doubt derive their force from their ability to maintain both positions in tension.

At other times, the tautological demonstrative description is made explicit as simple common sense. In "Composition as Explanation," a 1926 lecture published by the Woolfs' Hogarth Press, Gertrude Stein states crisply, "By this I mean this."[63] Meanwhile, in *In Search of Lost Time*, the tragedy of this is that it never *remains* this. Marveling at time's transformation of each person into a different one at the Prince de Guermantes's final matinée, Proust's narrator can hardly believe of an old woman whom he had known as a girl and whom he initially fails to recognize "that this [*ceci*] can ever have been that [*cela*], that the material of that [*cela*] has not taken refuge elsewhere but, thanks to the subtle manipulations of time, has itself become this [*ceci*]" (*SLT* 6:367, *RTP* 4:519).[64] From an unnamed old lady at one party to the aged Sally Seton at another, the result of time passing can be summed up in an inescapable equation: this *will* equal that.

In a 1922 letter to Roger Fry in which Woolf records having begun *In Search of Lost Time*, her response to reading Proust suggests one final point pertinent to the problem at hand. "Well—what remains to be written after that?" she wonders. "I am in a state of amazement. . . . How, at last, has someone solidified what has always escaped—and made it too into this beautiful and perfectly enduring substance? One has to put the book down and gasp."[65] The stupefaction Woolf experiences upon reading a work that captures the exact curve of the feeling or the thing is echoed and generalized by a later admirer of Proust. "In its perfect moments," Barthes remarks in his last lectures at the Collège de France, literature "tends to make us say 'That's it, that's absolutely it!' [*C'est ça, c'est tout à fait ça!*]" The context is a discussion of haiku, in particular one by the seventeenth-century Japanese poet Teishitsu, "'That, that' / Was all I could say / Before the blossoms of Mount Yoshino." Barthes comments, "saying you can't say, the whole haiku tends toward this, toward '*that.*' There's nothing to say, in short, other than the vertiginous limit of language, the *deictic Neutral* ('that')." He then poses a question, "Dare I extend this hypothesis around *Absolutely* to the whole of literature?"[66] If we take up Barthes's dare, ostension may be the end of literature in more than one way. A perfect description of what something is like, it would seem, can elicit only a response of speechlessness. In the face of so close a likeness, nothing remains to be uttered except perhaps a gasp of recognition at the familiar sight of an acquaintance. If that is the name of the indescribable, this is how Woolf points to the end of description.

Acknowledgments

This project began under the guidance of Daniel Heller-Roazen, who did much to clarify and sharpen my thinking. Michael Wood and Maria DiBattista helped to shape a number of my initial ideas, and all three lent their support when it was most needed. I'm grateful, too, for Peter Brooks's feedback on early incarnations of the project. Ann Banfield opened up new intellectual worlds for me, and the last chapter of the book in particular would not have been possible without her pioneering work. Eileen Reeves read much more of my work than she should ever have had to, and her care and commitment to graduate education meant more to me than she knows. My gratitude also extends to Ben Conisbee Baer, Sandie Berman, and Wendy Belcher, who all provided support beyond the call of duty in various departmental administrative capacities. Two earlier teachers deserve thanks here as well, Rebecca Comay and Julian Patrick, in whose classrooms the seeds of this project were first planted and whose support I've never forgotten.

It was at the University of California, Berkeley, that this book really took shape, and writing it would not have been possible without the conditions of stable employment, which I had only because I effectively won the lottery that is the academic job market. So many colleagues at Berkeley, in both English and comparative literature, read and engaged with the ideas in this book while making room for it to develop in its own way. At a pivotal juncture, Elizabeth Abel, Dan Blanton, Rob Kaufman, and Michael Lucey read the entire manuscript and gave me the push I needed to take the argument where it wanted to go. Their feedback has helped to sharpen many of the book's specifics, and they have also been exemplary mentors since I arrived here. I've also benefited from conversations with Charlie Altieri, Stephen Best, Eric Falci, Catherine Flynn, Anne-Lise François, Mark Goble, Suzanne Guerlac, Dori Hale, Vicky Kahn, Marianne

Kaletzky, Niklaus Largier, Steven Lee, Colleen Lye, David Marno, Eric Naiman, Kent Puckett, and Katie Snyder as well as the graduate students in two seminars where I discussed some of the ideas presented here. In their capacities as chairs of the Departments of English and of Comparative Literature, Steve Justice, Katherine O'Brien O'Keeffe, Genaro Padilla, Miryam Sas, and Sophie Volpp have all lent instrumental support during my time as junior faculty. I'm especially grateful to Steve and Sophie for their support and guidance as I navigated maternity leave and the tenure process. Many thanks, too, to Wendi Bootes for her conscientious research assistance, which saved me from many errors.

So much of the work of writing and thinking is done in solitude, but it wouldn't have been possible without the camaraderie of friends and interlocutors in graduate school, the Bay Area, and beyond. For cheer and sustenance of various kinds, my thanks to David Atkin, Alexis Cohen, Henry Cowles, Adrian Daub, Sergio Delgado, Nika Elder, Nadia Ellis, Julia Fawcett, Caroline Fowler, Colin Garretson, Anna Katz, Nico Lefevre-Marton, Anneka Lenssen, Abra Levenson, Duncan MacRae, Ivan Ortiz, Zakir Paul, Alyssa Pelish, Rebecca Porte, Kristin Primus, Poulomi Saha, Namwali Serpell, Kathryn Stergiopoulos, Michelle Wang, Ron Wilson, and Damon Young. Jeff Lawrence, Luis Othoniel, and Danny Braun talked through ideas and read parts of the project in various incarnations, and I count myself lucky that some of my most long-standing and trusted readers are also some of the best literary critics I know. Nick Gaskill and Johanna Winant both read earlier versions of different chapters and helped me wrangle them into shape with their customary brilliance. I had the good fortune of meeting Hannah Freed-Thall in my last year at Princeton, and I'm grateful to her for reading the entire manuscript at a late stage and helping me make a number of improvements. Having interlocutors like these in the field has given me the gift of that wonderful thing, intellectual community, which makes up for so much else in the profession.

Books take material resources to write, and support for this one was provided by the Townsend Center for the Humanities, the Humanities Research Fellowship, and the Regents' Junior Faculty Fellowship at Berkeley. A grant from the Institute for International Studies here made it possible to hold a manuscript workshop, and I'm greatly indebted to Michael Levenson and Mark McGurl for their thoughtful and incisive engagements with the manuscript. Their feedback was invaluable during the revision process. Additionally, conversations with Jonathan Flatley and Paul Saint-Amour helped to spark thoughts that ended up in the book, and Paul's astute comments on my proposal helped me frame the arc of the book as a whole.

I owe an immense debt to David Kurnick, who is an exemplar of critical brilliance and verve. It was a dream to discover that he had been a press reader, and his discerning, detailed, uncompromising yet generous comments were nothing short of transformative. I am also tremendously grateful to John Lurz for his sensitive, generous reading of the manuscript and his probing questions and formulations, which helped me clarify many threads of the argument. At the University of Chicago Press, thanks to Alan Thomas for taking the book on and expertly shepherding it through the publication process and to Randy Petilos and the entire team for their help in many pragmatic matters. I couldn't be more thrilled that the book is appearing in Nan Da and Anahid Nersessian's new Thinking Literature series. Nan and Anahid's indefatigable energy and razor-sharp intelligence are a force to behold, and I'm glad for the field that they're wielding both on behalf of literary criticism.

Finally, I could not have finished this book without the support of those who in many ways cared very little about it because they cared much more about me. Matt Gloyd and Shanelle Smith have known me since long before I ever wrote a piece of scholarship, and their reminders of that fact buoyed me during difficult periods of writing. Sandy and Jim Giordano welcomed me into their family with the utmost warmth and cheered me along as I spent one visit after another "finishing my book," while the Eklunds (Carrie, Scott, Oliver, Nolan, and Miles) provided much needed breaks with chaos and fun. My parents supported me in embarking on the study of comparative literature even when they didn't quite know what it was, and their belief in me has been unwavering. Above all, I'm grateful to and for Ryan, who first entered my life at this project's inception and then propitiously again at the start of its second life. In addition to his steadying love and intellectual partnership, he also gave me the crucial material resource of caring for our son so that I could have time to write. And last but not least, to Kai, my thanks for showing up when the book was almost finished and showing me a whole new world.

Portions of chapter 5 first appeared as "Naming the Indescribable: Woolf, Russell, James, and the Limits of Description" in *New Literary History* 45, no. 1 (Winter 2014): 41–70. A few sentences in chapter 1 are drawn from "Notes on Atmosphere," which first appeared in *Qui Parle* 27, no. 1 (June 2018): 121–55. Thanks to Johns Hopkins University Press and Duke University Press for allowing me to think through some of the ideas in this book first in their journals.

Notes

Introduction

1. Balzac, *Père Goriot*, 16–17.
2. Wall, *Prose of Things*, 13. Wall's study is one of a few notable exceptions. For a discussion of description in an eighteenth-century French context, see Stalnaker, *Unfinished Enlightenment*. See also Philippe Hamon's more theoretical study, *Introduction à l'analyse du descriptif*, which takes nineteenth-century French fiction, especially Zola and Verne, as its primary corpus.
3. Brian Glavey argues vis-à-vis one of description's oppositional pairs, performance: "This is the lesson of the post-structuralist reception of J. L. Austin's theory of performativity: though the performative utterance is held to be that which transforms a state of affairs rather than that which 'merely describes' it, under scrutiny it becomes clear that performativity is most powerful in those instances that purport to be purely descriptive." *Wallflower Avant-Garde*, 13.
4. Foucault, *Order of Things*, 129. See also Daston, "Description by Omission," 11–24.
5. Foucault, *Order of Things*, 130.
6. Stewart, *On Longing*, 25–26.
7. Beaujour, "Some Paradoxes of Description," 47.
8. See Propp, *Theory and History of Folklore*; Genette, *Figures* and *Narrative Discourse*. See also Bal, *On Storytelling*. Both Genette and Bal acknowledge that description is understudied.
9. Ruth Ronen makes this point in "Description, Narrative, and Representation," 280. As she rightly notes, these ideas were influential on the study of narrative from early Barthes to poststructuralism.
10. See Brooks, *Reading for the Plot*. Similarly, Amy M. King points out that most canonical theories of realism—those of Brooks, Roland Barthes, René Girard, and Fredric Jameson—"center on desire: the reader's desire to get to the end of the reading experience, the protagonist's desire to get to some goal. . . . What drops out of this dominant critical tradition is description—not only the fact of it, but precisely how in the reading experience description works against the headlong thrust toward closure." King, "Dilatory Description and the Pleasures of Accumulation," 163.
11. See Lukács, "Narrate or Describe?"
12. In a review of Jameson's *The Antinomies of Realism*, Catherine Gallagher writes,

"the most thrilling thing about the book is its exploration of that previously unmapped continent of nonnarrative novelistic features that increasingly cluster around the pole of affect." Gallagher, "Affective Realism," 129.

13. To my knowledge the only work on description in modernist fiction specifically is Mieke Bal, "Over-writing as Un-writing." Brian Glavey's *Wallflower Avant-Garde* deals with ekphrasis primarily in modernist poetry (with the exception of *Nightwood*), which he reads together with queer theory. In contrast, my book takes up nonekphrastic forms of description in the modernist novel.

14. Genette, *Figures of Literary Discourse*, 136.

15. Genette, 133.

16. See, for instance, Gérard Genette's comments on description in Proust discussed in chapter 3. Genette, *Narrative Discourse*.

17. Wittgenstein, *Philosophical Investigations*, §291.

18. For a history of description in rhetoric from antiquity to the nineteenth century, see Hamon, *Introduction á l'analyse du descriptif*, and Wall, *Prose of Things*.

19. Balzac, *Père Goriot*, 6. In contrast to this harmony, Christopher Prendergast argues that Balzac ultimately loses confidence in the ability of clothing, physiognomy, and objects to reveal the truth of social realities, which is "a sign of the developing opaqueness of the modern city." Prendergast, *Order of Mimesis*, 95.

20. See Jameson, *The Antinomies of Realism*, chapter 3.

21. I take this phrase from the title of Ian Hacking's essay "Making Up People." Influenced by Foucault, Hacking suggests that the development of certain ways of describing and classifying people (such as homosexuality or multiple personality disorder or being a waiter) also "creates new ways for people to be." Hacking, *Historical Ontology*, 100. I am grateful to David Kurnick for making the connection to Hacking.

22. I am drawing here on Wittgenstein's discussion of aspect-seeing in *Philosophical Investigations*, which has been influential for philosophy of action, philosophy of history, and philosophy of science, among other fields.

23. Hacking, *Historical Ontology*, 108.

24. See Anscombe, *Intention*, 28. Similar ideas are at work in midcentury philosophy of history, as in Arthur Danto's idea that "phenomena *as such* are not explained, it is only phenomena as *covered by a description* which are capable of explanation," and any explanation of a phenomenon must always be relativized to a particular description of it. See Danto, *Narration and Knowledge*, 218, italics in original. Something similar is also at stake in Clifford Geertz's famous call for "thick descriptions" in cultural anthropology, a term that he borrows from the ordinary language philosopher Gilbert Ryle. See Geertz, *The Interpretation of Cultures*. Anscombe, Danto, and Ryle are all directly influenced by Wittgenstein.

25. Hacking, *Historical Ontology*, 108. Hacking's example is the category of "multiple personality disorder," and he is drawing on Foucault's famous work on the invention of the identity of the homosexual. I do not focus specifically on the issue of "how kinds of people come into being," but the point about the feedback loop between discourse and reality is one on which I am drawing. See Hacking, *Rewriting the Soul*, 6. For related discussions, see Geertz, *The Interpretation of Cultures*, 6; and Ryle, *Collected Papers* 2:474–81.

26. Bal, "Over-Writing as Un-writing," 578.

27. David Kurnick suggested the term *expression*. Barbara Maria Stafford writes, "All

of analogy's simile-generating figures are thus incarnational. They materialize, display, and disseminate an enigma that escapes words." Stafford, *Visual Analogy*, 24.

28. These potentialities may be characterized as what Hacking calls "dynamic nominalism," where giving a name to something actively shapes that kind of thing's coming into being such that "our classifications and our classes conspire to emerge hand in hand, each egging the other on." Hacking, *Historical Ontology*, 106.

29. Cynthia Wall writes, "Domestic interiors—the furniture and fabric and object details of particularized rooms as part of ordinary life and action—rarely appear in the high-level hierarchies of poetry or prose until later in the eighteenth century, but then dominate nineteenth-century novels and poetry." Wall, *Prose of Things*, 10.

30. Flaubert, *Bouvard et Pécuchet*, 506.

31. See James, *Art of Criticism*, 75, for first citation.

32. This formulation is Beckett's. See Beckett, *Proust and Three Dialogues*, 78.

33. Breton, *Manifestoes of Surrealism*, 7.

34. Breton, 8.

35. Aragon, *Je n'ai jamais appris à écrire*, 55, my translation. The first long descriptive section of *Le paysan de Paris*, "Passage de l'Opéra," famously inspired Walter Benjamin's *Arcades Project*.

36. Beckett, *Three Novels*, 31.

37. Beckett, 392.

38. This was a response to Sainte-Beuve's complaint both of the tediousness of the descriptions in that novel and the fact that Flaubert included details that couldn't have been known, such as mentioning "blue stones" when the pavement was seen at night. Flaubert retorted that in fact it was perfectly possible to see the color of the stones by moonlight. A point-by-point critique of *Salammbô*'s historical accuracy was also mounted in an article by Guillaume Froehner, the chief conservationist of the Department of Antiquities at the Louvre, to which Flaubert responded, also point by point, with a list of his unimpeachable sources. The exchange is printed, along with details of Flaubert's extensive research, in Flaubert, *Oeuvres completes*, 2:377. For more details about this exchange, see Jehlen's *Five Fictions in Search of Truth*.

39. This is explicitly the case with the later *Nouveau Roman*, where writers like Alain Robbe-Grillet explicitly limited themselves to description in an effort to reinvent the novel and especially to move it beyond its indebtedness to psychological depth. See Robbe-Grillet, *For a New Novel*.

40. Leon Edel, introduction to Dujardin, *We'll to the Woods No More*, xx.

41. See, inter alia, Mao, *Solid Objects*; Brown, *Sense of Things*; and, on an earlier period, Freedgood, *Ideas in Things*.

42. Wittgenstein, *Philosophical Investigations*, §290. The idea of language games is to remind us that we tend to think that "language always functions in one way, always serves the same purpose: to convey thoughts—which may be about houses, pains, good and evil, or anything else you please" (§304).

43. Wall, *Prose of Things*, 7. Ruth Webb argues that the idea of ekphrasis as a verbal representation of a visual image is an entirely modern definition that only became popular in the second half of the twentieth century. The goal of classical ekphrasis, according to her, was to produce specific emotions in the audience, and it was not tied specifically to visual images. See Webb, *Ekphrasis, Imagination, and Persuasion*. See also Alex Potts's argument that ancient ekphrasis was always about the rhetorical power of

language, rather than visuality in "Disparities between Part and Whole." Similarly, Michael Baxandall claims that when we describe a visual image, we're really describing our process of thinking *about* that image. See Baxandall, *Patterns of Intention*. The classic discussion of ekphrasis and other questions of visual and verbal representation is W. J. T. Mitchell's *Picture Theory*.

44. To mention just a few points of connection, James speculated about the ways in which the photographs on the frontispieces of the New York edition of his novels did not function as illustrations; Proust drew copiously on the history of painting and the metaphorics of photography in *In Search of Lost Time*; and Woolf's connections to post-impressionism via her sister Vanessa Bell and Roger Fry are well known. For secondary scholarship, see, among many others, McWhirter, "Photo-Negativity"; Bal, *Mottled Screen*; and Goldman, *Feminist Aesthetics*. Elsewhere in modernism, writers like Gertrude Stein and Wyndham Lewis looked to Paul Cézanne and Cubism for ways to remake their literary portraits, while Dorothy Richardson was among the first to engage seriously with film, contributing regularly to the journal *Close Up*, and many surrealist works exploited both visual and verbal mediums, including, as I discuss in this chapter, André Breton's photo-novel *Nadja*. See Lewis, *Tarr*; Stein, *Tender Buttons*, and "Three Portraits of Painters"; Friedberg, Donald, and Marcus, *Close Up 1927–1933*.

45. Nancy Armstrong, *Fiction in the Age of Photography*.

46. Forster, *Howard's End*, 171. As Peter Brooks argues, clothing, tools, furniture, accessories—these were, for the realist, "part of the very definition of 'character,' of who one is and what one claims to be," and thus necessary for the depiction of a person. Brooks, *Realist Vision*, 16.

47. See Daston and Galison, *Objectivity*; Jay, *Downcast Eyes*; Crary, *Techniques of the Observer*; and Jacob, *The Eye's Mind*.

48. Jay, *Downcast Eyes*, 135–36. See also Sheppard, "The Problematics of European Modernism," on the demotion of the epistemic authority of visual knowledge.

49. Gillian Beer summarizes: "The authenticity of the eye's insight was put in question.... The eye itself, in Helmholtz's work, proved to be an imperfect instrument incapable of stable resolution. Far from dominating explanation or experience in this new mind-set, sight must welter in a world strung through with energy that declares itself equally as heat, light, sound." Beer, "Authentic Tidings of Invisible Things," 85. See also "Wave Theory and the Rise of Literary Modernism" in Beer, *Open Fields*, and Theodore M. Porter, "Death of the Object."

50. Russell, *The Analysis of Mind*, 5. Valéry echoed, "From the day when the enclosure of apparently rigid and inert elements had been breached—when the atom was split open displaying the energy inside—physical explanations were over, the world of *direct* experience had no more models to offer us." Valéry, cited in Crow, *Paul Valéry*, 162, my translation.

51. Conrad, *Collected Letters*, 2:94–95.

52. Conrad, 2:96.

53. See Brian Glavey's discussion of "queer ekphrasis" in Barnes, *Wallflower Avant-Garde*, chapter 2.

54. See Bal, "Over-Writing as Un-writing," for more on Albertine's descriptive elusiveness in particular.

55. See Jacob, *The Eye's Mind*, and Danius, *Senses of Modernism*, for extended discussions of this discontinuity.

56. Lessing, *Laocoön*. See Albright, *Untwisting the Serpent*, on the revival of the debate in the early twentieth century.

57. For instance, as Jonathan Foltz puts it, "film has proven a key figure through which novelists reckoned with their dissatisfaction with the narrowness of aesthetic propriety and came to credit a host of eccentric narrative modes that the dominant strain of the novel, with its commitment to psychological realism, seemed most to repudiate." Foltz, *Novel after Film*, 5.

58. Valéry, "Centenaire de la photographie," 366. All translations from this text are mine.

59. Valéry, 366. For Valéry the "purification" of language leads to two paths: one toward the expression of abstract thought, the other to the expression of poetic patterns.

60. Valéry, 371.

61. See "The Salon of 1859," in Baudelaire, *Art in Paris*, 162.

62. It is, for instance, close to André Bazin's early and influential theorization of the photographic image. For a classic critique of photography's documentary or objective status, see Krauss, "The Photographic Conditions of Surrealism."

63. *Nadja* was first published in 1928 and reissued in a revised edition with additional images in 1963. It contains forty-four illustrations, including photographs by Jacques-André Boiffard, Man Ray, and a commercial photographer, Henri Manuel. Two other novels by Breton, *Les vases communicants* (1932) and *L'amour fou* (1937), also include images.

64. Breton, *Nadja*, 5–6, my translation.

65. Rosalind Krauss calls Boiffard's images for *Nadja* "absolutely banal"; "The Photographic Conditions of Surrealism," 17. Michel Beaujour refers to their willful dullness as a "voluntary banality"; "Qu'est-ce que *Nadja*," 797. For more on photography in surrealist aesthetics, see Krauss and Livingston, *L'amour fou*.

66. Breton, who had been a medical student, wrote in the later preface that he modeled the tone of the book on that of clinical observation. *Nadja*, 6. This leads Dawn Ades to suggest that although Breton had critiqued the idea of photography as a faithful reproduction of reality elsewhere, the images in *Nadja* have a documentary function, operating as "record and verification" and guaranteeing the text from becoming a fiction. Dawn Ades, "Photography and the Surrealist Text," in Krauss and Livingston, *L'amour fou*, 161.

67. Breton, *Nadja*, trans. Howard, 151–52.

68. Breton, trans. Howard, 38.

69. Kittler, *Gramophone, Film, Typewriter*, 173. See also Foltz, *Novel after Film*, for a measured assessment of Kittler's categorical claim. I discuss the relationship between cinema and the novel more extensively in chapter 4.

70. The classic version of this critical narrative is Andreas Huyssen, *After the Great Divide*. See also McGurl, *Novel Art*, for an account of the establishment of the "art novel" in the United States.

71. Cather, *Willa Cather on Writing*, 35.

72. Cather, 36.

73. See Yeazell, *Art of the Everyday*. See also Alpers's classic study, *Art of Describing*.

74. Valéry, "Degas, Dance, Drawing," 76.

75. For a fuller history of James and Besant, see Spilka, "Henry James and Walter Besant." For Woolf and Bennett, see Hynes, "Whole Contention."

76. Besant founded the Incorporated Society of Authors in 1883, which aimed to maintain, define, and defend literary property and promote domestic and international copyright laws. Besant, *Society of Authors*, 4. In an essay on Flaubert, James alludes to a distinction between "writers" who wrote to live and those who were merely "authors." "The latter, indeed, the mere authors, simply did not exist for [Flaubert], and with Mr. Besant's Incorporated Society he would have had nothing whatever to do" (*LC* 2:303).

77. Jesse Matz makes this point with reference to James and Woolf in *Literary Impressionism and Modernist Aesthetics*, 42.

78. See Wendell, "English at Harvard University (1895)," 129, and Genung, *Practical Elements of Rhetoric*. As J. B. Fletcher and G. R. Carpenter summarize, "Description produces in the mind of the reader a picture, as it were, of certain objects or persons; Narration gives an account of an event or a series of events; Exposition explains the theory underlying a group of connected facts; Argument convinces the reader of the truth of a proposition, or propositions; and Persuasion induces the reader to adopt a certain line of action." Fletcher and Carpenter, *Introduction to Theme-Writing*, 2.

79. As Genung, the "Quintilian of Amherst," describes the late nineteenth-century composition class, it began with subjects requiring simple observation and imagination progressing to those requiring exercises in thought. See Genung, "The Study of Rhetoric in the College Course."

80. Cather herself attended the University of Nebraska and graduated in 1894 with a BA in English, so she would have been acquainted with the course of composition instruction.

81. Hamon, *Introduction à l'analyse du descriptif*, 26. The major reform took place in 1880 under Jules Ferry, who made primary education free, nonclerical, and mandatory. He also greatly reduced the influence of the clergy in universities. See Savatovsky, "French as a Discipline."

82. Austin, *Proust, Pastiche, and the Postmodern*, 10; see 9–24 for an extended discussion of Proust's schooling in relation to the writing of pastiche. See also Freed-Thall, *Spoiled Distinctions*, 40–45.

83. Gérard Genette, *Figures*, 2:26. Savatovsky notes that the hermeneutic paradigm was not really institutionalized until 1900; "French as a Discipline," 188.

84. Savatovsky, "French as a Discipline," 184. These amplifying exercises were separated into *narrative*, where a synopsis of a story would be given, and *discourse*, which involved an oratorical passage. Savatovsky understands them as a kind of translation.

85. Albalat, *La formation du style*, 87. This text went through numerous editions, and Albalat continued to write other highly popular instruction manuals into the 1930s.

86. We might compare this with something like Auerbach's practice in *Mimesis* of beginning each chapter with a long textual extract. His subsequent analysis could be considered a description of what is happening in the text. We might want to call his analysis a redescription, but my point is that every description already has the interpretive valence that we associate only with redescription.

87. Besant, *The Art of Fiction*, 17–18. On the injunction to write from experience in American literature stemming from the modernist period as well as its counterpart responses in Latin American literature, see Lawrence, *Anxieties of Experience*.

88. Besant, *The Art of Fiction*, 20.

89. Besant, 21.

90. For accounts of shifts in the meanings and practices of observation in the sci-

ences, see Patrick Singy, "Huber's Eyes," and Daston and Lunbeck, *Histories of Scientific Observation*.

91. In a moment of genre competition, Woolf argues that lyric poetry, with its delicacy and pursuit of beauty, is no longer adequate to express the complexity and ugliness of the modern condition, which requires instead the toughness of prose, unafraid to get its hands dirty, "serv[ing] the needs of business men, shopkeepers, lawyers, soldiers, peasants." (*E* 4:434). It will not escape notice that Woolf's critique of the limits of lyric poetry closely resembles the charges that critics have leveled at the kinds of novels she herself wrote, whose prose is anything but workmanlike and whose characters are rarely peasants. Nevertheless, I think it would be wrong to dismiss this statement as simply written in bad faith.

92. Scarry, *Dreaming by the Book*, 6.

93. Scarry, 6.

94. Scarry, 6.

95. See Scarry, 36–7, where she interpolates a passage from Hardy with these implicit imperatives.

96. Hardy, *Far From the Madding Crowd*, 11. Scarry cites this passage as an example of how Hardy directs us to focus our attention on a single patch on the surface of the composition, "the northern side," followed by an extensive description of the effects of a storm there. Scarry, *Dreaming by the Book*, 55.

97. Compare the image of Adam Verver with a description of Wemmick in Dickens, *Great Expectations* (163–64) that is similar in some ways: "His mouth was such a post-office of a mouth that he had a mechanical appearance of smiling. We had got to the top of Holborn Hill before I knew that it was merely a mechanical appearance, and that he was not smiling at all." I would argue that Dickens's comedic rendering of Wemmick actually undermines the strangeness of the metaphor here by acknowledging it as explicitly outlandish or unreal, in contrast to James, whose description of Adam Verver is operating more realistically, as it were, and paradoxically emerges as all the stranger for it. Compounding the strangeness is the fact that whereas Dickens tends to associate characters with particular objects (as with Wemmick and his post-office mouth), which underscores the allegorical nature of especially his physiognomic descriptions, this description of Mr. Verver is unmarked or, to use a term from chapter 3, passing. I'm grateful to David Kurnick for bring this instructive comparison to my attention.

98. I do not mean to suggest that typically realist physiognomic descriptions disappear entirely in James, or that such abstract formulations have never before appeared in literary history. I speak rather in terms of dominant trends and of distinctive features. Once again we can see that modernism inherits and intensifies the undoing of certain mimetic effects already present in realism, and of course James is usually considered a transitional figure between the two.

99. See Jameson, *The Antinomies of Realism*. He calls the temporality of affect the "eternal present." I will return to Jameson's argument about the temporality of affect and description in chapter 4.

100. Jameson, 10.

101. Often affect that eludes language is contrasted with "emotion," which can be named. See Jameson, *The Antinomies*, 29. For a helpful glossary of terms surrounding affect, including *mood* and *emotion*, see Flatley, *Affective Mapping*, 11–27.

102. Mieke Bal, *Narratology*, 27. In "Over-Writing as Un-writing," she calls it

"thoughts about particular states, objects, and individuals expressed in the subject-predicate form" (571).

103. See Latour, *Reassembling the Social*. The term *assemblage* is the English translation of *agencement*, a term used by Deleuze and Guattari in *A Thousand Plateaus*. For an attempt to more systematically theorize this concept, see DeLanda, *New Philosophy of Society*.

104. Timothy Morton, *The Ecological Thought*. Especially salient for me is Morton's emphasis on ecological thinking as that which is always spilling over; in similar fashion, the writers of my study perpetually struggle to contain and to circumscribe the relations they see in the field of experience, a struggle that expresses itself formally in a variety of ways.

105. Sedgwick, *Tendencies*, xii. See also Glavey's recent discussion of "relational formalism" in *Wallflower Avant-Garde*, under which he includes Gertrude Stein, Djuna Barnes, Frank O'Hara, and John Ashbery.

106. Christoff, *Novel Relations*, 3.

107. Christoff, 6. I am not working within a psychoanalytic framework, but my discussion of affect attunement via the developmental psychologist Daniel Stern in chapter 4 is especially resonant with Christoff's focus on the phenomenology of reading. I regret that Christoff's book came out only after the completion of my manuscript, so my engagement with it is limited.

108. Altieri, "Modernist Poetry's Encounter with Epistemic Models of Value," 335–36.

109. See Thomson, *The Seasons*. For the history of description in poetry, see E. R. Curtius, *European Literature and the Latin Middle Ages*, chapter 10, and Koelb, *Poetics of Description*. On modernist poetry's engagement with ekphrasis, see Glavey, *Wallflower Avant-Garde*.

110. Balzac, *La vieille fille* in *La comédie humaine*, 4:257, cited in Jameson, *Political Unconscious*, 155.

111. Jameson, *Political Unconscious*, 156.

112. Jameson, 156.

113. Jameson, 156–57.

114. Jameson, 157.

115. Jameson, 156.

116. Auerbach, *Mimesis*, 550.

117. Auerbach, 550. For a classic account of the changes wrought by modernity, see Berman, *All That Is Solid Melts into Air*.

118. For more on Helmholtz and modernism, see Brain, *Pulse of Modernism*, and Ryan, *Vanishing Subject*.

119. Williams, *The Long Revolution*, 287–88.

120. Williams, 288, first ellipsis in the original, second ellipsis mine. Williams does not mention Helmholtz, but I would argue his discoveries belong to what Williams refers to as "modern discoveries in perception and communication." It should be noted that Williams's vision of an authentic realism is one in which individual and society are integrated, and he did not see the authors I discuss as examples of this, although Proust comes closest.

121. Helmholtz, *Popular Lectures on Scientific Subjects*, 308–9.

122. Helmholtz effectively distinguishes here between a visual portrait, which seems

capable of substituting for the actual person and leading to knowledge in the sense of *das Kennen*, and language, which is restricted to the realm of *das Wissen*. Incidentally, French makes a similar distinction between these two senses of "to know" (*connâitre* and *savoir*) as does Spanish (*conocer* and *saber*), although English does not. For Helmholtz, this fact poses a challenge to research in the physiology of perception. "Indeed, it is just the impossibility of describing sensations, whether actual or remembered, in words, which makes it so difficult to discuss this department of psychology at all." *Popular Lectures on Scientific Subjects*, 308.

123. Lorraine Daston and Peter Galison call this desire to escape the ambiguity of ordinary language and to avoid the uncertainty of subjective experience the epistemic paradigm of "structural objectivity." See Daston and Galison, *Objectivity*, chapter 5.

124. Williams, *The Long Revolution*, 288.

125. Russell, *Human Knowledge*, 105.

126. Auerbach, *Mimesis*, 549. At the end of *Mimesis*, Auerbach singles out Woolf, along with Proust and a few others, as writers who nevertheless reach for a "synthesized cosmic view" amid the "overlapping, complementing, and contradiction." *Mimesis*, 549.

127. Jameson, *Political Unconscious*, 160.

Chapter One

1. As Ruth Ronen comments, the opposition between the two is "accepted as almost axiomatic in different theoretical contexts and at distant times" despite the difficulty of actually separating the two in textual practice. She argues that the "almost canonical description of description as non-narrative should be given up." Ronen, "Description, Narrative, and Representation," 274.

2. The example comes from Genette, *Figures of Literary Discourse*, 133-134.

3. This is the phrase of Otto Ludwig, a German novelist and dramatist whom Lukács cites. See Lukács, "Narrate or Describe?," 126.

4. Lukács, 117.

5. It is worth noting that Zola himself stressed the need to make description serve the ends of representing the environment that "completes" characters. "Description is not our goal: we want simply to complete and to determine.... We believe that man cannot be separated from his milieu, that he is completed by his clothing, his house, his town, his province." Zola, *Le roman experimental*, 228, my translation. He praises Flaubert— and to a lesser extent the Goncourt brothers—for never describing for its own sake, unlike Theophile Gautier (230-31).

6. Lukács, "Narrate or Describe?," 113-14.

7. Lukács, "The Ideology of Modernism," 1218-19, see also 1226.

8. See Hamon, "Rhetorical Status of the Descriptive," and Wall, *Prose of Things*, chapter 1.

9. Lukács, "Narrate or Describe?," 135.

10. Hamon, "Rhetorical Status of the Descriptive," 5. In a similar vein, Mieke Bal writes, "[Descriptive units] come to stand out as the *cores*, foci, or centralizing sites of fictional worlds, rather than as the *sores* of the narrative pestilence that both traditional narrative theory and rhetoric have made of them." Bal, "Over-Writing as Unwriting," 573.

11. As Michael Levenson has noted of the modernist tendency toward dualistic op-

position and radical polarities, "'Good' and 'evil' may disappear from the modernist vocabulary, but the Manichean habit remains"; *Genealogy of Modernism*, ix.

12. Lukács, "Ideology of Modernism," 1231. "The modern literary schools . . . from Naturalism to Surrealism . . . all have one feature in common. They all take reality exactly as it manifests itself to the writer and the characters he creates." Lukács, "Realism in the Balance," 36. For him the negation of outward reality is ubiquitous among modernists whether it results in lament for or exaltation of subjectivity. "In Kafka, the descriptive detail is of an extraordinary immediacy and authenticity. But Kafka's artistic ingenuity is really directed towards substituting his angst-ridden vision of the world for objective reality. The realistic detail is the expression of a ghostly un-reality, of a nightmare world, whose function is to evoke *angst*." Lukács, "Ideology of Modernism," 1222.

13. As he famously writes, "The novel is the epic of an age in which the extensive totality of life is no longer directly given, in which the immanence of meaning in life has become a problem, yet which still thinks in terms of totality." Lukács, *Theory of the Novel*, 36. For an illuminating discussion of Lukács's narrative theory alongside those of James and Auerbach, see Puckett, *Narrative Theory*, chapter 4.

14. On the modernist turn to subjective experience as the repository of truth and epistemological certainty, see Levenson, *Genealogy of Modernism*.

15. When Rancière takes issue with twentieth-century Marxist critics, he seems more often to have in mind instead Sartre. However, he does name Lukács in a critique of the overreliance on the concept of reification in political interpretations of literature. See Rancière, *Lost Thread*, xxxii–xxxiii. He also juxtaposes Lukács and Auerbach in the more recent *Les bords de la fiction*; see especially 11–13 and the section "Le moment quelconque."

16. As Davide Panagia notes in his explication of this term, it relies on the dual meaning of *partager* that refers "at once to the conditions for sharing that establish the contours of a collectivity (i.e. '*partager*' as sharing) and to the sources of disruption or dissensus of that same order (i.e. '*partager*' as separating)." Thus there is always a tension between "a specific act of perception and its implicit reliance on preconstituted objects deemed worthy of perception." Panagia, "*Partage du sensible*," 95–6. For Rancière, democratic politics occurs when certain elements of society deemed insensible—that is, unable to be sensed, noticed, or accounted for—come to challenge the governing political order. "The task of political action, therefore, is aesthetic in that it requires a reconfiguration of the conditions of sense perception so that the reigning configuration between perception and meaning is disrupted by those elements, groups or individuals in society that demand not only to exist but indeed to be perceived." Panagia, 96.

17. Rancière, *Lost Thread*, xxx.

18. Rancière, xxxi.

19. Rancière, 8.

20. Rancière, 8. See Aristotle, *Poetics*, 1451b2.

21. "The inflation of description over and against action . . . comprises the singularity of the realist novel." Rancière, *Lost Thread*, 7.

22. Barbey d'Aurevilly, *Le roman contemporain*, 103; cited in Rancière, *Lost Thread*, xxvii. Barbey's critique goes on suggestively, "No! [Flaubert] proceeds like an infant, drawn by an object to describe, *seized* by this object of frivolous [*futile*] interest, the interest of a sensation. The sensations of this book are not even selected. They are the

sensations that the most common soul receives from the most common milieu" (*Le roman contemporain*, 103).

23. Armand de Pontmartin, "Le roman bourgeois et le roman démocrate: MM. Edmond About et Gustave Flaubert," *Le correspondant*, June 25, 1857, cited in Rancière, *Lost Thread*, 10.

24. Rancière, *Lost Thread*, 6 and 17. Susan Stewart makes a similar critique of the emergence of exactness as an ideal in realism. "Exactness is a mirror, not of the world, but of the ideology of the world. And what is described exactly in the realistic novel is 'personal space,' the space of property, and the social relations that take place within that space." Stewart, *On Longing*, 5.

25. Rancière, *Lost Thread*, 17. We could add that Barthes's framework of analysis in his earlier essay, "An Introduction to the Structural Analysis of Narrative," was an explicitly Aristotelian project of understanding the relation between different parts of a narrative in relation to the whole.

26. Rancière, *Lost Thread*, 18. In Barthes's case it is articulated in a structuralist framework "that identifies literary modernity and its political impact with a purification of the narrative structure, sweeping away parasitic images of the 'real.'" Rancière, *Lost Thread*, 18.

27. In many respects this is also strikingly similar to the problem Caroline Levine points out in *Forms* when she shows the common investment of the seemingly opposed New Critics and new historicists in the form of the bounded whole. Levine, *Forms: Whole, Rhythm, Hierarchy, Network*, 24-48.

28. Rancière, *Lost Thread*, 9.

29. Rancière, xxxiii.

30. Rancière, 20.

31. See Rancière, *The Politics of Literature*, 4.

32. Rancière, 18-19. In Rancière's idiosyncratic model of "politics" in opposition to "the police" (the latter of which encompasses most of what we ordinarily mean by politics), democracy is not "a particular constitution that determines different ways of assembling people under a common authority" but the essence of politics. Insofar as democracy is a "rupture in the logic of *arche*," that is, a foundational ordering principle, especially for determining qualifications for ruling, it "is *the* institution of politics—the institution of both its subject and its mode of relating." Rancière, "Ten Theses on Politics," thesis 4.

33. Rancière, *Lost Thread*, 13.

34. Rancière, 15.

35. Rancière, 14.

36. Rancière, 10-11. "Certainly the little people have always had their place in fiction. But it was exactly the subalternate place or inferior genre in which it was permissible for them to amuse the audience by acting and talking as befits people of their kind. It is this distribution of roles that the new fiction destroys" (11-12). This tracks Auerbach's definition of realism as the "serious representation of the everyday" in *Mimesis*, where he also notes that for the first time, lower-class characters were presented not in the low genres of satire or comedy.

37. Rancière, 14. He does not mean that all individuals, objects, and sensations are equivalent but that "any one of them can trigger for any woman of the lower classes

the vertiginous acceleration that opens her to experiencing the depths of passion." Importantly, as these new "subversive demonstrations of the power of the anonymous" develop, they become separated from their agents (the lower-class characters) and on the one hand become decomposed "into a dust of impersonal sensible micro-events" and on the other hand become identified with "the impersonal power of writing." (21).

38. See Hamilton, *America's Sketchbook*, discussed briefly in Bal, "Over-Writing as Un-writing," 582–83.

39. Mitchell, *Picture Theory*, 185. Mitchell is pointing to the visual metalanguage of "windows" and "mirrors" providing "transparent access" that attends the understanding of description in these texts, which also encodes the desire for authenticity and the "unvarnished truth" (186). See also Davis and Gates, *The Slave's Narrative*.

40. For an essay that considers Rancière's ideas in a postcolonial context, see Vallury, "Incalculable Rupture."

41. Woolf, *The Waves*, cited in Rancière, "Thread of the Novel," 196. The ways in which novelists after Flaubert negotiated the relationship between the logic of the plot and the logic of the succession of things as they happen is crucial to Rancière's account of modern fiction. Although I discuss it in chapter 4, I will not be following it in detail. More recently he has proposed intriguingly that the detective novel emerges in the late nineteenth and early twentieth centuries in order to restore the fictional rationality that the realist novel was eroding. Rancière, *Les bords de la fiction*, 16.

42. Rancière, *Lost Thread*, 18.

43. "Narration recounts the past. One describes what one sees, and the spatial 'present' confers a temporal 'present' on men and objects." Lukács, "Narrate or Describe?," 130.

44. Fleissner, *Women, Compulsion, Modernity*, 32.

45. Fleissner, 50. Fleissner defends naturalism against the charge of stuckness (whose formal correlate is the preponderance of description) via an ingenious rewriting of determinism as "compulsion," which she shows actually holds the potential for creativity and change.

46. Fleissner, 9.

47. Thanks to David Kurnick for some of this phrasing. Naomi Schor points out Lukács's "implicitly phallocentric" poetics with reference to his condemnation of Flaubert's overabundance of details in rendering Emma's death in *Madame Bovary*. See Schor, *Reading in Detail*, 197–98n33. Schor draws here on Michael Danahy's critique of Lukács's identification of epic with masculinity and the novel with a woman who is a failed man such that what has been lost in the passage from epic to novel is a vigorous hero. See Michael Danahy, "Le roman est-il chose femelle?," *Poetique* 25 (1976): 85–106, cited in Schor, *Reading in Detail*, 197–98n33.

48. See Schor, *Reading in Detail*.

49. Dames, *Physiology of the Novel*, 11.

50. See Dames, chapter 1.

51. Dames, 11. Although my aim in turning to this earlier tradition is not to make a historical argument about the persistence of these earlier ideas in modernism, connections can certainly be found. Dames notably names Valéry as a late inheritor of the physiological tradition, and temporal concepts such as rhythm and speed remain central to the vorticists and futurists. *Rhythm* was the name of a short-lived magazine (1911–1913), edited by J. Middleton Murry and Katherine Mansfield, that was a major precursor

of vorticism. See Martin, *Modernism and the Rhythms of Sympathy*, for a discussion of rhythm in fiction. Nor indeed is it so clear that Lubbock, whom Dames casts as the vanquisher of physiological novel theory, excised these ideas from his own work as thoroughly as Dames suggests.

52. Dames, 11.
53. Dames, 49.
54. Dames, 33–34.
55. See Frank, *Idea of Spatial Form*.
56. Kent Puckett also notes the dissonance between two temporal aspects of narrative form: "narrative experienced immanently as a sequence of discrete events and narrative experienced only after the fact as a whole aesthetic design." Puckett, *Narrative Theory*, 136.
57. Genette, *Figures of Literary Discourse*, 134.
58. For Mieke Bal (*Narratology*, 27), since description is defined by the function of attribution, any textual fragment can be considered descriptive when this function is predominant. Although I want to widen the scope of descriptive functions, Bal's approach allows textual fragments to be considered more or less descriptive in ways amenable to my suggestions here.
59. Genette, *Narrative Discourse*, 100.
60. Genette, 100.
61. That is Bal's aim in "Over-Writing as Un-writing," 571. Her goal is to show that description is generative of narrative rather than opposed to it.
62. Genette, *Narrative Discourse*, 93–94.
63. On motivation, see Bal, *Narratology*, 27–29.
64. King, "Natural History and the Novel."
65. Jarvis, *Exquisite Masochism*, 7–8.
66. This resists a now customary association of deep attention with moral virtue propounded by critics from F. R. Leavis to Martha Nussbaum. See Dames, *Physiology of the Novel*, 16–22.
67. See Christoff, *Novel Relations*, chapter 1.
68. *Der Angriff der Gegenwart gegen die übrige Zeit* [The assault of the present on the rest of time] (1985) is the title of a film written and directed by Kluge, cited in Jameson, *The Antinomies of Realism*, 10.
69. Doty, *Art of Description*, 10.
70. Bal, "Over-Writing as Un-writing," 576. In her view, this development has occurred because "the history of the novel has privileged a certain kind of literature—say, to use an overextended term, 'realist'—whereas narratology took its initial lead from folktales" ("Over-Writing as Un-writing," 576).
71. Hamon, *Introduction à l'analyse du descriptif*, 5.
72. Moretti, *The Bourgeois*, 71.
73. Zola is another writer whose descriptions, especially in their length, are much wilder than is typically attributed to him under the rubric of naturalist objectivity and precision.
74. In his later work Barthes frequently turns to the descriptive form of the haiku as a model for a particular kind of representational ethics that he does not find in Western literature. See Barthes, *Preparation of the Novel*. See also Shirane, *The Bridge of Dreams: A Poetics of 'The Tale of Genji,'* especially chapter 9.

75. Wegner, *Imaginary Communities*, xviii. I am grateful to David Kurnick for pointing out this reference to me.

76. Wegner, xix.

77. Toral Jatin Gajarawala, "Fictional Murder," 295.

78. Gajarawala, 291.

79. Gajarawala, 293.

80. See Wolf and Bernhart, *Description in Literature*.

81. Lubbock, *The Craft of Fiction*, 69–70.

82. Lubbock, 70.

83. Thorne, *Harry Potter and the Cursed Child*.

84. Although James recorded in his notebooks in 1896 that "the *scenic* method is my absolute, my imperative, my *only* salvation" (*Notebooks*, 263), in the preface to *The Ambassadors* he acknowledges that "the finest proprieties and charms of the non-scenic may, under the right hand for them, still keep their intelligibility and assert their office" (*LC* 2:1379–80). For a brilliant account of James's relationship to drama, see Kurnick, *Empty Houses*.

85. Beaujour, "Some Paradoxes of Description," 47.

86. See Best and Marcus, "Surface Reading."

87. Best and Marcus, 9.

88. Best and Marcus, 11. See also Latour, "Why Has Critique Run Out of Steam," and Felski, *The Limits of Critique*. There have also been plenty of dissenters and robust critiques of the critique of critique. See in particular Rooney, "Live Free or Describe," and Robbins, "Not So Well Attached."

89. See Love, "Close but Not Deep."

90. Ricoeur, *Freud and Philosophy*, 26. Best and Marcus do mention Ricoeur's distinction, although their exemplary symptomatic reader is Fredric Jameson.

91. Ricoeur, 33–34.

92. See Strowick, "Comparative Epistemology of Suspicion."

93. Best, Marcus, and Love, "Building a Better Description," 3. I do, however, wholeheartedly concur with their assessment that "the strange status of description—valued in practice, but often publicly disavowed or dismissed—has made it hard to account for its full range of meanings, effects, techniques, and potentials" (3–4). My sense is that the methodological issues articulated in Best, Marcus, and Love's introduction may be more salient to disciplines other than literary criticism, as in fact the range of the special issue itself suggests.

94. Glavey, *Wallflower Avant-Garde*, 15. Glavey argues that "queer ekphrasis" provides both a model for and object of criticism that is able to move between paranoid or reparative styles (15–16). While I don't share the aspiration to make description a critical model, I do find persuasive Glavey's argument that "a more useful way of addressing the matter . . . might involve framing it not in terms of ethics . . . but in terms of pedagogy and aesthetics" (13). He writes, "Ekphrasis is not simply about seeing; it is also about showing and sharing. It is, in this sense, pedagogical. Queer ekphrasis in particular is dedicated to the proliferation of an unpredictable spectrum of relationality, multiplying ways of desiring, identifying with, attaching to, loving, imitating, envying, and sometimes ignoring works of art" (6).

95. Daston, "Description by Omission," 13.

96. See Baxandall, *Patterns of Intention*, and Alex Potts, "Disparities between Part and Whole."

97. Hamon, *Introduction à l'analyse du descriptif*, 7. See Best, Marcus, and Love, "Building a Better Description," 4–6 for a summary of the objections raised against description.

98. Best, Marcus, and Love, "Building a Better Description," list Nancy Hartsock, Donna Haraway, Mary Louise Pratt, and Bruno Latour in his early work as "among the first to expose the particularities and limits of objectivity, detachment, and distance" (4). I would add that it was also central to mid-twentieth-century philosophy of science and philosophy of history debates about whether observation (and by extension description) was inevitably "theory-laden." See Danto, *Narration and Knowledge*, and the discussion in the introduction to this book.

99. Related ideas include Gianni Vattimo's "weak thought (*il pensiero debole*)"; Gianni Vattimo and Pier Aldo Rovatti, *Weak Thought*. Paul Saint-Amour discusses modernism in light of Vattimo and Silvan Tomkins's weak theory in *Tense Future: Modernism, Total War, Encyclopedic Form*. See also Wai-Chee Dimock's use of the term with respect to genre in "Weak Theory: Henry James, Colm Tóibín, and W. B. Yeats."

100. Tomkins, *Affect, Imagery, Consciousness*, 2:433, cited in Sedgwick, *Touching Feeling*, 134.

101. Sedgwick, *Touching Feeling*, 145.

Chapter Two

1. For an extended discussion of setting, see Hannah Freed-Thall and Dora Zhang, eds. "Modernist Setting," a cluster in *Modernism/modernity Print Plus*.

2. For comparison, take the passage describing Monsieur Grandet's house in Balzac's early novel *Eugénie Grandet*: "The room, whose two windows gave on to the street, had a wooden floor. Grey, wooden paneling with antique moulding lined the walls from top to bottom. The ceiling consisted of exposed beams, also painted grey, the spaces between them being filled with a yellowing mixture of whitewash and sand. An old copper clock, inlaid with tortoiseshell arabesques, adorned the white, badly carved, stone chimneypiece.... In each corner of the room stood a corner cupboard, a kind of side board with grimy shelves above. An old marquetry card-table, whose top was used as a chess-board top, was placed in the space between the two windows." *Eugénie Grandet*, 17–18.

3. Levenson, *Modernism and the Fate of Individuality*, 27. Similarly, Bill Brown remarks how little the eponymous spoils of Poynton actually appear in the descriptive register of *The Spoils of Poynton* such that the mise-en-scène is "a matter of aura, not artifacts." Brown, *Sense of Things*, 147.

4. Kurnick, *Empty Houses*, 129, my emphases. Michael Irwin also observes the absence of precise physiognomic descriptions in James compared with Dickens or Hardy. Irwin, *Picturing*, 41.

5. The examples from *The Other House* and *The Awkward Age* are cited in Kurnick, *Empty Houses*, 129. Kurnick reads the fogginess of these descriptions as conveying the sense of being a preliminary or incomplete version of itself leading to the experience of "reading a play—one that has not yet been cast with the actors who will give these names bodily density."

6. Scott, *Biographical Memoirs of Eminent Novelists*, 1:379. Scott compares Radcliffe to her contemporary Mrs. Charlotte Smith, "whose sketches are so very graphical, that an artist would find little difficulty in actually painting from them" (*Biographical Memoirs of Eminent Novelists*, 1:379). Lewis discusses a related passage in *Air's Appearance*, 193. In *What We See When We Read*, the graphic designer and now novelist Peter Mendelsund shows the inadequacy of this logic by literalizing it when he makes a police sketch of Anna Karenina.

7. Scarry, *Dreaming by the Book*, 37; Kurnick, *Empty Houses*, 128.

8. That the air is "upper" and "finer" here serves to sanction on aesthetic grounds, if not to purify on moral ones, the adulterous nature of the events that are taking place. See McGurl, *Novel Art*, for the importance of dimensionality in signifying social distinctions, which James recodes as intellectual distinctions.

9. These were developed influentially by Hippocrates in *Waters, Airs, and Places* (400 BCE). The Hippocratic model remained influential in eighteenth-century ideas about climates. Lewis, *Air's Appearance*, 27. So, for instance, Densher is changed by his cosmopolitan upbringing: "But brave enough though his descent to English earth, he had passed, by the way, through zones of air that had left their ruffle on his wings—he had been exposed to initiations indelible" (*WD* 67).

10. According to Lewis, the concept of literary atmosphere emerged over the long eighteenth century interdependently with studies of the physical atmosphere in natural philosophy. During this period, the visual medium of writing "openly aspired to the ubiquity, liberty, and commonality of air" while also absorbing many of the occult powers attributed to it. Lewis, *Air's Appearance*, 1. Leaping forward, we could track how the intertwining of writing and the air—that double figure of ephemerality and evanescence—develops in modernism in the mysterious letters traced by the airplane in *Mrs. Dalloway*, now in the service of advertising.

11. See Lewis, *Air's Appearance*, 9–11; Castle, "The Female Thermometer"; and Pizzo, "Atmospheric Exceptionalism in *Jane Eyre*."

12. As Lorraine Daston writes, "If modern facts have an incarnation, it is as rocks: hard, jagged, plain rocks—the kind you might hurl at a window or stub your toe against." Daston, "Hard Facts," 680.

13. Although I do not focus on forms of media or technology in James, there are interesting resonances between my discussion of atmospheres as influential environments and contemporary work in environmental media. See, for instance, John Durham Peters, *The Marvelous Clouds: Towards a Philosophy of Elemental Media* (Chicago: University of Chicago Press, 2015), which considers media as environments and vice versa. I'm grateful to Paul Saint-Amour for bringing this connection to my attention.

14. Evans, "Relating in Henry James," 2. Evans discusses Jamesian relations in light of Latourian actor-network theory.

15. Simmel, *Essays on Sociology*, 327.

16. See Leo Spitzer's classic essay "Milieu and Ambiance."

17. Böhme, "Atmosphere as the Fundamental Concept," 114. For a discussion of atmosphere in a social and political rather than aesthetic context, see my "Notes on Atmosphere."

18. Böhme, 114.

19. For ecocritical approaches, see, among others, Menely, "Anthropocene Air," and Taylor, *Sky of Our Manufacture*. On Dickens and smog in mid-nineteenth-century Lon-

don, see Yeats, "Dirty Air." On differentially distributed olfactory atmospheres in naturalism, see Hsu, "Naturalist Smellscapes and Environmental Justice."

20. Joseph Conrad, *The Nigger of the "Narcissus,"* 14. In that same preface, Conrad describes art as an appeal of "one temperament to all the other innumerable temperaments whose subtle and resistless power endows passing events with their true meaning, and creates the moral, the emotional atmosphere of the place and time" (13).

21. See Matz's *Literary Impressionism and the Modernist Aesthetics* for a discussion of both Conrad and James in this context. Matz argues persuasively that contrary to popular belief, writerly and painterly forms of impressionism are actually antonyms. I am here observing a similarity in subject matter only, not technique or underlying philosophy. As Matz notes, "impression" hovers in the borderlands between sense and intellect, unable to be reduced to or fully captured by either; in this respect it shares something with atmosphere. However, whereas impression is for Matz a "mercurial metaphor for perception" (18), I take the air and the atmosphere as the *site* of perceptual attention in James, a fertile place where impressions are received and information circulated.

22. Conrad, *Heart of Darkness*, 3.

23. Justine Pizzo argues that Dickens's use of ether in *Bleak House* differs from the examples here. "Dickens's atmospheric representation discloses the perceived corporeal and mental unpredictability of a realistic female body rather than the questionable materiality of an apparition." Pizzo, "Esther's Ether," 82.

24. Conrad, *Heart of Darkness*, 44. This veiling effect extends beyond the visual field to speech and sound, most famously in the ambush scene in *Heart of Darkness*, when the thick fog provides both visual and sonic cover for the arrows attacking Marlow's boat. For a related discussion to the one here but focusing on sound, see Napolin, "'A Sinister Resonance.'"

25. Anna Jones Abramson argues that unlike many Victorian novels in which the resolution of the plot is akin to the lifting of the fog, in Conrad the fog does not clear even when it lifts. See Abramson, "Joseph Conrad's Atmospheric Modernism."

26. A comparable moment of self-conscious foreshadowing via the pathetic fallacy happens in the climatic confrontation between Charlotte and Maggie toward the end of *The Golden Bowl* when Maggie tries to make small talk by saying, "The air's heavy as if with thunder—I think there'll be a storm" (GB 493). See Brooks, *Melodramatic Imagination*.

27. I take inspiration from Teresa Brennan's question, "is there anyone who has not, at least once, walked into a room and felt the 'atmosphere'?" Brennan, *The Transmission of Affect*, 1.

28. She also feels an atmospheric apprehension of being on the brink of a "crisis," which she reports to the Prince when she asks him to secure a chance for her to talk with Fanny Assingham. "She had already accepted her consciousness, as we have already noted, that a crisis for them all was in the air" (GB 217). She wants Mrs. Assingham to see her and the Prince together at the party alone and to "square" their appearing together without the Ververs with her, which is to say she also senses in the air the potential appearance of impropriety.

29. Cameron, *Thinking in Henry James*, 97. This is in particular with respect to the second half of *The Golden Bowl*, where thought displaces speech as the "medium in which meaning is made audible" while speech becomes "the medium in which it is blocked" (96).

30. For more on modernist dialogue, see Alsop, *Making Conversation in Modernist Fiction*.

31. Georg Simmel, *Essays on Sociology*, 326–27.

32. Simmel, 326 and 327. Presaging Raymond Williams's notion of "structures of feeling," Simmel observes that these minor processes are difficult for sociology to study because "as a rule they are not yet fixated as rigid, superindividual structures, but exhibit society, as it were, *statu nascendi*" (327).

33. Simmel, 327–28. These relations "are the actual occurrences that are concatenated or hypostatized into those macrocosmic, solid units and systems" (327).

34. Simmel, 327.

35. This structure anticipates in miniature what Willa Cather, a careful reader of James, claimed she wanted to do on a larger scale with the middle section of *The Professor's House* (1925), the first novel she wrote after "The Novel Démeublé." "Tom Outland's Story" is marked off within the novel, which is otherwise set in a bourgeois midwestern household, and Cather envisioned this section as a window opening from Godfrey St. Peter's stuffy house onto the open cliffs of New Mexico, infusing the novel with a breath of air. See Cather, "On *The Professor's House*," in *Willa Cather on Writing*, 31–32.

36. For instance, in another atmospheric context, when Maggie first begins to suspect her husband's infidelity as she awaits his return from Matcham, she sits, growing confused "in the thick air that had begun more and more to hang, for our young woman, over her accumulations of the unanswered." These unanswered questions "were like a roomful of confused objects, never as yet 'sorted,' which for some time now she had been passing and re-passing, along the corridor of her life" (*GB* 334). After an extended discussion of this figurative corridor and room, the passage culminates in "the final sharp extinction of the inward scene by the outward. The quite different door had opened and her husband was there" (*GB* 335).

37. I am of course alluding to William James's later philosophy of radical empiricism, which is characterized by a rejection of any substantial distinction between subject and object in favor of his theory of "pure experience," bits of which occupy positions that we call subjective or objective in particular situations but which could change. For William, the relations that connect experiences are not secondary connective tissue between two more important terms but objects of knowledge and parts of experience no less than what they connect. See James, *Essays on Radical Empiricism* and *The Meaning of Truth*. For a discussion of the radical empiricism of both James brothers, see Grimstad, *Experience and Experimental Writing*, and David Lapoujade, *Fictions du pragmatisme*. Lapoujade notes the importance of nineteenth-century developments of postal and rail networks for both James's thinking about relationality. We could add that the widespread installation of public utilities (gas, electricity, and water) in the latter half of the nineteenth century in metropolises all over Western Europe and the United States formed another important way in which they were "networked" and "related." See Schivelbusch, *Disenchanted Night*.

38. Gillian Beer argues something similar about the interludes in Woolf's *The Waves*. She reads them as part of Woolf's growing interest in physics, which led to her sense that what was "real" was different from what was substantial. See Beer, "Physics, Sound, and Substance." Elsewhere Beer shows that in the wake of developments in the empirical sciences in the nineteenth century, a number of scientists were also seeking different

means of describing more accurately natural phenomena—waves, molecules, electrical currents—that were neither visible nor substantial and were unlike anything known in ordinary experience. Gillian Beer traces the efforts of Maxwell, Tyndall, and Eddington in this regard, noting the shared problems of literary and scientific description. See "Problems of Description in the Language of Discovery," in Beer, *Open Fields*, 173–95.

39. So keen is Maggie's perception in particular that in her vigilance of her husband after she begins to suspect his affair, "It would be a question but of the most trivial act of surrender, the vibration of a nerve, the mere movement of a muscle. . . . She knew more and more—every lapsing minute taught her—how he might by a single rightness make her cease to watch him" (*GB* 366). Lambert Strether would be an exception to the otherwise female cast of sensitive feelers, although in a way, *The Ambassadors* is an entire novel about Strether's inability to read a room, where his assumption of his own interactional competence is shown to be wrong.

40. See Castle, "The Female Thermometer."

41. Recalling Henry James Sr.'s Swedenborgianism, Joan Richardson calls Jamesian epistemology closer to revelation in *A Natural History of Pragmatism*, 145. Sharon Cameron has suggested it is akin to "mind reading" in *Thinking in Henry James*, 96.

42. Dorothy Richardson, *Pilgrimage*, 3:257. In a 1938 foreword, Richardson singles out James as a "pathfinder" for her artistic project (*Pilgrimage*, 1:11).

43. I owe this phrasing to Michael Lucey. For a related discussion of this subject in the context of the late nineteenth century's professionalization of taste and aesthetic judgment, see Freedman, *Professions of Taste*.

44. For a comprehensive account of the ways in which this occurs, see McGurl, *Novel Art*.

45. Goble, *Beautiful Circuits*, 20.

46. With regard to ideas about mediumship and telepathy, in which air figured so centrally, the boundaries between occult pseudosciences and "proper" science around the turn of the twentieth century were not so clear. See Enns and Trower, *Vibratory Modernism*. See also the fascinating catalog of telepathy and visual representation in Rousseau, *Cosa Mentale*.

47. The history of the ether is of course a long one, stretching back to classical antiquity. For a history, see Cantor and Hodge, *Conceptions of the Ether*. For futurists like Boccioni, the atmosphere was synonymous with the ether, which underpinned "the electric theory of matter" where matter was energy. He states in his 1911 Circolo Artistico lecture, "solid bodies are only atmosphere condensed"; Boccioni, "Futurist Painting," cited in Henderson, "Vibratory Modernism, 135.

48. See Enns and Trower, *Vibratory Modernism*; Clarke and Henderson, *From Energy to Information*; Steven Connor on "nebular modernism" in *Matter of Air*, 183; and Jesse Oak Taylor on "climactic modernism" in *Sky of Our Manufacture*, chapter 8.

49. Enns and Trower, *Vibratory Modernism*, 2.

50. Steven Connor remarks of Tyndall that his writings were "one of the most important conduits of scientific ideas into literary and artistic life" (*Matter of Air*, 190). Tyndall was also an important influence on William James. See Richardson, *Natural History of Pragmatism*, 128–29. For more on Tyndall's influence on late nineteenth- and early twentieth-century British writers, see Beer, *Open Fields*.

51. Although James's review is of Tyndall's mountaineering memoir, in it he alludes to an image comparing the mind to a photographic plate, which was employed by Tyn-

dall in his earlier essay collection, *Fragments of Science for Unscientific People*, suggesting he knew of this book. That enormously popular essay collection contains the work on ether cited later in this paragraph.

52. Tyndall, 4.

53. Tyndall, 178. He writes similarly in the opening essay "Men's minds, indeed, rose to a conception of the celestial and universal atmosphere through the study of the terrestrial and local one. From the phenomena of sound as displayed in the air, they ascended to the phenomena of light as displayed in the *aether*; which is the name given to the interstellar medium" (9–10).

54. Tyndall, 140. For similar ideas expressed by Herbert Spencer and others, see Connor, *Matter of Air*, 150–74; Clarke and Henderson, *From Energy to Information*; Enns and Trower, *Vibratory Modernism*.

55. Michael Levenson notes that James wrote to Hugh Walpole not long after finishing *The Ambassadors* that it is "a picture of relations." Levenson comments, "'relation,' as it stands, bestows no content on any human tie; it escapes the definition of love, envy, respect or loathing, and allows James to arrange his characters as though they were colors and masses in a pictorial composition." Levenson, *Modernism and the Fate of Individuality*, 29. Evoking Mallarmé's description of himself as a *syntaxier*, implying that "relations between words matter more than words themselves," Maud Ellmann writes, "James could be described as a syntaxer of love, whose sexual combinations are determined by a grammar of relations, rather than by any personal endowments of the characters." Ellmann, *Nets of Modernism*, 37.

56. Virginia Woolf, *Roger Fry*, 273–74.

57. T. S. Eliot, "On Henry James," 110.

58. Eliot, 110.

59. James, *The Ambassadors*, 173.

60. Although I focus here on relations within an immediate proximate environment, in a more global sense of atmosphere, the weather has also long been a way to imagine relations across distances. See Favret's argument that as a result of developments in meteorology and modern warfare in the late eighteenth and early nineteenth centuries, "scientists and poets together produced a *georgics* of the sky, fusing the *work* of war and that of weather to highlight questions of mediation, especially between bodies and events at great removes from each other." Favret, "War in the Air," 533.

61. Conrad, *Heart of Darkness*, 1.

62. Conrad, 38. In a later letter to Edward Garnett in 1902, Conrad thanks the latter for his "brave attempt to grapple with the foggishness of H of D." Conrad, *Collected Letters*, 2:467–68.

63. Taylor, *Sky of Our Manufacture*, 171.

64. Taylor, 172 and 173.

65. Connor, *Matter of Air*, 38. Connor uses this phrase to draw a contrast with a new sense in the nineteenth century that the air was no longer a vacancy or "the privileged bearer of the idea of the open" but something that was increasingly becoming crowded and contaminated (37).

66. Taylor, 8.

67. See, for instance, Frank, *Literary Architecture*. Anna Kornbluh offers an alternative reading of James's interest in architecture, one that resonates in a number of ways with my reading although in a more Marxian framework, in "The Realist Blueprint."

68. As Böhme observes, architecture shapes "the character of the space in which we find ourselves," but this is something we sense only by being physically present *in* a space, not merely by seeing it. Böhme, "Atmosphere as the Subject Matter of Architecture," 402. This is why architecture is an apt figure for what exceeds the visual.

69. See Lefebvre, *The Production of Space*, trans. Donald Nicholson-Smith (Cambridge, MA: Blackwell, 1991), and Bachelard, *The Poetics of Space*, trans. Maria Jolas (New York: Penguin, 1994). I do not mean to equate Lefebvre's materialist and Bachelard's phenomenological approaches but merely to highlight their shared emphasis on space considered in terms of relations.

70. Michel Foucault, "Of Other Spaces," 23–24. Whereas utopias are "sites with no real place," what Foucault calls "heterotopias" are "counter-sites, a kind of effectively enacted utopia in which the real sites, all the other real sites that can be found within the culture, are simultaneously represented, contested, and inverted" (24).

71. As Kornbluh writes of James's architectural invocations, "to comprehend sociality in all its treachery and banality is to experience architecture." Kornbluh, "The Realist Blueprint," 200.

72. Bill Brown, *Sense of Things*, 167.

73. On the objectification and commodification of people in James, see Agnew, "Consuming Vision of Henry James."

74. Brown writes, "Whereas Lukács understood the commercialization of fiction—the complete transformation of the book into a commodity and the writer 'into a salesman of his merchandise'—as the reason for the triumph of description in the novel, James posits commercialization as the reason for its absence," suggesting that "the novel registers the effects of reification that accompany the ubiquity of the commodity form: that it conceals above all the immediate—qualitative and material—of things as things." Brown, *Sense of Things*, 154.

75. I am grateful to Mark McGurl for posing this question.

76. Simmel, *Essays on Sociology*, 315.

77. Simmel, 317.

78. Simmel, *On Individuality and Social Forms*, 127.

79. This is the meaning of his famous statement, "Every definite image in the mind is steeped and dyed in the free water that flows round it. With it goes the sense of its relations, near and remote, the dying echo of whence it came to us, the dawning sense of whither it is to lead. The significance, the value, of the image is all in this halo or penumbra that surrounds and escorts it,—or rather that is fused into one with it and has become bone of its bone and flesh of its flesh; leaving it, it is true, an image of the same thing it was before, but making it an image of that thing newly taken and freshly understood." (*PP* 1:255).

80. Thus, the symbol leaves an absence that is filled as soon as it is asserted. See, for instance, Eve Kosofsky Sedgwick's queer reading of "The Beast in the Jungle" in *Epistemology of the Closet*. Brad Evans observes a similar gesture in Robert Pippin's quite different moral philosophical reading of James. See Evans, "Relating in Henry James," 3.

81. In theorizing social forms, Simmel himself turns to geometry as an analogy. See, for instance, *On Individuality and Social Forms*, 26. See also Leo Bersani's discussion of James's social geometry in "The Jamesian Lie," 53–79.

82. Kornbluh, "The Realist Blueprint," 201–2. Kornbluh's point is that architecture—

both as a medium and as a metaphorics in James—is not about representation of what is already there but instead about "productions of unindexable social space" (202).

83. This is especially true for phenomenological thinkers such as Susanne Langer and Mikel Dufrenne, both of whom are discussed by Sianne Ngai in her chapter on "tone" in *Ugly Feelings*.

84. Simmel, "Philosophy of Landscape," 26; "Philosophie der Landschaft," 149. He also writes, "We say that a landscape arises when a range of natural phenomena spread over the surface of the earth is comprehended by a particular kind of unity . . . the most important carrier of this unity may be the 'mood' [*Stimmung*], as we call it, of a landscape" ("Philosophy of Landscape," 26). On *Stimmung* and literature, see Gumbrecht, *Atmosphere, Mood, Stimmung*.

85. Ezra Pound, "I Gather the Limbs of Osiris (I-II)," *New Age* 10, no. 6 (1911): 130-31, cited in Natalia Cecire, *Experimental: American Literature and the Aesthetics of Knowledge*, 51. Cecire calls the desire to comprehend the whole in the fragment the epistemic virtue of the "flash," one that is valorized by experimental writing and which she discusses in light of various fin-de-siècle attempts to represent and account for the social body. See Cecire, *Experimental*, chapter 2.

86. Rancière, *Lost Thread*, 29.

Chapter Three

1. Edme-François Mallet and Louis Jaucourt, "Description," in Diderot and d'Alembert, *Encyclopédie*, 4:878, my translation.

2. *SLT* 6:284, *RTP* 4:463-64. I have silently modified the translations in *SLT* at a number of points, sometimes considerably.

3. On the common opposition between surface and depth during this period, see Schwartz, *Matrix of Modernism*. Importantly, Schwartz points out that this topology persists even when the meaning of the terms differs; for example, for Bergson, depth means immediate intuitive sensation, whereas for Nietzsche, it is a matter of imposing a different set of concepts.

4. Hayden White, "Narrative, Description, and Tropology in Proust," in *Figural Realism*, 126-46, 129. See also Eve Kosofsky Sedgwick's discussion of the fountain at the opening of *The Weather in Proust*, 1-3.

5. Genette, *Narrative Discourse*, 100. Accordingly, Genette states that Proust is in fact not a lavishly descriptive writer at all and that his reputation for being one is due to the prominence of these isolated ekphrastic excerpts in anthologies used in French schools (*Narrative Discourse*, 99).

6. Genette, 100.

7. This is especially true for defenders of naturalist writers, for instance, J. H. Matthews, "The Art of Description in Zola's *Germinal*," and Susan Harrow, "Exposing the Imperial Cultural Fabric." For a brilliant reading of description in American naturalism, see Fleissner, *Women, Compulsion, Modernity*.

8. Genette, *Narrative Discourse*, 102.

9. This is exacerbated by the assumed binary of narrate/describe.

10. As Christie McDonald writes in a related discussion of the principle of "association" in Proust, "Association is a mode of thinking that functions by deviation and

digression[,] ... a process of learning to comprehend the self and the world based upon the repetition of events inscribed through memory and association from the very first pages of the book." McDonald, *Proustian Fabric*, 6.

11. See Ullman, *Image in the Modern French Novel*, for a fuller list and observations about each field.

12. In *Du côté de chez Swann* alone, Ullmann counts well over 750 metaphorical or analogical images, an average of nearly three every two pages. Ullman, *Image in the Modern French Novel*, 129.

13. Ullmann counts roughly seven examples every four pages in the "Combray" and "Nom de pays: Le nom" sections of *Swann's Way*, but only one per page in "Un Amour de Swann," which he attributes to the fact that Swann's story is told from a third-person perspective, whereas the first and last sections are narrated by the narrator in the first person. Ullman, *Image in the Modern French Novel*, 129. My further hunch is that with regard to the novel as a whole, analogies are particularly concentrated in the early volumes and then again in the final one, with certain fields appearing with greater frequency at different moments. As the novel proceeds, for instance, there is an increase in the number of comparisons to actual artworks, suggesting that as the narrator acquires greater knowledge about painting, music, and literature, he increasingly turns to them as means of assimilating and comprehending the world he observes around him (a characteristic shared by certain other characters, such as Mme de Guermantes and especially Swann).

14. See Luckhurst, *Science and Structure*, 134.

15. Proust, *Correspondance*, 21:652, cited in Luckhurst, *Science and Structure*, 134, my translation.

16. See Genette, *Figures*, 3:41–63, 1:39–67, and De Man, *Allegories of Reading*. This debate follows Roman Jakobson's distinction between the metaphoric and metonymic poles of language, operating on principles of resemblance and contiguity, respectively. Jakobson identifies metaphor with poetry and metonymy with prose. See "Two Aspects of Language and Two Types of Aphasic Disturbances," 90–96. As recent commentators have pointed out, however, it seems clear that both elements coexist. See Landy, *Philosophy as Fiction*, and Kristeva, *Time and Sense*.

17. "Metaphor is the transference of a name from the object to which it has a natural application; this transference can take place from genus to species or species to genus or from species to species or by analogy." Aristotle, *Poetics*, 1457b18-21. Sometimes there is no standard name for the analogous relation (to scatter seeds is to sow, but the scattering of the sun's rays has no name), but nevertheless the related elements will be spoken of by analogy.

18. Aristotle, *Poetics*, 1457b18-22. For Aristotle, the distinction between what we now call *simile* and *metaphor* is not sharply drawn. In the *Poetics* he calls metaphor simply an abbreviated simile, but the former term remains the more dominant and broader term encompassing a range of comparative thinking in the *Rhetoric*. For an extended discussion, see Ricoeur, *Rule of Metaphor*. In French the word for simile is *comparaison*, which can also refer broadly to metaphor, simile, analogy, and parallel. In the French rhetorical tradition, simile is rarely considered to be an autonomous figure separate from metaphor, and it is usually considered an inferior one. See Michel, "Introduction."

19. I adopt this basic definition from Griffiths, *Age of Analogy*, 28. Relatedly, analogy

is of course also a form of logical reasoning. The cognitive scientists Douglas Hofstadter and Emanuel Sander propose it is central to all conceptualization in *Surfaces and Essences*.

20. Reino Virtanen notes that Balzac used scientific metaphors as frequently, but whereas he makes "substantive" comparisons, for example, the will to physical energy, or magnetism to hypnotism, Proust's analogies tend rather to be "formal." See Virtanen, "Proust's Metaphors," 1057. See also Nicola Luckhurst, *Science and Structure*, and Stephen Ullmann, *Image in the Modern French Novel*.

21. As Aristotle writes, "I mean by transference by analogy the situation that occurs whenever a second element is related to a first as a fourth is to a third." *Poetics*, 1457b31–33. For example, evening is to day as old age is to life; or, a cup is related to Dionyus as a shield is to Ares. "The poet will, therefore, speak of the cup as the shield of Dionysus and the shield as the cup of Ares." *Poetics*, 1457b38–39. In the *Topics*, he comments in a similar vein: "As for similarity, this should be examined, first, in the case of things in different genera: as the one is to the one, so the other is to the other (e.g., as knowledge is to the known, so is perception to the perceptible); and, as one thing is in one, so is another in another (e.g., as sight is in the eye, so intelligence is in the soul, or as a calm is in the sea, so is a stillness in the air)." *Topics*, 108a 6–11.

22. Barthes calls "inversion [*le renversement*]," with homosexuality as its paradigm, a Proustian law and principle of cognition, one with surprise as its ethos. "Une idée de recherche," 38. See also note 45 on p. 202, below.

23. See Griffiths, *Age of Analogy*, 33, and Hesse, *Models and Analogies in Science*.

24. Although the entomologist Jean-Henri Fabre is cited here, the more likely source is Élie Metchnikoff's *Études sur la nature humaine*, which Proust mentions in his correspondence. See *RTP*, 1:1159.

25. As Christie McDonald writes in a related discussion of associations in Proust, "The beauty of what [associations] convey, as Proust says of Giotto, is not so much the ideas but a *feeling of form*." McDonald, *Proustian Fabric*, 16.

26. Walter Benjamin, "On the Image of Proust," in Benjamin, *Selected Writings*, vol. 2, pt. 1. He develops this further in the short piece "On the Mimetic Faculty" in *Selected Writings*, vol. 2, pt. 2.

27. Benjamin, "On the Mimetic Faculty," in Benjamin, *Selected Writings*, vol. 2, pt. 2, 722. It is worth noting that an astral analogy appears in *Within a Budding Grove* when the narrator dines at Rivebelle. The tables that fill the restaurant appear to him "like so many planets, as the latter are represented in old allegorical pictures" (*SLT* 2:532, *RTP* 2:168). The parallel is developed and sustained throughout the scene as the diners at each table seem drawn by an irresistible force to have eyes only for the other tables while waiters circulate around "the harmony of these astral tables" in dizzying revolutions. All of this leads the narrator to pity those who "had not cut through things in such a way as to clear their habitual appearances and enable us to perceive analogies" (*SLT* 2:533, *RTP* 2:168). The analogical nature of the narrator's perception is thus not only a feature of his conscious search for general laws but also how he perceives when he is less possessed of his wits, as here, when he is a little tipsy.

28. Benjamin, "Doctrine of the Similar," in Benjamin, *Selected Writings*, vol. 2, pt. 2, 694. For Benjamin the perception of similarity is a mode of reading closely linked to language: "Language may be seen as the highest level of mimetic behavior and the most complete archive of nonsensuous similarity: a medium into which the earlier powers

of mimetic production and comprehension have passed without residue, to the point where they have liquidated those of magic." Benjamin, "On the Mimetic Faculty," in Benjamin, *Selected Writings*, vol. 2, pt. 2, 722.

29. See Buck-Morss, "Aesthetics and Anaesthetics." I adopt here the gloss of Buck-Morss discussed in Jonathan Flatley with respect to Warhol's practices of liking. See Flatley, *Like Andy Warhol*, 18–20.

30. I am alluding to Sedgwick's idea of reparative modes of reading, which are oriented toward aesthetic pleasure and are "frankly ameliorative." See "Paranoid Reading and Reparative Reading, or, You're so Paranoid, You Probably Think This Essay Is about You" in Sedgwick, *Touching Feeling*, 144. In this essay Sedgwick names Proust as an example of a reparative orientation.

31. Silverman, *Flesh of My Flesh*, 2.

32. Joan Richardson notes the influence of reading *Heaven and Hell* on Henry James Sr. and the entire James family, writing that both William and Henry Jr. "loosened Swedenborg's cosmology from its theological moorings." Richardson, *Natural History of Pragmatism*, 139.

33. See Silverman, *Flesh of My Flesh*. See also Griffiths, *Age of Analogy*, which traces the nineteenth-century combination of previously separate ideas of comparison and analogy into a new way of thinking about the past that he calls "comparative historicism."

34. Proust makes several appearances in Silverman's book, although he is not discussed at length. See especially *Flesh of My Flesh*, 9–10.

35. Kachler, "L'analogie des symbolistes," 251. This danger was posed not only in the realm of literature and language but also with regard to social organization (251).

36. Kachler, 252.

37. On the penchant for generating similarities, however, it is worth noting the famous closing lines of the opening poem, "To the Reader," in *The Flowers of Evil*: "hypocrite reader—my like—my brother! [—*hypocrite lecteur,—mon semblable,—mon frère!*]." Baudelaire, *Les fleurs du mal*, 6 and 84, translation modified.

38. See Charles Baudelaire, "Réflexions sur quelques-uns de mes contemporains, Victor Hugo," in Baudelaire, *Oeuvres complètes*, 2:129–41, and Kachler, "L'analogie des symbolistes," 252–55. Kachler notes that Baudelaire, leaning on Fourier and Swedenborg, adopts the idea of a "universal analogy." In Kachler's schema, correspondence and analogy refer back to one another without being entirely synonymous—correspondence implies the idea of *accord* whereas analogy insists on *relation*, or "the dissimilarity at the heart of similarity" (253).

39. Silverman, *Flesh of My Flesh*, 1–2.

40. Eve Kosofsky Sedgwick also discusses the relief that can come from momentarily escaping the "omnipotence plot" in Proust, the toxic "all-or-nothing understanding of agency." Sedgwick, *The Weather in Proust*, 20. See also Christoff's discussion of moments of respite in the context of Hardy's doomed plots in chapter 1 of *Novel Relations*.

41. Flatley, *Like Andy Warhol*, 5.

42. As Kaja Silverman writes of Gerhard Richter's work in her book on analogy, the balance of similarity and difference can vary across works, "but regardless of the form they take, these couplings neutralize the two principles by means of which we are accustomed to think: identity and antithesis." Silverman, *Flesh of My Flesh*, 173.

43. Flatley, *Like Andy Warhol*, 6. Although I am more focused on *likening* than *liking*,

I have learned a great deal from Flatley's theorization of this group of concepts. See also Moon, *A Small Boy and Others*.

44. Flatley, *Like Andy Warhol*, 5.

45. On sexuality in Proust, see, among others, Sedgwick, *Epistemology of the Closet*; Michael Lucey, *Never Say I*; and Ladenson, *Proust's Lesbianism*. Importantly, Ladenson points out that in the novel, lesbianism, unlike male homosexuality, is organized around a desire for likeness rather than being subject to a logic of inversion that reinstates the male-female gender binary.

46. Flatley, *Like Andy Warhol*, 44. I am also grateful to Dan Blanton for his phrasing of some of these ideas, some of which has been woven into this paragraph.

47. In these condemnations of observation, Proust may also have had in mind Zola's call for the writer to model himself on the physician and the chemist and to "replace novels of pure imagination with novels of observation and experimentation." Zola, *Le roman experimental*, 17, my translation.

48. Proust first wrote a pastiche of the Goncourts' style in 1908, and the one included in *Time Regained* is directed mostly at the last volumes of the *Journal*, those covering 1878-1895 and written by Edmond de Goncourt alone after the death of his brother Jules. See Milly, "Le pastiche Goncourt," 826. Milly also argues that contrary to the common idea that Proust wrote the pastiche after he was awarded the Goncourt Prize in 1919, it was most likely drafted at least a year earlier (816).

49. "The only true voyage, the only bath in the fountain of youth, would not be to visit other lands but to possess other eyes, to see the world with the eyes of another" (*SLT* 5:343, *RTP* 3:762).

50. See Milly, "Le pastiche Goncourt," 828-30, for a list of principle traits highlighted by Proust.

51. What Mayor and Kilmartin translate as a "Chinese" plate is in the original a "Tching hon" plate, which the Pléiade editors note refers not to an emperor (presumably during the Qing dynasty) but to a particularly obscure type of ceramic. This whole gastronomic scene refers especially to the volume titled *La maison d'un artiste*, where Goncourt describes the meals he and his brother served in their dining room on rue Saint-Georges. See *RTP* 4:1193n1 and n3.

52. Milly, "Le pastiche Goncourt," 830. All translations from this text are mine.

53. See Milly, 831, for the reading that it is a cautionary tale about the perils of aestheticism as represented by the Goncourts and by Ruskin. He adds that it is a real "temptation" because Proust shares this orientation and that "it is necessary to underline this kinship, even if he ultimately rejects it" (828).

54. Freed-Thall, *Spoiled Distinctions*, 41. Paul Aron also emphasizes the intimacy entailed by the pastiche form itself, which incorporates the words of another within the body of one's own text. Aron, *Histoire du pastiche*, 232.

55. A common interpretation of Proust's pastiches (of Balzac, Flaubert, Chateaubriand, Maeterlinck, and Saint-Beuve, among many others)—published in two early collections, *Pastiches et mélanges* (1919) and *L'affaire Lemoine* (1919)—is that they were exercises he wrote in order to rid himself of influences. See Austin, *Proust, Pastiche, and the Postmodern*, 50-52, for a summary of critical responses. In *Spoiled Distinctions*, Freed-Thall argues convincingly contra this standard view that Proust wrote pastiches rather to "multiply his connections and attachments" (27). So "the occasion of narrative redoubling" in the Goncourt excerpt "reveals Proust's love of per-

spectival variety, and interest in the invigorating multiplicity of the perceptual world" (44).

56. In a different take on this passage, Michael Lucey reads the narrator's interest in the manner of speech rather than what is said as suggesting Proust's interest in "language-in-use," that is, with reference to the "social indexicality" of language, the meaning and knowledge registered in and produced by the *how* of what is said rather than the *what*. See Lucey, "Proust and Language-in-Use."

57. We should not forget, of course, that Proust grew up in a distinguished medical household comprising not only his father, Adrien Proust, but also later his brother, Robert.

58. On photography and literary description, see Armstrong, *Fiction in the Age of Photography*. On painting, see Yeazell, *Art of the Everyday*, and Alpers, *Art of Describing*. See also Alpers, "Describe or Narrate?," for a discussion that incorporates literature.

59. Indeed, Bal writes, "the snapshot's vocation is to become the *mise en abyme* of description and its limitations according to Proust." Bal, "Over-Writing as Un-writing: Descriptions, World-Making and Novelistic Time," 591. For Bal, however, both are denaturalizing. "Photography challenges any simple idea of description as distinct from narration. With its glossy, shiny, flat surface, it is neither 'profound'—it has no *depth*— nor stable; it resists any attempt to subordinate description to the service of the humanistic ideal of 'dense' characters, as advocated by Proust's younger contemporary, E. M. Forster" (590–91).

60. See Glasser, *Wilhelm Conrad Röntgen*, and Lisa Cartwright, *Screening the Body*.

61. See Henderson, "X-Rays and the Quest for Invisible Reality."

62. "Lily Briscoe knew all that. Sitting opposite [Charles Tansley] could she not see, as in an X-ray photograph, the ribs and thigh bones of the young man's desire to impress himself lying dark in the mist of his flesh—that thin mist which convention had laid over his burning desire to break into the conversation" (*TL* 90–91).

63. Mann, *The Magic Mountain*, 207.

64. In the "Technical Manifesto of Futurist Painting" (1910), Umberto Boccioni, Carlo Carrà, Luigi Russolo, Giacomo Balla, and Gino Severini state, "Who can still believe in the opacity of bodies, since our sharpened and multiplied sensibilities have already grasped the obscure manifestations of mediums? Why should we continue to create works that don't take into account our growing visual powers which can yield results analogous to those of the X-rays?" Rainey, Poggi, and Wittman, *Futurism: an Anthology*, 65.

65. See Henderson, "X-Rays"; Danius, *Senses of Modernism*, especially 71–82; and Cartwright, *Screening the Body*, who singles out the gendered dimension of early radiographic images, which often depicted a woman's hand.

66. Henderson, "X-Rays and the Quest for Invisible Reality," 326 and 329.

67. Laszló Moholy-Nagy, *Vision in Motion*, 252. Cited in Lippit, "Phenomenologies of the Surface," 39.

68. Lippit, "Phenomenologies of the Surface," 39.

69. Moholy-Nagy, *Vision in Motion*, 252, cited in Lippit, "Phenomenologies of the Surface," 39. "X-ray texts, despite their semblance of total penetration and absolute lucidity, require a form of mediation—they must be read before they can be understood. In this light, the X-ray can be seen as having reversed the trajectory of Enlightenment writing from inscription to *exscription*." (Lippit, "Phenomenologies of the Surface," 40).

204   Notes to Pages 105–110

70. Proust was especially seen as apolitical in relation to World War I. When the Académie Goncourt awarded À l'ombre des jeunes filles en fleur its prestigious prize in 1919 over Roland Dorgelès's war novel Les croix de bois, they "enshrined an image of Proust and his world as feminine, pre-war and peaceful." Mahuzier, "The First World War," 176. As Edward J. Hughes writes, "The unavailability of tidy labels for the author of A la recherche du temps perdu derives substantially from Proust's capacity both to identify with and assume the tribal mindset and to demonstrate a countervailing will to transcend and often disown group identities." Hughes, Proust, Class, and Nation, 4.

71. See Griffiths, Age of Analogy, for a discussion of analogy and historical thinking.

72. See Zhang, "Lens for an Eye," for an extended discussion of the function of photography in this scene. Proust also makes reference to the mendacity of perception with reference to his grandmother in the opening of this section (SLT 6:323–24, RTP 4:491).

73. Benjamin, Selected Writings, vol. 2 pt. 1, 245.

74. Stafford, Visual Analogy, 24.

75. Elaine Scarry discusses imagining one thing passing over another surface, especially vis-à-vis the magic lantern projecting images on the narrator's room, in Dreaming by the Book. She argues this is a way to create the sense of solidity.

76. Bidou-Zachariasen, Proust sociologue, 16. All translations from this text are mine. So for instance Mme Verdurin champions Wagner and the Ballet Russes while Oriane de Guermantes fails to recognize the merits of the avant-garde.

77. This point follows a Bourdieusian approach to aesthetic taste. See Bourdieu, Distinction. For a reading of Proust and aesthetic judgment that combines Bourdieu and Kant, see Freed-Thall, Spoiled Distinctions.

78. Proust had an early reputation as simply a politically conservative lover of the aristocracy, which was one reason André Gide refused to seriously consider the manuscript of Du côté de chez Swann for publication in 1912. That view was revised in subsequent decades by critics, who have drawn attention to his "demystification of the Faubourg St-Germain." See Hughes, Proust, Class, and Nation, 4.

79. See Descombes, Proust, 171. He also refers to these world systems as cosmologies and also as "rhetorical societies" (172).

80. See Hesse, Models and Analogies in Science, for a classic discussion of the role of analogies in scientific discovery. In the context of the Search, see Luckhurst's incisive analysis in Science and Structure. Descombes also observes the narrator's analogical method of knowledge seeking in other areas, for example, seeking to understand the dynamics of power in the social life of the Faubourg Saint-Germain by looking to the realm of politics and reading press coverage of the perverse unpredictability of parliamentary proceedings in order to comprehend the Duchesse de Guermantes's arbitrary verdicts on acquaintances. Descombes, Proust, 178.

81. Roland Barthes, "Une idée de recherche," 37, my translation.

82. Heather Love, "Close but Not Deep," 375. Bruno Latour, particularly his work in actor-network theory, is the other exemplar of a descriptive sociologist in this essay. Love marshals Goffman's and Latour's descriptive practices in an effort to resist the humanism of literary studies. I do not see Proust as part of this project.

83. I am referring to the turn to description as a critical method in the postcritical or symptomatic reading debates. See my discussion of my project in relation to these debates in chapter 1.

84. Bidou-Zachariasen suggests, for instance, that the ethnographic quality of

Proust's descriptions of "les scènes mondaines" is supported by a theory of social relations that is akin to that of Norbert Elias. Bidou-Zachariasen, *Proust sociologue*, 15.

85. Bidou-Zachariasen, 15.

86. Dorothy Richardson, *Pilgrimage*, 3:257.

87. Bidou-Zachariasen, *Proust sociologue*, 17. Plenty of men are present, Bidou-Zachariasen argues, but only as husbands to their wives, for example, Swann, the duc de Guermantes, and Monsieur Verdurin. Charlus is the only man to affect the course of things by his acts, but as an "invert," she argues, he also represents the feminine.

88. Bidou-Zachariasen, 17.

89. Bidou-Zachariasen, 18. Framing this in different terms, Kristeva also comments, "By unraveling the intricacies of high society along with the fashions that it dictates, [Proust's] narrator does not uncover their 'essence.' . . . When the essence of the spectacle is described through metaphor, it disintegrates into images, appearances, and blind imitation. . . . Indeed, the carefully crafted pages of *In Search of Lost Time* form one of the first modern visions of the society of the spectacle." Kristeva, *Time and Sense*, 223.

90. See Schor, *Reading in Detail*.

91. Proust, preface to *Nouvelles complètes*, by Paul Morand, 1:11. He also warned against didactic images, sounding like his symbolist contemporaries. In a 1907 letter to Maurice Duplay, he takes issue with writers who consider the image "the purely practical and utilitarian servant of reason, equal to those abstracts that serve to make students better understand a lesson. No, the image should have its raison d'être in itself, its sudden birth entirely divine." Proust, *Correspondance*, 7:167, my translation.

92. T. E. Hulme, *Selected Writings*, 82. For more on Hulme's role in English modernism as well as the influence of French letters on his thought via his initial apprenticeship to Bergson and subsequent engagement with the anti-Romanticism of Pierre Lasserre and the reactionary political positions of Charles Maurras and the *Action Française*, see Levenson, *Genealogy of Modernism*, especially chapter 3. See also Shusterman, "Remembering T. E. Hulme."

93. Stevens, *Necessary Angel*, 114. This chapter takes its title from the title of Stevens's essay "The Effects of Analogy."

94. Samuel Beckett, *Proust and Three Dialogues*, 88.

95. In other words, they are metonymic even when they are ostensibly metaphoric. Thus, for Genette, Proust intends metaphors to discover the essences of things, but in fact they end up constructing mirages, contingent instead of necessary links. This failure, however, he sees as a sign of the novel's modernity. See Genette, *Figures*, "Proust Palimpseste," 1:39–68, and "Métonymie chez Proust," 3:41–63.

96. There is no better illustration of this in the history of the work's composition than the irruption of World War I, which completely upended the original tripartite plan, while the suspension of publishing during the war gave Proust time to revise and caused the manuscript to more than double in size. For an overview of the history of the text's composition, see Jean-Yves Tadié's introduction to the Pléiade edition of the novel. See also Schmid, "Birth and Development of *À la recherche du temps perdu*," and Dyer, *Proust inachevé*.

97. McDonald, *Proustian Fabric*, 3. This understanding of Proust as straddling two centuries was first influentially developed by Antoine Compagnon in *Proust between Two Centuries*.

98. I'm inspired here by Eve Kosofsky Sedgwick's account of "the grounded reality-

level of surprise and plenitude" in Proust that is "radically different from the demystifying, propositional level of knowingness and lack." Sedgwick, *The Weather in Proust*, 5.

99. Rainer Maria Rilke, *Letters*, 2:313.

100. Sedgwick, *The Weather in Proust*, 5. See also the chapter on Proust in Kate Stanley, *Practices of Surprise*.

Chapter Four

1. In this regard I am sympathetic to Eugenie Brinkema's spirited call, made within the context of cinema studies, for the affective turn to recognize the need to read for form, that is, to treat affect as "a problematic of structure, form, and aesthetics." Brinkema, *Forms of the Affects*, xvi.

2. The distinction between *emotion* and *affect* is by no means uniform among affect theorists, some of whom use the terms interchangeably, others of whom insist on strict opposition. Typically, however, emotion is identified with a conscious, cognitively laden state that is personal and subject centered, whereas affect is identified with nonconscious bodily or physiological processes and said to be resistant to naming. Although my concern is with affect insofar as I emphasize the way in which feelings drift away from characters and present a challenge to description, I use the terms *feeling*, *affect*, and occasionally *emotion* interchangeably. This is in part because Woolf herself frequently uses both *feeling* and *emotion* without distinction, and the term *affect* was not then in widespread use. When I do distinguish between one term and another, it is usually to mark a difference of emphasis and connotation rather than one of ontology. For a helpful overview of terms, see Jonathan Flatley's glossary in *Affective Mapping*, 11–27, Sianne Ngai's introduction to *Ugly Feelings*, and Eric Shouse, "Feeling, Emotion, Affect."

3. The context of this essay as a polemic should not be forgotten in evaluating Woolf's categorical pronouncements on description. Bennett had written an unfavorable review of *Jacob's Room* shortly before, and her essay was both a defense and a counterattack. See Hynes, "Whole Contention."

4. Genette, *Narrative Discourse*, 100. See my discussion of this idea in chapter 3.

5. This is especially the case in *Mrs. Dalloway* and the main sections of *To the Lighthouse* and *The Waves*. It is less true of *The Years* in part because of the much greater predominance of dialogue in that novel relative to other works. *The Years* is also the most explicit rewriting of the Victorian family chronicle or the Balzacian social panorama, and there the descriptions are very much centered on the weather, the seasons, and the cityscape.

6. In this respect Woolf also intensifies a tradition already begun in realism with Eliot and Flaubert and especially Hardy. Several recent critics of Victorian literature have discussed the prominence of descriptions of sensations and (although they do not always identify it this way explicitly) the descriptive as a countermovement to plot. See Cohn, *Still Life*, and Christoff, "Alone with *Tess*."

7. I focus on the latter problem here, but see "Poetry, Fiction, and the Future" (1927) and "Impassioned Prose" (1926) for two essays where she discusses the relation between prose and poetry.

8. Rancière, "Thread of the Novel," 197, my emphasis. Arriving at a somewhat similar conclusion in a very different consideration of Woolf, Alex Zwerdling observes that the real difference between her and Bennett lies not in the fact that Bennett's descrip-

tions are all about the external world while Woolf's are about the internal one but in the economy of her method. Her descriptions take the form of selective snapshots rather than a continuous exhaustive list, and they are typically focalized, which makes them illuminate the processes of perception as much as their ostensible object. Zwerdling, *Virginia Woolf and the Real World*, 17–18.

9. Rancière, "Thread of the Novel," 200. In a diary entry from 1928, Woolf writes of "this appalling narrative business of the realist: getting on from lunch to dinner: it is false, unreal, merely conventional" (*D* 3:209).

10. Rancière, "Thread of the Novel," 200.

11. See, among others, Sim, *Virginia Woolf*, especially chapter 2, and Dalgarno, *Virginia Woolf and the Visible World*.

12. Critics have drawn parallels between her work and postimpressionist aesthetics, but I am focused specifically on the relationship of visuality and emotion. Daniel Tiffany separates the notion of the "image" from visuality in helpful ways. "The idea of a nonvisual image is paradoxical. Yet pictures of all kinds, including graphic images, frequently resist, contest, or subvert visuality by a variety of formal means." For Tiffany, "The aggressive visualization of the unseen that characterizes modern culture frequently produces images that are distinguished, paradoxically, by a resistance to visuality and a persistent quotient of the invisible." Tiffany, *Radio Corpse*, 1 and 2. Whereas he is interested in the opacity and discursive negativity of modernity's "scopic regime," I am interested rather in the displacement of visuality when it comes to descriptions of feelings and sensations.

13. The first postimpressionist exhibit in London was organized by Fry in 1910 and is frequently cited as one of the reasons for Woolf's famous line "On or about 1910, human character changed." In a delivery to the Memoir Club, a society of close friends, in 1921 or 1922, Woolf herself wrote, "The Post-Impressionist movement had cast—not its shadow—but its bunch of variegated lights upon us." Woolf, *Moments of Being*, 200. For the relationship between Fry and Woolf, see Banfield, *Phantom Table*. For more on Woolf and the visual arts, see, among others, Goldman, *Feminist Aesthetics*, and Humm, *Modernist Women*.

14. See Hornby, *Still Modernism*; Trotter, *Cinema and Modernism*; Marcus, *Tenth Muse*; Gillespie, *Multiple Muses*; and Caughie, *Virginia Woolf*. I have learned a great deal especially from Foltz, *Novel after Film*.

15. In this way she completes the circle of intermedial influence by suggesting that film could exploit its own language only by freeing itself from the novel, in particular, from its reliance on the narratives supplied by novels. "The Cinema" was first published in *Arts* in June 1926, in revised form a month later in *The Nation & Athanaeum* in July 1927, and again (although without her permission) in *The New Republic* in August 1927, this time under the title "The Movies and Reality." I will be citing from the revised version published in *The Nation & Athanaeum*, which is included in an appendix to volume 4 of Woolf, *Essays of Virginia Woolf*. Although that essay was published a year after *Mrs. Dalloway*, some of Woolf's earliest notes for the essay appear on the back of holograph manuscripts of *The Voyage Out*, and she continued to work out her ideas on this topic throughout the period of *Mrs. Dalloway*'s composition. For a comprehensive history of the pre-texts, see Hankins, "Virginia Woolf's 'The Cinema.'"

16. See Ellmann, *Poetics of Impersonality*.

17. See Rives, *Modernist Impersonalities*, which includes a chapter on Woolf, and

Walter, *Optical Impersonality*. Walter writes that "optical impersonality," which she derives from contemporaneous discourses of vision, offers "a sort of prehistory for current affect theory" (258).

18. Cited in Hankins, "Virginia Woolf's 'The Cinema,'" 146. These are from partial holograph drafts titled "The Movies" from 1925. Especially suggestive of the threat of obsolescence literature faced next to film is the crossed-out comparison of a horse to the motor car.

19. See the holograph fragment reproduced in Hankins, "Virginia Woolf's 'The Cinema,'" 143.

20. These are also examples of what Fredric Jameson calls the rise of the "affect" in the modern European novel as, beginning with Flaubert and Zola, "global waves of generalized sensations" take on a growing autonomy from narrative and allegorical meaning. Jameson, *The Antinomies of Realism*, 28.

21. Although Woolf refers scathingly to a film adaptation of *Anna Karenina* as an example of the failures of film adaptation in the published version of "The Cinema," in earlier drafts she substitutes a series of literary texts, including *Oliver Twist*, *Lorna Doone*, and *Tess of the D'Urbervilles*, as examples of failed adaptations, suggesting that she had no actual film adaptation (of *Anna Karenina* or any other text) in mind. See Hankins, "Virginia Woolf's 'The Cinema,'" 157–63.

22. Returning to the medium specificity of the visual and literary arts, Woolf qualifies, "but obviously the images of a poet are not to be cast in bronze or traced by pencil. Even the simplest image 'My luve's like a red, red rose, that's newly-sprung in June' presents us with impressions of moisture and warmth and the glow of crimson and the softness of petals inextricably mixed and strung upon the lift of a rhythm which is itself the voice of the passion and hesitation of the lover" (*E* 4:594). She warns in no uncertain terms, "all this, which is accessible to words and to words alone, the cinema must avoid" (*E* 4:351).

23. Jonathan Foltz writes similarly of this passage, "What the moment reveals for Woolf is less the remarkable power of the cinema to capture what words cannot, than the recognition of the way that emotion temporarily attaches to visual forms, discovering analogies, correspondences, evocative 'likenesses' of thought that animate the visual field." Foltz, *Novel after Film*, 89.

24. "[vaguely—dimly we are ~~thinking of/have thoughts of things~~ which are not in words and not in writing & not in shape: we also have a sense of]." Hankins, "Virginia Woolf's 'The Cinema,'" 151.

25. Preminger, Warnke, and Hardison, *Princeton Encyclopedia of Poetry and Poetics*, 767. For a discussion of classical concepts of comparison and the argument that there is no specific ancient theory of simile in the restricted sense that it has in English today, see McCall, *Ancient Rhetorical Theories*. Among contemporaries of Woolf, I. A. Richards writes that metaphor includes all "those processes in which we perceive or think of or feel about one thing in terms of another—as when looking at a building it seems to have a face and to confront us with a peculiar expression." Richards, *Philosophy of Rhetoric*, 116–17. All thought, Richards suggests, is in some way metaphoric.

26. Water imagery is of course everywhere in Woolf's work, associated with dissolution of individuality and an impersonal nature. Jane Marcus reads *The Waves* as offering a critique of imperial Britannia as ruler of the sea, and Jessica Berman argues that Woolf uses oceanic images to critique fascism, drawing on Klaus Theweleit's idea that

oceanic images "ultimately *threaten* the fascist desire to 'stand with both feet and every root firmly anchored in the soil.'" See Marcus, "Britannia Rules *The Waves*," and Theweleit, *Male Fantasies*, vol. 1, *Women, Floods, Bodies, History*, trans. Stephen Conway, Erica Carter, and Chris Turner (Cambridge: Polity, 1987), 230, cited in Berman, *Modernist Fiction*, 141.

27. See Buxton, "Similes and Other Likenesses."

28. This is something that I have observed especially in teaching *Mrs. Dalloway* to first-time readers.

29. A linguistic account of free indirect discourse as well as its history are given by Ann Banfield in *Unspeakable Sentences*. She uses the term "represented speech and thought." For a discussion of Woolf's particular use of this technique, see Banfield, *Phantom Table*, 307-11. For other important discussions of free indirect style, see Pascal, *Dual Voice*, and Cohn, *Transparent Minds*.

30. "I am arrayed, I am prepared. This is the momentary pause; the dark moment" (*W* 101). In Mrs. Ramsay's case this anticipatory pause is balanced by a pause after dinner as she looks back from the threshold of the room, Eurydice-like, knowing that the scene "had become . . . already the past" (*TL* 111). For further examples of such moments of suspense, see *MD* 37, *TL* 82, and *W* 170.

31. William C. Scott, *Artistry of the Homeric Simile*, 6. Here is an example from the *Iliad*:

[Hector] leaped into the crowd as when beneath the clouds a rushing wave
churned by the wind falls upon a swift ship. The whole ship
is hidden in the spray, and the fearful blowing of the wind
roars in the sails; the sailors tremble in their hearts,
fearing—for only by a little have they escaped death.
So were the hearts of the Achaeans split . . .
(Homer, *Iliad* 15.624-28, cited in Scott, 7)

32. Scott, 8 and 4.

33. See George Whalley's entry in Preminger, Warnke, and Hardison, *Princeton Encyclopedia of Poetics*, 767, which also asserts that all extended similes in the European tradition may be traced to Homer's epic similes: "Whereas metaphor is a mode of condensation and compression, [simile] through its descriptive function readily leads to diffuseness and extension, even to the digressive development of the figurative scene, action, or object as an object of beauty in itself."

34. See Lukács, *Theory of the Novel*. For an account of modernist poetry's engagement with epic, see Blanton, *Epic Negation*.

35. See Hoff, "Pseudo-Homeric World."

36. Steven Monte observes of this passage that it "sounds more like a hyperliteral translation of the Greek formula ὡς . . . ὡς than like a colloquial English rendering, say, 'Just as . . . so,'" although we should note that the latter construction also appears frequently in the novels. Monte, "Ancients and Moderns," 590. Monte notes that when critics mention such similes at all in Woolf's work, they tend to label them mock heroic. He argues that the extended similes in the novel work, like flashback memories, to "bring to mind paths in life not taken" (592-93).

37. Other examples include Septimus and Lucrezia crossing the street in Portland

Place being likened to visitors to a house when the family is away (*MD* 83) and Mr. Ramsay thinking of a talk he will give in *To the Lighthouse*: "All this would have to be dished up for the young men at Cardiff next month, he thought; here, on his terrace, he was merely foraging and picknicking (he threw away the leaf that he had picked so peevishly) like a man who reaches from his horse to pick a bunch of roses, or stuffs his pockets with nuts as he ambles at his ease through the lanes and fields of a country known to him from boyhood" (*TL* 43). The passage goes on with an uncertain boundary between the figurative world of the simile and diegetic world of the narrative.

38. Jack Myers and Michael Simms characterize epic similes as "develop[ing] the vehicle into an independent set of images that exclude the tenor, as well as temporarily obscuring the main thread of the narrative." Myers and Simms, *Longman Dictionary*, 100. G. P. Shipp argues that Homeric similes are not typically vehicles that move the action forward, as others have claimed. See Shipp, *Studies in the Language of Homer*, 218.

39. Woolf has often been read alongside psychoanalysis. Key works include Abel, *Virginia Woolf*; Bowlby, *Feminist Destinations*; and Jacobus, "The Third Stroke." In turning to Stern's work I want to move away from a focus on Freudian models of psychic development or subject formation. Stern's work has not been taken up much by psychoanalytically minded literary critics, but he has been discussed by some affect theorists, including Sara Ahmed in *Cultural Politics of Emotion* and "Not in the Mood," and Jonathan Flatley in "How a Revolutionary Counter-Mood is Made." Stern himself cites Silvan Tomkins as an influence, and Félix Guattari has recorded his debt to Stern's work on the preverbal subjective formation of infants in contrast to the Freudian view of "stages." See Guattari, *Chaosmosis*, 6.

40. This is not to say that imitation is not important, especially in the first six months, as, citing extensive empirical studies, Stern acknowledges. What I am emphasizing here, however, is how the transposed, nonimitative modes of matching in affect attunement provide a way to understand how affects can be evoked in literature without being represented.

41. Stern, *Interpersonal World*, 140.

42. Stern, 140. See 140–41 for more examples.

43. Stern, 141.

44. Stern, 142. See Roger Fry's statement about the postimpressionists, quoted by Woolf in her biography of him: "They do not seek to imitate form, but to create form, not to imitate life, but to find an equivalent for life." Woolf, *Roger Fry*, 178.

45. Stern, *Interpersonal World*, 146–49. Furthermore, "we tend automatically to transpose perceptual qualities into feeling qualities," so the qualities of rapid acceleration and speed in someone's arm gesture will be experienced directly as "forceful" rather than in terms of timing, intensity, and shape (158). Qualities such as explosiveness or fading belong to what Stern calls "vitality affects," which accompany but are distinct from the "categorical affects" such as joy and sadness.

46. Critics have pointed out that riding the bus and the landmarks Elizabeth sees on her ride (Somerset House, Chancery Lane, Fleet Street) mark her generation and indicate a new world of work open to her. See, for instance, Squier, *Virginia Woolf and London*.

47. A similar shape appears earlier with Clarissa, when, amid the feeling that "it was all over for her. The sheet was stretched and the bed narrow," the thought of her husband lunching with Lady Bruton appears, too, as an abandonment. "And Richard,

Richard! she cried, as a sleeper in the night starts and stretches a hand in the dark for help" (*MD* 47).

48. I am grateful to Hannah Freed-Thall for helping me make the connection to pastiche here.

49. Stern, *Interpersonal World*, 161, situates the experiences of nonverbal affect attunement in the middle stage on the trajectory from imitation to analogue to symbol. Insofar as it applies to art, Stern's argument would seem to be more pertinent to music, dance, painting, or film than literature, and indeed those other arts become the explicit topic of a later book, *Forms of Vitality: Exploring Dynamic Experience in Psychology, Art, Psychotherapy, and Development*, in which he acknowledges the conspicuous absence of literature. Stern, *Forms of Vitality*, 77.

50. Myers and Simms, *Longman Dictionary*, 278, write that simile "displays a characteristic tentativeness, while the metaphor displays a sense of directness and certainty." The other two ways they differentiate simile from metaphor are "(1) The simile does not attempt to use its vehicle as an identity or substitution, but simply as a comparison, [and] (2), [simile] is a form of extension while metaphor is a form of compression." There is a large body of work on metaphor in a variety of disciplines, although less work specifically on simile, and there is no consensus about the absoluteness of the distinction between the two. For philosophy, see Black, *Models and Metaphors*, and Ricoeur, *Rule of Metaphor*. For an overview from the perspective of cognitive science, psychology, and linguistics, see Ortony, *Metaphor and Thought*. For linguistics and literary criticism, see Roman Jakobson's classic discussion of metaphor and metonymy in "Two Aspects of Language and Two Types of Aphasic Disturbances."

51. Barthes, *Empire of Signs*, 83.

52. For a discussion of the grammar of *as* and aspectual thinking in modernist poetry, see Altieri, *Wallace Stevens*.

53. Burt, "Like: A Speculative Essay," 17.

54. Jonathan Flatley, *Like Warhol*, 6–7. For Flatley, embedded in Warhol's "tendency toward liking and promotion of likenesses" is a wish to be liked and to know that there are others "like me" (7). I would not, however, characterize Woolf's descriptive project as utopian in the way Flatley understands Warhol's.

55. Burt playfully imagines an unwritten but easily drafted essay, "'The Queer Simile,' in which comparisons using *like* or *as* stand for same-sex and non-procreative sexual pleasure, while metaphor, comparison using the copula, stands for heterosexual intercourse." She adds, "Romantic and modernist preferences for metaphor could look, from this angle, like assertions of straight privilege, while the obvious artifice in simile (this is not really that, this ≠ that; it's only like that, this ≈ that) makes it akin to camp, and to drag." Burt, "Like: A Speculative Essay," 18. I am arguing that Woolf does prefer simile over metaphor, although in her work it does not take the form of a camp or drag aesthetic, with the possible exception of *Orlando*. My reading accords with the generative forms of shyness and reserve that Brian Glavey finds in a strain of formalism he aligns with "queer ekphrasis," although he does not discuss Woolf. See Glavey, *Wallflower Avant-Garde*.

56. Woolf, *Room of One's Own*, 108.

57. Stern makes reference to all of these examples; see *Interpersonal World*, 155. For more on the fascinating history of "color music," see Moritz, "Abstract Film and Color Music." In a broader aesthetic history than I can provide here, opera—conceived by

Wagner as the *Gesamtkunstwerk*—would no doubt be an important part of this story. Jane Marcus comments of Woolf's search for a form of the novel that would dispose of plot in *The Years*: "she longed to *compose* her novel, to score arias, duets, trios, quartets, as for voices and orchestra; above all to bring forward the chorus." Marcus, "*The Years* as Greek Drama," 296.

58. Stern, *Interpersonal World*, 155.

59. Stern, 142. As Stern points out, citing a stanza of Baudelaire's "Correspondances," "most poetry could not work without the tacit assumption that cross-sensory analogies and metaphors are immediately apparent to everyone" (155).

60. This is very similar to the view of texts in the mid-nineteenth-century physiological novel theory rehabilitated by Nicholas Dames in *Physiology of the Novel*, which I discuss in chapter 1.

61. This desire for common ground is why she does not pursue the more radically defamiliarizing strategies of the surrealists, Stein, or Joyce or the alienating effects of a Brecht. "And thus though the rhythmical is more natural to me than the narrative, it is completely opposed to the tradition of fiction and I am casting about all the time for some rope to throw to the reader." Woolf, *Letters* 4:204.

62. What I am calling accompaniment is related to D. W. Winnicott's idea that the capacity to be alone paradoxically requires the presence of others, which is sensitively explored in the context of the phenomenology of reading in Christoff, "Alone with *Tess*," where she discusses feeling accompanied in solitude in Winnicott and Hardy. My ideas in this section are inspired by Christoff's discussion.

63. I am specifically thinking of our attachment to texts rather than characters here. For instance, it is possible to be deeply attached to a novel without especially liking or identifying with any of the individual characters. Deirdre Lynch's *Loving Literature* recounts the emergence of the attachment to texts over the course of the eighteenth century.

64. Stern, *Interpersonal World*, 145. That recasting is also what makes attunement dangerous, as Sara Ahmed has warned and to which I return below. Work on empathy is especially prominent in cognitive literary studies, for instance, Suzanne Keen, *Empathy and the Novel*. It also forms part of a broader argument, made by moral philosophers as much as by literary critics, that such experiences of empathy lead to greater altruism or serve some kind of moral pedagogical purpose, as in the work of Martha Nussbaum.

65. Stern reports that the mothers in his study gave as their largest single reason for performing an attunement "being with" the infant, "participating in" or "joining in" with the infant. This group of reasons he calls "communing" as opposed to a second group of reasons, such as "to jazz the baby up or to quiet, to restructure the interaction, to reinforce," and so forth, that fall under the category of "communication." This latter generally includes the desire "to exchange or transmit information with the attempt to alter another's belief or action system," in contrast to the noninterventionist character of communion. Stern, *Interpersonal World*, 148.

66. Thomas Hardy describes Tess of the D'Urbevilles as "an existence, an experience, a passion, a structure of sensations." Cited in Christoff, *Novel Relations*, 27.

67. Sara Ahmed, "Not in the Mood," 18. Ahmed reads one of Stern's examples of attunement, the child and her toy, with a scene from *The Bluest Eye* in which Claudia feels alienated from a blue-eyed doll she receives for Christmas.

68. An exception is Jennifer Fleissner, who made the connection between Jameson's

and Rancière's parallel arguments about temporality in a talk titled "Form, Temporality, and the Novel" at the 2016 meeting of the American Comparative Literature Association.

69. Jameson uses the word *affect* in idiosyncratic ways, but he joins a number of theorists in understanding it in terms of "bodily feelings" in contrast to "conscious states" that characterize emotions, which can thus be named whereas affect cannot. Jameson, *The Antinomies of Realism*, 32.

70. Jameson discusses the use of cataphora in Faulkner and other early twentieth-century writers, which reintroduces narrativity. Jameson, *The Antinomies of Realism*, 165ff.

71. Catherine Gallagher credits Jameson for pointing out that affect *has* a temporality instead of being simply atemporal. See Gallagher, "Affective Realism."

72. Rancière, "Thread of the Novel," 199.

73. Rancière, 199. In Rancière's account, along with the novel, the other formerly minor genre that rises at the beginning of the nineteenth century claiming to be "the proper language of life" is lyric poetry (198). French postwar literature in particular seems to have pursued the expansion of the lyrical into the prosaic. For instance, the prose poems of Francis Ponge in *Le parti pris des choses* (1942), the vignettes that make up Nathalie Sarraute's early work *Tropismes* (1939), and the subsequent works of the *Nouveau Roman*.

74. Meanwhile, as discussed in chapter 1, other critics have further read the "stillness" of descriptive temporality as providing respite and a sense of plenitude that counters the sense of doom or apprehension created by the plot. See Amy M. King on Mary Mitford's *Our Village* in "Natural History and the Novel," and the chapter "Finding a Scale for the Human: Plot and Writing in Thomas Hardy" in Beer, *Darwin's Plots*, although she does not explicitly take description as a key term. Citing Beer, Christoff discusses the oscillation of "plot and description" in Hardy's *Tess of the D'Urbevilles* as one "between doom and reprieve, between Tess's paranoia and her sense of well-being, but also . . . the reader's experience oscillating between anxiety and joy, terror and release." Christoff, "Alone with *Tess*," 32.

75. See Berman, *Modernist Fiction*, 114ff. Mosley formed the New Party out of disaffection with the coalition government created by Ramsay MacDonald in response to the economic crisis, a move that divided the Labour Party in two. My understanding of Woolf's political stances during the interwar years (including her involvements with the Fabians, the Labour Party, and the Women's Co-Operative Guild) is indebted to Berman's account.

76. The newspaper folded by the end of the year in order to preserve party funds. As Mosley, who initially split from Labour, steered the New Party increasingly to the right, Nicolson and other left-leaning intellectuals defected, leaving the party to become folded into the National Union of Fascists. *Action* was relaunched in 1936. For an overview, see Lewis, *Illusions of Grandeur*, 276.

77. Oswald Mosley, "Crisis," *Action* 1, no. 1 (1931), cited in Berman, *Modernist Fiction*, 117. Berman reads *Orlando* and *The Waves* in particular as constructing alternate models of community based on a cosmopolitan ideal that "creates an alternative discourse of feminist action and power, one which seeks to intervene directly in the political life of Britain" (117).

78. Gajarawala, "Fictional Murder," 293. Gajarawala emphasizes description's role

Chapter Five

1. Chalmers, *Conscious Mind*, 4.

2. Dennett, "Quining Qualia," 519, italics in original. In this essay, Dennett argues *against* the idea that subjective conscious experience has special properties such as being ineffable, intrinsic, private, and directly apprehensible. In contrast, Chalmers is one of the foremost proponents of qualia. See also Thomas Nagel's classic essay "What Is It Like to Be a Bat?" Nagel does not actually use the term *qualia*, but his argument that consciousness has an essentially subjective character irreducible to a purely physicalist explanation is a touchstone in this debate.

3. Hulme, *Selected Writings*, 78.

4. These are, however, not homogenous among themselves. Demonstratives and pronouns number among the class of indexicals, while proper names, whose nature has been subject to great debate in twentieth-century philosophy of language, seem to contain more descriptive content even if their function is purely to designate or refer.

5. Chalmers, *Conscious Mind*, 197.

6. Historians of science Lorraine Daston and Peter Galison argue that during the late nineteenth and early twentieth centuries, the worry about epistemic privacy and the unshareability of sense perceptions was intimately related to perceived threats to achieving objectivity among philosophers, mathematicians, and scientists (including Helmholtz, Henri Poincaré, and Frege in addition to Russell). See Daston and Galison, *Objectivity*, chapter 5.

7. Forster, *Abinger Harvest*, 130.

8. And as Lily Briscoe wonders while sitting at Mrs. Ramsay's knee, "What art was there, known to love or cunning, by which one pressed through into those secret chambers? . . . How then, she had asked herself, did one know one thing or another thing about people, sealed as they were?" (*TL* 51).

9. I borrow this term from Sanford Schwartz, who writes that the notion of a matrix "makes it possible, for instance, to compare individuals who have no direct ties to one another but exhibit similar patterns of thought. It can also illuminate specific features of a writer's work that influence cannot explain." Schwartz, *Matrix of Modernism*, 9.

10. The Woolfs possessed Russell's works in their library and also knew him socially. After a dinner party in 1924, Woolf records in her diary, "One does not like him. Yet he is brilliant of course; perfectly outspoken; familiar; talks of his bowels; likes people. . . . Nevertheless, I should like the run of his headpiece" (*D* 2:295). On Russell's influence on Eliot, see Shusterman, *T. S. Eliot and the Philosophy of Criticism*.

11. Banfield, *Phantom Table*. Other exceptions include Rosenbaum, "Philosophical Realism of Virginia Woolf"; Hintikka, "Virginia Woolf and Our Knowledge of the External World"; Wood, "Lighthouse Bodies"; Quigley, *Modernism and Vagueness*, and Kronfeld, "Spontaneous Form."

12. Jakobson, "Shifters, Verbal Categories, and the Russian Verb." Incidentally,

Jakobson takes this term from the linguist Otto Jespersen, a German linguist who was also the first to identify free indirect style in German, coining the term *erlebte Rede*, or "reported speech."

13. Benveniste, *Problèmes de linguistique générale*, 1:253, my translation. Similarly, the spatial and temporal indexicals *here* and *now* delimit the spatial and temporal instance coextensive and simultaneous with the present instance of discourse.

14. On the role of indexicals in free indirect discourse, see Banfield, *Unspeakable Sentences*, 26–27, 98–99, and 151–55.

15. James, *The Meaning of Truth*, 19.

16. James, 17.

17. Russell, *Logic and Knowledge*, 134.

18. Such acquaintance by introspection, which we more commonly call self-consciousness, "is the source of all our knowledge of mental things," and by extension, others' minds. "But for our acquaintance with the contents of our own minds, we should be unable to imagine the minds of others, and therefore we could never arrive at the knowledge that they have minds" (*PPH* 49). Although less relevant to the present discussion, Russell holds that we also have acquaintance with universals (general qualities like "brotherhood" or "redness") and abstract ideas (such as the facts of logic or mathematics).

19. I leave aside here Russell's actual theory of descriptions, which concern their logical structure in propositions and are less relevant to the present discussion. For more on the role of sense-data in Woolf, see Banfield, *Phantom Table*, particularly chapter 3.

20. Like Russell's epistemology, Banfield writes, "Woolf's aesthetic is similarly acquaintance-based." Banfield, *Phantom Table*, 297. Banfield's account emphasizes the way in which "atomic propositions" like "this is here," "this is now," and "this is what I see" are part of a primitive "nursery language" that forms a departure point for a more complete language of description in Woolf (302). My argument does not disagree, but, like a contrastive stress, it highlights the way in which such words also mark the limit of describing experience.

21. Ludwig Wittgenstein, *Zettel*, no. 191. Hegel already cautioned against naive acceptance of the immediacy of sensory knowledge in the first chapter of *Phenomenology of Spirit*, although he also affirms the unique relation of such knowledge to demonstratives like *this*.

22. See Sellars, *Empiricism and the Philosophy of Mind*, and Derrida, *Of Grammatology*.

23. The Aristotelian Society, for instance, held two symposia on the subject, one in 1919 and one in 1949. See Hicks et al., "Symposium"; and Hart, Hughes, and Findlay, "Symposium."

24. As the contemporary philosopher Gareth Evans remarks, "Russell introduced us to the idea that demonstrative identification is a mode of identification quite unlike descriptive identification." Evans, *The Varieties of Reference*, 143.

25. Russell, *An Inquiry*, 109. In addition to *naming*, Russell also uses interchangeably the terms *referring, denoting,* and *designating*. All are opposed to *describing*.

26. This view was challenged most importantly by Saul Kripke in a series of lectures in 1970 published subsequently as *Naming and Necessity*. Kripke argues that ordinary proper names, which he calls "rigid designators," do name directly, in the manner of the demonstrative *this*. Although a full explication of Kripke's objection is beyond the scope

of the present discussion, I treat ordinary proper names in this chapter, contra Russell, as nondescriptive. But although this difference is philosophically significant, it does not negate the ability of his ideas to elucidate the general problematic or Woolf's text.

27. Russell's own term for indexicals is *egocentric particulars*, words whose "denotation is relative to the speaker." He speculates that all indexicals can be defined in terms of *this*. "Thus 'I' means 'The biography to which this belongs'; 'here' means 'The place of this'; 'now' means 'The time of this'; and so on." Russell, *An Inquiry*, 108.

28. Russell, *Logic and Knowledge*, 201.

29. Russell, *Human Knowledge*, 105. Wittgenstein attacks this position in the "private language argument" in the *Philosophical Investigations*. For a summary of the debate about the privacy of language, see Hacking, *Historical Ontology*, chapter 8. It is worth noting that philosophers, including Wittgenstein, consistently (though not always self-consciously) use demonstratives to characterize first-person experiential qualities even when they are arguing against any special epistemological access to these.

30. Russell, *An Outline of Philosophy*, 13. Russell's concern is to draw attention to the fact that "there is thus something subjective and private about what we take to be external perception," which is not to suggest that we can never proceed from our private perceptions to public knowledge of the external world (11).

31. Russell, *Human Knowledge*, 441 and 17.

32. John Lyons calls a speaker's use of proximal and distal indexicals *empathetic* or *non-empathetic* deixis, encoding within it the expression of psychological proximity or distance from the referent. See Lyons, *Semantics*, 677.

33. Woolf, *Moments of Being*, 65.

34. Woolf, 110.

35. Barthes, *Fragments of a Lover's Discourse*, 19.

36. There seems to be something desirous about description whether it is conceived in amatory, consumptive, or ideological terms. Recall Jameson's reading of the generalized anonymous desire produced by Balzacian description discussed in the introduction. Mark Doty also writes, "Description is fueled by HUNGER for the world, the need to taste, to name, to claim what's seen." But he adds that we should not "conceive of such hunger as simply celebratory or affirmative. . . . It's very often true that what we are compelled to describe is terrible, or oppressive, or heartbreaking." Doty, *Art of Description*, 84.

37. In a 1944 letter to Malcolm Cowley, Faulkner writes that his primary goal is to tell a story, "which is myself and the world. . . . This I think accounts for what people call the obscurity, the involved formless 'style,' endless sentences. I'm trying to say it all in one sentence, between one Cap and one period. I'm still trying to put it all, if possible, on one pinhead." Malcolm Cowley, *The Faulkner-Cowley File*, 14.

38. Hulme, *Selected Writings*, 82.

39. Gass, *Fiction and the Figures of Life*, 17.

40. I am grateful to Dan Blanton for suggesting I put these figures together and for talking through many of the ideas developed about this odd grouping in this section.

41. Williams, *The Long Revolution*, 288

42. Mieke Bal, "Over-writing as Un-writing," 600.

43. Bal, 600. Ultimately, Bal's point is that "the description that stages the withdrawal of the focalizer affirms the impossibility of zero-focalization" (604).

44. Bal, 602.

45. Banfield, "L'imparfait de l'objectif," 177. See also Banfield, *Phantom Table*, 70ff, where she elaborates Russell's notion of "sensibilia," the sense-data perceived subjectively but from unoccupied perspectives. She reads the anonymous narrative passages in the "Time Passes" section of *To the Lighthouse* in these terms.

46. Jameson, *Political Unconscious*, 160.

47. Fredric Jameson, *Signatures of the Visible* (New York: Routledge, 1992), 101 and 102, cited in Galloway, "History Is What Hurts," 129.

48. See Fleissner, *Women, Compulsion, Modernity*.

49. According to Kaufman, for Marx the key to transcending the conceptual abstraction of labor time as the ultimate determinant of value would happen through "what aesthetic judgment by definition (since Kant at least) offers the *form* or *semblance* but not the *substance* of: an already extant, determined, determining concept." Crucially, "aesthetic judgment thus begins to enact, in form or semblance, the experience and process of forming, making, or constructing something not conceptually predetermined." Kaufman, "Lyric Commodity Critique," 209. See also Kaufman, "Nothing If Not Determined." In formulating the achievements of modernist description in these terms I have benefited greatly from these essays and from conversations with Rob Kaufman. Although I have not used the framework of the Frankfurt School, it is worth noting that this ability to assert a nonpredetermined mode of conceptuality—which I discuss here in terms of relationality—is for Marxian thinkers such as Walter Benjamin and Theodore Adorno the crucial critical capacity of art.

50. On Woolf's response to and depiction of the war see, among others, Saint-Amour, *Tense Future*; Hussey, *Virginia Woolf and War*; and Levenback, *Virginia Woolf and the Great War*.

51. See Armstrong, *Fiction in the Age of Photography*, 245; and Bowlby, *Feminist Destinations*, especially chapter 6. To be sure, physical appearances and objects in the realist novel also often play us false in what they reveal about their possessors—the assumption of a new identity by means of external accoutrements is often an essential narrative generator.

52. Bowlby suggests that *Jacob's Room* "is both an interrogation of the notion of individuality and, at the same time, a demonstration of the inescapability of 'typing' in the making—autobiographically and as perceived by others—of what is thought of as an individual self." Bowlby, *Feminist Destinations*, 86.

53. See Banfield, *Phantom Table*, for an extended discussion of this issue.

54. In addition to William Bradshaw's worship of "Proportion," Doris Kilman's religion and Peter Walsh's love are also perceived as coercive forces ("clumsy, hot, domineering, hypocritical, eavesdropping, jealous, infinitely cruel and unscrupulous" [*MD* 126]).

55. See Barthes, *The Neutral*, especially 174, where he discusses "Ah, this!" as the key term of satori, the Zen Buddhist notion of sudden enlightenment.

56. It also continues a tradition of what Anne-Lise François has theorized in a Romantic context as a literature of "recessive action." See François, *Open Secrets*, especially chapter 1.

57. Barthes, *Fragments of a Lover's Discourse*, 20-1.

58. This is essentially the realization of sense-certainty in Hegel's *Phenomenology of Spirit*, where the immediacy with which deictics offer up the subject is realized to be illusory.

59. "Y por las calles la sangre de los niños / corría simplemente, como sangre de niños." Pablo Neruda, "I'm Explaining a Few Things [Explico algunas cosas]," in *Pablo Neruda: Selected Poems*, a bilingual edition, 152 and 153. Mark Doty calls Neruda's lines an "anti-simile" in *Art of Description*, 105. Perhaps because it is unburdened by the ideology of character in the way the novel is and because of a more intensive preoccupation with problems of figuration, the descriptive tendency toward tautology is more evident after Woolf in twentieth-century poetry than in prose, from the example of Neruda to Theodore Roethke's observation of "the fieldness of fields, the weediness of weeds" to Wallace Stevens's self-conscious sliding between seeming and being in "Description Without Place," which culminates in the final line, "Like rubies reddened by rubies reddening." See Roethke, *On Poetry and Craft*, 120, and Stevens, *Collected Poems*, 346.

60. Barthes, *Fragments of a Lover's Discourse*, 222.

61. Levenson, *Modernism and the Fate of Individuality*, 69.

62. Levenson, 71.

63. Gertrude Stein, *Writings 1903–1932*, 520. *Tender Buttons* was originally titled "Studies in Description," and it was with William James's comments in mind that Stein composed the 1929 text, "An Acquaintance with Description," published by Robert Graves and Laura Riding's Seizin Press. For more on Stein's engagement with William James and her initial attempt at scientific, "complete description" in *The Making of Americans*, see Meyer, *Irresistible Dictation*.

64. For an illuminating discussion of how the demonstrative pronoun in Proust moves from individual to type ("*that* man" becomes "one of *those* men"), see Eagle, "On 'This' and 'That' in Proust." It is also hard not to hear echoes here of Victor Hugo's famous phrase, "this will kill that [*ceci tuera cela*]" in *Notre Dame de Paris* in reference to technological shifts (the printing press and architecture).

65. Woolf, *Letters*, 2:565–66.

66. Barthes, *Preparation of the Novel*, 80.

Bibliography

Abel, Elizabeth. *Virginia Woolf and the Fictions of Psychoanalysis.* Chicago: University of Chicago Press, 1989.
Abramson, Anna Jones. "Joseph Conrad's Atmospheric Modernism: Enveloping Fog, Narrative Frames, and Affective Attument." *Studies in the Novel* 50, no. 3 (2018): 336–58.
Agnew, Jean-Christophe. "The Consuming Vision of Henry James." In *The Culture of Consumption: Critical Essays in American History 1880–1980,* edited by Richard Wrightman Fox and T. J. Jackson Lears, 65–100. New York: Pantheon, 1983.
Ahmed, Sara. *Cultural Politics of Emotion.* Edinburgh: Edinburgh University Press, 2004.
———. "Not in the Mood." *New Formations* 82 (2014): 13–28.
Albalat, Antoine. *La formation du style par l'assimilation des auteurs.* Paris: A. Colin, 1901.
———. *L'art d'écrire: Enseigné en vingt leçons.* Paris: A. Colin, 1899.
Albright, Daniel. *Untwisting the Serpent: Modernism in Music, Literature, and Other Arts.* Chicago: University of Chicago Press, 2000.
Alpers, Svetlana. *The Art of Describing: Dutch Art in the Seventeenth Century.* Chicago: University of Chicago Press, 1983.
———. "Describe or Narrate? A Problem in Realistic Representation." *New Literary History* 8, no. 1 (1976): 15–41.
Alsop, Elizabeth. *Making Conversation in Modernist Fiction.* Columbus: Ohio State University Press, 2019.
Altieri, Charles. "Modernist Poetry's Encounter with Epistemic Models of Value." *Common Knowledge* 19 no.2 (2013): 334–50.
———. *Wallace Stevens and the Demands of Modernity: Towards a Phenomenology of Value.* Ithaca, NY: Cornell University Press, 2013.
Anscombe, G. E. M. *Intention.* Cambridge, MA: Harvard University Press, 2000.
Aragon, Louis. *Je n'ai jamais appris à écrire, ou Les incipit.* Geneva: Albert Skira, 1969.
Aristotle. *Poetics.* Translated by Leon Golden. Tallahassee: Florida State University Press, 1981.

———. *Topics: Books I and VIII, with Excerpts from Related Texts*. Translated by Robin Smith. Oxford: Clarendon, 1997.

Armstrong, Nancy. *Fiction in the Age of Photography: The Legacy of British Realism*. Cambridge, MA: Harvard University Press, 1999.

Aron, Paul. *Histoire du pastiche*. Paris: Presses universitaires de France, 2008.

Auerbach, Erich. *Mimesis: The Representation of Reality in Western Literature*. Translated by Willard R. Trask. New York: Anchor Books, 1957.

Austin, James F. *Proust, Pastiche, and the Postmodern, or Why Style Matters*. Lewisburg, PA: Bucknell University Press, 2013.

Bal, Mieke. *Narratology: An Introduction to the Theory of Narrative*. Translated by Christine Van Boheemen. Toronto: University of Toronto Press, 2017.

———. *On Storytelling: Essays in Narratology*. Edited by David Jobling. Sonoma, CA: Polebridge, 1991.

———. "Over-writing as Un-writing: Descriptions, World-Making, and Novelistic Time." In *The Novel*. Vol. 2, *Forms and Themes*, edited by Franco Moretti, 571–610. Princeton, NJ: Princeton University Press, 2006.

———. *The Mottled Screen: Reading Proust Visually*. Translated by Anna-Louise Milne. Palo Alto, CA: Stanford University Press, 1997.

Balzac, Honoré de. *La comédie humaine*. 12 vols. Paris: Bibliothèque de la Pléiade, 1976–1981.

———. *Eugénie Grandet*. Translated by Sylvia Raphael. Oxford: Oxford University Press, 2003.

———. *Père Goriot*. Translated by A. J. Krailsheimer. New York: Oxford University Press, 1991.

Banfield, Ann. "L'imparfait de l'objectif: The Imperfect of the Object Glass." *Camera Obscura* 8.3, no. 234 (1990): 64–87.

———. "Mrs. Dalloway." In *The Novel*, vol. 2, *Forms and Themes*, edited by Franco Moretti, 888–95. Princeton, NJ: Princeton University Press, 2007.

———. *The Phantom Table: Woolf, Fry, Russell and the Epistemology of Modernism*. Cambridge: Cambridge University Press, 2000.

———. *Unspeakable Sentences: Narration and Representation in the Language of Fiction*. New York: Routledge, 2015.

Barbey d'Aurevilly, J. *Le roman contemporain*. Paris: A. Lemerre, 1902.

Barthes, Roland. *Empire of Signs*. Translated by Richard Howard. New York: Hill and Wang, 1982.

———. *Fragments of a Lover's Discourse*. Translated by Richard Howard. New York: Hill and Wang, 1978.

———. "An Introduction to the Structural Analysis of Narrative." Translated by Lionel Duisit. *New Literary History* 6, no. 2 (Winter 1975): 237–72.

———. *The Neutral: Lecture Course at the Collège de France (1977—1978)*. Translated by Rosalind E. Krauss and Denis Hollier. New York: Columbia University Press, 2005.

———. *The Preparation of the Novel: Lecture Courses and Seminars at the Collège de France, 1978-1979 and 1979-1980*. Translated by Kate Briggs. New York: Columbia University Press, 2011.

———. "The Reality Effect." In *The Rustle of Language*, translated by Richard Howard, 141–48. Berkeley: University of California Press, 1989.

———. "Une idée de recherche." In *Recherche de Proust*, edited by Gérard Genette and Tzetvan Todorov, 34–39. Paris: Seuil, 1980.
Baudelaire, Charles. *Art in Paris, 1845–1862*. Translated and edited by Jonathan Mayne. London: Phaidon, 1965.
———. *Les fleurs du mal*. Translated by Richard Howard. Bilingual ed. Boston: David Godine, 1982.
———. *Oeuvres complètes*. 2 vols. Paris: Gallimard, 1975.
Baxandall, Michael. *Patterns of Intention: The Historical Explanation of Pictures*. New Haven, CT: Yale University Press, 1985.
Beaujour, Michel. "Qu'est-ce que *Nadja*." *Nouvelle Revue Française* 15, no. 172 (April 1967): 780–99.
———. "Some Paradoxes of Description." *Yale French Studies* 61 (1981): 27–59.
Beckett, Samuel. *Proust and Three Dialogues with Georges Duthuit*. London: John Calder, 1999.
———. *Three Novels: Molloy, Malone Dies, The Unnamable*. New York: Grove Press, 2009.
Beer, Gillian. "Authentic Tidings of Invisible Things: Vision and the Invisible in the Later Nineteenth Century." In *Vision in Context: Historical and Contemporary Perspectives on Sight*, edited by Teresa Brennan and Martin Jay, 83–98. New York: Routledge, 1996.
———. *Darwin's Plots: Evolutionary Narrative in Darwin, George Eliot, and Nineteenth Century Fiction*. Cambridge: Cambridge University Press, 2000.
———. *Open Fields: Science in Cultural Encounter*. Oxford: Oxford University Press, 1996.
———. "Physics, Sound, and Substance: Later Woolf." In *Virginia Woolf: the Common Ground; Essays by Gillian Beer*, 112–24. Ann Arbor: University of Michigan Press, 1996.
Bender, John, and Michael Marrinan, eds. *Regimes of Description: In the Archive of the Eighteenth Century*. Stanford, CA: Stanford University Press, 2003.
Benjamin, Walter. *Walter Benjamin: Selected Writings*. Vol. 2. Edited by Michael Jennings, Howard Eiland and Gary Smith. Cambridge, MA: Harvard University Press, 2005.
Benveniste, Émile. *Problèmes de linguistique générale*. 2 vols. Paris: Gallimard, 1966–1974.
Berman, Jessica. *Modernist Fiction, Cosmopolitanism, and the Politics of Community*. Cambridge: Cambridge University Press, 2001.
Berman, Marshall. *All That Is Solid Melts into Air*. New York: Simon and Schuster, 1982.
Bersani, Leo. "The Jamesian Lie." *Partisan Review* 36 (Winter 1969): 53–79.
Besant, Walter. *The Art of Fiction*. London: Chatto & Windus, 1884.
———. *The Society of Authors: A Record of Its Action from Its Foundation*. London: Society of Authors, 1893.
Best, Stephen, and Sharon Marcus, "Surface Reading: An Introduction." *Representations* 108 (Fall 2009): 1–21.
Best, Stephen, Sharon Marcus, and Heather Love. "Building a Better Description." *Representations* 135, no. 1 (Summer 2016): 1–21.
Bidou-Zachariasen, Catherine. *Proust sociologue: De la maison aristocratique au salon bourgeois*. Paris: Descartes, 1997.

Black, Max. *Models and Metaphors: Studies in Language and Philosophy*. Ithaca, NY: Cornell University Press, 1962.

Blanton, C. D. *Epic Negation: The Dialectical Poetics of Late Modernism*. Oxford: Oxford University Press, 2015.

Böhme, Gernot. "Atmosphere as the Fundamental Concept of a New Aesthetics." Translated by David Roberts. *Thesis Eleven* 36 (1993): 113–26.

———. "Atmosphere as the Subject Matter of Architecture." In *Herzog & de Meuron: Natural History*, edited by Philip Ursprung, 398–406. Montreal: Canadian Center for Architecture, 2002.

Bourdieu, Pierre. *Distinction: A Social Critique of the Judgment of Taste*. Translated by Richard Nice. New York: Routledge, 2015.

Bowlby, Rachel. *Feminist Destinations and Further Essays on Virginia Woolf*. Edinburgh: Edinburgh University Press, 1997.

Brain, Robert. *The Pulse of Modernism: Physiological Aesthetics in Fin-de-Siècle Europe*. Seattle: University of Washington Press, 2015.

Brennan, Theresa. *The Transmission of Affect*. Ithaca, NY: Cornell University Press, 2004.

Breton, André. *Manifestoes of Surrealism*. Translated by Richard Seaver and Helen R. Lane. Ann Arbor: University of Michigan Press, 1969.

———. *Nadja*. Paris: Gallimard, 1963.

———. *Nadja*. Translated by Richard Howard. New York: Grove Press, 1960.

Brinkema, Eugenie. *The Forms of the Affects*. Durham, NC: Duke University Press, 2014.

Brooks, Peter. *The Melodramatic Imagination: Balzac, Henry James, Melodrama, and the Mode of Excess*. New Haven, CT: Yale University Press, 1976.

———. *Reading for the Plot: Design and Intention in Narrative*. New York: A. A. Knopf, 1984.

———. *Realist Vision*. New Haven, CT: Yale University Press, 2005.

Brown, Bill. *A Sense of Things: The Object Matter of American Literature*. Chicago: University of Chicago Press, 2003.

Buck-Morss, Susan. "Aesthetics and Anaesthetics: Walter Benjamin's Artwork Essay Reconsidered." *October* 62 (1992): 3–41.

Burt, Stephanie. "Like: A Speculative Essay about Poetry, Simile, Artificial Intelligence, Mourning, Sex, Rock and Roll, Grammar, Romantic Love, William Shakespeare, Alan Turing, Rae Armantrout, Nick Hornby, Walt Whitman, William Carlos Williams, Lia Purpura, and Claire Danes." *American Poetry Review* 43, no. 1 (January/February 2014): 17–21.

Buxton, Richard. "Similes and Other Likenesses." In *Cambridge Companion to Homer*, edited by Robert Fowler, 139–55. Cambridge: Cambridge University Press, 2006.

Cameron, Sharon. *Thinking in Henry James*. Chicago: University of Chicago Press, 1989.

Cantor, G. N., and M. J. S. Hodge, eds. *Conceptions of the Ether: Studies in the History of Ether Theories, 1740–1900*. Cambridge: Cambridge University Press, 1981.

Cartwright, Lisa. *Screening the Body: Tracing Medicine's Visual Cultures*. Minneapolis: University of Minnesota Press, 1995.

Castle, Terry. "The Female Thermometer." *Representations* 17 (1987): 1–27.

Cather, Willa. *Willa Cather on Writing: Critical Studies on Writing as an Art*. Lincoln: University of Nebraska Press, 1988.

Caughie, Pamela L., ed. *Virginia Woolf in the Age of Mechanical Reproduction*. New York: Garland, 1993.

Cecire, Natalia. *Experimental: American Literature and the Aesthetics of Knowledge*. Baltimore: Johns Hopkins University Press, 2019.

Chalmers, David J. *The Conscious Mind: In Search of a Fundamental Theory*. Oxford: Oxford University Press, 1996.

Christoff, Alicia. "Alone with *Tess*." *Novel: A Forum on Fiction* 48, no. 1 (2015): 18–44.

———. *Novel Relations: Victorian Fiction and British Psychoanalysis*. Princeton, NJ: Princeton University Press, 2019.

Clarke, Bruce, and Linda Dalrymple Henderson, eds. *From Energy to Information: Representation in Science and Technology, Art, and Literature*. Stanford, CA: Stanford University Press, 2002.

Cohn, Dorrit. *Transparent Minds: Narrative Modes for Presenting Consciousness in Fiction*. Princeton, NJ: Princeton University Press, 1978.

Cohn, Elisha. *Still Life: Suspended Development in the Victorian Novel*. Oxford: Oxford University Press, 2015.

Compagnon, Antoine. *Proust between Two Centuries*. Translated by Richard E. Goodkin. New York: Columbia University Press, 1992.

Connor, Steven. *The Matter of Air: Science and the Art of the Ethereal*. London: Reaktion Books, 2010.

Conrad, Joseph. *Collected Letters*. 2 vols. Cambridge: Cambridge University Press, 1986.

———. *Heart of Darkness*. New York: Penguin, 2012.

———. *The Nigger of the "Narcissus."* New York: Doubleday, 1914.

Cowley, Malcolm. *The Faulkner-Cowley File: Letters and Memories 1944–1962*. Harmondsworth: Penguin, 1978.

Crary, Jonathan. *Techniques of the Observer: On Vision and Modernity in the Nineteenth Century*. Cambridge, MA: MIT Press, 1990.

Crow, Christine M. *Paul Valéry: Consciousness and Nature*. Cambridge: Cambridge University Press, 1972.

Curtius, E. R. *European Literature and the Latin Middle Ages*. Translated by Willard R. Trask. Princeton, NJ: Princeton University Press, 1990.

Dalgarno, Emily. *Virginia Woolf and the Visible World*. Cambridge: Cambridge University Press, 2007.

Dames, Nicholas. *Physiology of the Novel: Reading, Neural Science, and the Form of Victorian Fiction*. Oxford: Oxford University Press, 2007.

Danius, Sara. *The Senses of Modernism: Technology, Perception, and Aesthetics*. Ithaca, NY: Cornell University Press, 2002.

Danto, Arthur. *Narration and Knowledge*. New York: Columbia University Press, 1985.

Daston, Lorraine. "Description by Omission: Nature Enlightened and Obscured." In *Regimes of Description: In the Archive of the Eighteenth Century*, edited by John Bender and Michael Marrinan, 11–24. Stanford, CA: Stanford University Press, 2003.

———. "Hard Facts." In *Making Things Public: Atmospheres of Democracy*, edited by Bruno Latour and Peter Weibel, 680–85. Cambridge, MA: MIT Press, 2005.

Daston, Lorraine, and Peter Galison. *Objectivity*. New York: Zone Books, 2007.
Daston, Lorraine, and Elizabeth Lunbeck, eds. *Histories of Scientific Observation*. Chicago: University of Chicago Press, 2011.
Davis, Charles T., and Henry Louis Gates Jr., eds. *The Slave's Narrative*. Oxford: Oxford University Press, 1985.
DeLanda, Manuel. *A New Philosophy of Society: Assemblage Theory and Social Complexity*. London: Continuum, 2006.
Deleuze, Gilles, and Félix Guattari. *A Thousand Plateaus: Capitalism and Schizophrenia*. Translated by Brian Massumi. Minneapolis: University of Minnesota Press, 1987.
De Man, Paul. *Allegories of Reading: Figural Language in Rousseau, Nietzsche, Rilke, and Proust*. New Haven, CT: Yale University Press, 1979.
Dennett, Daniel, "Quining Qualia." In *Mind and Cognition: A Reader*, edited by William Lycan, 519–47. Cambridge: Blackwell, 1990.
Derrida, Jacques. *Of Grammatology*. Translated by Gayatri Spivak. Baltimore: Johns Hopkins University Press, 2016.
Descombes, Vincent. *Proust: Philosophy of the Novel*. Translated by Catherine Chance Macksey. Stanford, CA: Stanford University Press, 1992.
Dickens, Charles. *Great Expectations*. New York: Penguin, 2017.
Diderot, Denis, and Jean le Rond d'Alembert, eds. *Encyclopédie, ou Dictionnaire raisonné des sciences, des arts et des métiers, par une Société de Gens de lettres*. 17 vols. Paris, 1751–1772. http://encyclopedie.uchicago.edu.
Dimock, Wai-Chee. "Weak Theory: Henry James, Colm Tóibín, and W. B. Yeats." *Critical Inquiry* 39, no. 4 (Summer 2013): 732–53.
Doty, Mark. *The Art of Description: World into Word*. Minneapolis, MN: Graywolf, 2010.
Dujardin, Édouard. *We'll to the Woods No More*. Translated by Stuart Gilbert. New York: New Directions, 1957.
Dyer, Nathalie Mauriac. *Proust inachevé: Le dossier "Albertine disparue."* Paris: Champion, 2005.
Eagle, Christopher. "On 'This' and 'That' in Proust: Deixis and Typologies in *À la recherche du temps perdu*." *MLN* 121 (2006): 989–1008.
Eliot, T. S. "On Henry James." In *The Question of Henry James*, edited by F. W. Dupee, 108–19. New York: Henry Holt, 1945.
———. *The Wasteland and Other Writings*. New York: Modern Library, 2002.
Ellmann, Maud. *The Nets of Modernism: Henry James, Virginia Woolf, James Joyce, and Sigmund Freud*. Cambridge: Cambridge University Press, 2010.
———. *The Poetics of Impersonality*. Cambridge, MA: Harvard University Press, 1987.
Enns, Anthony, and Shelley Trower, eds. *Vibratory Modernism*. Basingstoke: Palgrave Macmillan, 2013.
Evans, Brad. "Relating in Henry James (The Artwork of Networks)." *Henry James Review* 36, no. 1 (2015): 1–23.
Evans, Gareth. *The Varieties of Reference*. Oxford: Oxford University Press, 1982.
Favret, Mary. "War in the Air." *Modern Language Quarterly* 65, no. 4 (2004): 531–59.
Felski, Rita. *The Limits of Critique*. Chicago: Chicago University Press, 2015.
Flatley, Jonathan. *Affective Mapping: Melancholia and the Politics of Modernism*. Cambridge, MA: Harvard University Press, 2008.

———. "How a Revolutionary Counter-Mood Is Made." *New Literary History* 43, no. 3 (2012): 503–25.
———. *Like Andy Warhol*. Chicago: University of Chicago Press, 2017.
Flaubert, Gustave. *Bouvard et Pécuchet*. Edited by Claudine Gothot-Mersch. Paris: Gallimard, 1979.
———. *Madame Bovary*. Translated by Lydia Davis. New York: Viking, 2010.
———. *Oeuvres completes de Gustave Flaubert*. 16 vols. Paris: Club de l'Honnête Homme, 1971–1975.
Fleissner, Jennifer. "Form, Temporality, and the Novel." Paper presented at the American Comparative Literature Association conference, Cambridge, MA, March 17–20, 2016.
———. *Women, Compulsion, Modernity: The Moment of American Naturalism*. Chicago: University of Chicago Press, 2004.
Fletcher, J. B., and G. R. Carpenter. *Introduction to Theme-Writing*. Boston: Allyn & Bacon, 1893.
Foltz, Jonathan. *The Novel after Film: Modernism and the Decline of Autonomy*. Oxford: Oxford University Press, 2018.
Forster, E. M. *Abinger Harvest*. London: Arnold, 1953.
———. *Howard's End*. New York: Knopf, 1921.
Foucault, Michel. "Of Other Spaces." Translated by Jay Miskowiec. *Diacritics* 16, no. 1 (1986): 22–27.
———. *The Order of Things: An Archaeology of Human Sciences*. Translated by Alan Sheridan. New York: Vintage, 1994.
François, Anne-Lise. *Open Secrets: The Literature of Uncounted Experience*. Palo Alto, CA: Stanford University Press, 2008.
Frank, Ellen Eve. *Literary Architecture: Essays Toward a Tradition; Walter Pater, Gerard Manley Hopkins, Marcel Proust, Henry James*. Berkeley: University of California Press, 1979.
Frank, Joseph. *The Idea of Spatial Form*. New Brunswick, NJ: Rutgers University Press, 1991.
Freedgood, Elaine. *The Ideas in Things: Fugitive Meaning in the Victorian Novel*. Chicago: University of Chicago Press, 2006.
———. "The Novelist and Her Poor." *Novel: A Forum on Fiction* 47, no. 2 (2014): 210–23.
Freed-Thall, Hannah. *Spoiled Distinctions: Aesthetics and the Ordinary in French Modernism*. New York: Oxford University Press, 2015.
Freed-Thall, Hannah, and Dora Zhang, eds. "Modernist Setting." *Modernism/modernity Print+* 3, cycle 1 (May 5, 2018). https://modernismmodernity.org/forums/modernist-setting.
Freedman, Jonathan. *Professions of Taste: Henry James, British Aestheticism, and Commodity Culture*. Stanford, CA: Stanford University Press, 1990.
Friedberg, James, Ann Donald, and Laura Marcus, eds. *Close Up, 1927–1933: Cinema and Modernism*. Princeton, NJ: Princeton University Press, 1998.
Gajarawala, Toral Jatin. "Fictional Murder and Other Descriptive Deaths: V.S. Naipaul's *Guerrillas* and the Problem of Postcolonial Description." *Journal of Narrative Theory* 42, no. 3 (Fall 2012): 289–308.
Gallagher, Catherine. "Affective Realism." *Novel: A Forum on Fiction* 48, no. 1 (2015): 126–30.

Galloway, Alexander R. "History Is What Hurts: On Old Materialism." *Social Text* 34 no. 2 (127) (2016): 125–41. https://doi.org/10.1215/01642472-3468014.
Gass, William. *Fiction and the Figures of Life*. Boston: David Godine, 1979.
Geertz, Clifford. *The Interpretation of Cultures*. New York: Basic Books, 1973.
Genette, Gérard. *Discours du récit*. Paris: Éditions du Seuil, 1983.
———. *Figures*. 5 vols. Paris: Éditions du Seuil, 1966–.
———. *Figures of Literary Discourse*. Translated by Alan Sheridan. New York: Columbia University Press, 1982.
———. *Narrative Discourse*. Translated by Jane Lewin. Ithaca, NY: Cornell University Press, 1983.
Genung, John F. *Practical Elements of Rhetoric*. Boston: Ginn, 1899.
———. "The Study of Rhetoric in the College Course." In *The Origins of Composition Studies in the American College, 1875–1925*, edited by John C. Brereton, 132–57. Pittsburgh: University of Pittsburgh Press, 1995.
Gillespie, Diane F., ed. *The Multiple Muses of Virginia Woolf*. Columbia: University of Missouri Press, 1993.
Glasser, Otto. *Wilhelm Conrad Röntgen and the Early History of the Roentgen Rays*. Springfield, IL: C. C. Thomas, 1934.
Glavey, Brian. *The Wallflower Avant-Garde: Modernism, Sexuality, and Queer Ekphrasis*. Oxford: Oxford University Press, 2015.
Goble, Mark. *Beautiful Circuits: Modernism and the Mediated Life*. New York: Columbia University Press, 2010.
Goldman, Jane. *The Feminist Aesthetics of Virginia Woolf: Modernism, Post-Impressionism and the Politics of the Visual*. Cambridge: Cambridge University Press, 1998.
Griffiths, Devin. *The Age of Analogy: Science and Literature between the Darwins*. Baltimore: Johns Hopkins University Press, 2016.
Grimstad, Paul. *Experience and Experimental Writing: Literary Pragmatism from Emerson to the Jameses*. Oxford: Oxford University Press, 2013.
Guattari, Felix. *Chaosmosis: An Ethico-Aesthetic Paradigm*. Translated by Paul Bains and Julian Pefanis. Bloomington: University of Indiana Press, 1995.
Gumbrecht, Hans Ulrich. *Atmosphere, Mood, Stimmung: On a Hidden Potential of Literature*. Translated by Erik Butler. Stanford, CA: Stanford University Press, 2012.
Hacking, Ian. *Historical Ontology*. Cambridge, MA: Harvard University Press, 2002.
———. *Rewriting the Soul: Multiple Personality and the Sciences of Memory*. Princeton, NJ: Princeton University Press, 1998.
Hamilton, Kristie. *America's Sketchbook: The Cultural Life of a Nineteenth-Century Literary Genre*. Athens: Ohio University Press, 1998.
Hamon, Philippe. *Introduction à l'analyse du descriptif*. Paris: Hachette, 1981.
———. "Rhetorical Status of the Descriptive." Translated by Patricia Baudoin. *Yale French Studies* 61 (1981): 1–26.
Hankins, Leslie Jane. "Virginia Woolf's 'The Cinema': Sneak Preview of the Holograph Pre-Texts Through Post-Publication Revision." *Woolf Studies Annual* 35 (2009): 135–75.
Hardy, Thomas. *Far from the Madding Crowd*. New York: W. W. Norton, 1986.
Harrow, Susan. "Exposing the Imperial Cultural Fabric: Critical Description in Zola's *La Curée*." *French Studies* 54, no. 4 (2000): 439–52.

Hart, H. L. A., G. E. Hughes, and J. N. Findlay. "Symposium: Is There Knowledge by Acquaintance?" Supplementary volumes, *Proceedings of the Aristotelian Society* 23, no. 1 (July 1949): 69–128.
Helmholtz, Hermann von. *Popular Lectures on Scientific Subjects*. Translated by E. Atkinson. New York: Appleton, 1873.
Henderson, Linda Dalrymple. "Vibratory Modernism: Boccioni, Kupka, and the Ether of Space." In *From Energy to Information: Representation in Science and Technology, Art, and Literature*, edited by Bruce Clarke and Linda Dalrymple Henderson, 126–49. Stanford, CA: Stanford University Press, 2002.
———. "X-Rays and the Quest for Invisible Reality in the Art of Kupka, Duchamp, and the Cubists." *Art Journal* 47, no. 4 (1988): 323–40.
Hesse, Mary. *Models and Analogies in Science*. London: Sheed and Ward, 1963.
Hicks, G. Dawes, G. E. Moore, Beatrice Edgell, and C. D. Broad, "Symposium: Is There Knowledge by Acquaintance?" Supplementary vols., *Proceedings of the Aristotelian Society* 2, no. 1 (July 1919): 159–220.
Hintikka, Jaakkao. "Virginia Woolf and Our Knowledge of the External World." *Journal of Aesthetics and Art Criticism* 38, no. 1 (1979): 5–14.
Hoff, Molly. "The Pseudo-Homeric World of Mrs. Dalloway." *Twentieth Century Literature* 45, no. 2 (Summer 1999): 186–209.
Hofstadter, Douglas, and Emmanuel Sander. *Surfaces and Essences: Analogy as the Fuel and Fire of Thinking*. New York: Basic Books, 2013.
Hornby, Louise. *Still Modernism: Photography, Literature, Film*. New York: Oxford University Press, 2017.
Hsu, Hsuan. "Naturalist Smellscapes and Environmental Justice." *American Literature* 88, no. 4 (2016): 787–814.
Hughes, Edward J. *Proust, Class, and Nation*. Oxford: Oxford University Press, 2011.
Hulme, T. E. *Selected Writings*. Edited by Patrick McGuinness. Manchester: Carcanet, 1998.
Humm, Maggie. *Modernist Women and Visual Cultures: Virginia Woolf, Vanessa Bell, Photography, and Cinema*. New Brunswick, NJ: Rutgers University Press, 2003.
Hussey, Mark, ed. *Virginia Woolf and War: Fiction, Reality, and Myth*. Syracuse, NY: Syracuse University Press, 1991.
Huyssen, Andreas. *After the Great Divide: Modernism, Mass Culture, Postmodernism*. Bloomington: Indiana University Press, 1986.
Hynes, Samuel. "The Whole Contention between Mr. Bennett and Mrs. Woolf." *Novel: A Forum on Fiction* 1, no. 1 (Autumn 1967): 34–44.
Irwin, Michael. *Picturing: Description and Illusion in the Nineteenth Century Novel*. London: Allen & Unwin, 1979.
Jacob, Karen. *The Eye's Mind: Literary Modernism and Visual Culture*. Ithaca, NY: Cornell University Press, 2001.
Jacobus, Mary. "The Third Stroke: Reading Woolf with Freud." In *Grafts: Feminist Cultural Criticism*, edited by Susan Sheridan, 93–110. London: Verso, 1988.
Jakobson, Roman. "Shifters, Verbal Categories, and the Russian Verb." In *Russian and Slavic Grammar: Studies 1931–1981*, edited by Linda Waugh and Morris Halle, 41–58. Berlin: Walter de Gruyter, 1984.
———. "Two Aspects of Language and Two Types of Aphasic Disturbances:" In

Roman Jakobson and Morris Halle, *Fundamentals of Language*, 69–96. Berlin: Mouton de Gruyter, 2002.

James, Henry. *The Ambassadors*. New York: Norton, 1994.

———. *The Art of Criticism: Henry James on the Theory and the Practice of Fiction*. Edited by William Veeder and Susan M. Griffin. Chicago: University of Chicago Press, 1986.

———. *The Golden Bowl*. New York: Penguin, 1987.

———. *Literary Criticism*. 2 vols. New York: Library of America, 1984.

———. *The Notebooks of Henry James*. Edited by F. O. Matthiessen and Kenneth B. Murdock. New York: Oxford University Press, 1962.

———. *The Wings of the Dove*. Oxford: Oxford University Press, 1998.

James, William. *Essays in Radical Empiricism*. Edited by Ralph Barton Perry. New York: Longmans, Green, 1912.

———. *The Meaning of Truth*. Cambridge, MA: Harvard University Press, 1975.

———. *Principles of Psychology*. 2 vols. New York: Dover, 1950.

Jameson, Fredric. *The Antinomies of Realism*. London: Verso, 2013.

———. *The Political Unconscious: Narrative as a Socially Symbolic Act*. Ithaca, NY: Cornell University Press, 1981.

Jarvis, Claire. *Exquisite Masochism: Marriage, Sex, and the Novel Form*. Baltimore: Johns Hopkins University Press, 2016.

Jay, Martin. *Downcast Eyes: the Denigration of Vision in Twentieth-Century French Thought*. Berkeley: University of California Press, 1993.

Jehlen, Myra. *Five Fictions in Search of Truth*. Princeton, NJ: Princeton University Press, 2008.

Kachler, Olivier. "L'analogie des symbolistes, un 'rhythme entre des rapports': Baudelaire, Mallarmé, Maeterlinck." In *La demon de l'analogie: Analogie, pensée et invention d'Aristote au xxᵉ siècle*, edited by Christian Michel, 251–69. Paris: Classiques Garnier, 2016.

Kaufman, Robert. "Lyric Commodity Critique, Benjamin Adorno Marx, Baudelaire Baudelaire Baudelaire." *PMLA* 123, no. 1 (2008): 207–15.

———. "Nothing If Not Determined: Marxian Criticism in History." In *A Companion to Literary Theory*, edited by David H. Richter, 203–17. Chichester: John Wiley & Sons., 2018.

Keen, Suzanne. *Empathy and the Novel*. Oxford: Oxford University Press, 2007.

King, Amy M. "Dilatory Description and the Pleasures of Accumulation: Towards a History of Novelistic Length." In *Narrative Middles: Navigating the Nineteenth Century British Novel*, edited by Caroline Levine and Mario Ortiz-Robles, 161–94. Columbus: Ohio State University Press, 2011.

———. "Natural History and the Novel: Dilatoriness and Length and the Nineteenth Century Novel of Everyday Life." *Novel: A Forum on Fiction* 42, no. 3 (2009): 460–66.

Kittler, Friedrich. *Gramophone, Film, Typewriter*. Translated by Geoffrey Winthrop-Young and Michael Wutz. Stanford, CA: Stanford University Press, 1999.

Koelb, Janice Hewett. *The Poetics of Description: Imagined Places in European Literature*. New York: Palgrave MacMillan, 2006.

Kornbluh, Anna. "The Realist Blueprint." *Henry James Review* 36 (2015): 199–211.

Krauss, Rosalind. "The Photographic Conditions of Surrealism." *October* 19 (1981): 3–34.
Krauss, Rosalind, and Jane Livingston, eds. *L'amour fou: Photography and Surrealism*. New York: Abbeville Press, 1985.
Kripke, Saul. *Naming and Necessity*. Cambridge, MA: Harvard University Press, 1980.
Kristeva, Julia. *Time and Sense: Proust and the Experience of Literature*. Translated by Ross Guberman. New York: Columbia University Press, 1996.
Kronfeld, Maya. "Spontaneous Form: Four Studies in Consciousness and Philosophical Fiction." PhD diss., University of California, Berkeley, 2019.
Kurnick, David. *Empty Houses: Theatrical Failure and the Novel*. Princeton, NJ: Princeton University Press, 2012.
Ladenson, Elisabeth. *Proust's Lesbianism*. Ithaca, NY: Cornell University Press, 1999.
Landy, Joshua. *Philosophy as Fiction: Self, Deception, and Knowledge in Proust*. Oxford: Oxford University Press, 2004.
Lapoujade, David. *Fictions du pragmatisme: William et Henry James*. Paris: Éditions de minuit, 2008.
Latour, Bruno. *Reassembling the Social: An Introduction to Actor-Network-Theory*. Oxford: Oxford University Press, 2007.
———. "Why Has Critique Run Out of Steam: From Matters of Fact to Matters of Concern." *Critical Inquiry* 30, no. 2 (Winter 2004): 225–48.
Lawrence, Jeff. *Anxieties of Experience: The Literature of the Americas from Whitman to Bolaño*. New York: Oxford University Press, 2018.
Lessing, Gottfried Ephraim. *Laocoön: An Essay on the Limits of Painting and Poetry*. Translated by Edward Allen McCormick. Baltimore: Johns Hopkins University Press, 1984.
Levenback, Karen L. *Virginia Woolf and the Great War*. Syracuse, NY: Syracuse University Press, 1999.
Levenson, Michael. *A Genealogy of Modernism: A Study of English Literary Doctrine 1908–1922*. Cambridge: Cambridge University Press, 1986.
———. *Modernism and the Fate of Individuality: Character and Novelistic Form from Conrad to Woolf*. New York: Cambridge University Press, 1991.
Levine, Caroline. *Forms: Whole, Rhythm, Hierarchy, Network*. Princeton, NJ: Princeton University Press, 2015.
Levine, Donald. Introduction to *On Individuality and Social Forms*, by Georg Simmel, ix–lxv. Edited by Donald Levine. Chicago: University of Chicago Press, 1971.
Lewis, David Stephen. *Illusions of Grandeur: Mosley, Fascism, and British Society 1931–1981*. Manchester: Manchester University Press, 1987.
Lewis, Jayne Elizabeth. *Air's Appearance: Literary Atmosphere in British Fiction 1660–1794*. Chicago: University of Chicago Press, 2012.
Lewis, Wyndham. *Tarr*. New York: Oxford University Press, 2010.
Lippit, Akira Mizuta. "Phenomenologies of the Surface: Radiation-Body-Image." Special issue on Lacan, *Qui parle* 9, no. 2 (1996): 31–50.
Love, Heather. "Close but Not Deep: Literary Ethics and the Descriptive Turn." *New Literary History* 41, no. 2 (2010): 371–91.
Lubbock, Percy. *The Craft of Fiction*. New York: Charles Scribner's Sons, 1921.

Lucey, Michael. *Never Say I: Sexuality and the First Person in Colette, Gide, and Proust.* Durham, NC: Duke University Press, 2006.

———. "Proust and Language-in-Use." *Novel* 48, no. 2 (2015): 261–79.

Luckhurst, Nicola. *Science and Structure in Proust's* À la recherche du temps perdu. Oxford: Oxford University Press, 2000.

Lukács, György. "The Ideology of Modernism." In *The Critical Tradition: Classic Texts and Contemporary Trends*, edited by David Richter, 1218–32. Boston: Bedford/St Martin's, 2007.

———. "Narrate or Describe?" In *Writer and Critic*. Edited and translated by Arthur Kahn, 110–48. London: Merlin, 1970.

———. "Realism in the Balance." In *Aesthetics and Politics*, edited by Ronald Taylor and translated by Rodney Livingstone, 28–59. London: Verso, 1980.

———. *Studies in European Realism.* New York: Grosset & Dunlap, 1964.

———. *The Theory of the Novel.* Translated by Anna Bostock. Cambridge, MA: MIT Press, 1971.

Lynch, Deirdre. *Loving Literature: A Cultural History.* Chicago: University of Chicago Press, 2015.

Lyons, John. *Semantics.* Cambridge: Cambridge University Press, 1977.

Mahuzier, Brigitte. "The First World War." In *Marcel Proust in Context*, edited by Adam Watt, 174–80. Cambridge: Cambridge University Press, 2013.

Mann, Thomas. *The Magic Mountain.* Translated by John E. Woods. New York: Knopf, 1995.

Mao, Douglas. *Solid Objects: Modernism and the Test of Production.* Princeton, NJ: Princeton University Press, 1998.

Marcus, Jane. "Britannia Rules *The Waves*." In *Decolonizing Tradition: New Views of Twentieth Century "British" Literary Canons*, edited by Karen R. Lawrence, 136–62. Urbana: University of Illinois Press, 1992.

———. "*The Years* as Greek Drama, Domestic Novel, and Götterdämmerung." In *Bulletin of the New York Public Library* 80 (1977): 276–301.

Marcus, Laura. *The Tenth Muse: Writing about Cinema in the Modernist Period.* Oxford: Oxford University Press, 2007.

Martin, Kirsty. *Modernism and the Rhythms of Sympathy: Vernon Lee, Virginia Woolf, and D. H. Lawrence.* Oxford: Oxford University Press, 2016.

Matthews, J. H. "The Art of Description in Zola's *Germinal*." *Symposium: A Quarterly Journal in Modern Literatures* 16, no. 4 (1962): 267–74.

Matz, Jesse. *Literary Impressionism and Modernist Aesthetics.* Cambridge: Cambridge University Press, 2001.

Maxwell, James Clerk. "Molecules." In *The Scientific Papers of James Clerk Maxwell*, edited by W. D. Niven, 2:361–78. Cambridge: Cambridge University Press, 1890.

McCall, Marsh H. *Ancient Rhetorical Theories of Simile and Comparison.* Cambridge, MA: Harvard University Press, 1969.

McDonald, Christie. *The Proustian Fabric: Associations of Memory.* Lincoln: University of Nebraska Press, 1991.

McGurl, Mark. *The Novel Art: Elevations of American Fiction after Henry James.* Princeton, NJ: Princeton University Press, 2001.

McWhirter, David. "Photo-Negativity: The Visual Rhetoric of James's and Coburn's

New York Edition Frontispieces." *English Language Notes* 44, no. 2 (2006): 101–16.
Menely, Tobias. "Anthropocene Air." *Minnesota Review* 83, no. 1 (2014): 93–101.
Mendelsund, Peter. *What We See When We Read: A Phenomenology*. New York: Vintage, 2014.
Meyer, Steven. *Irresistible Dictation: Gertrude Stein and the Correlations of Writing and Science*. Stanford, CA: Stanford University Press, 2001.
Michel, Christian. "Introduction: Petite histoire d'une disgrace." In *Le démon de l'analogie: Analogie, pensée et invention d'Aristote au XXe siècle*, edited by Christian Michel, 7–40. Paris: Classiques Garnier, 2016.
Milly, Jean. "Le pastiche Goncourt dans *Le Temps retrouvé*." *Revue d'histoire littéraire de la France* 71 (1971): 815–35.
Mitchell, W. J. T. *Picture Theory*. Chicago: University of Chicago Press, 1994.
Moholy-Nagy, Laszló. *Vision in Motion*. Chicago: Paul Theobald, 1947.
Monte, Steven. "Ancients and Moderns in *Mrs. Dalloway*." *Modern Language Quarterly* 61, no. 4 (December 2000): 585–616.
Moon, Michael. *A Small Boy and Others: Imitation and Initiation in American Culture from Henry James to Andy Warhol*. Durham, NC: Duke University Press, 1998.
Moretti, Franco. *The Bourgeois: Between History and Literature*. London: Verso, 2013.
———, ed. *The Novel*. 2 vols. Princeton, NJ: Princeton University Press, 2000.
Moritz, William. "Abstract Film and Color Music." In *The Spiritual in Art: Abstract Painting 1890–1985*, edited by Maurice Tuchman, 297–311. New York: Abbeville Press, 1986.
Morton, Timothy. *The Ecological Thought*. Cambridge, MA: Harvard University Press, 2010.
Myers, Jack, and Michael Simms. *The Longman Dictionary of Poetic Terms*. New York: Longman, 1989.
Nagel, Thomas. "What Is It Like to Be a Bat?" *Philosophical Review* 83 (1974): 435–56.
Napolin, Julie Beth. "'A Sinister Resonance': Vibration, Sound, and the Birth of Conrad's Marlow." In *Vibratory Modernism*, edited by Anthony Enns and Shelley Trower, 53–79. Basingstoke: Palgrave Macmillan, 2013.
Neruda, Pablo. *Pablo Neruda: Selected Poems*. Edited by Nathan Tarn and translated by Anthony Kerrigan, W. S. Merwin, Alastair Reid, and Nathan Tarn. Bilingual ed. Boston: Houghton Mifflin, 1970.
Ngai, Sianne. *Ugly Feelings*. Cambridge, MA: Harvard University Press, 2005.
Ogilvy, Brian. *The Science of Describing: Natural History in Renaissance Europe*. Chicago: University of Chicago Press, 2006.
Ortony, Andrew, ed. *Metaphor and Thought*. Cambridge: Cambridge University Press, 2003.
Otten, Thomas J. *A Superficial Reading of Henry James: Preoccupations with the Material World*. Columbus: Ohio State University Press, 2006.
Panagia, Davide. "*Partage du sensible*: The Distribution of the Sensible." In *Jacques Rancière: Key Concepts*, edited by Jean-Philippe Deranty, 95–103. Durham, NC: Acumen, 2010.
Pascal, Roy. *The Dual Voice: Free Indirect Speech and Its Functioning in the Nineteenth-Century Novel*. Manchester: Manchester University Press, 1977.

Pizzo, Justine. "Atmospheric Exceptionalism in *Jane Eyre*: Charlotte Brontë's Weather Wisdom." *PMLA* 131, no. 1 (2016): 84-100.

———. "Esther's Ether: Atmospheric Character in Charles Dickens's *Bleak House*." *Victorian Literature and Culture* 42, no. 1 (2014): 81-98.

Porter, Theodore M. "The Death of the Object: *Fin de siècle* Philosophy of Physics." In *Modernist Impulses in the Human Sciences 1870-1930*, edited by Dorothy Ross, 128-51. Baltimore: Johns Hopkins University Press, 1994.

Potts, Alex. "Disparities between Part and Whole in Description of Works of Art." In *Regimes of Description: In the Archive of the Eighteenth Century*, edited by John Bender and Michael Marrinan, 135-50. Stanford, CA: Stanford University Press, 2005.

Preminger, Alex, Frank J. Warnke, O. B. Hardison Jr., eds. *The Princeton Encyclopedia of Poetry and Poetics*. Princeton, NJ: Princeton University Press, 2015.

Prendergast, Christopher. *The Order of Mimesis: Stendhal, Balzac, Nerval, Flaubert*. Cambridge: Cambridge University Press, 1986.

Propp, Vladimir. *Theory and History of Folklore*. Edited by Anatoly Liberman and translated by Ariadna Y. Martin et al. Minneapolis: University of Minnesota Press, 1984.

Proust, Marcel. *À la recherche du temps perdu*. Edited by Jean-Yves Tadié. 4 vols. Paris: Bibliothèque de la Pléiade, 1989.

———. *In Search of Lost Time*. 6 vols. Translated by C. K. Scott Moncrieff, Terence Kilmartin, and D. J. Enright. New York: Random House, 1992.

———. *Correspondance*. Edited by Philip Kolb. 21 vols. Paris: Plon, 1970-1993.

———. Preface to *Nouvelles completes*, by Paul Morand, vol. 1. Edited by Michel Collomb, 867-70. Paris: Bibliothèque de la Pléiade, 1992.

Puckett, Kent. *Narrative Theory: A Critical Introduction*. Cambridge: Cambridge University Press, 2016.

Quigley, Megan. *Modernism and Vagueness: Philosophy, Form, and Language*. Cambridge: Cambridge University Press, 2015.

Rainey, Lawrence, Christine Poggi, and Laura Wittman, eds. *Futurism: An Anthology*. New Haven, CT: Yale University Press, 2009.

Rancière, Jacques. *Les bords de la fiction*. Paris: Éditions du Seuil, 2017.

———. *The Lost Thread: The Democracy of Modern Fiction*. Translated by Steven Corcoran. London: Bloomsbury, 2016.

———. *The Politics of Literature*. Translated by Julie Rose. Cambridge: Polity, 2011.

———. "The Thread of the Novel." *Novel: A Forum on Fiction* 47, no. 2 (2014): 196-209.

———. "Ten Theses on Politics." Translated by Davide Panagia, and Rachel Bowlby. *Theory & Event* 5 no. 3 (2001). https://doi.org/10.1353/tae.2001.0028.

Richards, I. A. *The Philosophy of Rhetoric*. Oxford: Oxford University Press, 1950.

Richardson, Dorothy. *Pilgrimage*. 4 vols. London: Virago, 1979.

Richardson, Joan. *A Natural History of Pragmatism*. Cambridge: Cambridge University Press, 2007.

Ricoeur, Paul. *Freud and Philosophy*. Translated by Denis Savage. New Haven, CT: Yale University Press, 1970.

———. *The Rule of Metaphor: The Creation of Meaning in Language*. Translated by Robert Czerny. Toronto, NY: University of Buffalo Press, 1981.

Rilke, Rainer Maria. *Letters.* Translated by Jane Bannard Greene and M. D. Herter Norton. 2 vols. New York: W. W. Norton, 1947–1948.
Rives, Rochelle. *Modernist Impersonalities: Affect, Authority, and the Subject.* New York: Palgrave Macmillan, 2012.
Robbe-Grillet, Alain. *For a New Novel: Essays on Fiction.* Translated by Richard Howard. Evanston, IL: Northwestern University Press, 1996.
Robbins, Bruce. "Not So Well Attached." *PMLA* 132, no. 2 (2017): 371–76.
Roethke, Theodore. *On Poetry and Craft: Selected Prose.* Port Townsend, WA: Copper Canyon Press, 2001.
Ronen, Ruth. "Description, Narrative, and Representation." *Narrative* 5, no. 3 (October 1997): 274–86.
Rooney, Ellen. "Live Free or Describe: The Reading Effect and the Persistence of Form." *differences: A Journal of Feminist Cultural Studies* 21, no. 5 (2010): 112–39.
Rosenbaum, S. P. "The Philosophical Realism of Virginia Woolf." In *English Literature and British Philosophy*, edited by S. P. Rosenbaum, 316–56. Chicago: University of Chicago Press, 1971.
Rousseau, Pascal. *Cosa Mentale: Art et télépathie au XXeme siècle.* Paris: Gallimard, 2015.
Russell, Bertrand. *The Analysis of Mind.* London: Allen & Unwin, 1921.
———. *Human Knowledge: Its Scope and Its Limits.* New York: Routledge, 2003.
———. *An Inquiry into Meaning and Truth.* New York: Routledge, 1992.
———. *Logic and Knowledge.* Edited by Robert Charles Marsh. London: Allen & Unwin, 1956.
———. *An Outline of Philosophy.* New York: Routledge, 2009.
———. *Problems of Philosophy.* Oxford: Oxford University Press, 1912.
Ryan, Judith. *The Vanishing Subject: Early Psychology and Literary Modernism.* Chicago: University of Chicago Press, 1991.
Ryle, Gilbert, *Collected Papers.* 2 vols. London: Hutchinson, 1971.
Saint-Amour, Paul. *Tense Future: Modernism, Total War, Encyclopedic Form.* Oxford: Oxford University Press, 2015.
Savatovsky, Dan. "The Founding and Recasting of French as a Discipline." Translated by Mary Jane Cowles. *Yale French Studies* 113 (2008): 183–96.
Scarry, Elaine. *Dreaming by the Book.* New York: Farrar, Strauss and Giroux, 1999.
Schivelbusch, Wolfgang. *Disenchanted Night: The Industrialization of Light in the Nineteenth Century.* Translated by Angela Davies. Berkeley: University of California Press, 1988.
Schmid, Marion. "Birth and Development of *À la recherche du temps perdu.*" In *The Cambridge Companion to Proust*, edited by Richard Bales, 58–73. Cambridge: Cambridge University Press, 2001.
Schor, Naomi. *Reading in Detail: Aesthetics and the Feminine.* New York: Methuen, 1987.
Schwartz, Sanford. *The Matrix of Modernism: Pound, Eliot, and Early Twentieth Century Thought.* Princeton, NJ: Princeton University Press, 1985.
Scott, Walter. *Biographical Memoirs of Eminent Novelists.* 2 vols. London: Whittaker, 1834.
Scott, William C. *The Artistry of the Homeric Simile.* Lebanon, NH: Dartmouth College Press, 2009.

Sedgwick, Eve Kosofsky. *The Epistemology of the Closet*. Berkeley: University of California Press, 1990.

———. *Tendencies*. Durham, NC: Duke University Press, 1993.

———. *The Weather in Proust*. Edited by Jonathan Goldberg. Durham, NC: Duke University Press, 2011.

———. *Touching Feeling: Affect, Performativity, Pedagogy*. Durham, NC: Duke University Press, 2003.

Sellars, Wilfred. *Empiricism and the Philosophy of Mind*. Edited by Robert Brandom. Cambridge, MA: Harvard University Press, 1997.

Sheppard, Richard. "The Problematics of European Modernism." In *Theorizing Modernism: Essays in Critical Theory*, edited by Steve Giles, 1–51. New York: Routledge, 1993.

Shipp, G. P. *Studies in the Language of Homer*. Cambridge: Cambridge University Press, 1972.

Shirane, Haruo. *The Bridge of Dreams: A Poetics of* The Tale of Genji. Stanford, CA: University of Stanford Press, 1987.

Shouse, Eric. "Feeling, Emotion, Affect." *M/C Journal* 8, no 6 (2005). http://journal.media-culture.org.au/0512/03-shouse.php.

Shusterman, Richard. "Remembering T. E. Hulme: A Neglected Philosopher-Critic-Poet." *Journal of the History of Ideas* 46, no. 4 (1985): 559–76.

———. *T. S. Eliot and the Philosophy of Criticism*. New York: Columbia University Press, 1988.

Silverman, Kaja. *Flesh of My Flesh*. Stanford, CA: Stanford University Press, 2009.

Sim, Lorraine. *Virginia Woolf: The Patterns of Ordinary Experience*. Farnham: Ashgate, 2010.

Simmel, Georg. *Essays on Sociology, Philosophy, and Aesthetics*. Edited by Kurt H. Wolff. New York: Harper & Row, 1959.

———. *On Individuality and Social Forms*. Edited by Donald N. Levine. Chicago: University of Chicago Press, 1971.

———. "Philosophie der Landschaft." In *Brücke und Tür: Essays des Philosophen zur Geschichte, Religion, Kunst und Gesellschaft*, edited by Michael Landmann with Margarete Susman, 141–52. Stuttgart: K. F. Koehler, 1957.

———. "Philosophy of Landscape." Translated by Josef Bleicher. *Theory, Culture & Society* 24 no. 7/8 (2007): 20—29.

Singy, Patrick. "Huber's Eyes: The Art of Scientific Observation before the Emergence of Positivism." *Representations* 95, no. 1 (2006): 54–75.

Spilka, Mark. "Henry James and Walter Besant: 'The Art of Fiction' Controversy." *Novel: A Forum on Fiction* 6, no. 2 (1973): 101–19.

Spitzer, Leo. "Milieu and Ambiance: An Essay in Historical Semantics." *Philosophy and Phenomenological Research* 3, no. 1 (1942): 1–42.

Squier, Susan Merrill. *Virginia Woolf and London: The Sexual Politics of the City*. Chapel Hill: University of North Carolina Press, 1985.

Stafford, Barbara Maria. *Visual Analogy: Consciousness as the Art of Connecting*. Cambridge, MA: MIT Press, 1999.

Stalnaker, Joanna. *The Unfinished Enlightenment: Description in the Age of the Encyclopedia*. Ithaca, NY: Cornell University Press, 2010.

Stanley, Kate. *Practices of Surprise in American Literature after Emerson*. Cambridge: Cambridge University Press, 2018.
Stein, Gertrude. *Tender Buttons*. San Francisco: City Light Books, 2014.
———. "Three Portraits of Painters." In *Selected Writings of Gertrude Stein*, edited by Carl Van Vechten, 327-36. New York: Vintage, 1990.
———. *Writings 1903-1932*. New York: Library of America, 1998.
Stern, Daniel. *Forms of Vitality: Exploring Dynamic Experience in Psychology, Art, Psychotherapy, and Development*. Oxford: Oxford University Press, 2010.
———. *The Interpersonal World of the Infant: A View from Psychoanalysis and Developmental Psychology*. New York: Basic Books, 1985.
Stevens, Wallace. *Collected Poems*. New York: Vintage, 1990.
———. *The Necessary Angel: Essays on Reality and the Imagination*. New York: Random House, 1951.
Stewart, Susan. *On Longing: Narratives of the Miniature, the Gigantic, the Souvenir, the Collection*. Durham, NC: Duke University Press, 1993.
Strowick, Elisabeth. "Comparative Epistemology of Suspicion: Psychoanalysis, Literature, and the Human Sciences." *Science in Context* 18, no. 4 (2005): 649-69.
Taylor, Jesse O. *The Sky of Our Manufacture: The London Fog in British Fiction from Dickens to Woolf*. Charlottesville: University of Virginia Press, 2016.
Thorne, Jack. *Harry Potter and the Cursed Child*. New York: Arthur A. Levine Books, 2016.
Tiffany, Daniel. *Radio Corpse: Imagism and the Cryptaesthetics of Ezra Pound*. Cambridge, MA: Harvard University Press, 1995.
Thomson, James. *The Seasons*. New York: Oxford University Press, 1981.
Tomkins, Silvan. *Affect, Imagery, Consciousness*. 4 vols. New York: Springer, 1962-1992.
Trotter, David. *Cinema and Modernism*. Malden, MA: Blackwell, 2007.
Tyndall, John. *Fragments of Science for Unscientific People*. New York: D. Appleton, 1871.
———. *Hours of Exercise in the Alps*. London: Longmans, Green, 1871.
Ullmann, Stephen. *The Image in the Modern French Novel: Gide, Alain-Fournier, Proust, Camus*. Cambridge: Cambridge University Press, 1960.
Valéry, Paul. "Centenaire de la photographie." In *Vues*, 365-75. Paris: Table Ronde, 1948.
———. "Degas, Dance, Drawing." In *Degas, Manet, Morisot*. Translated by David Paul, 5-102. New York: Pantheon Books, 1960.
Vallury, Raji. "An Incalculable Rupture: The Aesthetics and Politics of Postcolonial Fiction." *Novel: A Forum on Fiction* 47, no. 2 (2014): 242-60.
Vattimo, Gianni, and Pier Aldo Rovatti, eds. *Weak Thought*. Translated by Peter Carravetta. Albany: State University of New York Press, 2012.
Virtanen, Reino. "Proust's Metaphors from the Natural and the Exact Sciences." *PMLA* 69, no. 5 (1954): 1038-59.
Wall, Cynthia. *The Prose of Things: Transformations of Description in the Eighteenth Century*. Chicago: University of Chicago Press, 2006.
Walter, Christina. *Optical Impersonality: Science, Images, and Literary Modernism*. Baltimore: Johns Hopkins University Press, 2014.
Webb, Ruth. *Ekphrasis, Imagination, and Persuasion in Ancient Rhetorical Theory and Practice*. Burlington, VT: Ashgate, 2009.

Wegner, Phillip E. *Imaginary Communities: Utopia, Nation, and the Spatial Histories of Modernity*. Berkeley: University of California Press, 2002.
Wendell, Barrett. "English at Harvard University (1895)." In *The Origins of Composition Studies in the American College*, edited by John C. Brereton, 127–31. Pittsburgh: University of Pittsburgh Press, 1995.
White, Hayden. *Figural Realism: Studies in the Mimesis Effect*. Baltimore: Johns Hopkins University Press, 1999.
Williams, Raymond. *The Long Revolution*. New York: Columbia University Press, 1961.
Wittgenstein, Ludwig. *Philosophical Investigations*. Translated by G. E. M. Anscombe. Oxford: Blackwell, 2001.
———. *Zettel*. Edited by G. E. M. Anscombe and G. H. von Wright. Berkeley: University of California Press, 1970.
Wolf, Werner, and Walter Bernhart, eds. *Description in Literature and Other Media*. Amsterdam: Rodopi, 2007.
Wood, Joanne. "Lighthouse Bodies: The Neutral Monism of Virginia Woolf and Bertrand Russell." *Journal of the History of Ideas* 55, no. 3 (1994): 483–502.
Woolf, Virginia. *Between the Acts*. New York: Harcourt, Brace, 1941.
———. *The Diary of Virginia Woolf*. Edited by Anne Olivier Bell. 5 vols. San Diego, CA: Harcourt Brace Jovanovich, 1977–1984.
———. *The Essays of Virginia Woolf*. Edited by Andrew McNeillie. 6 vols. San Diego, CA: Harcourt Brace Jovanovich, 1986–2011.
———. *Jacob's Room*. San Diego, CA: Harcourt Brace Jovanovich, 2008.
———. *The Letters of Virginia Woolf*. Edited by Nigel Nicolson and Joanne Trautmann. 6 vols. San Diego, CA: Harcourt Brace Jovanovich, 1975–1982.
———. *Moments of Being*. Edited by Jeanne Schulkind. San Diego, CA: Harcourt Brace Jovanovich, 1985.
———. *Mrs. Dalloway*. San Diego, CA: Harcourt Brace Jovanovich, 1985.
———. *Roger Fry: A Biography*. London: Hogarth Press, 1940.
———. *A Room of One's Own and Three Guineas*. Oxford: Oxford University Press, 2000.
———. *The Waves*. San Diego, CA: Harcourt Brace Jovanovich, 1959.
———. *The Years*. San Diego, CA: Harcourt Brace Jovanovich, 1965.
———. *To the Lighthouse*. San Diego, CA: Harcourt Brace Jovanovich, 1981.
Yeats, George. "Dirty Air: *Little Dorrit*'s Atmosphere." *Nineteenth-Century Literature* 66, no. 3 (2011): 328–54.
Yeazell, Ruth. *The Art of the Everyday: Dutch Painting and the Realist Novel*. Princeton, NJ: Princeton University Press, 2009.
Zhang, Dora. "A Lens for an Eye: Proust and Photography." *Representations* 118, no. 1 (Spring 2012): 103–25.
———. "Notes on Atmosphere." *Qui Parle* 27, no. 1 (2018): 121–55.
Zola, Émile. *Le roman experimental*. Paris: Bibliothèque-Charpentier, 1902.
Zwerdling, Alex. *Virginia Woolf and the Real World*. Berkeley: University of California Press, 1986.

Index

action: and exclusion, 40; and significance, 39; under a description, 6
Ades, Dawn: on Breton and photography, 181n66
affect: affect attunement (Stern), 33, 121, 131–34, 137–40, 210n40, 211n49, 212n65; affective mimesis, 24, 126; and description, 49–51; vs. emotion, 183n101, 206n2; and form, 206n1; and reading, 45; and temporality, 132, 213n71; "vital affects" (Stern), 210n45; and Woolf, 117–43
Ahmed, Sara: on affective description, 139; on the dangers of attunement, 212n64
Albalat, Antoine: on writing pedagogy, 20
Altieri, Charles: on the Nietzschean strain of modernism, 27
analogy: vs. metaphor, 92–93; and proportion, 93–94; and Proust, 33, 51, 87–116, 199n13, 200n27, 203n57; and scale, 105; and the surrealists, 94; universal, 201n38
Anscombe, Elizabeth: on intentional actions, 6
appearance: description as mere, 38; as essential (Proust), 107–8; and the social, 108, 111, 166–67. See also surface/depth binary
Aragon, Louis: *Le paysan de Paris*, 8
Aristotle: on metaphor, 93, 126, 135;
199nn17–18; poetic rationality of, 39–40
Armstrong, Nancy: on photography and realist fiction, 12
atmosphere: and Conrad, 66–67, 78, 193nn24–25; and gender, 64, 73–74, 111; and James, 32–33, 61–86; and knowledge, 64; and mood, 86; and relations, 78–79. See also ether
Auerbach, Erich, 29, 182n86
Austin, J. L., 62
authorship, 18, 182n76; as gendered (James), 73

Bachelard, Gaston, 79
Bain, Alexander, 45
Bal, Mieke: on description, 6–7, 25, 51, 185n10, 189n58, 189n61; on photography, 203n59; on Zola, 162
Balzac, Honoré de, 1–3, 5, 7–8, 66; *Eugénie Grandet*, 191n2; excessive description of, 51–52; and fiction's claim to truth, 9; *History of the Thirteen*, 141; *La Recherche de l'absolu*, 90; and relationality (and social totality), 26; *La vieille fille*, 28–29, 31, 163; *Père Goriot*, 1–2, 5, 47–48, 90
Banfield, Ann: on Russell and Woolf, 147; on Woolf, 163, 215n20
Barbey d'Aurevilly: on *Sentimental Education*, 40, 186n22

Barnes, Djuna: *Nightwood*, 14, 47, 52
Barthes, Roland, 134, 170; on haiku, 172, 189n74; on the lover's discourse, 159, 169; on "the neutral," 168–69, 172; on Proust's work, 110, 112–13, 200n22; on the "reality effect," 40; on semiosis, 55
Baudelaire, Charles, 96–97, 201n38; "Correspondances," 136; *The Flowers of Evil*, 201n37
Baxandall, Michael: on ekphrasis, 179n43
Beaujour, Michel: on the history of description, 3
Beckett, Samuel: description in *Molloy* and *The Unnamable*, 8–9; on Proust, 113
Beer, Gillian: on scientific description, 194n38; on skepticism about visual knowledge, 180n49; on *The Waves*, 194n38
Bell, Clive: and Woolf, 122
Bell, Vanessa: and Woolf, 122, 169
Benjamin, Walter: "mimetic faculty," 51, 95–99, 200n28; on observation and the novelist, 99; on Proust's writing, 95–96, 110
Bennett, Arnold, 8, 18, 206n8; *Hilda Lessways*, 118
Benveniste, Émile: on indexicals, 149–50
Berman, Jessica: on Woolf's politics, 142, 208n26, 213n77
Besant, Walter: and intellectual property/authorship, 18, 182n76; on observation and writing, 20
Best, Stephen: on surface and symptomatic reading, 56–58
Bidou-Zachariasen, Catherine: on culture and the late-nineteenth-century bourgeoisie, 108, 111; on women and the social in *In Search of Lost Time*, 112
Boccioni, Umberto: and atmosphere, 195n47; and electromagnetic waves, 75; and the X-ray, 103, 203n64
Böhme, Gernot: and the concept of atmosphere, 65, 197n68
Bowlby, Rachel: on *Jacob's Room*, 217n52
Breton, André: on description and the visual, 14–17, 124; on Dostoevsky, 8; *Nadja*, 15–17, 181n63; on photography, 181n66; on the realist novel, 8, 16
Brinkema, Eugenie: on affect and form, 206n1
Brooks, Peter: on narrative, 3
Brown, Bill: on the pagoda image in *The Golden Bowl*, 82; on *The Spoils of Poynton*, 191n3
Brunetière, Ferdinand, 19
Buck-Morss, Susan: on the mimetic faculty, 96
Burt, Stephanie: on the simile, 134, 211n55

Cameron, Sharon: on James, 69
Cather, Willa: as against description, 18–19, 57; *The Professor's House*, 194n35
Cecire, Natalia, 198n85
Cézanne, Paul, 123, 180n44
Christoff, Alicia Mireles, 27, 49
cinema, 17: contingency in, 125; and literature, 14, 122, 181n57; Woolf on, 121–26, 157, 208nn22–23
Collins, Wilkie: *The Woman in White*, 67
commodity fetishism: and description, 37, 82
Connor, Steven: on atmosphere and relations, 78–79, on Tyndall, 195n50
Conrad, Joseph: on the aim of art (as to make you *see*), 66; atmospheric interests of, 66–67, 78, 193nn24–25; *Heart of Darkness*, 52, 66, 78, 193n24; on matter and vibration, 13
contingency: in film, 125; and Proust, 113–15, 205n95

Daireaux, Max: and Proust, 92
Dallas, E. S., 45
Dames, Nicholas: on physiological novel theory and novel form, 44–45, 49
Danto, Arthur: on description and explanation, 178n24
Darwin, Charles, 96
Daston, Lorraine: on modern facts, 192n12; on transformations of descriptions in natural history, 58

demonstratives, 34, 146, 148–50, 153–64, 171, 216n27, 216n29. *See also* indexicals
Descombes, Vincent, 109
description: and affect 49–51, 67, 80–85, 90, 95–96, 107, 119–21, 124–26, 131–39; and the camera (Proust), 33; and commodity fetishism, 37, 82; and critique, 108, 110; vs. definition, 87; and desire, 216n36; as determining its object, 2, 6–7; devaluation of, 3–4, 18–19, 52, 112; as egalitarian (Rancière), 38–43; enumerative, 25, 90–91, 157, 169; and ethics of nonimposition, 164–69; and gender, 43–44, 64, 73–74, 108, 111–12, 127, 141–43; as inseparable from narrative, 44, 47; and knowledge, 29–31, 64, 67–74, 102–6, 146–47, 150–53, 155, 158, 160–61, 170–71; limits of, 30, 33–34, 144–72; and modernism, 5, 7, 9–11, 25–28, 29–32, 37, 47, 57, 78, 147, 157, 160–64; vs. naming, 153, 156; vs. narration, 3–4, 19, 32, 35–53, 118, 127–31, 182n78, 185n1, 189n61, 203n59; *as* narrative, 90; and novel form, 44–47; and painting, 18, 122–25; and photography, 203n59; pleasure of, 51, 56; and poetry, 27–28; and point of view, 28–29, 31–32, 162–64; politics of, 17–18, 21, 36–44, 163–64; postcolonial, 55, 139, 142–43, 213n78; and precision, 15, 25, 108–10, 112–14, 153–61; as reading method, 56–9; and realism, 2–5, 7, 10–14, 29–30, 36–37, 39–40, 43–45, 64–65, 140–41, 177n10; vs. *récit*, 24, 48, 140; relational, 25–26, 76–85, 91–94, 114–16; and the social, 3, 5–7, 28–32, 38, 147, 160–67; and social relations, 25–27; and sociology, 110; as superficial, 33, 37, 87–88, 100, 103, 118; surface, 89–91; as symptomatic of reification (Lukács), 36–38; and temporality, 4, 24, 35, 43–50, 87, 90, 118–19, 140–43, 164, 213n74; as threatening the unity of the text, 92, 115, 143; as translation, 2; as ubiquitous, 3, 46; and the visual, 11–17, 33, 122; and weak theory, 59–60; as world making, 2, 6–7; and writing pedagogy, 18–20
desire: in Balzac, 28–29; and description, 216n36; and plot, 3
detail: absence of, 7, 68; in description, 100–101, 106, 120, 129–30; as (potentially) excessive, 49, 51–53, 142–43; as gendered, 43, 112; "Luminous Detail" (Pound), 86; nineteenth-century proliferation of, 36, 40–41; omission of, 58; vs. ostension, 159–60; in realist fiction, 7–10, 18, 118; selection of, 20; useless, 40
detective fiction, 67
Dickens, Charles: *Bleak House*, 66, 193n23; *Great Expectations*, 183n97; and relationality (and social totality), 26
domestic, the: and description, 43; and detail, 112; "domestic air," 81
Dos Passos, John: *U.S.A.*, 52
Dostoevsky, Fyodor: the "school-boy description" of (Breton), 8
Doty, Mark: on "antisimile," 218n59; on description, 51, 216n36
Douglas, Mary, 109
Doyle, Arthur Conan: *The Hound of the Baskervilles*, 67
Dreiser, Theodore: *Sister Carrie*, 31, 163
d'Urfé, Honoré: *L'Astrée*, 90
Duchamp, Marcel: and electromagnetic waves, 75; and the X-ray, 103
Dujardin, Édouard: *Les lauriers sont coupés*, 10

Edel, Leon: on Dujardin's *Les lauriers sont coupés*, 10
Eisenstein, Sergei, 137
ekphrasis, 11, 14, 47, 179n43, 190n94, 198n5. *See also* visual, the
Eliot, George: and relationality (and social totality), 26
Eliot, T. S., 124; on James's writing, 77; and Russell, 147
Ellmann, Maud: on James as a syntaxer of love, 196n55

ether, 75–76, 193n23, 195n47. *See also* atmosphere
Evans, Brad: on description of relation, 65
exactitude: and description, 15, 25, 108–10, 112–14, 153–55, 160; in language, 30, 32, 160; in Proust, 112–16; in Woolf, 155–60

Faulkner, William, 159, 216n37
Favret, Mary: on war and weather, 196n60
Fitzgerald, F. Scott: *The Great Gatsby*, 52
Flatley, Jonathan: on liking and likening in the work of Warhol, 98, 135, 211n54
Flaubert, Gustave, 36, 111, 123; *Bouvard et Pécuchet*, 8; *bovarysme*, 31; on description, 8; descriptive meanderings of, 40; and fiction's claim to truth, 9; James on, 8; *Madame Bovary*, 5, 7, 41, 56; on the novel, 19; and plot, 42; *Salammbô*, 9, 179n38; *Sentimental Education*, 40–41, 186n22; "A Simple Heart," 41
Fleissner, Jennifer: on naturalism, description, and gender, 43, 164, 188n45
focalization, 28–29, 31–32, 80, 162–64, 206n8
Foltz, Jonathan: on film and the novel, 181n57; on Woolf, 208n23
Ford, Ford Madox, 13; *The Good Soldier*, 52; *Parade's End*, 52
form: and affect, 206n1; and air, 85; novel form and description, 44–47; spatial, 45
Forster, E. M.: on the nineteenth century as "the Age of Property," 12; on Woolf, 146
Foucart, André: and Proust, 92
Foucault, Michel: on description and natural history, 2; on "heterotopias," 79, 197n70; "sites" of, 81, 83
Fourier, Charles: and correspondences, 96
François, Anne-Lise, 217n55
Frank, Joseph: on spatial form, 45
free indirect discourse, 55, 128, 148–49, 156, 162, 167

Freed-Thall, Hannah: on pastiche in Proust's style, 101, 202n55
Frege, Gottlob: on ideal languages, 30
Fry, Roger: on the postimpressionists, 210n44; on reading James, 77; and Russell, 147; and Woolf, 122, 171

Gajarawala, Toral: on description and discursive violence, 142–43; on description and the other, 55, 213n78
Gass, William: on "constructions" in fiction, 160
gender: and appearance, 108, 111; and atmosphere, 64, 73–74, 111; and detail, 43, 112; and history, 43, 142–43, 164; in Lukàcs, 188n47; and *Orlando*, 127
Genette, Gérard, 3; on descriptions and temporality, 47–48, 90, 118–19; on the division between narration and description, 4, 35, 46–47, 90; on Proust, 90, 198n5, 205n95
Genung, John: and writing pedagogy, 19
Glavey, Brian: on description and performance, 177n3; on "queer ekphrasis," 190n94, 211n55; on surface reading debates, 58
Goble, Mark: on the "circuitry" of Jamesian relations, 75
Goffman, Erving, 57, 110
Goncourt, Jules and Edmond: *Journal*, 8

H.D., 27
Hacking, Ian: on description and "making it up," 6, 178n21, 179n28; on dynamic nominalism, 179n28
Hamon, Philippe: on description, 19, 52, 58–59
Hardy, Thomas, 123; *Far from the Madding Crowd*, 22–23, 49
Harry Potter and the Cursed Child (play), 56
Helmholtz, Hermann von: and the physiology of sensation, 29–30, 146, 180n49, 184n122
Henderson, Linda Dalrymple: on the X-ray, 103
hesitation: in Woolf, 127–28, 132

Hippocrates, 192n9
history, 141–43: and description (Foucault), 2; and fiction (for James), 64; as gendered, 43, 142–43, 164; and photography, 15; vs. poetry, 39–41; and realism, 43
Hulme, T. E.: on analogy and linguistic precision, 113, 157; on a new "classical" poetry, 145–46

impersonal, the, 124–25, 128
indexicals, 31–32, 149, 161, 215n13. *See also* demonstratives
Irwin, Michael: on physiognomic descriptions in James, 191n4

Jakobson, Roman, 3, 199n16; on "shifters" (indexicals), 149–50, 153
James, Henry: *The Ambassadors*, 77–78, 82, 190n84, 196n55; "The Art of Fiction," 18, 35, 72–73; atmosphere in, 32–33, 61–86; *The Awkward Age*, 62; on Balzac, 8; on the commercialization of fiction (and description), 197n74; and the demonstrative, 161, 171; on depth, 38; on description, 35; on experience, 72; on fiction, 64; on Flaubert, 8; *The Golden Bowl*, 1–3, 22–23, 53, 62–65, 68–71, 74, 80–86, 171, 183n97, 193n26, 193nn28–29, 194n36, 195n39; house of fiction, 9, 79, 84–85; length of description of, 53, 128; length of novels of, 85; on the novel, 18, 51; on observation, 20; *The Other House*, 62; *The Princess Casamassima*, 74; and relations, 65, 70, 75–86, 114, 196n55; and the social, 32–33, 65, 68–74; and the spatial, 65, 80–86; *The Spoils of Poynton*, 191n3; and tautology, 170; on Tyndall, 75–76, 195n51; as underdescriber, 23, 32, 61–63; *What Maisie Knew*, 23, 74; *The Wings of the Dove*, 61–62, 67–68, 72–73, 76, 79, 165
James, William, 78, 83–84, 146–47; on demonstratives, 157–58; on description and language, 31, 34, 147, 160; on knowledge by acquaintance and knowledge by description, 150–52, 157–158; on relations and experience, 95, 146, 160, 194n37; and Tyndall, 195n50
Jameson, Fredric: and affect, 213n69, 213n71; on description in Balzac's works, 28–29, 31, 163; on description in Zola's works, 5, 208n20; on point of view, 31, 163; on the *récit* vs. description in the realist novel, 24; on temporality and description, 140–43, 183n99
Jarvis, Claire: on "exquisite masochism" in Victorian fiction, 48–49
Jay, Martin: on skepticism toward visual knowledge, 13
Joyce, James, 27, 38, 114; on Dujardin's *Les lauriers sont coupés*, 10; and the Homeric tradition, 129; *Ulysses*, 52, 74, 129

Kachler, Olivier: on analogy, 96; on Baudelaire's "universal analogy," 201n38
Kaufman, Robert: on Marx, 164, 217n49
King, Amy M.: on description in Victorian works, 48; on desire in theories of realism, 177n10
Kittler, Friedrich: on "non-filmability" and literature, 17
Kluge, Alexander: on the present, 49
knowledge, 30–31: by acquaintance/description, 30–31, 34, 146, 150–52; and atmospheres, 64; immediate, 153, 215n21; and language, 150–55; and sense, 30
Kornbluh, Anna: on James and architecture, 84–85, 196n67, 197n82
Kripke, Saul: on "rigid designators," 215n26
Kristeva, Julia: on Proust's writing, 205n89
Kupka, Frantisek: and the X-ray, 103
Kurnick, David: on James's underdescription, 62–63

language: ideal (Frege and Russell), 30; and knowledge: 150–55; private, 155; pure (Valéry), 17, 181n59; of shapes (and film), 124; and the social, 155, 203n56

Index

Larsen, Nella: *Passing*, 52
Latour, Bruno: and relationality, 26
Lee, Vernon: on the novel as a process, 45
Lefebvre, Henri: "social space," 79
Lessing, G. E.: on painting and poetry, 14–15, 122
Levenson, Michael: on dualistic thinking in modernism: 185–86; on "the great provocation" of James's late work, 62; on "relation" in James, 196n55; on the tautological utterances in James's dialogues, 170
Lewes, G. H.: on the novel as a process, 45
Lewis, Wyndham: *Tarr*, 47; and visual art, 180n44
likeness, 9, 25–28, 85, 166; queerness of, 134–35; in Warhol's work, 98, 135, 211n54; in Woolf, 121, 125–39. *See also* analogy; simile
Lippit, Akira Mizuta: on the impossible perspective of the X-ray, 104
Love, Heather: on "close but not deep" reading, 57, 110
Loy, Mina, 27
Lubbock, Percy: on the novel, 45, 51, 56
Lucey, Michael: on Proust's interest in "language-in-use," 203n56
Lukács, Georg, 35–44: on the authentic realist novel, 26, 36, 43; on Balzac, 36, 108, 111; on description, 4, 26, 32, 35–44, 51, 57, 82–83, 100, 108, 111, 140–43, 160–61, 164, 197n74; and history, 43; on/and modernism, 31, 37, 38, 57; on narration, 37, 65, 111, 160; on naturalism, 36–38; on the novel, 129, 186n13; on social relations, 65, 111; on Zola's description, 51
Lumière brothers, 17

Man Ray: and the X-ray, 103
Mann, Thomas, 114; *The Magic Mountain*, 103
Marcus, Jane: on *The Waves*, 208n26; on *The Years*, 211n57
Marcus, Sharon: on surface and symptomatic reading, 56–58
matching, 161; affective, 23–24, 122, 126, 131–34, 137–40. *See also* affect: affect attunement (Stern)
Matz, Jesse, 182n77; on impressionism, 193n21
Maxwell, James Clerk, 13
McDonald, Christie: on association for Proust, 114, 198n10, 200n25
Melville, Herman: *Bartleby, the Scrivener*, 169
memory: acquaintance by, 151; déjà vu, 133; involuntary, 87, 98, 104, 133
metaphor, 199n17, 208n25; vs. analogy, 92–93; vs. description (Proust), 87–88, 104; and madness, 135; vs. metonymy, 199n16, 205n95; vs. simile, 126, 134, 199n18, 209n33, 211n50; and temporality, 87; and the X-ray (Proust), 33, 91
Milly, Jean: on Proust's Goncourt pastiche, 100
mimesis: affective, 24, 126; "mimetic faculty" (Benjamin), 51, 95–99; perceptual, 22–24, 28, 62–63
Mitchell, W. J. T.: on slave narratives, 42
Mitford, Mary: descriptive stillness of, 48
modernism: and the epic, 129; and exactitude in language, 113, 160; and impersonality, 124; and the indescribable, 145, 152, 157; "inward turn" of, 10; Nietzschean strain of, 27; and point of view, 31, 160–64; and realism, 10–11, 54; relational, 25–28; and suspicion of surfaces, 57; vibratory, 75; and the whole, 37–38, 40–43, 86
Moholy-Nagy, Laszló: on X-ray photos, 103–4
Monet, Claude: and nebular phenomena, 67
morality: and the body, 12; and the realist novel, 8
Morand, Paul: *Tendres Stocks*, 113
Morton, Timothy: on "the ecological thought" and relationality, 26
Mosley, Oswald: and the New Party, 142, 213nn75–76
Musil, Robert, 114; *The Man Without Qualities*, 52

Muybridge, Eadweard, 13
Myers, Jack: on similes, 210n38, 211n50

narration: vs. description, 3–4, 19, 32, 35–53, 118, 127–31, 182n78, 185n1, 189n61, 203n59; and strong theory, 59
natural theology, 48–49
naturalism, 36–38, 43, 164, 188n45; and modernism (Lukács), 37
Neruda, Pablo: antisimile in the Spanish Civil War poem of, 170, 218n59
Nicolson, Harold: and the New Party, 142, 213n76
Nietzsche, Friedrich, 27

observation, 99–100; and Proust, 21, 102, 202n47; and writing pedagogy, 20–21
Ovid, 96–97

pastiche: and Proust, 91, 99–101, 133, 202n48, 202n55
pedagogy of writing, 18–21
perception: as felt, 140; and impressionism, 193n21; indirect, 113–14; inseparability of discrete senses, 79; keenness of, 20–21, 64, 72–74, 195n39; as narrative: 47; reconfiguration of, 14, 21–24, 28, 103; subjectivity of, 99–100, 105–6, 204n72. *See also* mimesis: perceptual
perfunctory, the, 84–85
photography, 12–17, 33, 91, 103, 181n66, 203n59. *See also* X-ray
Pizzo, Justine: on the use of ether in *Bleak House*, 193n23
poetic rationality, 39–40, 42
Ponge, Francis, 28
Pontmartin, Armand de: on detail in Flaubert's work, 40
Potts, Alex: on ancient ekphrasis, 179n43
Pound, Ezra, 27, 113, 124; and electromagnetic waves, 75; on "the method of the Luminous Detail," 86; "In a Station of the Metro," 128
Prendergast, Christopher: on Balzac's description, 178n19
Propp, Vladimir, 3
prose of things: description and, 5, 10–11, 13–4, 32, 65, 84–85; and prose of sensations, 119, 121
Proust, Marcel, 123; analogies of, 33, 51, 87–116, 199n13, 200n27, 203n57; and contingency, 113–15, 205n95; correspondence of, 92; critique of identity in, 51, 88, 97–99; demonstratives in, 171; on description vs. metaphor, 33, 104; on didactic images, 205n91; drafts of, 92; education of, 19; ekphrasis in the work of, 14; and exactitude, 112–16; on indescribability, 145; length of *In Search of Lost Time*, 52, 205n96; on Morand's *Tendres Stocks*, 113; and music, 157; narrative descriptions in, 47; and observation, 21, 102, 202n47; and pastiche, 91, 99–101, 133, 202n48, 202n55; politics of, 204n70, 204n78; practices of likening in, 91–99, 101; queerness of, 98; on realists and naturalists, 8; repetition in, 115; sexuality in, 202n45; the social in, 107–12, 203n56; on women's work, 111–12
psychoanalysis, 27, 210n39

qualia, 145, 151, 164, 214n2
queerness: and ekphrasis, 190n94, 211n55; and likeness, 134–35; and relationality, 26–27; and resemblance, 98

Radcliffe, Ann, 62–63; mists of, 66
Rancière, Jacques: on Barthes, 40; on democratic politics, 186n16; on description and "literary democracy," 21, 32, 35–36, 38–44; on lyric poetry, 213n73; "microsensory events," 52; on nineteenth-century growth of description, 52; on the redistribution of the sensible, 112; on reification, 42–43; on temporality and description, 140–43; on types of wholes, 86; on Woolf, 74, 120
reading: for description, 53–56; experience of, 45–46, 48–49, 51; and the imagination, 63; paranoid, 57–59; surface, 56–57, 110; suspicious/symptomatic, 57–58

realist novel, the, 7–8, 36; and morality, 8; and photography (Armstrong), 12; *récit* vs. description in, 24

récit: vs. description, 24, 48, 140

relations/relationality, 6, 9, 23, 33, 38; and James, 65, 70, 75–86, 114, 196n55; and Proust, 88, 91; relational descriptions, 25–26, 70, 76–86, 91–94, 114–16; relational modernism, 25–28

reparative reading/instinct, 96–97, 201n30

repetition: and naturalism, 43; in Proust, 115

resemblance: as description, 1–2; and queer theory, 98

Richards, I. A.: on metaphor, 208n25

Richardson, Dorothy: on atmosphere and gender, 111; on James, 195n42; *Pilgrimage*, 52, 73

Ricoeur, Paul: on the hermeneutics of suspicion, 57, 59

Rilke, Rainer Maria: on Proust, 115

Robbe-Grillet, Alain, 179n39

Roethke, Theodore: antisimile in, 218n59

Ronen, Ruth: on description vs. narration, 185n1

Röntgen, Wilhelm Conrad, 103. *See also* X-ray

Russell, Bertrand, 214n10; on the demonstrative/indexical, 150, 153, 216n27; on description, 159–60; on external perception, 216n30; on knowledge by acquaintance and description, 146–47, 150–53, 160; on language, 30–31, 155; on the materiality of "matter" after Einstein, 13; and modernism, 147; on naming vs. describing, 153–56

Sackville-West, Vita, 142

Sartre, Jean-Paul, 40

scale: and description, 44–49, 118–19; temporal, 50

Scarry, Elaine: on imagining solidity, 204n75; on "perceptual mimesis," 22–24, 28, 62–63

Schor, Naomi: on the gendered devaluation of the detail, 43, 112; on Lukàcs, 188n47

Scott, Walter: on Ann Radcliffe, 62–63

Sedgwick, Eve Kosofsky, 57; on likeness, 98; on Proust's work, 115, 201n40; on queerness and relationality, 26–27; on the reparative, 96, 201n30; on strong vs. weak theory, 59

Sellars, Wilfred: on the "myth of the given," 153

sensible: redistribution of the, 39, 41–42, 74, 112

sensory experience: as potentially private, 6, 29–30; as shared, 161, 168n16

Shipp, G. P.: on Homeric similes, 210n38

Silverman, Kaja: on analogy, 96–97, 201n42

simile, 24; antisimile, 170, 218n59; epic, 25, 121, 129–30, 135–36, 140, 209n31, 209n33, 210n38; vs. metaphor, 126, 134, 199n18, 209n33, 211n50; queer, 211n55; and Woolf, 126–43

Simmel, Georg: on "forms of sociation," 83, 194n32; on the "microscopic-molecular" level of sociality, 65, 69–70, 83, 194n32; on *Stimmung*, 86

Simms, Michael: on similes, 210n38, 211n50

social, the, 26, 36; and description, 147, 166; in James, 32–33, 65, 68–74; language and, 155, 203n56; in Proust, 107–112; in Woolf, 128, 166

social space, 79; as "unindexable," 197n82

Stafford, Barbara: on analogy, 106, 178n27

Stein, Gertrude, 84; on the tautological demonstrative, 171; *Tender Buttons*, 24, 218n63

Stern, Daniel: on "affect attunement," 33, 121, 131–34, 137–40, 210n40, 211n49, 212n65; "misattunement," 139; "vital affects," 210n45

Stevens, Wallace: antisimile in, 218n59; on the effects of analogy, 113

Stewart, Susan: on literary description, 2

Strachey, Lytton: and Russell, 147

surface/depth binary, 38, 57, 101–12, 136

Swedenborg, Emanuel: *Heaven and Hell*, 96, 201n32; and the James family, 201n32
synesthesia, 136–37

Tale of Genji, The, 55
tautology, 169–71
Taylor, Jesse Oak: on atmospheres in Conrad, 78–79
Teishitsu, Yasuhara, 172
temporality: and affect, 132, 213n71; description and, 4, 24, 35, 43–50, 87, 90, 118–19, 140–43, 164, 213n74; eternal present (Jameson), 140–41, 183n99; hypothetical, 129; and indexicals, 215n13; and metaphor, 87; and the novel, 44–46, 49; and postmodernism, 140; in Proust, 97
Thomson, James: *The Seasons*, 27
Tiffany, Daniel: on the resistance to visuality in modernist images, 207n12
Tomkins, Silvan: on weak theory, 59
Toomer, Jean, 27
Tyndall, John, 195nn50–51; on the ether, 75–76, 196n53

Ullman, Stephen: on images in Proust, 199n13

Valéry, Paul: on description and the visual, 14–18, 124; on description as unintellectual, 18; on photography, 15, 124; on "pure" language, 17, 181n59
visual, the, 207n12; and art (for Conrad), 66; and description, 11–17, 33, 122; and language, 184n122; and literature, 180n44, 208n22. *See also* ekphrasis

Wall, Cynthia: on eighteenth-century description, 177n2, 179n29
weak theory, 59–60
Webb, Ruth: on ekphrasis, 179n43
Wegner, Phillip: on utopias, 55
Wendell, Barrett: and writing pedagogy, 19
Whistler, James: and nebular phenomena, 67

White, Hayden: on Proust, 90
Whitman, Walt: and likeness, 96
Williams, Raymond, 194n32; on art as integrating social and personal, 160–61; on a new kind of realism, 29–30, 184n120
Williams, William Carlos, 27
Winnicott, D. W., 212n62
Wittgenstein, Ludwig: demonstratives, use of, 216n29; on description, 4–5, 10, 29; on expression and knowledge, 152; on language games, 179n42; on the possibility of a private language, 155
Woolf, Leonard, 147
Woolf, Virginia, 117–43; and affect, 49–51, 117, 125–34, 136–39; on Arnold Bennett, 8, 118; *Between the Acts*, 119, 167; on *The Cabinet of Dr. Caligari*, 124, 133–34; "Character in Fiction," 167; "The Cinema," 121–25, 207n15, 208n21; on cinema, 33, 121–26, 157, 208nn22–23; on Conrad, 123; on constraints and the "proper stuff of fiction," 39, 207n9; "Craftsmanship," 117; and the critique of description, 7–8, 118–20; and the demonstrative/indexical, 146–60, 163, 168; and the ethics of nonimposition, 164–69; and feminism, 44; on Flaubert, 123; and free indirect discourse, 128, 148–49, 155–56, 162–63, 167, 209n29; on Hardy, 123; hesitation in, 127–28, 132; on the impersonality of emotion, 124–25; *Jacob's Room*, 18, 141, 165–69, 217n52; on James, 23, 76–77; on Joyce, 38; and the limits of description, 30–31, 144–50, 154–61, 169–72; on the limits of lyric poetry, 183n91; "Modern Fiction," 118, 120; "Mr. Bennett and Mrs. Brown," 8, 18, 118, 123, 137–38, 165–66; *Mrs. Dalloway*, 24, 52, 74, 125–36, 139, 141, 146–49, 154–65, 167–68, 206n5; *Night and Day*, 169; *Orlando*, 127, 213n77; "Phases of Fiction," 23, 114; "Pictures," 122, 125; "Poetry, Fiction, and the Future," 124; politics of, 142; on postimpressionism's influence, 207n13; and prose of sen-

Woolf, Virginia (*continued*)
sations, 119, 121; on Proust, 114, 123, 171; on reading, 45–46, 137; *A Room of One's Own*, 135; and Russell, 147, 214n10; "A Sketch of the Past," 159; social types in, 165–69; *Three Guineas*, 141; *To the Lighthouse*, 47, 103, 119, 121, 128, 137, 144–45, 154, 206n5; on *Tristram Shandy*, 137; water images in, 208n26; *The Waves*, 47, 49–51, 117, 119–20, 124–25, 128, 136, 142, 158, 169, 194n38, 206n5, 208n26, 213n77; on writing, 137–38; *The Years*, 119, 142, 167, 206n5, 211n57

X-ray, 13–14, 101–6, 110, 203n69; vs. camera, 102–3, 106; and metaphor (for Proust), 33, 91. *See also* photography

Yeats, W. B., 27

Zola, Émile, 5, 36, 111, 189n73; *The Belly of Paris*, 162; *La bête humaine*, 7; *Le roman experimental*, 19, 185n5, 202n47; *Nana*, 51, 162; and relationality (and social totality), 26

Zwerdling, Alex: on the use of description in Woolf vs. Bennett, 206n8

www.ingramcontent.com/pod-product-compliance
Lightning Source LLC
Chambersburg PA
CBHW051354290426
44108CB00015B/2007